Certificate Stage

Module C

Audit Framework

Revision Series

9205/F99

British Library Cataloguing-in-Publication Data

A catalogue record for this book is available from the British Library.

Published by AT Foulks Lynch Ltd
Number 4
The Griffin Centre
Staines Road
Feltham
Middlesex
TW14 0HS

ISBN 0 7483 3920 5

© AT Foulks Lynch Ltd, 1999

Acknowledgements

The past ACCA examination questions are the copyright of the Association of Chartered Certified Accountants. The answers to the questions from June 1994 onwards are the answers produced by the examiners themselves and are the copyright of the Association of Chartered Certified Accountants. The answers to the questions prior to June 1994 have been produced by AT Foulks Lynch Ltd.

We are grateful to the Chartered Institute of Management Accountants and the Institute of Chartered Accountants in England and Wales for permission to reproduce past examination questions. The answers have been prepared by AT Foulks Lynch Ltd.

CONTENTS

PREFACE

The new edition of the ACCA Revision Series, published for the June and December 1999 examinations, contains a wealth of features to make your prospects of passing the exams even brighter.

Examiner Plus

This book contains all the new syllabus examinations from June 1994 up to and including December 1998 plus the examiner's official answers. All the exams are set out in chronological order at the back of the book.

We have cross referenced all these questions to their topic headings in the contents pages so you can see at a glance what questions have been set on each syllabus area to date, topic by topic.

The inclusion of these questions and answers really does give students an unparalleled view of the way the new syllabus examinations are set and, even more importantly, a tremendous insight into the mind of the Examiner. The Examiner's answers are in some cases fairly lengthy and whilst the Examiner would not necessarily expect you to include all the points that his answers include, they do nevertheless give you an excellent insight into the sorts of things that the Examiner is looking for and will help you produce answers in line with the Examiner's thinking.

Features

Step by Step Answer Plans and *'Did you answer the question?'* checkpoints will be fully explained on the following two pages.

Tutorial Notes

In some situations the examiner's official answers benefit from a little extra explanation when they are to be used as a learning aid. Where appropriate, we have incorporated extra workings or explanatory notes, so that you derive the maximum benefit from these answers in preparation for your own exam.

Topic Index

The topics covered in all the answers have been indexed. This means that you can easily access an answer relating to any topic which you want to consider by use of the index as well as by reference to the contents page at the front of the book.

The Revision Series also contains the following features:

- Practice questions and answers - a total bank of around 80 questions and answers

- An analysis of the new syllabus exams from June 1994 to December 1998

- Update notes to bring you up to date for new examinable documents and any changes to legislation as at 1st December 1998.

- The syllabus and format of the examination

- General Revision Guidance

- Examination Technique - an essential guide to ensure that you approach the examinations correctly

- Key Revision Topics

- Formulae and tables where appropriate

HOW TO USE THE ANSWER PLANS AND 'DID YOU ANSWER THE QUESTION?' CHECKPOINTS

STEP BY STEP ANSWER PLANS

A key feature in this year's Revision Series is the Step by Step Answer Plans, produced for all new syllabus exam questions from June 1995 to June 1998.

Students are always being told to plan their answers and this feature gives you positive assistance by showing you how you should plan your answer and the type of plan that you should produce before you attempt the question.

Of course, in the exam, your answer Plan can be less fully written than ours because you are writing it for yourself. We are producing an answer plan which communicates the details to you the student and therefore is of necessity much fuller. However, all the detail is there, written in a way which shows you the lines along which you should be thinking in order to produce the answer plan.

You will notice that the Answer Plans start and finish with the exhortation that you must make sure that you have read the question and that you are answering it correctly. Each time you write down the next step in the Answer Plan, you must ask yourself - 'Why am I including this step?' 'Is it relevant?' 'Is this what the Examiner has asked me to do and expected me to do?'

Help with the answer

In addition, if you really do get stuck with the question and cannot see how to approach it, you may find it helpful to turn to the answer page, **cover up the answer itself!,** and start to read the Answer Plan. This may trigger your memory such that you can then return to the question itself and gain all the benefit of doing the question properly without reference to the answer itself.

Practice makes perfect

Like all elements of examination technique the time to learn how to plan your answers is not in the examination itself. You have to practise them now - every time you produce an answer - so that when you come to the examination itself these answer plans will be second nature.

It is probably a good idea to sketch out your answer plans in the way we have produced them here (but remember they can be briefer) and then compare them swiftly to our Answer Plan at the back of the book (don't look at the answer itself at this stage!).

This may indicate that you have completely missed the point of the question or it might indicate one or two other areas that you might wish to explore.

Then, without having yet looked at the answer itself, start writing your answer proper and then compare that with the examiner's own answer.

'DID YOU ANSWER THE QUESTION?' CHECKPOINTS

This is another feature included in this year's edition of the Revision Series. They are included in the new syllabus exam answers from June 1995 to June 1998.

At various points of the answers, you will come across a box headed **'Did you answer the question'**, followed by a brief note which shows you how the printed answer is answering the question and encourages you to make sure that your own answer has not wandered off the point or missed the point of the question completely.

This is an invaluable feature and it is a discipline you must develop as you practise answering questions. It is an area of examination technique that you must practise and practise again and again until it becomes second nature. How often do we read in an Examiner's report that candidates did not answer the question the Examiner had set but had simply answered the question that they wanted him to set or simply wandered off the point altogether? You must make sure that your answers do not fall into that particular trap and that they do rigorously follow the questions set.

A good way of practising this aspect of examination technique is to imagine an empty box headed up 'Did you answer the question?' at the end of the paragraph or paragraphs you are about to write on a particular topic. Try and imagine what you are going to write in that box; what are you going to say in that box which justifies the two or three paragraphs that you are about to write. If you can't imagine what you are going to put in that box, or when you imagine it you find that you are struggling to relate the next few paragraphs to the question, then think very hard before you start writing those paragraphs. Are they completely relevant? Why are you writing them? How are they relevant to the question?

You will find this 'imagining the box' a very useful way of focusing your mind on what you are writing and its relevance to the question.

SUMMARY

Use the two techniques together. They will help you to produce planned answers and they will help you make sure that your answers are focused very fully and carefully on the question the Examiner has actually set.

1 SYLLABUS AND EXAMINATION FORMAT

FORMAT OF THE EXAMINATION

	Number of marks
Section A: 3 compulsory questions	60
Section B: 2 (out of 3) questions of 20 marks each	40
	————
	100
	————

Section A will contain questions on core auditing topics such as stock, verification of balance sheet items, internal controls and computer systems.

Section B will contain questions on both core and non-core topics.

Generally students should assume that accounting systems included in exam questions are computerised.

Time allowed: 3 hours

Certificate stage - Module C Paper 6: THE AUDIT FRAMEWORK

(1)   THE NATURE, PURPOSE AND SCOPE OF AN AUDIT

(a)   Development of auditing.

(b)   The ethical base of auditing.

(c)   Notion of accountability, stewardship and agency.

(d)   The social concept of an audit and its changing role.

(2)   THE REGULATORY FRAMEWORK OF AUDITING

(a)   Auditing standards, their nature, purpose, scope and development.

(b)   Legislation and the auditor; the development and impact of statute law, case law, European Directives, Financial Services Act.

(c)   The role of the government and the DTI in relation to auditing.

(d)   Supervision and monitoring of auditors.

(e)   The role and responsibilities of bodies which set Auditing Standards and Guidelines.

(f)   The roles of parties in relation to auditing including the Audit Commission, National Audit Office, Recognised Supervisory Bodies, Directors' responsibilities and Audit Committees (with reference to their contribution to corporate governance).

(3)   FUNDAMENTAL PRINCIPLES AND CONCEPTS

(a)   Independence, objectivity and integrity.

    (b)   Confidentiality.

    (c)   Audit evidence and documentation.

    (d)   Due care, skill and competence.

    (e)   Audit risk.

    (f)   Materiality and judgement.

    (g)   True and fair view.

    (h)   Audit reporting as a communication medium.

    (i)   Audit planning and supervision.

(4)   THE FRAMEWORK OF AUDITING

    (a)   The application of fundamental auditing principles and concepts.

    (b)   The application of auditing standards and guidelines.

    (c)   The audit requirements of the Companies Acts.

    (d)   The legal liability of auditors and their professional obligations.

    (e)   The auditors' responsibility for the detection and reporting of fraud.

    (f)   The statutory and ethical considerations, relating to the acceptance and continuance of audit clients.

    (g)   Terminating professional engagements and factors affecting such decisions.

    (h)   Preparing, issuing and revising engagement letters.

(5)   AUDIT EVALUATION AND PLANNING

    (a)   Establishing the objectives, scope and critical aspects of an audit.

    (b)   Developing the audit plan to meet those objectives.

    (c)   The identification of sources of audit evidence and its relationship to critical audit objectives.

    (d)   Establishing materiality levels, statistical sampling, and sampling size.

    (e)   Determining the areas of audit risk and the consideration of inherent risk, control risk and detection risk.

    (f)   Analysing the consistency of financial and related information by substantive analysis (including analytical procedures).

    (g)   Designing, documenting and re-evaluation of the audit plan.

    (h)   Evaluating the management information systems.

(6)   EVIDENCE COLLECTION AND ANALYSIS

    (a)   Collecting evidence using a variety of sources and methods.

    (b)   Selecting audit procedures appropriate to the business.

(c)   Identifying and applying sampling techniques.

(d)   Evaluating the evidence collected.

(e)   Recognising mutual co-operation, similarities and differences in the work of the internal and external auditors.

(f)   Recognising the needs and limitations of the use of specialists.

(7)   PERFORMANCE OF AN AUDIT

(a)   Determining the internal control systems and documenting the system.

(b)   Designing the audit programme.

(c)   Evaluating internal controls.

(d)   Performing tests of control on the system.

(e)   Evaluating the results of tests and the re-evaluation of inherent and control risk.

(f)   Applying substantive analysis, substantive sampling and the evaluation of test results.

(g)   Determining and analysing the inter-relationship of tests.

(h)   Altering/modifying tests in the light of test results.

(i)   Comparing test results with evidence from other tests, critical audit objectives, risk evaluation and materiality levels.

(j)   Responding to potential weaknesses in the system and areas of concern evidenced by substantive tests.

(k)   Utilising CAATs and testing Management Information System (MIS) controls.

(l)   Impact of relevant legislation on the performance of an audit.

(m)   Performing substantive procedures in relation to balance sheet items, and evaluating the sufficiency, relevance and reliability of evidence, and the amendment of the audit plan.

(n)   Evaluating the quality of the audit.

(8)   REPORTING FRAMEWORK

(a)   Evaluating the sufficiency, relevance and reliability of audit evidence.

(b)   Reviewing subsequent events, going concern status, management representations and the truth and fairness of financial statements.

(c)   Identifying and recommending appropriate action on weaknesses found during the audit.

(d)   Formulating an audit opinion.

(e)   Issuing management letters, the principles and practices.

(f)   Advising management of improvements in business systems.

(g)   Preparing a formal audit report, and the form of audit qualifications.

(h)   Determining the potential effects of audit qualifications.

(i)   Evaluating and determining the circumstances in which it is necessary to qualify audit reports.

2 ANALYSIS OF PAST PAPERS

Topics	J94		D94		J95		D95		J96		D96		J97		D97		J98		D98	
Computer assisted audit techniques	1	□									1	□	5	○			2	■		
Audit of stocks	2	□			1	□	1	□			3	□	1	□	1	□	1	□	1	□
Controls in a purchases system	3	□	2	□			2	■	3	□	2	□							3	□
Reliability of audit evidence	4	○																		
Consideration of going concern	5	●									5	○							6	●
Forms of audit reports	5	●	4	○																
Liability of the auditor, fraud and ethics	5	●			6	●			4	○	4	○					5	●		
Audit of a small enterprise/non-company	6	○					6	○			6	○								
Controls in a computerised system			1	□			2	■	2	□					2	□	2	■		
Audit of sundry creditors and accruals			2	■																
Audit of a wages system			3	□			2	■									3	□		
Investigate a fall in gross profit margin			5	○																
Audit planning, controlling and recording			6	○													5	○	5	○
Audit of fixed assets, development costs					2	□			6	○					3 4	□ ●			6	●
Controls in a sales system					3	□			1	□					2	□	6	○		
Appointment as an auditor					4	○			4	●			6	●						
Audit of subsequent events, contingencies					5	○									4	●	5	○		
Quality of audit work					6	●	5	○							4	○				
Debtors' circularisation							3	□											2	□
Audit risk, other theoretical topics							4	○					6	●	6	○				
Audit exemption for small companies									5	○										
Audit of bank reconciliation, petty cash															3	□				
Internal audit																	4	○	4	○

Key

The number refers to the number of the question where this topic was examined in the exam.

Topics forming the whole or a substantial part of a question:

☐   Compulsory   O   Optional

Topics forming a non-substantial part of a question

■   Compulsory   ●   Optional

3 GENERAL REVISION GUIDANCE

PLANNING YOUR REVISION

What is revision?

Revision is the process by which you remind yourself of the material you have studied during your course, clarify any problem areas and bring your knowledge to a state where you can retrieve it and present it in a way that will satisfy the Examiners.

Revision is not a substitute for hard work earlier in the course. The syllabus for this paper is too large to be hastily 'crammed' a week or so before the examination. You should think of your revision as the final stage in your study of any topic. It can only be effective if you have already completed earlier stages.

Ideally, you should begin your revision shortly after you begin an examination course. At the end of every week and at the end of every month, you should review the topics you have covered. If you constantly consolidate your work and integrate revision into your normal pattern of study, you should find that the final period of revision - and the examination itself - are much less daunting.

If you are reading this revision text while you are still working through your course, we strongly suggest that you begin now to review the earlier work you did for this paper. Remember, the more times you return to a topic, the more confident you will become with it.

The main purpose of this book, however, is to help you to make the best use of the last few weeks before the examination. In this section we offer some suggestions for effective planning of your final revision and discuss some revision techniques which you may find helpful.

Planning your time

Most candidates find themselves in the position where they have less time than they would like to revise, particularly if they are taking several papers at one diet. The majority of people must balance their study with conflicting demands from work, family or other commitments.

It is impossible to give hard and fast rules about the amount of revision you should do. You should aim to start your final revision at least four weeks before your examination. If you finish your course work earlier than this, you would be well advised to take full advantage of the extra time available to you. The number of hours you spend revising each week will depend on many factors, including the number of papers you are sitting. You should probably aim to do a minimum of about six to eight hours a week for each paper.

In order to make best use of the revision time that you have, it is worth spending a little of it at the planning stage. We suggest that you begin by asking yourself two questions:

- How much time do I have available for revision?
- What do I need to cover during my revision?

Once you have answered these questions, you should be able to draw up a detailed timetable. We will now consider these questions in more detail.

How much time do I have available for revision?

Many people find it helpful to work out a regular weekly pattern for their revision. We suggest you use the time planning chart provided to do this. Your aim should be to construct a timetable that is sustainable over a period of several weeks.

Time planning chart

	Monday	Tuesday	Wednesday	Thursday	Friday	Saturday	Sunday
00.00							
01.00							
02.00							
03.00							
04.00							
05.00							
06.00							
07.00							
08.00							
09.00							
10.00							
11.00							
12.00							
13.00							
14.00							
15.00							
16.00							
17.00							
18.00							
19.00							
20.00							
21.00							
22.00							
23.00							

1   First, block out all the time that is **definitely unavailable** for revision. This will include the hours when you normally sleep, the time you are at work and any other regular and clear commitments.

2   Think about **other people's claims on your time**. If you have a family, or friends whom you see regularly, you may want to discuss your plans with them. People are likely to be flexible in the demands they make on you in the run-up to your examinations, especially if they are aware that you have considered their needs as well as your own. If you consult the individuals who are affected by your plans, you may find that they are surprisingly supportive, instead of being resentful of the extra time you are spending studying.

3   Next, give some thought to the times of day when you **work most effectively**. This differs very much from individual to individual. Some people can concentrate first thing in the morning. Others work best in the early evening, or last thing at night. Some people find their day-to-day work so demanding that they are unable to do anything extra during the week, but must concentrate their study time at weekends. Mark the times when you feel you could do your best work on the

timetable. It is extremely important to acknowledge your personal preferences here. If you ignore them, you may devise a timetable that is completely unrealistic and which you will not be able to adhere to.

4   Consider your **other commitments**. Everybody has certain tasks, from doing the washing to walking the dog, that must be performed on a regular basis. These tasks may not have to be done at a particular time, but you should take them into consideration when planning your schedule. You may be able to find more convenient times to get these jobs done, or be able to persuade other people to help you with them.

5   Now mark some time for **relaxation**. If your timetable is to be sustainable, it must include some time for you to build up your reserves. If your normal week does not include any regular physical activity, make sure that you include some in your revision timetable. A couple of hours spent in a sports centre or swimming pool each week will probably enhance your ability to concentrate.

6   Your timetable should now be taking shape. You can probably see obvious study sessions emerging. It is not advisable to work for too long at any one session. Most people find that they can only really concentrate for one or two hours at a time. If your study sessions are longer than this, you should split them up.

What do I need to cover during my revision?

Most candidates are more confident about some parts of the syllabus than others. Before you begin your revision, it is important to have an overview of where your strengths and weaknesses lie.

One way to do this is to take a sheet of paper and divide it into three columns. Mark the columns:

OK   **Marginal**   **Not OK**

or use similar headings to indicate how confident you are with a topic. Then go through the syllabus (reprinted in Section 1) and list the topics under the appropriate headings. Alternatively, you could use the list of key topics in Section 5 of this book to compile your overview. You might also find it useful to skim through the introductions or summaries to the textbook or workbooks you have used in your course. These should remind you of parts of the course that you found particularly easy or difficult at the time. You could also use some of the exercises and questions in the workbooks or textbooks, or some of the questions in this book, as a diagnostic aid to discover the areas where you need to work hardest.

It is also important to be aware which areas of the syllabus are so central to the subject that they are likely to be examined in every diet, and which are more obscure, and not likely to come up so frequently. Your textbooks, workbooks and lecture notes will help you here, and section 2 of this book contains an analysis of past papers. Remember, the Examiner will be looking for broad coverage of the syllabus. There is no point in knowing one or two topics in exhaustive detail if you do so at the expense of the rest of the course.

Writing your revision timetable

You now have the information you need to write your timetable. You know how many weeks you have available, and the approximate amount of time that is available in each week.

You should stop all serious revision 48 hours before your examination. After this point, you may want to look back at your notes to refresh your memory, but you should not attempt to revise any new topics. A clear and rested brain is worth more than any extra facts you could memorise in this period.

Make one copy of this chart for each week you have available for revision.

Using your time planning chart, write in the times of your various study sessions during the week.

In the lower part of the chart, write in the topics that you will cover in each of these sessions.

Example of a revision timetable

Revision timetable Week beginning:	Monday	Tuesday	Wednesday	Thursday	Friday	Saturday	Sunday
Study sessions							
Topics							

Some revision techniques

There should be two elements in your revision. You must **look back** to the work you have covered in the course and **look forward** to the examination. The techniques you use should reflect these two aspects of revision.

Revision should not be boring. It is useful to try a variety of techniques. You probably already have some revision techniques of your own and you may also like to try some of the techniques suggested here, if they are new to you. However, don't waste time with methods of revision which are not effective for you.

- Go through your lecture notes, textbook or workbooks and use a highlighter pen to mark important points.

- Produce a new set of summarised notes. This can be a useful way of re-absorbing information, but you must be careful to keep your notes concise, or you may find that you are simply reproducing work you have done before. It is helpful to use a different format for your notes.

- Make a collection of key words which remind you of the essential concepts of a topic.

- Reduce your notes to a set of key facts and definitions which you must memorise. Write them on cards which you can keep with you all the time.

- When you come across areas which you were unsure about first time around, rework relevant questions in your course materials, then study the answers in great detail.

- If there are isolated topics which you feel are completely beyond you, identify exactly what it is that you cannot understand and find someone (such as a lecturer or recent graduate) who can explain these points to you.

- Practise as many exam standard questions as you can. The best way to do this is to work to time, under exam conditions. You should always resist looking at the answer until you have finished.

- If you have come to rely on a word processor in your day-to-day work, you may have got out of the habit of writing at speed. It is well worth reviving this skill before you sit down in the examination hall: it is something you will need.

- If you have a plentiful supply of relevant questions, you could use them to practise planning answers, and then compare your notes with the answers provided. This is not a substitute for writing full answers, but can be helpful additional practice.

- Go back to questions you have already worked on during the course. This time, complete them under exam conditions, paying special attention to the layout and organisation of your answers. Then compare them in detail with the suggested answers and think about the ways in which your answer differs. This is a useful way of 'fine tuning' your technique.

- During your revision period, do make a conscious effort to identify situations which illustrate concepts and ideas that may arise in the examination. These situations could come from your own work, or from reading the business pages of the quality press. This technique will give you a new perspective on your studies and could also provide material which you can use in the examination.

4 EXAMINATION TECHNIQUES

THE EXAMINATION

This section is divided into two parts. The first part considers the practicalities of sitting the examination. If you have taken other ACCA examinations recently, you may find that everything here is familiar to you. The second part discusses some examination techniques which you may find useful.

The practicalities

What to take with you

You should make sure that you have:

- your ACCA registration card
- your ACCA registration docket.

You may also take to your desk:

- pens and pencils
- a ruler and slide rule
- a calculator
- charting template and geometrical instruments
- eraser and correction fluid.

You are not allowed to take rough paper into the examination.

If you take any last-minute notes with you to the examination hall, make sure these are not on your person. You should keep notes or books in your bag or briefcase, which you will be asked to leave at the side of the examination hall.

Although most examination halls will have a clock, it is advisable to wear a watch, just in case your view is obscured.

If your calculator is solar-powered, make sure it works in artificial light. Some examination halls are not particularly well-lit. If you use a battery-powered calculator, take some spare batteries with you. For obvious reasons, you may not use a calculator which has a graphic/word display memory. Calculators with printout facilities are not allowed because they could disturb other candidates

Getting there

You should arrange to arrive at the examination hall at least half an hour before the examination is due to start. If the hall is a large one, the invigilator will start filling the hall half an hour before the starting time.

Make absolutely sure that you know how to get to the examination hall and how long it will take you. Check on parking or public transport. Leave yourself enough time so that you will not be anxious if the journey takes a little longer than you anticipated. Many people like to make a practice trip the day before their first examination.

At the examination hall

Examination halls differ greatly in size. Some only hold about ten candidates. Others can sit many hundreds of people. You may find that more than one examination is being taken at the hall at the same time, so don't panic if you hear people discussing a completely different subject from the one you have revised.

While you are waiting to go in, don't be put off by other people talking about how well, or badly, they have prepared for the examination.

You will be told when to come in to the examination hall. The desks are numbered. (Your number will be on your examination docket.) You will be asked to leave any bags at the side of the hall.

Inside the hall, the atmosphere will be extremely formal. The invigilator has certain things which he or she must tell candidates, often using a particular form of words. Listen carefully, in case there are any unexpected changes to the arrangements.

On your desk you will see a question paper and an answer booklet in which to write your answers. You will be told when to turn over the paper.

During the examination

You will have to leave your examination paper and answer booklet in the hall at the end of the examination. It is quite acceptable to write on your examination paper if it helps you to think about the questions. However, all workings should be in your answers. You may write any plans and notes in your answer booklet, as long as you cross them out afterwards.

If you require a new answer booklet, put your hand up and a supervisor will come and bring you one.

At various times during the examination, you will be told how much time you have left.

You should not need to leave the examination hall until the examination is finished. Put up your hand if you need to go to the toilet, and a supervisor will accompany you. If you feel unwell, put up your hand, and someone will come to your assistance. If you simply get up and walk out of the hall, you will not be allowed to reenter.

Before you finish, you must fill in the required information on the front of your answer booklet.

Examination techniques

Tackling Paper 6

The examination will be divided into two parts. The first part will contain three compulsory questions which will generally be concerned with the practical aspects of auditing accounting systems and the financial statements. Each question will be worth 20 marks. In the second section, you must answer two out of three questions on other aspects of auditing. Once again, each question is worth 20 marks. It is possible that some topics mentioned in the first section will also occur in the second section.

At the start of the examination, you should decide which question you are going to leave out from the second section, and then spend equal time answering each of the five questions.

This paper will test your knowledge of certain examinable documents. These are listed periodically in the *Students Newsletter*.

Your general strategy

You should spend the first ten minutes of the examination reading the paper. If you have a choice of question, decide which questions you will do. You must divide the time you spend on questions in proportion to the marks on offer. Don't be tempted to spend more time on a question you know a lot about, or one which you find particularly difficult. If a question has more than one part, you must complete each part.

On every question, the first marks are the easiest to gain. Even if things go wrong with your timing and you don't have time to complete a question properly, you will probably gain some marks by making a start.

Spend the last five minutes reading through your answers and making any additions or corrections.

You may answer written questions in any order you like. Some people start with their best question, to help them relax. Another strategy is to begin with your second best question, so that you are working even more effectively when you reach the question you are most confident about.

Once you have embarked on a question, you should try to stay with it, and not let your mind stray to other questions on the paper. You can only concentrate on one thing at once. However, if you get completely stuck with a question, leave space in your answer book and return to it later.

Answering the question

All Examiners say that the most frequent reason for failure in examinations, apart from basic lack of knowledge, is candidates' unwillingness to answer the question that the Examiner has asked. A great many people include every scrap of knowledge they have on a topic, just in case it is relevant. Stick to the question and tailor your answer to what you are asked. Pay particular attention to the verbs in the question.

You should be particularly wary if you come across a question which appears to be almost identical to one which you have practised during your revision. It probably isn't! Wishful thinking makes many people see the question they would like to see on the paper, not the one that is actually there. Read a question at least twice before you begin your answer. Underline key words on the question paper, if it helps focus your mind on what is required.

If you don't understand what a question is asking, state your assumptions. Even if you do not answer in precisely the way the Examiner hoped, you may be given some credit, if your assumptions are reasonable.

Presentation

You should do everything you can to make things easy for the marker. Although you will not be marked on your handwriting, the marker will find it easier to identify the points you have made if your answers are legible. The same applies to spelling and grammar. Use blue or black ink. The marker will be using red or green.

Use the margin to clearly identify which question, or part of a question, you are answering.

Start each answer on a new page. The order in which you answer the questions does not matter, but if a question has several parts, these parts should appear in the correct order in your answer book.

If there is the slightest doubt when an answer continues on another page, indicate to the marker that he or she must turn over. It is irritating for a marker to think he or she has reached the end of an answer, only to turn the page and find that the answer continues.

Use columnar layouts for computations. This will help you to avoid mistakes, and is easier to follow.

Use headings and numbered sentences if they help to show the structure of your answer. However, don't write your answers in one-word note form.

If your answers include diagrams, don't waste time making them great works of art. Keep them clear, neat and simple. Use your rule and any templates or geometric instruments you have with you. Remember to label the axes of graphs properly. Make reference to any diagrams in the body of your text so that they form an integral part of your answer.

It is a good idea to make a rough plan of an answer before you begin to write. Do this in your answer booklet, but make sure you cross it out neatly afterwards. The marker needs to be clear whether he or she is looking at your rough notes, or the answer itself.

Essay questions

You must plan an essay before you start writing. One technique is to quickly jot down any ideas which you think are relevant. Re-read the question and cross out any points in your notes which are not relevant. Then number your points. Remember to cross out your plan afterwards.

Your essay should have a clear structure. It should contain a brief introduction, a main section and a conclusion. Don't waste time by restating the question at the start of your essay.

Break your essay up into paragraphs. Use sub-headings and numbered sentences if they help show the structure of your answer.

Be concise. It is better to write a little about a lot of different points than a great deal about one or two points.

The Examiner will be looking for evidence that you have understood the syllabus and can apply your knowledge in new situations. You will also be expected to give opinions and make judgements. These should be based on reasoned and logical arguments.

Case studies

A case study asks you to apply your knowledge in a particular situation. It is useful to spend up to a third of the time available for the question in planning your answer.

Start by reading the questions based on the case study. Then read the case study, trying to grasp the main points. Read the case study through again and make notes of the key points. Then analyse the case and identify the relevant issues and concepts. Before you start your answer, read the questions again along with relevant parts of the case study.

If alternative answers present themselves, mention them. you may sometimes find it helpful to consider short and long term recommendations separately.

Reports, memos and other documents

Some questions ask you to present your answer in the form of a report or a memo or other document. It is important that you use the correct format - there are easy marks to be gained here. Adopt the format used in sample questions, or use the format you are familiar with in your day-to-day work, as long as it contains all the essential elements.

You should also consider the audience for any document you are writing. How much do they know about the subject? What kind of information and recommendations are required? The Examiner will be looking for evidence that you can present your ideas in an appropriate form.

5 KEY REVISION TOPICS

The aim of this section is to provide you with a checklist of key information relating to this Paper. You should use it as a reminder of topics to be revised rather than as a summary of all you need to know. Aim to revise as many topics as possible because many of the questions in the exam draw on material from more than one section of the syllabus. You will get more out of this section if you read through Section 3, *General Revision Guidance* first.

Where appropriate, the key revision topics listed below have been extended to include information about the relevant SAS issued by the APB. You need to keep up to date in this area by reading the *Students' Newsletter* and the list of examinable material which will be published prior to your exam as the list may change.

1 THE NATURE, PURPOSE AND SCOPE OF AUDITING

You must be familiar with:

- the APB definition of an audit
- the purpose of an audit, as expressed in statute for the external audit of a company
- the advantages of having an audit
- the stages in a conventional external audit, including how satisfactory results to tests of control can lead to reduced substantive procedures
- the responsibilities of directors, compared with the responsibilities of auditors.

Refer to chapter 1 of the Lynchpin, and attempt the question shown under the heading The Nature, Purpose and Scope of Auditing on the contents page of this book.

2 THE REGULATORY FRAMEWORK AND PROFESSIONAL REQUIREMENTS

You must be familiar with:

- the concept of the ACCA as an RSB
- the concept of qualifying with an RQB before one can be a member of an RSB
- how auditing standards are developed
- the status of different documents from the APB: SASs, practice notes and bulletins
- the role of the APB as described in SAS 010
- how accounting standards are developed
- EC and international auditing bodies, and the effect of ISAs
- the ACCA's Rules of Professional Conduct, particularly in respect to independence of the auditor
- the increased importance of audit committees following the Cadbury Report.

Refer to chapter 1 and 2 of the Lynchpin, and attempt all the questions shown under the heading The Regulatory Framework and Professional Requirements on the contents page of this book.

3   THE LEGAL FRAMEWORK

You must be familiar with:

- the CA85 general requirement for companies to be audited, and the exemption from audit available to small companies
- how private companies may elect to dispense with the annual re-election of auditors
- the auditor's rights and duties under the CA85.

Refer to chapter 3 of the Lynchpin, and attempt all the questions shown under the heading The Legal Framework on the contents page of this book.

4   THE AUDIT APPOINTMENT PROCESS

You must be familiar with:

- the statutory rules of appointment
- the ethical rules of appointment
- the practical and commercial implications of appointment
- the procedures concerning removal, retirement and resignation of the auditor
- instituting client screening procedures to avoid potentially risky audit clients
- SAS 210's requirement for the auditor to obtain a knowledge of the client's business
- SAS 140's requirement for the sending of an engagement letter

Refer to chapters 3 and 5 of the Lynchpin, and attempt all the questions shown under the heading The Audit Appointment Process on the contents page of this book.

5   PLANNING, RISK AND AUDIT EVIDENCE

You must be familiar with:

- the general principles governing an audit in SAS 100
- SAS 200's requirement for auditors to develop and document an overall audit plan
- the use of a standard Planning Memorandum
- the categories of audit risk: inherent risk, control risk and detection risk
- the use of a client risk evaluation questionnaire to assess client risk (the combination of inherent risk and control risk)
- the planning of materiality levels
- the planning of the audit programmes
- using the work of an expert in accordance with SAS 520
- SAS 400's requirement for the auditor to obtain sufficient appropriate audit evidence
- the categories of financial statement assertions (a mnemonic such as COVER MP can be useful in this regard)
- SAS 230's requirement for auditors to document important matters
- SAS 240's requirement for auditors to establish quality control procedures

Refer to chapter 6 of the Lynchpin, and attempt all the questions shown under the heading Planning, Risk and Audit Evidence on the contents page of this book.

6   ACCOUNTING SYSTEMS AND INTERNAL CONTROL

You must be familiar with:

- the definition of the internal control system

- SAS 300's requirement for auditors to understand the accounting and internal control systems

- why the auditor tests internal controls (if satisfactory, he can then reduce the amount of substantive testing)

- drawing up a systems flowchart

- using an ICQ and an ICE document

Refer to chapter 7 of the Lynchpin, and attempt all the questions shown under the heading Accounting Systems and Internal Control on the contents page of this book.

7   COMPUTERS IN AUDITING

You must be familiar with:

- the role of the management information system
- the ways the auditor can use a microcomputer in his audit
- the features of computerised accounting systems
- the difference between general controls and application controls
- the use of CAATs: audit software and test data
- the special problems associated with auditing small computer systems

Refer to chapter 15 of the Lynchpin, and attempt all the questions shown under the heading Computers in Auditing on the contents page of this book.

8   INTERNAL CONTROL AND MANAGEMENT LETTERS

You must be familiar with:

- possible tests of control that can be applied
- controls to be found in the sales system
- controls to be found in the purchases system
- controls to be found in the payroll, cash and other areas
- the role of a management letter
- the guidance offered in this area by SAS 610

Refer to chapters 8 and 9 of the Lynchpin, and attempt all the questions shown under the heading Internal Control and Management Letters on the contents page of this book.

9   AUDIT SAMPLING

You must be familiar with:

- the definition of audit sampling
- the guidance offered in this area by SAS 430
- when sampling would not be appropriate
- the conditions for sampling to be acceptable
- the meaning of sampling risk and tolerable error
- the use of attribute sampling in tests of control

- the use of variables sampling in substantive procedures
- the stages to follow in monetary unit sampling

Refer to chapter 10 of the Lynchpin, and attempt all the questions shown under the heading Audit Sampling on the contents page of this book.

10   THE BALANCE SHEET AUDIT

You must be familiar with:

- the financial statement assertions listed in SAS 400. These were described earlier, and can be remembered using a mnemonic such as COVER MP

- the audit of stocks and work in progress. Valuation must be in accordance with SSAP 9. Attendance at the stocktake is an important source of evidence confirming existence of stock

- tests to ensure proper cut-off of sales and purchases

- the audit of fixed assets. Both the CA85 and accounting standards contain rules that must be complied with

- the audit of debtors. A debtors circularisation is a powerful source of audit evidence

- the audit of liquid assets. A bank certificate is a powerful source of audit evidence confirming year-end balances

- the audit of liabilities, capital and estimates. SAS 420 requires auditors to judge whether the management's accounting estimates are reasonable

Refer to chapters 11 to 14 of the Lynchpin, and attempt all the questions shown under the heading The Balance Sheet Audit on the contents page of this book.

11   FORMING AN AUDIT JUDGEMENT

You must be familiar with:

- the SAS 470 requirement to review the financial statements before expressing the audit opinion

- the analytical review procedures described in SAS 410

- the auditor's responsibilities for the going concern status of his client. SAS 130 requires the auditor to consider the client's ability to continue as a going concern

- the correct treatment of subsequent events in accordance with SAS 150

- the use of management representations as a source of audit evidence in accordance with SAS 440

- the definition of related parties

- the requirement of SAS 460 for auditors to obtain audit evidence concerning the disclosure of transactions with related parties

Refer to chapter 16 of the Lynchpin, and attempt all the questions shown under the heading Forming an Audit Judgement on the contents page of this book.

12   THE AUDIT REPORT AND OTHER REPORTS

You must be familiar with:

- the CA85 requirements on the content of the audit report

- the requirements of SAS 600 on the wording of the audit report, though note that you will **not** be asked to reproduce the audit report in full in an exam question

- when each form of audit report is appropriate: unqualified, unqualified with an explanatory paragraph, qualified 'except for', adverse, disclaimer

- the auditor's responsibilities for opening balances and comparatives, as laid down in SAS 450

- the auditor's responsibilities for other information in documents containing audited financial statements (eg, the directors' report) as laid down in SAS 160

- the filing of abbreviated accounts by small and medium-sized companies

- the exemption from audit of small companies

- the issue of summary financial statements to shareholders in place of full accounts

- the issue of revised accounts

- the auditors' statement on distributions following an audit qualification

Refer to chapters 17 and 18 of the Lynchpin, and attempt all the questions shown under the heading The Audit Report and Other Reports on the contents page of this book.

13   RESPONSIBILITIES AND LEGAL LIABILITIES

You must be familiar with:

- the auditor's responsibilities under statute
- the concept of due care and negligence
- key cases identifying the auditor's liability, particularly the Caparo case
- ways of avoiding negligence by improving the quality of audits, as specified in SAS 240
- the auditor's responsibility for detecting fraud and error, as specified in SAS 110

Refer to chapters 19 and 20 of the Lynchpin, and attempt all the questions shown under the heading Responsibilities and Legal Liabilities on the contents page of this book.

6 UPDATES

INTRODUCTION

Examinable documents

Every six months (on 1 July and 1 December) the ACCA publish a list of 'examinable documents' which form the basis of the legislation and accounting regulations that will be examinable at the following diet.

The ACCA Official Textbooks published in July 1998 were fully up-to-date for these examinable documents published by the Association on 1 July 1998 and this section gives details of additional examinable documents listed by the ACCA at 1 December 1998.

The only new examinable document issued between 1 June 1998 and 1 December 1998 is FRS 12, on which some notes are set out below.

ACCOUNTING FOR PROVISIONS AND CONTINGENCIES

FRS 12 *Provisions, contingent liabilities and contingent assets* was issued in September 1998 to introduce new standard accounting for provisions (there was no previous standard in this area) and to replace SSAP 18 in the accounting for contingencies.

Provisions are defined as liabilities of uncertain timing or amount. FRS 12 therefore deals with those sorts of items that might appear in a balance sheet under 'Provisions for liabilities and charges', for example provisions for repairs and renewals. It does not deal with provisions for depreciation or provisions for doubtful debts.

A provision should only be set up where:

- an entity has an obligation.
- it is probable that a transfer of economic benefits will be required to settle the obligation, and
- a reliable estimate can be made of the amount of the obligation.

The amount set up for a provision should be the best estimate of the expenditure required to settle the present obligation at the balance sheet date.

A contingent liability is either:

- a possible obligation arising from past events whose existence will be confirmed only by the occurrence of one or more uncertain future events not wholly within the entity's control, or

- a present obligation that arises from past events but is not recognised because it is not probable that a transfer of economic benefits will be required to settle the obligation or because the amount of the obligation cannot be measured with sufficient reliability.

A contingent asset is a possible asset arising from past events whose existence will be confirmed only by the occurrence of one or more uncertain future events not wholly within the entity's control.

Contingent assets and liabilities should not be recognised in the balance sheet.

Unless remote in possibility, a contingent liability should be disclosed in a note to the accounts.

Where an inflow of economic benefits is probable, details of a contingent asset should be disclosed in a note to the accounts.

SSAP 18 *Accounting for contingencies* has been withdrawn, so entities should now follow the standard accounting in FRS 12.

7 PRACTICE QUESTIONS

1 ADVANTAGES OF AUDIT

Only certain types of entities are legally required to have an audit; others may choose to do so.

You are required to discuss the advantages of an audit.

(12 marks)

2 REGULATION AND PROFESSIONALISM

The auditing profession has been criticised recently by politicians for its role in monitoring potential corporate failure. Radical reforms have been called for in the way the audit is regulated. For example, politicians have stated that there should be a change of legislation in the following ways:

(i) Auditing standards

Auditing standards should be set and enforced independently from the accounting profession.

(ii) Fraud

Auditing firms should have a duty to detect and report fraud.

(iii) Non audit services

Non auditing services supplied to an audit client should be stopped.

(iv) The duration of the appointment of auditors

The appointment of auditors should be for a maximum period of seven years.

You are required:

(a) to describe the current regulatory and professional requirements relating to each of the main headings listed above.

(12 marks)

(b) to discuss the reasons why you feel that the audit profession has been criticised over the current regulations in the above areas.

(8 marks)
(Total: 20 marks)
(ACCA Dec 93)

3   AB & CO

It is important that an auditor's independence is beyond question and that he should behave with integrity and objectivity in all professional and business situations. The following are a series of questions which were asked by auditors at a recent update seminar on professional ethics.

(a)   Can I audit my brother's company?

(4 marks)

(b)   A B & Co the previous auditors, will not give my firm professional clearance or the usual handover information because they are still owed fees. Should I accept the client's offer of appointment?

(5 marks)

(c)   Can I prepare the financial statements of a public company and still remain as auditor?

(4 marks)

(d)   My client has threatened to sue the firm for negligence. Can I still continue to act as auditor?

(5 marks)

(e)   I am a student of the Association of Chartered Certified Accountants. Am I bound by the ethical guidelines of the Association?

(2 marks)

You are required to discuss the answers you would give to the above questions posed by the auditors.

(Total: 20 marks)
(ACCA June 93)

4   GROWFAST PLC

Growfast plc was formed on 1 August 19X0 in order to manufacture minicomputers. The directors are unsure as to their responsibilities, and the nature of their relationship with the external auditors. The audit partner has asked you to visit the client and explain to the directors the more fundamental aspects of the accountability of the company and their relationship with the auditor.

You are required: to explain to the directors of Growfast plc

(a)   why there is a need for an audit;

(5 marks)

(b)   how the auditor of a public company may be appointed under the CA85;

(5 marks)

(c)   what the auditor's rights are under the CA85;

(6 marks)

(d)   the responsibilities of the directors in relation to the accounting function of the company.

(4 marks)
(Total: 20 marks)
(ACCA Dec 90)

5   ABLE PLC

Mr White is a partner in a small four partner accounting practice, which is registered to carry out audits under the Companies Act 1989. One of his clients, Able plc has asked him if he would like to join the board of directors of a subsidiary company, Dale Ltd. They have suggested that he leaves the practice, joins the board of Dale Ltd and continues to audit the holding company Able plc in his own right. The client incorrectly informed Mr White that if he left his practice, the partnership would automatically be dissolved and become ineligible to act as auditors of Able plc, so that he could audit Able plc without offending his previous colleagues.

Unfortunately Mr White, not having studied in detail the provisions of the Companies Acts, agrees to join the board of directors of Dale Ltd and to carry out the audit of the holding company Able plc. The former auditors were not re-elected at the annual general meeting of Able plc and Mr White was elected in their place.

You are required:

(a)   to explain the reasons why Mr White is ineligible, under the Companies Acts, to act as auditor of Able plc.

(7 marks)

(b)   to explain what steps the auditor should take when he becomes ineligible to act in that capacity.

(3 marks)

(c)   to explain the consequences under the Companies Acts of an accountant acting in the capacity as auditor when being ineligible to do so.

(3 marks)

(d)   to describe the powers of the Secretary of State in relation to an audit that has been carried out by an ineligible person.

(4 marks)

(e)   to comment on the directors' statement that the previous auditors would become ineligible to act when Mr White left the practice because the partnership would automatically be dissolved.

(3 marks)
(Total: 20 marks)
(ACCA Dec 92)

---

6   MATERIALITY

You have been asked by the partner in charge of your firm to provide guidance to audit staff about materiality; he believes that if this guidance is provided to staff it will allow them to carry out audits more effectively.

You are required

(a)   to provide a definition of the term 'material' and explain why the concept of materiality is important to auditors;

(4 marks)

(b)   to provide guidance on materiality. You answer should consider:

(i)   errors in tests of control on accounting systems;
(ii)   errors in the profit and loss account;
(iii)   errors in balance sheet items;
(iv)   compliance with the Companies Acts and Accounting Standards;
(v)   aggregation of errors and uncertainties.

(16 marks)
(Total: 20 marks)
(ACCA Dec 91)

7   ACCOUNTANCY WORK AND AUDIT EVIDENCE

An audit firm which is the auditor of a small business may also be engaged to carry out a significant amount of accountancy work. This accountancy work may comprise writing up books of account, drawing up a trial balance and producing financial statements. In carrying out this accountancy work, the auditor may obtain audit evidence relevant to meeting certain audit objectives. For example, the auditor may himself calculate a balance for inclusion in the financial statements. One of the objectives which the auditor will wish to achieve in respect of any balance under audit is to establish that the item is complete. The auditor will be particularly concerned with establishing the completeness of income, stock and purchases, and the auditor may be met with special difficulties when trying to establish the completeness of an item in the case of a small business. The causes of these difficulties may include lack of internal controls and dominant management.

You are required:

(a)   to outline the criteria which must be satisfied before the auditor can rely upon evidence derived from accountancy work carried out by the audit firm.

(5 marks)

(b)   to describe the limitations of relying upon accountancy work as a prime source of audit evidence.

(6 marks)

(c)   to describe the forms and types of audit evidence which the auditor will gather in order to satisfy himself of the completeness of an item when auditing a small business.

(9 marks)
(Total: 20 marks)
(ACCA June 93)

8   WAGES AND SALARIES ICQ

The following questions have been selected from an internal control questionnaire for wages and salaries.

Internal control questionnaire – wages and salaries

		Yes	*No*
(1)	Does an appropriate official authorise rates of pay?		
(2)	Are written notices required for employing and terminating employment?		
(3)	Are formal records such as time cards used for time keeping?		
(4)	Does anyone verify rates of pay, overtime hours and computations of gross pay before the wage payments are made?		
(5)	Does the accounting system ensure the proper recording of payroll costs in the financial records?		

You are required:

(a)   to describe the internal control objective being fulfilled if the controls set out in the above questions are in effect.

(5 marks)

(b)   to describe the audit tests which would test the effectiveness of each control and help determine any potential material error.

(10 marks)

(c)   to identify the potential consequences for the company if the above controls were not in place.

(5 marks)

Students may answer in columnar form under the headings

ICQ question	Internal control objective	Audit tests	Consequences

(Total: 20 marks)
(ACCA Dec 93)

9   COTGRAVE DISTRIBUTORS

You are the senior in charge of the audit of Cotgrave Distributors Ltd, and a junior member of your audit team has asked you the controls which you would expect to see in the company's sales system. Cotgrave Distributors is a large private company which purchases products from manufacturers and sells them to retailers. It operates from a single warehouse where the products are received from suppliers, stored, and sent to customers. You understand that there should be sufficient staff to ensure that there are strong internal controls in the sales system. The company's sales ledger is maintained on a computer, and it is integrated into the stock control system so that goods are deducted from the book stock records when they are dispatched to customers.

You are aware that the following departments or individuals are involved in the sales system and receipt of cash from customers:

(a)   the sales department
(b)   the credit controller
(c)   the sales accounting department
(d)   the cashier
(e)   the dispatch department.

All sales are made on credit and there are no cash sales.

You are aware that the documents in the sales system include:

(a)   customer order
(b)   order confirmation
(c)   dispatch note
(d)   sales invoice
(e)   credit note
(f)   sales day book
(g)   sales ledger
(h)   cash book
(i)   remittance advice and cheque from the customer
(j)   statements sent to customers.

The junior member of the audit team has asked you the questions listed below.

You are required to describe the controls which you would expect to be in operation:

(a)   to ensure that goods are only sent to authorised customers:

   (i)   who have placed an order with the company, and
   (ii)   who the company expects to pay for these goods (ie, they will not be a bad debt);

(10 marks)

(b)   to ensure cash is received promptly from customers and it is accurately recorded in the company's accounting records.

(10 marks)
(Total: 20 marks)
(Pilot Paper)

10   BULWELL MANUFACTURING PLC

Bulwell Manufacturing plc is proposing to install a new computer system, and the financial director has asked you to suggest the controls which should be exercised over access to the computer system from remote terminals. All accounting data will be input into the computer from terminals and data from remote factories and branches will be transmitted to the main computer through the national telephone system (ie, British Telecom in the UK).

You are required:

(a)   to describe the general controls which can be exercised to prevent unauthorised access to the computer system from remote terminals. Your answer should consider the effectiveness and limitations of each of the types of control;

(7 marks)

(b)   to describe the additional procedures which can be exercised to prevent unauthorised access to the computer through the national telephone system;

(5 marks)

(c)   to briefly describe the controls which should be exercised in the purchases and payroll systems over:

   (i)   retrieval of information
   (ii)   input of transaction data
   (iii)   updating of standing data files.

(8 marks)
(Total: 20 marks)
(Pilot Paper)

11   HYSON HOTELS PLC

SAS 500 has been issued on 'Considering the work of internal audit'. You have recently been appointed auditor of Hyson Hotels plc which owns and runs about 100 hotels in the UK. The company has an established internal audit department, which both operates at the head office and visits the hotels.

Each hotel has a computer which records the bookings of rooms for overnight accommodation and the accounts for each guest.

You are required:

(a) to list and briefly describe the work you would expect to be carried out by the internal audit staff of Hyson Hotels;

(11 marks)

(b) to describe the factors you would consider and the work you would perform to enable you to assess the extent to which you could rely on the work of the internal auditors;

(5 marks)

(c) assuming that you conclude that the work of the internal audit department is reliable, to describe the effect this would have on your audit work.

(4 marks)
(Total: 20 marks)
(Pilot Paper)

---

12 MANAGEMENT LETTERS

The management letter should be clear, concise and constructive. Careful presentation will help the recipient to understand the significance of the comments and devise corrective action. The letter may contain matters of varying levels of significance and may well be read by a person who does not have an accounting background. The following paragraphs are extracts from draft management letters prepared by inexperienced members of audit teams.

(i) *Extract from a management letter to the managing director of a large privately owned company.*

At present there is no control over amendments to the master file data in either the creditors or wages system. Because of this, unauthorised amendments to the data could be made, thus affecting all related transactions processed. Somebody should check amendment data before it is input through the master file suite of programs.

(ii) *Extract from a management letter to the managing director of a medium sized public limited company*

Calculations of the net monthly and weekly payroll figures should be independently checked on a random sample basis. At present there is no evidence that checks of this nature are carried out. Independent checks are an essential element of internal control and will help eliminate the possibility of computational errors remaining undetected.

You are required:

(a) to discuss the weaknesses in the above extracts from management letters and redraft the extracts in a more suitable form.

(14 marks)

(b) to describe the principal purposes of a management letter.

(6 marks)
(Total: 20 marks)
(ACCA Dec 92)

13 HEALTHY MILK LTD

Healthy Milk Ltd buys milk from dairy farmers, processes the milk and delivers it to retail outlets. You are currently auditing the debtors system and determine the following information:

(i)   The company employs 75 drivers who are each responsible for delivering milk to customers. Each driver delivers milk to between 20 and 30 shops on a daily basis. Debtors normally amount to approximately £450,000. Payments by customers are not normally made to the drivers but are sent directly to the head office of the company.

(ii)   The sales ledger is regularly reviewed by the office manager who prepares a list for each driver of accounts with 90 day balances or older. This list is used for the purpose of intensive collection by the drivers. Each driver has a delivery book which is used for recording deliveries of milk and those debtors with 90 day balances.

(iii)   The audit program used in previous audits for the selection of debtor balances for direct confirmation stated: 'Select two accounts from each driver's customers, one to be chosen by opening each driver's delivery book at random and the other as the fourth item on the list of 90 day or older accounts.' Each page of the driver's delivery book deals with a single customer.

Having reviewed the debtors system, you conclude that statistical sampling techniques should be used to assist your audit work. On the completion of your review and testing of the 2,000 debtor balances, your statistical sample of 100 accounts disclosed 10 errors. You therefore conclude that there must be 200 accounts in the entire population which are in error as you are sure that the errors detected in the sample will be in exact proportion to the errors in the population.

You are required:

(a)   to explain the reasons why the audit procedure used in the previous audit for the selection of debtors for audit confirmation would not produce a valid statistical sample;

(4 marks)

(b)   to explain briefly the audit objectives in selecting a sample of 90 day accounts for direct confirmation;

(3 marks)

(c)   to discuss whether the application of statistical sampling techniques would help in the attainment of the audit objectives set out in (b) above;

(5 marks)

(d)   to discuss whether it is reasonable to assume that the errors detected in the sample of debtor balances tested are in exact proportion to the errors in the total population of debtors;

(4 marks)

(e)   to discuss the view that since statistical sampling techniques do not relieve the auditor of his responsibilities in the exercise of his professional judgement, then they are of no benefit to the auditor.

(4 marks)
(Total: 20 marks)
(ACCA Dec 90)

14   AUDIT SAMPLING

It is important to recognise that audit sampling may be constructed on a non-statistical basis. If the auditor uses statistical sampling, probability theory will be used to determine sample size and random selection methods to ensure each item or £1 in value of the population has the same chance of selection. Non-statistical sampling is more subjective than statistical sampling, typically using haphazard selection methods and placing no reliance upon probability theory. However, in certain circumstances statistical sampling techniques may be difficult to use. The auditor will review the circumstances of each audit before deciding whether to use statistical or non-statistical sampling.

You are required:

(a)   to list three situations where the auditor would be unlikely to use audit sampling techniques.

(3 marks)

(b)   to explain what you understand by the following terms:

   (i)   attribute sampling
   (ii)   monetary unit sampling.

(6 marks)

(c)   to describe the factors which the auditor should consider when determining the size of a sample.

(6 marks)

(d)   to describe to what extent statistical sampling enhances the quality of the audit evidence.

(5 marks)
(Total: 20 marks)
(ACCA June 93)

15   TRENT TEXTILES

Your firm is the auditor of Trent Textiles Ltd, and you are planning your audit work on the stocktake, which will be carried out at the firm's year end of 31 May 19X3.

Trent Textiles manufactures knitted garments, including pullovers. The production process comprises:

(a)   knitting the individual components (eg, body and arms)
(b)   sewing the components together to form the finished garment
(c)   cleaning, finishing, pressing and folding the garments
(d)   packing the garments, ready for dispatch to the customer.

Trent Textiles does not have a perpetual inventory system, so the value of the stock in the accounts is found from the stocktake at the year end. For management purposes, Trent Textiles carries out a full stocktake every three months.

Your permanent file of the company confirms that it has a single factory and no internal audit department.

You have been asked by the manager in charge of the audit to suggest the work you will perform at the stages listed below.

You are required:

(a)   to describe the work you will carry out prior to the commencement of the stocktake;

(5 marks)

(b)   to describe the procedures you will check during the stocktake to ensure the company's staff have accurately recorded the stock;

(8 marks)

(c)   to describe the work you will carry out and the matters you will record at the stocktake.

(7 marks)
(Total: 20 marks)
(Pilot Paper)

16   STOCK VALUATION

An important part of the audit of stocks and work in progress is to perform procedures to make certain that stocks are properly valued and compiled. Valuation, amongst other things, includes all the tests of the clients unit prices to determine whether they are correct. Compilation includes all the tests relating to the physical stock counts and the summarisation of the results of the counts.

The following are examples of specific audit objectives relating to the physical stock count and the valuation of stock.

Audit objectives

Physical stock count

(i)   The stock is owned by the company.

(ii)   The stock count is carried out accurately and records obsolete stock.

(iii)   Information is obtained to ensure sales and purchases are recorded in the proper period.

Valuation of stock

(i)   Stock items shown on the stock evaluation sheets are valid.

(ii)   All existing stock items are included on the stock evaluation sheets.

(iii)   Stock is properly priced.

You are required:

(a)   to list the audit procedures which would be carried out in order to ensure that the above audit objectives are fulfilled.

(15 marks)

(b)   to list five audit procedures which would be undertaken in order to verify a material amount of stock which is held at third parties.

(5 marks)
(Total: 20 marks)
(ACCA Dec 93)

17   GOING CONCERN

There is evidence that the public interest would be best served by the inclusion of fuller information about risks facing companies in audited financial statements. The Auditing Practices Board intends to ensure that doubts about the going-concern presumption are detected and adequately disclosed in financial statements and auditors reports. SAS 130 explains what can reasonably be expected of auditors in this regard.

You are required:

(a)   to explain what you understand by the term 'going-concern basis' in relation to the preparation of financial statements.

(4 marks)

(b)   to describe the audit procedures necessary in order to gain sufficient audit evidence to be able to form an opinion on the going-concern status of a company.

(6 marks)

(c)   to list six factors which might cast doubt on the going-concern status of a company.

(6 marks)

(d)   to discuss, briefly, whether and how the present responsibilities of the auditor regarding the going-concern status of a company could be extended.

(4 marks)
(Total: 20 marks)
(ACCA June 93)

18   LAMBLEY PROPERTIES PLC

SAS 440 has been issued on 'Management representations'. You are the manager in charge of the audit of Lambley Properties plc and you have been asked to prepare the letter of representation which will be signed by the company's directors.

You are aware that there are two material items in the accounts for the year ended 31 January 19X3 on which you want the company's directors to confirm that the treatment in the accounts is correct:

(a)   One of the company's subsidiaries, Keyworth Builders Ltd, is experiencing going concern problems, and you want the directors' confirmation that they intend to support the company for the foreseeable future.

(b)   Eastwood Manufacturing plc is in dispute with Lambley Properties over repairs required to a building they purchased from Lambley. Lambley Properties constructed the building for Eastwood, and three years after it was sold to Eastwood, the customer is claiming that repairs are required which will cost £3 million, and that Lambley is liable to pay for these repairs, as they are as a result of negligent construction of the building. In addition, Eastwood is claiming £2 million for the cost of disruption of its business due to the faults in the building and in the period when the repairs take place. Lambley Properties has not included any provision in its accounts for this claim. Lambley Properties have obtained the advice of a lawyer and a surveyor, and the directors believe there are no grounds for the claim and any court action will find in their favour. However, Lambley Properties has included a note in its accounts concerning this contingency.

You are required:

(a)   to prepare a letter of representation which the directors will sign and send to you, as auditors. In the letter, you should include the two items above and any other matters which you believe should be included;

(9 marks)

(b)   to discuss the reliability of a letter of representation as audit evidence and the extent to which an auditor can rely on this evidence;

(5 marks)

(c)   to describe the work you will perform to check whether a provision should be included in the accounts for the legal claim from Eastwood Manufacturing plc.

(6 marks)
(Total: 20 marks)
(Pilot Paper)

---

19   JONES, ROBERTS, WILLIAMS, GRIFFITHS AND EVANS

You are currently engaged in reviewing the working papers of several audit assignments recently carried out by your audit practice. Each of the audit assignments is nearing completion, but certain matters have recently come to light which may affect your audit opinion on each of the assignments. In each case the year end of the company is 30 September 19X4.

(a)   **Jones Ltd** (Profit before tax £150,000)

On 3 October 19X4 a letter was received informing the company that a debtor, who owed the company £30,000 as at the year end had been declared bankrupt on 30 September. At the time of the audit it was expected that unsecured creditors, such as Jones Ltd, would receive nothing in respect of this debt. The directors refuse to change the accounts to provide for the loss, on the grounds that the notification was not received by the balance sheet date.

Total debts shown in the balance sheet amounted to £700,000.

(4 marks)

(b)   **Roberts Ltd** (Profit before tax £500,000)

On 31 July 19X4 a customer sued the company for personal damages arising from an unexpected defect in one of its products. Shortly before the year end the company made an out-of-court settlement with the customer of £10,000, although this agreement is not reflected in the financial statements as at 30 September 19X4. Further, the matter subsequently became known to the press and was extensively reported. The company's legal advisers have now informed you that further claims have been received following the publicity, although they are unable to place a figure on the potential liability arising from such claims which have not yet been received. The company had referred to the claims in a note to the financial statements stating, however, that no provision had been made to cover them because the claims were not expected to be material.

(4 marks)

(c)   **Williams plc** (Net loss for the year £75,000)

Three directors of this manufacturing company owed amounts totalling £50,000 at the end of the financial year, and you have ascertained that such loans were not of a type permissible under the Companies Act 1985. These amounts had been included in the balance sheet with other items under the heading 'Debtors collectable within one year'. The directors did not wish to disclose these loans separately in the accounts as they were repaid shortly after the year end, as soon as they were made aware that the loans were not permissible. The directors have argued that the disclosures could prove embarrassing and that no purpose would be served by revealing this information in the accounts.

(4 marks)

(d)   **Griffiths Ltd** (Net profit before tax £250,000)

The audit work revealed that a trade investment stated in the balance sheet at £500,000 had suffered a permanent fall in value of £300,000. The company admitted that the loss had occurred, but refused to make a provision for it on the grounds that other trade investments (not held for resale) had risen in value and were stated at amounts considerably below their realisable values.

(4 marks)

(e)   **Evans plc** (Net profit before tax £100,000)

This client is a construction company, currently building a warehouse on its own premises, and using some of its own workforce. The cost of labour and materials has been included in the cost of the fixed asset in the balance sheet, the total figure being based on the company's costing records. The warehouse is almost complete and the cost shown in the balance sheet includes direct labour costs of £10,000. However, during audit testing it was discovered that the costing records, showing the direct labour costs for the warehouse in the early part of the year, had been destroyed accidentally.

(4 marks)
(Total: 20 marks)

You are required to complete the task below:

Discuss each of the cases outlined above, referring to materiality considerations and, where appropriate, relevant accounting principles and appropriate accounting standards. You should also indicate, with reasons, the kind of audit report (including the type of qualification, if necessary) which you consider would be appropriate in each case.

You are not required to produce the full audit reports, and you may assume that all matters other than those specifically mentioned are considered satisfactory.

---

20   DUTY OF CARE

For many years the law had adopted an approach whereby no action for negligence could be brought if the parties concerned had no contractual relationship with each other, unless the negligent act caused physical injury or was fraudulent misrepresentation. Thus, the auditor had a contractual relationship with his clients' shareholders only and owed a duty of care to them alone. However, the courts have increasingly sought to extend the liability of the auditor to other (even potential) users of financial statements. The view of the judiciary appears to be that the time is ripe for the auditing profession to assume a greater responsibility for its actions. The risk attaching to users of audited financial statements has been reduced and, at the same time, there has been an increase in the risk carried by the auditing profession.

You are required:

(a)   to describe the judicial decisions which have altered the range of the auditors' duty of care to third parties;

(10 marks)

(b)   to explain how the auditor can ensure that the risk attaching to an audit is reduced to a minimum;

(7 marks)

(c)   to comment on the view that much of the litigation and allegations of negligence directed against the auditors may be more appropriately aimed at the directors of a company.

(3 marks)
(Total: 20 marks)
(ACCA June 89)

8 ANSWERS TO PRACTICE QUESTIONS

---

1   ADVANTAGES OF AUDIT

(Tutorial note: in each section a short paragraph is written on each point. This breaks the answer up, and is much easier to mark, as well as improving presentation. The examiner does not want to see a long verbose essay.

The main advantage common to all forms of audit is that the accounts have been subjected to independent review and an independent and professional opinion obtained on their truth and fairness.

Incidental advantages are the detection of irregularities, the moral deterrent against fraud and error, and the availability of expert technical advice on such matters as the improvement of systems, taxation and accountancy. More specifically, the advantages depend on the types of audit.)

(a)   **Limited companies**

In the case of limited companies, shareholders must of necessity place great reliance upon a review of the accounts by an independent qualified auditor since they do not have access to the books and records of the company and they are not always familiar with the businesses in which they have an interest, nor indeed with the accounting practices adopted.

Moreover, the audit ensures that the directors have fulfilled their statutory obligations, and acts as a precaution against fraud on the part of employees.

Additional benefits deriving include the improvement of the company's control and information systems, and possibly advice on improvement in standards of the company's reporting to its members.

(b)   **Partnerships**

Audited accounts in the case of a partnership provide a reliable basis for the division of profits and for the settling of accounts between partners, reducing the possibility of disputes and facilitating their settlement should they arise. Effect is therefore given to the rights of partners in accordance with the provisions of the partnership agreement, or in the absence of such, with the provisions of the Partnership Act 1890.

Audited accounts will assist in settling the partnership income tax assessments and provide a basis for negotiation in the case of an incoming partner or the sale of the business.

On the death of a partner the total amount due to him should be more readily determined and agreed, and the settlement of death duties facilitated.

The provision of reliable audited accounts presents a more acceptable basis for the negotiations involved in raising additional finance.

In the special situation of a firm which has 'sleeping' or limited partners, an audit is of particular importance and advantage as such persons take no part in the management of the business.

(c)   **Sole traders**

Similar advantages accrue to the business of a sole trader, since there is a likelihood of a breakdown in internal control and accounting systems.

An incidental but important advantage of an audit is that the professional firm of accountants acting as auditors will be available to provide other services eg, advice and assistance on accounting, costing, management, taxation and systems problems.

2   REGULATION AND PROFESSIONALISM

The purpose of this question is to examine students on current and potential changes in practice within the profession.

(a)   (i)   Auditing standards are set by the Auditing Practices Board (APB). The accountancy bodies adopt all of the auditing standards promulgated by the APB. Failure by auditors to comply with auditing standards lends them open to disciplinary action by their own accountancy body. The Companies Act 1989 requires the Recognised Supervisory Bodies (such as the Association of Chartered Certified Accountants) to have rules and practices as to the technical standards to be applied in company audit work and as to the manner in which these standards are to be applied in practice. Each Recognised Supervisory Body adopts auditing standards in order to meet the Companies Act requirement, and each body is required to have arrangements in place for the effective monitoring and enforcement of compliance with those standards. Failure to apply relevant auditing standards is a factor which an RSB will take into account when deciding whether persons are fit and proper to be eligible for appointment as company auditor.

(ii)   Currently the responsibility within a company for the prevention and detection of fraud rests with management. As part of their business responsibilities, the directors of a company have a fiduciary duty to safeguard the assets. The Cadbury Committee has recently recommended that the auditor should check that the board of a company has established a system which ensures compliance with its legal requirements. The auditor is not responsible for preventing fraud but audit procedures should be designed to give the auditor a reasonable expectation of detecting any material misstatements, whether intentional or unintentional in a company's financial statements. This responsibility is set out in SAS 110 'Fraud and error' (January 1995).

(iii)   The auditor should always strive to be objective in his professional judgement. He should not only be independent in fact but he must be clearly seen to be independent in practice. The RSBs have no objection in principle to a practice providing services to a client, additional to the audit. Care must be taken not to perform management functions or make management decisions. The auditor should not assist in the preparation of financial statements for public company clients unless the work is of a routine clerical nature or in emergency situations. Any fee paid to the auditor for non-audit work should be shown in the financial statements in addition to amounts paid for audit work.

Under the provisions of the Companies Act 1985, an auditor may not be an officer or employee of a client company. Thus it is necessary for the auditor to ensure that he does not make executive decisions. For example if he recruits key financial and administrative staff, it could be construed as the performance of a management function. The auditor's objectivity may be threatened in such situations and he should be careful that he is not seen as acting as anything other than an independent adviser.

(iv)   Under the Companies Act 1985 (s385), a company shall at each general meeting of the company at which accounts are laid, appoint an auditor to hold office from the conclusion of that meeting until the conclusion of the next general meeting at which accounts are laid. Under the 'elective regime' established by the Companies Act 1989 in relation to small companies, a company may elect to dispense with the obligation to appoint auditors annually. In this case the auditor will be deemed to be re-appointed for each succeeding financial year on the expiry of the time for re-appointing the auditors for that year (unless the company becomes dormant, or the appointment is brought to an end by resolution of the members). The ethical guidance issued by the RSBs does not specifically deal with the length of audit appointments. However, the auditor should always be aware of any potential threat to his independence which may be caused by an audit appointment which has lasted for a disproportionate length of time.

(b)   (i)   Auditing standards are set by the Auditing Practices Board whose members are mainly drawn from the members of the auditing profession. The disciplinary procedures applied against an auditor for non-compliance with an auditing standard are enforced by the professional bodies of accountants.

Thus politicians have criticised this self regulatory procedure believing it to be open to abuse and lacking independence. The argument put forward is that the consequences of auditing affect society and therefore in order to ensure that audits achieve social goals, auditing standards should be set by an independent body.

(ii)   It is quite apparent from the press and audit research that the public believe that the auditor should and in fact does search for fraud during the conduct of an audit. In view of the recent scandals, particularly BCCI and the Maxwell affair, the public expectation of the extent of an audit has increased. It is not surprising, given the nature of these scandals, that the public finds it difficult to accept that an auditor has no responsibility for the detection and reporting of fraud, especially when one sees the high social cost of these scandals.

(iii)   Audit firms do not act exclusively in the capacity of auditors for their clients. Audit work is in some cases, not the main business of audit firms. Auditors provide many other services to their clients including tax advice, brand name valuation and recruitment advice. Audit firms are dependent upon the fees earned from non-audit services, and this dependency can affect the auditors attitude to the audit. If an audit firm loses the audit, the financial loss to the auditors can be significantly more than just the audit fee if he provides other services to the client. Thus a significant amount of pressure can be exerted upon the auditor if he supplies other services to the client. A significant amount of an auditor's fee income derives from non-audit work and in an environment where the audit work is declining, fees for other services are becoming increasingly important.

(iv)   It has been argued that the long-term nature of the company audit engagement can lead to a loss in auditor independence due to an increasing familiarity with the company's management. In many European countries, the audit appointment has, by law, to be terminated after a fixed number of years. If the audit appointment was for a fixed maximum period, then auditors would not be under the same pressure to maintain their client base if they know that their relationship with the company was for a limited period, and that audit appointments would be rotated.

3   AB & CO

The purpose of this question is to examine students on professional ethics.

(a)   The statement on independence warns that personal relationships with a client can affect objectivity. There is a particular need therefore for a practice to ensure that its objective approach to an assignment is not endangered as a result of a personal relationship. Problems of this nature can arise if an officer or senior employee of an audit client is so closely connected with the partner or senior member of staff responsible for the conduct of the audit as to give rise to real fears of a lack of independence. 'Closely connected' in this context includes spouses and cohabitees, children and their spouses, brothers and sisters and their spouses and any dependent relative. It follows therefore that one should not audit the company of one's brother because of the circumstances set out above.

(b)   This question raises two particular issues. Firstly, the previous auditor of a company cannot give 'professional clearance' to the auditor who intends to succeed him. It is for the latter after making the necessary enquiries with the previous auditor to decide, having taken into account all of the circumstances, whether he should act. Secondly, the detailed guidance on changes in professional appointment does include a requirement for the previous auditor to co-operate promptly and reasonably in the provision of handover information.

However, if fees are still owing to the previous auditor, the prospective auditor is not on that account expected to refuse to act. Whether he does so or not is entirely a matter for his own judgement, and so too, is the related question of how far he may go in assisting the previous auditor to recover those fees. Additionally there is no pressure on the previous auditor to provide information about a client if fees are owing from that client. The previous auditor should be prepared to show confidence in his level of charging by taking relevant action to recover his fees. The prospective auditor will ask the client the reasons why the fee has not been paid.

(c)   There is no objection in principle to a practice providing services to a client additional to the audit. However, care must be taken not to perform management functions. In the case of many audit clients, it is common to provide a range of accountancy services which may include the preparation of financial statements. However, in the case of public companies, a practice should not participate in the preparation of the company's accounts except in relation to assistance of a routine clerical nature or in emergency situations. Such assistance might include for example, work on the finalisation of statutory accounts including consolidations and tax provisions. It is important that the scale and nature of such work is regularly reviewed, that the client accepts responsibility for the records as its own, and that the practice makes appropriate audit tests even where it has processed certain records.

(d)   A firm's objectivity may be threatened or appear to be threatened when it is involved in, or threatened with, litigation in relation to a client. Litigation between an auditor and his client could represent a breakdown of the trust which should exist between them. When a client company expresses an intention to commence legal action against an audit firm, the firm and the company may be placed in adversarial positions which could call into question the objectivity of the auditor and thus his ability to report fairly and impartially on the company's accounts. At the same time, the management of the company may not be willing to disclose relevant information to the auditor.

The issue by the audit client of a writ for negligence against the auditor would be considered to impair independence. It is not possible to specify the point at which it would be improper to act as auditors. In this case the client company has only threatened to sue the firm for negligence. A firm should have regard to circumstances where litigation, or potential litigation might reasonably be perceived by the public as adversely affecting the auditor's independence.

(e)   Student members are bound by the ethical requirements of the Association. They also remain bound during the period between the successful completion of the examinations and their admission to membership at which point they become subject to the same requirements in their new capacity.

4   GROWFAST PLC

(Tutorial note: a question where it is easy to pick up marks if the basic facts are known. Remember that some questions in the examination are factual and that you will score highly if the basic facts have been learnt before the exam.)

(a)   The need for an audit arises from the division in many companies between ownership of the company, and the day-to-day running of the company.

In many companies, particularly plc's, the owners of the company, that is the shareholders, will not normally be involved in the actual running of the company. The company will be run by the directors, who are elected by the shareholders at the annual general meeting (AGM) of the company. The owners of the company thus buy shares in the company, and expect a return of their loan to the company in the form of dividends, whilst the directors run the company and are paid a salary for doing this.

At the end of each year, the directors will produce the financial statements to show the results of the company. The shareholders need confidence that these financial statements are correct ie, that the directors have actually told the truth regarding the company's results. To ensure that the financial statements are correct the shareholders employ an auditor. The job of the auditor is to 'audit' or check the financial statements, and then report back to the shareholders whether these financial statements are correct, or show a 'true and fair view'. By having this independent check the shareholders gain confidence that the accounts are correct and therefore that their investment in terms of money, is being handled properly.

(b)   The auditor of a plc is appointed in different ways, depending on the situation, as noted below.

Initial appointment - new company

In a company that has just commenced trading, the directors have the power to appoint the auditors, who will remain in office until the end of the first AGM. The appointment of auditors can be made at a general meeting by the shareholders, if they wish to do this. If the directors or the shareholders do not appoint auditors, then the Secretary of State will, although this is rare in practice.

Ongoing appointment

All companies, in their AGM, appoint auditors to serve from the end of that meeting until the end of the next AGM. The auditor's term of office therefore allows him to report back to the meeting that initially appointed him. The appointment of auditors is a statutory requirement of an AGM. If the meeting does not appoint auditors then the Secretary of State must be informed within seven days and he will then appoint auditors. If the company does not inform the Secretary of State then both the company and the directors are liable to fines.

Appointment to fill a casual vacancy

At certain times the office of auditor may fall vacant eg, a sole practitioner may die, or the current auditor resigns, perhaps due to a conflict of interest that has been brought to light. In this situation, the directors may appoint a new auditor whose term of office will cease at the end of the next AGM of the company. Alternatively, the members in general meeting may appoint a new auditor, or failing both of these the Secretary of State will appoint.

Note that where a new auditor is being appointed at an AGM where the directors previously made the appointment, special notice is required of the resolution. This is to try and ensure that the members always have the final choice in who audits the financial statements.

(c)   The rights of an auditor under the CA85 are as follows:

The auditor has the right:

(i)   to receive information and explanations from the directors and officers of the company. It is a criminal offence to provide the auditor with false information (s389);

(ii)   of access to the company's books and records at all times (s389);

(iii)   to receive notice of all general meetings of the company as if he were a member of the company (s390);

(iv)   to attend and to be heard at any general meeting of the company concerning matters affecting him as auditor or former auditor (s390);

(v)   where the company is attempting to remove the auditor, to make written representations to the members, and to attend and speak at the meeting where he is being removed and the meeting where his term of office would otherwise have expired if he was previously removed (Ss 390 and 391);

(vi)   where the auditor resigns, to make written representations to the members of the company, and to require the directors to convene an extraordinary general meeting to consider the circumstances of his resignation (s392);

(vii)   to give notice to the company in writing that a general meeting should be held to lay the accounts and auditor's report before the members of the company (s253).

(d)   The responsibilities of the directors in relation to the accounting function of the company are as follows:

(i)   to safeguard the company's assets and to prevent fraud and errors in the company;

(ii)   to ensure that the company keeps proper accounting records as defined in s221 CA85;

(iii)   to prepare annual financial statements to show the results of the company for the year and the state of affairs of the company at the balance sheet date. These accounts must show a true and fair view (s228 CA85);

(iv)   to deliver to the Registrar of Companies a copy of the company's audited financial statements within (for a plc) seven months of the end of the accounting year;

(v)   to set up an internal control system in the company to ensure that all of the above are carried out. The directors cannot run the company by themselves; they must employ staff to carry out many of the accounting and other duties in the company. The system of internal control tries to ensure that the directors' other responsibilities above are met.

5	**ABLE PLC**

The purpose of this question is to examine students on the provisions of the Companies Acts relating to the ineligibility of auditors to act in that capacity.

(a)   A person is ineligible for appointment, as auditor of a company, if he is an officer or employee of that company, or if he is a partner or employee of such a person, or a partnership of which such a person is a partner. From the above it appears as though Mr White is eligible to act as auditor of Able plc. However, Mr White cannot act as auditor of Able plc if by 'virtue of the above rules he is ineligible for appointment as company auditor of any "associated undertaking" of the company': CA 89, s.27. Thus, Mr White is ineligible to act as auditor of Dale Ltd as he is a director of that company; as a result he then becomes ineligible to act as auditor of the holding company Able plc.

There are further provisions in the Companies Act 1989 which might preclude Mr White from acting as auditor; Schedule 11 of the Act requires that any auditor should be 'free of any interest likely to conflict with the proper conduct of the audit'. Obviously holding a directorship in a subsidiary company would conflict with the conduct of an audit of a holding company. Further Schedule 11 requires auditors to be free from any influence exerted by individuals outside 'the firm'. Mr White could easily be influenced by the holding company's directors who appointed him.

A person is also ineligible for appointment as auditor of a company if there exists between him (or any associate of his) and the company (or any associated undertaking) a connection of any description as may be specified by regulations made by the Secretary of State. At the time of writing these regulations have not been published but there is no doubt that the directorship of a subsidiary company would fall into the category of a connected person. Finally, a person is only eligible for appointment as a company auditor if he is eligible for appointment under the rules of the recognised supervisory body of whom he is a member. The independence rules of the RSBs would dictate that the relationship which exists between Mr White and Able plc is unacceptable and he should not accept appointment and therefore, he would be ineligible to act as auditor.

(b)   If during his term of office a company auditor became ineligible for appointment to that office, he must thereupon vacate office and forthwith give notice in writing to the company concerned that he has vacated it by reason of ineligibility: CA 89, s.28(2). Vacation of office through ineligibility requires a statement of any circumstances which the outgoing auditor considers should be brought to the attention of members or creditors of the company or statement that there are no such circumstances.

(c)   Contravention of the rules regarding ineligibility carries a penalty under the Companies Acts but it is a defence for a person to show that he did not know and had no reason to believe that he was, or had become ineligible for appointment. The onus of proof is thus on the defendant. Any costs of a second audit may be recovered from the ineligible auditor.

(d)   Where a person appointed auditor of a company was, for any part of the period during which the audit was conducted, ineligible for appointment as auditor of the company, the Secretary of State may require the company to engage the services of someone who is eligible for that appointment. The company has three weeks in which to comply with the direction: CA 89, s.29. The person engaged must either audit the relevant accounts again or review the first audit and report (giving reasons) whether a second audit is needed.

The company must send a copy of the latter report to the Registrar of Companies within 21 days of receiving it. If a second audit is recommended, the company must forthwith take steps to comply with this recommendation. This audit may be carried out by the firm which has recommended it. The Secretary of State is required to send a copy of the direction requiring a second audit to the Registrar of Companies.

(e)   When a partnership of accountants is appointed as auditor of a company, the appointment is of the partnership as such and not of the partners: CA 89, s.26(2).

Where the partnership changes, effectively the partnership ceases but the appointment is treated as extending to any partnership which succeeds to the practice of that partnership, and which is eligible for appointment. For this purpose a practice can only succeed if the members of the successor partnership are substantially the same as those of the former partnership. In this case three of the partners of the old practice would form the new partnership and would be eligible to succeed to the practice of the old partnership. Hence the directors views expressed to Mr White were incorrect and misleading.

6   MATERIALITY

(a)   The APB definition of 'Materiality' in SAS 220 is as follows:

'Materiality is an expression of the relative significance or importance of a particular matter in the context of financial statements as a whole. A matter is material if its omission would reasonably influence the decisions of an addressee of the auditors' report; likewise a misstatement is material if it would have similar influence. Materiality may also be considered in the context of any individual primary statement within the financial statements or of individual items included in them. Materiality is not capable of general mathematical definition as it has both qualitative and quantitative aspects.'

Materiality is an important concept for auditors, as it acknowledges the fact that accounts cannot be perfectly accurate, and so allows small errors. If accounts had to be perfectly accurate, auditors would have to check every transaction (even then it is unlikely the accounts would be perfectly accurate). However, materiality allows an auditor to check only a sample of items, as he will be relying on statistics and the fact that small items are unlikely to contain significant errors. In this way the number of items checked in an audit is a small percentage of the total transactions, and the audit is completed at a reasonable cost.

(b)   (i)   In relation to tests of control, normally all errors are material, irrespective of their value. This is because these tests are to check that the controls in the accounting system are being applied as prescribed, so any error indicates a weakness in the control. So, if an auditor requires a sample size of 58 items and no errors to satisfy himself that the system is reliable (ie, that he has 95% confidence that the error rate is less than 5%), then one error in this sample will mean that his confidence of the accuracy of the system in recording transactions is less than he requires. In order to satisfy himself that the system is sufficiently reliable, he will have to increase his sample size to about 88 items and find no further errors (ie, the maximum error rate of the population is the same if the auditor finds no errors in a sample of 58 items or one error in a sample of 88 items).

However, some controls are more important than others, so a higher level of errors may be acceptable where controls are less important, or where other controls detect errors where controls are weak. For instance, checking suppliers' statements to the balances on the purchase ledger will detect errors in posting invoices and cash to the purchasing ledger and missing purchase invoices.

Many auditors conclude that errors found in processing small value items are less important than errors in large items. Also, small errors in computations are less important than large ones. These conclusions appear to be reasonable provided the auditor is satisfied that these errors arise only in small value items and not large ones. This may be true if large value items are subject to more detailed checks, or there are other controls which would detect large errors. However, controls over processing sales transactions will probably have to be more reliable than controls over purchase transactions, as suppliers' statements will highlight errors in posting purchases transactions, whereas there is no similar control over sales transactions. A customer is unlikely to tell you that you have either not invoiced a sale or that the invoice value is only a tenth or a hundredth of its correct value! So, it can be concluded that all errors found in tests of control are usually material. However, these errors may not be material if the control being tested is considered to be of only secondary importance, or the weakness only applies to low value items, or the error is detected by other controls.

(ii)   In relation to the profit and loss account and balance sheet, an error is normally not material if it is 5% or less, and it is material if it is 10% or more of either:

•   the profit before tax; or
•   the value of the item.

If the error is between 5% and 10% of these figures, it may be material. For simplicity, from now onwards in this discussion I will say that a material error is one where the error is more than 10% and it is immaterial if it is less than 10%.

In relation to the profit and loss account, an error is material if it is more than 10% of the profit before tax or the value of the item. However, if the profit is low it would be unreasonable for profit to be stated within 10%, as it is not possible or economic to produce accounts to this degree of accuracy (ie, normal uncertainties, errors and matters which arise after the audit are likely to be more than 10% of profit). So, many auditors suggest that a material error should be more than 10% of the 'normal' profit before tax. The 'normal' profit is the product of the turnover and the 'normal' net profit margin. For example, if the profit margin is about 10%, then a material error is one which is more than 1% of turnover (ie, net profit is 10% of turnover and a material error is 10% of net profit). For food supermarkets the normal net profit margin is about 4%, so a material error will be 0.4% of turnover.

Frequently, it is argued that if the effect of the error is to change a profit into a loss, or vice versa, then an error is likely to be material, even though it is less than 10% of the normal profit before tax. However, if the profit or loss is very small, the normal uncertainties in preparing accounts mean it is probably not possible to be certain whether the company is making a profit or loss, so this additional criteria may not apply.

If the value of an item is small, then an error of more than 10% of the item will probably be acceptable provided it is less than 10% of the profit before tax.

Any error in the value of dividends in the profit and loss account would normally be material, as one would expect these to be stated accurately (ie, as the product of the dividend per share and the number of shares ranking for dividend).

(iii)   For the balance sheet, similar principles apply to those for the profit and loss account. An error in a balance sheet item is normally material if it is more than 10% of either the value of the item or the profit before tax.

If the item is small (eg, petty cash balance) then an error of more than 10% of the item's value may be acceptable provided it is less than 10% of the profit before tax.

Some items in the balance sheet can be valued more accurately than others. So, one would expect the bank overdraft to be more reliable than the value of debtors, and debtors to be more accurate than the stock value. However, all these items should be within the lower of 10% of their value and 10% of the profit before tax. For many balance sheet items 10% of profit before tax is less than 10% of the value of the item, so profitability is the more important criteria. One would expect the value of share capital and loan stock issued by the company to be stated accurately, and no error, or only a very small error, would be acceptable.

(iv)   In relation to the Companies Act, one would expect the accounts to comply with them, and the figures disclosed in the accounts should be within the lower of 10% of their value and 10% of the profit before tax. Normally, if the Companies Act requires an item to be disclosed, the accounts should include this item, unless the value of the item is immaterial (eg, very small). Also, it is acceptable for certain items not to comply with the Companies Act if complying with the Companies Act means the accounts do not show a true and fair view, and with the method used in the accounts they do show a true and fair view.

Similarly, accounts should comply with Accounting Standards, and the auditor should report if there is non-compliance. Sometimes it can be difficult for auditors to decide whether to qualify their audit report for non-compliance with Accounting Standards. For instance, if a company does not depreciate its freehold properties, then it is not complying with SSAP 12 on depreciation (and the Companies Act), but the effect on profit of not depreciating fixed assets may be immaterial. It appears that some auditors report such a non-compliance in their audit report while others give no qualification, so no firm guidance can be given on this matter.

It appears that if the Companies Act or Accounting Standards require an item to be valued or disclosed, then a material error in the item is likely to be a smaller figure than if there is no specific disclosure requirement. However, the 10% principle normally applies to items required by the Companies Act or Accounting Standards.

(v)   So far the discussion has considered the effect of a single error. However, in most sets of accounts there will be a number of errors and uncertainties. So, during the audit the staff should record errors or uncertainties they have found in a schedule of unadjusted errors, which shows the effect of the error on the profit and loss account and balance sheet. From this schedule the total error on profit and on each profit and loss account and balance sheet item is found. Then the principles described above are applied, that is the total error is material if it affects profit before tax by more than 10%, or the value of any item in the profit and loss account or balance sheet is affected by more than 10%. However, if the value of the item is small, an error may not be material even if it is misstated by more than 10%.

Uncertainties are slightly different from errors. For instance, one may be uncertain about the value of the stock or a legal claim against the company. To convert an uncertainty into a potential error, one would normally multiply the uncertainty by the probability that it will arise (eg, in the case of contingencies) or one could say that a material uncertainty would be twice the value of a material error (ie, 20% of the profit before tax, in the case of stock), This appears to be a very subjective way of converting uncertainties into errors, but it does seem reasonable that one would accept larger uncertainties before qualifying the audit report.

Finally, it appears that auditors are more concerned that profit is not overstated, so one may accept a larger error which understates profit than one which overstates profit before qualifying one's audit report. So, a material error may be one which overstates profit by more than 10%, or one which understates profit by more than 15%. Two reasons can be found for auditors taking this approach. Firstly, they can argue they are using prudence, and secondly they are more likely to be sued for negligence if profits are overstated than if they are understated.

7   ACCOUNTANCY WORK AND AUDIT EVIDENCE

The purpose of this question is to examine students on the audit of a small company, where the accounts are prepared by the audit firm.

(a)   Before the auditor may rely upon accountancy work carried out by his firm, the following criteria must be satisfied.

   (i)   The accountancy work must be relevant to the audit work being carried out. For example the auditor, when carrying out accountancy work, will examine prime documentation in preparing the accounts. This documentation may support a transaction or a balance such as the purchase of raw material or a fixed asset.

   (ii)   The audit staff carrying out the accountancy work should understand the relevant audit objectives and be aware that reliance is being placed upon them. For example where they are dealing with sales invoices, they must ensure that sales are made only to bona fide customers.

   (iii)   The accountancy work should be carried out by someone with relevant training and experience. In addition this work should be subject to review by persons other than those staff who have actually performed the work. The purpose of this review is to assess the reliability of the accounting work for audit purposes.

(b)   The audit evidence derived from accountancy work will only normally provide some of the evidence required to determine the completeness of the population or the value of the item in the financial statements. Certain important audit tests will not have been performed when preparing the financial statements. For example when preparing the financial statements it may not be necessary to circularise debtors, and investigate their recoverability. The valuation and existence of stock will be investigated by the auditor but probably not when preparing the accounts.

The auditor will need to derive audit evidence for the entire accounting period. The accountancy work carried out is unlikely to cover the whole period under review and is more likely to be concentrated around the financial year end. Specific audit work must be carried out in respect of the period not covered by the accountancy work. For example, the auditor may obtain all sales invoices for the final month of the accounting year and check them to the sales day book when preparing the accounts but he would not derive any audit evidence in respect of transactions for the remainder of the accounting period. When preparing the audit plan, this should be taken into account.

Small businesses are usually dependent upon the proprietor to ensure that all transactions are recorded. The proprietor may be so closely involved with the transactions that he may have little difficulty in excluding transactions from the accounting records. Accountancy work is likely to provide the assurance that the auditor requires to ensure full inclusion of transactions.

(c)   The auditor should consider the audit evidence available in respect of the completeness of an item. Sufficient audit evidence will normally be gathered in two ways. If the business has a system of internal control in operation, then the auditor may test the controls and rely upon them. This reliance will lead to a reduction in the amount of the substantive testing required. If there are no internal controls which can be relied upon, then the auditor must obtain evidence from substantive testing. If the auditor utilises a substantive testing approach, he may obtain reasonable assurance from the following sources.

(i)   Independent evidence

Third parties may be contacted in order to verify the balance of the item in the financial records. For example a bank letter may be requested from the company's bankers. Certain transactions may be recorded independently of the item being audited and from these transactions data relevant to the item can be predicted or calculated. For example issues of finished stock recorded in the physical stock records should give rise to sales income. Obviously the auditor must ensure that he can rely upon the physical stock records before using them to provide evidence of sales income.

(ii)   Reconciliations

The auditor may reconcile total quantities of goods bought and sold. He may prepare control accounts for debtors and creditors in order to verify their respective balances in the financial statements. This technique may be more feasible in the case of smaller business with smaller quantities of goods.

(iii)   Analytical review

Analytical review procedures are often an effective means of testing for completeness provided that the results can be predicted with reasonable accuracy. Variations from expected results may indicate potential omissions which have not been detected by other substantive tests. Predictive analytical review procedures will be more reliable where at least one variable can be independently proven. For example a property company's rental income can be proven by taking the number of units let and multiplying it by the average rental income per unit. The number of units let could be independently verified by circularisation techniques.

(iv)   Post balance sheet review

A review of transactions after the balance sheet date would further assist the auditor in determining the completeness of an item. For example a review of the cash book would give additional evidence of the completeness of sales income.

(v)   Representations by the proprietor

A limited amount of evidence of completeness may be provided by general representations by the proprietor but these representations would never provide all of the necessary evidence required by an auditor. Where the auditor has knowledge of the proprietor and the business from previous audits, he may be able to assess the reliability of management representations as corroboration of other audit evidence.

8   WAGES AND SALARIES ICQ

The purpose of this question is to examine students on the audit of wages and salaries.

ICQ	Internal control objective	Audit tests		Potential consequences
(1) Does an appropriate official authorise rates of pay?	All elements of the payroll cost should be authorised	Test check from payroll to personnel files or trade union agreements for wage rate authorisation and directors authorisation of wage rates	Test details on clock record cards as regards rates of pay, to payroll	Employees could be over/underpaid and wage costs in profit/loss account could be misstated
(2) Are written notices required for employing and terminating employment?	Amounts recorded on the payroll are for non-fictitious employees	Review personnel policies. Test check from payroll to personnel files for authorisation of employment and termination of employment	Compare cheque payments/credit transfer payments to personnel records	Fictitious employees could be on the payroll of the company
(3) Are formal records, such as time cards, used for time keeping?	Amounts recorded on the payroll are for work actually performed	Examine time record cards and review the control of time record cards. Observe time recording procedures	Review the wages account and payroll records for large, unusual amounts	Employees could be paid for work not performed and the payroll costs overstated
(4) Does anyone verify rates of pay, overtime hours, and computation of gross pay before wage payments are made?	Verification of calculation of wages and amounts to be paid	Examine evidence of internal verification of wage calculations	Recompute hours worked from time cards and agree to payroll. Compare pay rates to union agreement, and formal documentation of pay rates signed by the directors. Recompute gross pay and agree to payroll	Payroll costs could be misstated and employees under or overpaid
(5) Does the accounting system ensure the proper recording of payroll costs in the financial records?	Payroll transactions are properly included in the accounting records	Check the procedures for recording payroll costs	Test clerical accuracy of payroll and trace postings to the wages account in the nominal ledger	Payroll costs may be incorrectly recorded in the accounting records

9   COTGRAVE DISTRIBUTORS

Answer Plan

(a)   Receipt of order; authorisation of order; order confirmation to customer; dispatch on authorised dispatch note; note signed by customer; sales invoice generated and checked; periodic check on orders and invoices; periodic stocktakes; analytical review; division of responsibilities.

(b)   Cash received promptly; credit checks; cash on delivery in certain cases, credit limits, 'stop' notice; monthly statements; debt chasing procedures; legal action.

      Accurately recorded; receipt procedures, pre-list; uncrossed cheques; prompt banking; cash book record; bank reconciliation; sales ledger procedures.

(Tutorial note: the likely marking scheme with such a question is one mark for one point so make sure you clearly identify the points made. Although part (a) seems to have two parts, it is more sensible to treat these as one. Ironically part (b) can easily be answered in two parts. Some of the points in part (b) concerning credit control could have been made in part (a).)

(a)   The following controls are required:

     (i)   Initial order from customer processed by sales department. For telephone orders, the employee in the sales department should record the date and time the order is received and its details.

     (ii)   Order confirmation prepared which should be authorised by the sales manager.

     (iii)   Before the goods are dispatched, they should be authorised by the credit controller. As the company uses a computerised sales system, the computer may accept dispatches of goods to good credit risk companies (where the credit limit is not exceeded) without the authorisation of the credit controller.

               In this situation the credit controller will authorise dispatch of goods to poor credit risk companies and those where the credit limit is being exceeded. With this system, the credit controller should ensure that the standing data files of good credit risk companies and customers' credit limits are kept up to date.

     (iv)   The goods should only be dispatched to customers when the dispatch department receives an authorised dispatch note.

     (v)   A copy of the dispatch note should be signed by the customer and retained by Cotgrave Distributors as this is evidence that the customer (or carrier) has received the goods (in cases where there is a dispute over a delivery).

     (vi)   The computerised sales system presumably produces a sales invoice when the goods are dispatched. The prices on the sales invoice should agree with the order confirmation (or the company's authorised price list) and it should be posted to the sales ledger.

     (vii)   Depending on the sophistication of the computerised system, the pricing needs to be checked in the accounts department.

     (viii)   A person independent of the dispatch, sales and sales accounting department should check that:

            -      a sales invoice is issued for every dispatch of goods
            -      all customer orders are satisfied within a reasonable time

               This person should check any cases of a dispatch of goods with no invoice and any old orders where no goods have been sent to the customer.

(ix)   There should be periodic stocktakes to check that the quantities of goods in stock are the same as those shown by the book stock records. Any differences should be investigated. This check should either prevent or detect any unauthorised dispatches of goods (or misappropriation of stock).

(x)   A responsible official should perform an analytical review of sales and profit margins. This should highlight any cases of customers being charged the incorrect price. Also, it will highlight misappropriation of stock and goods being dispatched without an invoice being raised.

(xi)   The following duties should be carried out by different staff:

- authorisation of the customer order, and raising the dispatch note
- credit control checks
- dispatch of goods to the customer
- processing of sales invoice.

(b)   **Procedures to ensure cash is received promptly**

(i)   The credit worthiness of new customers needs to be established. The company may ask for recent accounts of the customer, bank and other customer references. Also, a credit rating agency could be used to obtain an independent assessment.

(ii)   For poor credit risk customers the company should require payment in advance or cash on delivery.

(iii)   The credit limits for a new customer will be subject to clear criteria and will be based on its reputation and other information described in part (i) above.

(iv)   The credit limit of existing customers should be reviewed periodically. It will be increased if the company pays its account promptly and sales are increasing. For slow payers the credit limit may be reduced, or credit may be withdrawn.

(v)   The credit controller should put accounts on 'stop' where the account is over the credit limit or in arrears. Further dispatches should only be permitted with the authorisation of the credit controller.

(vi)   Monthly statements should be promptly sent to customers.

(vii)   Action for chasing of debts when the credit period has expired should be prompt with laid down procedures.

(viii)   There should be a procedure for following up old debts. This should start with the customer being sent a reminder, then dispatch of goods should be stopped, legal action should be threatened and finally the debt should be dealt with by a debt collection agency or by a lawyer.

Procedures to ensure accurate recording in accounting records

(i)   Cash received in the post should be opened by two persons, in order to reduce the risk of theft.

(ii)   A listing of receipts should immediately be prepared.

(iii)   Any uncrossed cheques should be crossed 'a/c payee' (thus only being able to be paid into the company's bank account).

(iv)   The cheques and remittance advices should be passed to the cashier who will record them in the cash book and pay them into the bank promptly.

(v)   Periodically, an independent person should check the pre-list of cash received to the cash book to ensure all items are entered in the cash book and banked.

(vi)   A bank reconciliation statement should be regularly prepared. An independent person (eg, the chief accountant) should check the bank reconciliation and ensure that cash received is banked promptly as late banking of this cash could indicate that a teeming and lading fraud is taking place.

(vii)   A sales ledger control account should be maintained by a person independent of the sales accounting department and cashier. The independent person should check the posting of the sales ledger control account and that the balance either agrees (or can be reconciled) to the total of the balances on the sales ledger.

10   BULWELL MANUFACTURING PLC

Answer Plan

(a)   Security of terminals; turnkey systems; accessible from terminal; passwords; access to main computer

(b)   Systems protocols; call back systems; incorrect passwords; secure telephone lines

(c)   Purchases system; retrieval of information; input of transaction data; updating of standing data files. Payroll system; same headings

(Tutorial note: you need to give a variety of controls wherever possible in order to maximise the chances of earning marks. In part (c) there are two systems under consideration. The controls will be different. The payroll system for example must be more secure than the purchases system. It is important to bring out this difference in your answer.*)*

(a)   General controls that can be exercised to prevent unauthorised access to Bulwell Manufacturing's computer system from remote terminals will include the following:

(i)   **Security of terminals**

The terminals used to communicate with the main computer should be kept in secure rooms at each location. Access to the room and therefore the terminal should be limited to known key holders. A list of authorised key holders should be updated regularly and staff encouraged to lock the computer room when they leave it, even if they are only going to get a cup of coffee.

This control will be effective as long as procedures are maintained. The limitations of the control are that keys can be duplicated relatively easily, and staff may leave the computer room open by accident. The locks to the room could be changed regularly to ensure that duplicate keys have limited use.

(ii)   **Turnkey systems**

As well as keys being required to access the computer room, the terminal itself could be designed to be active only when a special key is used. Even if unauthorised staff gained access to the computer room, they could not necessarily gain access to the computer system. Again a register of authorised users should be kept, and staff trained to remove their key from the computer when they have completed their processing.

The effectiveness and limitations of this control are the same as for (i) above.

(iii)   **Computer systems accessible from the terminal**

Terminals can be configured so that they access only those parts of the main computer system that the employees at that particular branch are actually required to use.

This will effectively preclude unauthorised staff from gaining access to any part of the computer that they do not have to use. For example, if all wages processing is done centrally, then no individual at the branch will be able to access the wages system.

(iv)   **Passwords**

Passwords can be used in two ways. A single password could be used to access the whole computer system; this password would be known to all authorised users. Alternatively, each user could have his/her own password. Each individual's password would allow access to only those systems that the individual is required to use. Employees should be instructed to memorise their own password and not to write the password down or disclose the password to any other individual.

Passwords are effective unless the password becomes generally known. It is unlikely that an unauthorised individual will guess the password and thereby gain access to the computer system. The password should be changed regularly to try and maintain system integrity.

A single password has the limitation that it will quickly become common knowledge and it is therefore likely that unauthorised individuals will learn it. Passwords that are specific to each employee are less likely to be shared in conversation, and will therefore provide greater security for the computer system.

(v)   Terminal access to main computer

The terminal itself could be allowed access to the main computer only during normal working hours.

This will be an effective control because staff where the terminal is located are more likely to note use of the terminal out of hours. The control will provide the limitation in that working out of hours for authorised staff will not be possible; inputting urgent or backlog of data will therefore be difficult.

(b)   Procedures that can be employed to prevent access to the company's computer via the national telephone system can include the following:

(i)   Systems protocols

When the main computer is accessed, the terminal is required to send various passwords and other coded data to show that this is bona fide access. If this data was not sent then the request for access from the outside source would be denied.

(ii)   Call back systems

The main computer is informed that the terminal wishes to communicate with it; this will be by the terminal in effect telephoning the main computer. After this initial contact, the terminal rings off and the main computer then calls the terminal back. After contact is re-established, a full link is created between the terminal and the main computer.

This system has the benefit in that if an unauthorised source calls the main computer, this source will not be called back by the main computer. Access to the main computer will therefore be denied.

(iii)   Incorrect passwords used

The main computer may receive repeated requests for access in the space of a few minutes, but the passwords given could be incorrect. In this situation, the computer should be instructed to stop accepting incoming calls until the human controller has established the reasons for the incorrect passwords. This situation would be indicative of an unauthorised user trying to gain access to the main computer by guessing the system password.

(iv)   Secure telephone lines

The use of telephone lines dedicated to the company will also minimise the risk of unauthorised access to the main computer. Dedicated telephone lines are more difficult for third parties to gain access to than non-dedicated lines on the telephone network.

(c)   **Purchases system - controls over**

(i)   Retrieval of information

Information on the purchases system is not normally confidential; a simple password is therefore likely to be sufficient.

(ii)   Input of transaction data

Controls will be required to ensure that all transaction data is correctly entered into the purchases system. Input of the data could be limited to the purchases department (only terminals in this department being able to accept input of this type of data). Batch totals could be used to ensure the completeness of input of data. In more recent systems allowing real time input and processing, the completeness and accuracy of input could be checked by regular reconciliation of purchase ledger balances to suppliers' statements.

Care must be taken to ensure that data input is bona fide; hence the requirement for only the purchasing department terminals to be available for input.

(iii)   **Updating of standing data files**

Standing data files must be regularly updated to add new suppliers and delete suppliers no longer dealt with. The latter should be deleted to ensure that invoices are not allocated to these accounts in error (or fraudulently) thereby providing the possibility of payment to unauthorised suppliers. Any changes in supplier details like a change in invoice address will also require actioning.

Controls over these updates should be tight to ensure that the supplier details are correct. It is likely that only a few responsible officials, such as the purchase ledger controller, will be allowed to change the standing data files. All changes should be authorised on manually produced change forms, and these forms kept as written evidence of the alteration. Similarly, the amended standing data file should be printed out and attached to the change form to show that the amendment was processed correctly. Greater security can also be provided by requiring additional passwords to access the computer programme which will process the changes.

Payroll system

Controls over the payroll system are likely to be more stringent to reflect the increased sensitivity of this data.

(i)   **Retrieval of information**

Access will be limited to terminals in the wages department, and other responsible officials such as the chief accountant.

(ii)   **Input of transaction data**

Input will again be limited to the wages department. As input will be on a regular weekly or monthly basis, and errors in inputting will not be noted by comparison with third party documentation (such as suppliers' statements for checking purchase invoices), batch controls will be used to check the completeness and accuracy of input. It is also likely that a full printout of the wages payable will be printed out and reviewed by the chief accountant. He/she will investigate any unusually large, or small payments, as well as checking that the totals appear correct compared to previous payrolls. The chief accountant will then authorise the payroll and the cheques or bank credit transfers before printing of the payslips.

(iii)   **Updating of standing data files**

Payroll standing data files will be amended for employees joining and leaving the company, as well as for changes in bank details (for bank credit payments) and salary and/or overtime rates at various times throughout the year. As well as the data being confidential, it is also essential that the data is correct. The wages personnel could, for example, use the account of an employee who has left the company, to extract moneys from the company and direct this to their own bank accounts.

As with purchases, all amendments will be performed by responsible officials, with printouts of the changes made attached to authorised change forms. In addition, every few months, a full printout of the payroll standing data could be produced and agreed to the personnel details by a responsible official. Any discrepancies between these two sets of data will be investigated and adequate explanations obtained.

11   HYSON HOTELS PLC

Answer Plan

(a)   List typical tasks: checks on computer system; room booking system; returns to head office; other accounting areas; ad hoc work.

(b)   Qualifications and experience; reporting to; independence; limitations; documentation; management response to recommendations.

(c)   Accounting system recording; verification of assets; nominal ledger analysis.

(Tutorial note: the answer to part (a) can start off by stating the general work performed in any organisation by internal auditors but must also consider the particular work relevant to an hotel company.

A general answer is all that is required in part (b) ie, no particular reference needs to be made to the hotels.*)*

(a)   The scope and objectives of the internal audit department are set by management and will vary from one organisation to another. However, common areas of activity of any internal audit department will include:

   (i)   reviewing accounting systems and internal control

   (ii)   examining financial and operating information for management, including detailed testing of transactions and balances

   (iii)   reviewing the economy, efficiency and effectiveness of operations and of the functioning of non-financial controls

   (iv)   reviewing the implementation of corporate policies, plans and procedures

   (v)   any other special investigative procedures.

With regard to the internal auditors of Hyson Hotels plc the work that would be carried out should include:

   (i)   checks on the operation of the computer system including:

   •   controls over input, processing and distribution of output

   •   controls over access to the computer and computer records

   •   procedures for the maintenance of back-up files and the provision of emergency facilities in the event of hardware or software failure

   •   appropriate separation of duties and proper training and supervision of staff.

   (ii)   checks on the system for room bookings and guests' accounts including:

   •   procedures for recording reservations
   •   procedures for accounting and handling deposits received and payments in advance
   •   cancellations.

   (iii)   test checks on the day-to-day computer transactions, including:

   •   completeness and accuracy checks by examining accounts for each guest and comparing the receipts and entries in the cash book

   •   sequence checks, on pre-numbered documents, especially purchase orders and sales invoices. Investigations should be carried out for any missing documents

- checks on closing entries in guests' accounts to ensure that charges are not made to guests who have left or to new guests occupying the same room.

(iv)   checks and tests of transactions contained in returns to head office, noting:

- adjustments for inter-hotel transactions
- amounts written off for spoilage, equipment losses and damages.

(v)   checks on other accounting systems at the hotel including:

- system of accounting for income relating to meals, drinks, snacks, etc

- with regard to the payroll system, ensuring the existence of employees, including casual staff, and ensuring that all employees' salaries truly reflect their entitlement

- for the purchase system, authorisation of purchase orders, payments to suppliers, and ensuring the correct treatment of returns

- with regard to petty cash expenditure, ensuring that all payments are supported by duly authorised vouchers and that regular reconciliations take place.

(vi)   special ad hoc investigations into matters such as:

- suspected fraud
- proposed acquisitions of other hotels
- improvements to existing control systems.

(b)   The factors which the external auditor should consider, and the work which he would perform to enable him to assess the extent to which he could place reliance on the work of the internal auditor would include:

(i)   the qualifications and experience of the head of the internal audit department and his staff - this is likely to affect the quality of their work

(ii)   the level to which the internal auditor reports. Ideally, it should be directly to the board of directors

(iii)   the degree of independence with which the internal auditor works. Quite obviously, the overall objective of the internal auditor will be the same as that of the hotel, and in this respect he can never be as independent as the external auditor. However, within his own area of activity he should demonstrate an objective approach

(iv)   the extent to which there are any limitations on the scope of the work of the internal auditor. This would involve discussions with the internal auditor to ascertain the extent of management influence over his work

(v)   the quality of the internal auditor's documentation and working papers, as these will indicate the quality of the work performed

(vi)   the extent of management response to the internal auditor's recommendations. This would involve examining both the internal auditor's reports and also minutes of board meetings

(vii)   the re-performance of tests already carried out by the internal auditor to verify the accuracy of results and ultimately the conclusions drawn.

(c)   The external auditor would be able to rely on the work of the internal audit department in the following ways:

(i)   As the internal auditor would have recorded the system of accounting and internal control, and evaluated it, the external auditor may use the schedules produced and consider the tests carried out and the conclusions drawn. This will obviously avoid a duplication of work which should reduce costs.

The external auditor would probably carry out some walk-through tests, but his level of testing would be greatly reduced.

(ii) In addition to systems verification, the external auditor may call on the internal auditor to assist in the final audit in terms of verification of assets. In respect of Hyson Hotels, this may involve verification of:

- cash balances
- stocks held
- fixed assets.

Any co-ordination of effort must be carefully planned to ensure a wide exposure of all of the hotels.

(iii) The internal auditor may be able to prepare working papers for the external auditor of analysis of nominal ledger accounts.

However, the external auditor must always be aware that the responsibility of reporting on the truth and fairness of the financial statements rests with him. He should always play a dominant role in determining materiality levels, considering audit risk and evaluating areas of judgement.

12 MANAGEMENT LETTERS

(a) The purpose of this question is to examine students on the form and content of management letters. Part (i) of the question illustrates a situation where the management letter is too brief, part (ii) illustrates the situation where the letter is too verbose.

(i) It is important that management letters are understood by the client. In this large privately owned company, the management letter was addressed to the managing director, and many phrases used in the extract may be incomprehensible to such a reader. The phrase 'amendments to master file' may not mean much to the reader, although the reader may have a vague notion of what it means. The phrases used in the extract would not alert a reader, who was not fully familiar with the principles of internal control, to all of the implications of such a weakness, nor would it encourage corrective action. The extent of the explanation of the weakness will depend upon the knowledge level of the recipient of the letter, but at present the explanations of the implications of the weakness are not comprehensive enough.

The extract does not recommend the officials who should check amendment data before it is input. This is an important omission because the auditor can nominate officials to review the amendments and preserve the segregation of duties within the organisation. If the company is left to delegate this responsibility, they may not take into account this aspect of internal control. The letter also uses phrases which could be classified as vague and unhelpful. 'Somebody should check' is an obvious example. Management letters should not contain such words but should use clear and concise English phraseology.

Redrafted extract

The company relies upon computer print-outs to show the payments made to creditors for goods supplied and to employees for wages. In producing these print-outs, the computer uses stored information which is usually common to each transaction (master file data). For example, wage rates, discounts etc.

If that information is not accurate, a supplier or an employee may be under/overpaid. The master file data may not be correct because it is out of date, has been tampered with, or was set up incorrectly. It is important that such errors in master file data do not arise. We recommend that all amendments updating the master file should first be approved and that the print-out of amendments which have been inputted should be reviewed. This could be done by the personnel manager for payroll master file changes and by the accountant for creditors' master file data. This would reduce the risk of loss from overpayment of creditors or wages or fraudulent activity.

(ii) The extract utilises a large number of words and lengthy phrases to describe the weakness. This could cause confusion for the audit client. For example, 'checked independently on a random sample basis' and 'eliminate the possibility of computational errors remaining undetected'. Further the recommendation does not indicate to the reader how and by whom the checks on the payroll figures should be carried out. Finally, the letter does not point out the potential loss which could arise from computational errors on the payroll.

Redrafted extract

At present it is possible that more will be paid for wages than is actually due, because some of the important figures used in calculating the wages, such as the overtime, bonus and holiday pay calculations prepared by the wages clerk, are not checked by another person.

We recommend that this should be done by someone other than the wages clerk who prepares the payroll. This check could be carried out by the assistant accountant, Mr X.

(b)   The principal purposes of management letters are as follows:

   (i)   To enable the auditor to comment on the accounting records, systems and controls that he has examined during the course of his audit. Areas of weakness in systems and controls which might lead to material errors will be highlighted, and brought to management's attention, together with advice as to their improvement.

   (ii)   To provide management with other constructive advice as regards areas where efficiency may be improved or economies made.

   (iii)   To communicate matters which have come to the auditors' attention during the audit that might have an impact on future audits.

   (iv)   To document important matters arising during the audit in order that there is a written record of these matters in the event of litigation.

   (v)   To formally document matters which have informally been discussed with management. This record should include management's responses and any intended action.

   (vi)   To ensure that the comments on the accounting systems reach those members of the management team who have the power to act on the findings.

   (vii)   To inform the client of other services the auditor can provide.

13   HEALTHY MILK LTD

(Tutorial note: Parts (b) and (c) are likely to provide the most problems in this question. By remembering the auditor objectives for any asset, the objectives of a debtors circularisation may be determined. This provides a framework for part (b) which can be used again in (c), along with some ideas on non-sampling risk.)

(a)   A basic principle of statistical sampling is that each item in the population must have an equal chance of being selected. If this is not the case then there is a possibility that the sample selected will be biased in some way, and valid statistical results will not be obtainable.

The method of selection being used for Healthy Milk Ltd does not allow random selection of items for two reasons:

   (i)   each roundsman is likely to have a different number of customers on his round. Choosing one customer from each book from a 'random' page means that customers on the smaller rounds have a higher chance of being picked. Taking one item from each book also assumes that the population is homogeneous (ie, all items are the same). This may not be the case because each route is different and will have different drivers;

   (ii)   taking the fourth item on each list of older debtors automatically precludes the picking of other debtors on that list; again the choice is not random.

The audit procedure will therefore not produce a valid statistical sample.

(b)   Audit objectives in circularising old debtors:

Valuation -   provide evidence on any provision for bad debts (if circularisation request answered by liquidator or administrator) and also provide evidence as to the completeness of the balance. This ensures the value of the debtor is correctly stated in the financial statements.

Existence -   provide evidence that the debtor balance actually exists and is therefore a bona fide debt.

Ownership -   provide evidence that the debt is due to Healthy Milk Ltd.

Disclosure -   provide some evidence on the value to be included for debtors in the balance sheet and the amount of any bad debt provision - especially if material.

(c)   Statistical sampling techniques may help attain the audit objectives in (b) as noted below:

Valuation -   evidence on the completeness of the debtor balance, and therefore the accuracy of the recording of the sales system can be gained by circularising some debtors. This audit objective would otherwise be met by depth testing a statistical sample of sales invoices;

-      evidence on the bad debt provision can again come from the circularisation, although an after-date cash review is likely to provide the auditor with his main evidence.

Existence, -   statistical evidence will be of use here because the auditor has identified potentially risky
ownership   debtor balances. If these debtors are shown to be in existence, owned by the company and
and   correctly disclosed, then the auditor has some evidence that the less risky, less old debtor
disclosure   balance will also be correctly treated;

-      stratification of the sample chosen will also assist the auditor because he can then concentrate on the larger balances for audit testing. Similarly increasing the confidence level will provide additional assurance that these balances are correctly stated.

The statistical technique in this situation will assist the auditor in meeting his audit objectives, as noted above, although it will suffer from additional non-sampling risk problems as follows:

(i)   debtors may fill the circularisation request form in incorrectly giving the auditor incorrect audit evidence;

(ii)   the auditor could use an incorrect audit test, or an incorrect confidence level meaning that the wrong number of items are tested;

(iii)   the auditor could also make mistakes in interpreting the results of his testing, especially regarding the number of errors found.

These factors will detract from the attainment of the audit objectives.

(d)   It is unlikely that the percentage of errors found in the sample testing will apply automatically to the whole population. Allowance must be made here for the level of precision, or movement away from this error percentage found in the sample when it is applied to the whole population. For example, a precision level of 2% would indicate that the error rate found would apply to the population, plus or minus 2%. The population error would therefore be in the range 8% to 12% for the sample error of 10% given in the question.

It is therefore possible that the error rate in the population is 10%, although this is unlikely and should not be relied upon. If the auditor wishes to be more precise regarding the population error rate, then the sample size of debtor balances tested must be increased. This will decrease the precision level to give a better estimate of the population error rate. To be 100% certain of the population error rate then all the items in the population must be tested.

In performing a statistical sample, the auditor accepts the (sampling) risk that his results may be different from those obtained from testing the whole population. As long as the maximum expected error does not exceed the tolerable error for this test, then the auditor can accept the results of the test, that is the correct degree of assurance has been achieved.

(e)   Statistical sampling techniques do not relieve the auditor of his responsibilities in the exercise of his professional judgement because:

   (i)   the auditor must still determine the confidence and precision levels, and the tolerable error to use in the statistical sample; and

   (ii)   in evaluating the results of the test, the auditor must still decide what constitutes an error and decide how this potentially affects the whole population,

Statistical sampling techniques do provide the following benefits to the auditor:

   (i)   results of the tests can be determined precisely using statistical techniques;

   (ii)   they decrease potential liability to clients and third parties by providing a precise audit methodology that can be defended in court;

   (iii)   it assists in audit planning and testing by making the auditor identify populations for testing and determining the testing method.

Statistical techniques do therefore provide some benefit to the auditor and do not completely relieve him of his professional judgement.

---

14   AUDIT SAMPLING

The purpose of this question is to examine students on audit sampling techniques.

(a)   The auditor would be unlikely to use audit sampling techniques in the following situations.

   (i)   Where the population size is so small that statistical sampling will create unacceptable margins of error. If the population is not sufficiently large then statistical methods are invalid. Also where transactions or balances are small in number and material in relation to the financial statements. For example all exceptional items should be verified.

   (ii)   Where the population is not homogeneous and requires stratification. For example stock and work in progress may need stratifying because of the diverse nature of the population and the need to increase the precision of the sampling unit. Raw material stocks, work in progress and finished good stocks are unlikely to represent a homogeneous population.

   (iii)   Where the population has not been maintained in a manner suitable for audit sampling. For example sales invoices may have been filed in customer order and not numerically. Audit sampling techniques would not be cost effective in these circumstances.

(b)   (i)   Attribute sampling is a statistical method used to estimate the proportion of items in a population containing a particular characteristic. This proportion is called the occurrence rate and is the ratio of items containing the specific attribute to the total number of population items. Auditors are usually interested in the occurrence of exceptions in populations and refer to the occurrence rate as a deviation rate or an error rate. An exception in attribute sampling may be a test of an internal control deviation or a monetary error. For example the signature of the credit controller on a sales order is an attribute and the absence of a signature is a deviation/error. By design, attribute sampling enables the auditor to conclude that the population contains errors (with an allowance for statistical error) in the same proportion as in the sample. Auditors use attribute sampling to determine the appropriateness of the assessed level of control risk, although it can be used for substantive tests particularly when tests of controls and substantive tests are performed concurrently.

(ii)   Monetary unit sampling is a method of sampling which attempts to place a value on the errors in a population. The auditor is interested not only in error rates but also in the monetary effects of those errors. The population is divided up into units of £1 and not into transactions or balances. The size of the sample is determined by the confidence level required and by the auditors tolerable error. Each transaction to which a £1 unit is attached is tested for accuracy and if there is an error in the transaction, the £1 unit is said to be 'tainted' by the percentage of the error in the transaction. Thus £500 recorded as £550 would be 'tainted' by 10%. This method of sampling enables the auditor to determine the value of the most likely error and the maximum possible error in the population.

(c)   The factors which the auditor should consider in determining the sample size are as follows:

(i)   The efficiency and effectiveness of the internal control systems to process transactions without error

The auditor has to determine the expected error rate. The auditor's estimate of this depends, amongst other things, upon his evaluation of internal control.

(ii)   The level of assurance which the auditor requires

The auditor has to determine the amount of the risk which he is prepared to accept. This would be determined by the auditor's assessment of the audit risk attached to a particular client. There is considerable information available to the auditor about the organisation, its management and the expectations of company performance, for example, and these factors would play a role in determining sample size.

(iii)   The results of previous audit work

The auditor has to assess the expected error rate based upon the results of audit work in this and previous years. The higher the expected error rate, the greater the sample size, although if very high error rates are expected it may not be appropriate to use a sampling approach.

(iv)   Stratification

This is the process of dividing a population into strata so that items in each sub-population are expected to have similar characteristics. Sample sizes can be made smaller because the auditor can spend more time on those strata deemed to be high risk.

(d)   Statistical sampling provides the auditor with a sound scientific basis for the generation of audit evidence. If the techniques are correctly employed, personal bias in the choice of sample size is reduced. The auditor is able to determine the reliability or precision of the sample and the risk inherent in relying upon the sample results. Thus greater reliance can be placed upon the audit evidence, with the result that the quality of the audit evidence is enhanced. Statistical sampling enables the auditor to generate audit evidence in a consistent manner over time and across different companies. This consistency of approach again improves the quality of the audit. The interpretation of the results of the test is more objective and is expressed in quantitative terms. As the sample result is objective, the audit evidence created is defendable in a court of law. This may not be the case if judgement sampling is used.

15   TRENT TEXTILES

Answer Plan

(a)   Review of the audit working papers for the previous year; date(s) of the stocktake; company's stocktaking procedures; deficiencies in the procedures; potential deficiencies; stocktakers provided with stocktaking instructions; stock held by third parties.

(b)   Staff properly briefed by company's management; stocksheets prepared; sequentially numbered; control over issue of sheets to staff; stock and description clearly recorded; changes to sheets; stocksheets completely filled; staff signing the bottom of sheet; which staff to count (are they responsible for stock?); supervision by management; systematic approach to counting of stock; marking system; damaged stock; balls of wool (weighed?); work-in-progress; management - test counts; stock movements; last goods despatched and received.

(c)   Checks on procedures in (b); test counts; record details of the counts; discrepancies between test counts and actual count; unopened containers; last goods issued and received; record stocksheets details; audit firm's checklist; conclusion on the count.

(Tutorial note: a standard question to be expected in the Audit Framework exam. Stock is an important audit area and a question on stock is to be expected in nearly every exam. Many of the points made are standard to any stocktake, but some of your points should relate to the specific circumstances of the question.*)*

(a)   Work to be carried out prior to the stocktake includes:

- a review of the audit working papers for the previous year including the company's system for the stocktake. Note the problems that arose if any

- establish the date(s) the stocktake is being carried out

- obtain the company's stocktaking procedures and review these with the procedures for the previous year. Consider whether there are deficiencies in the procedures

- any problems with the stocktake last year and potential deficiencies this year should be raised with the company's management. The problems should be resolved, if possible, before the stocktake commences

- check that the stocktakers have been provided with the stocktaking instructions

- check whether any stock is likely to be held by third parties. If so, then special procedures will be required to confirm the amount of stock so held. If there is a material amount of stock for example, attendance at the stocktaking at the premises of the third party will be required

(b)   Procedures to be checked to ensure the accurate recording of the stock include:

- the staff have been properly briefed by the company's management

- stocksheets have been prepared and these are sequentially numbered. Control is exercised over the issue of the sheets to staff with a record of the issues and returns. One employee would be responsible for control in this area

- the quantity of stock and description, if necessary, should be clearly recorded (eg, by black pen). Any changes should be initialed by the member of the staff or the relevant manager.

- the stocksheets should be completely filled with the staff member signing the bottom of each sheet. If a sheet is incomplete it should be ruled off so that no more items can be added

- consideration needs to be given to the staff members counting particular parts of the stock. From an internal control point of view, staff should not count stock for which they are responsible. However such members are more likely to be able to record the stock accurately and therefore are often used. If so, the actual supervision by management should be monitored

- a systematic approach to the counting of stock should be used eg, shelves counted from top to bottom. A marking system should be used to identify those areas which have been counted.

- if any stock is damaged, this fact needs to be recorded on the stocksheets. If the staff responsible for a particular type of stock are also doing the stocktaking, they should note which stock is slow moving. This will indicate stock which may need to be stated at net realisable value

- Trent Textiles' raw materials stock will include balls of wool. This may be weighed rather than counted and therefore the weighing procedures need to be checked

- the company may have a considerable amount of work-in-progress. A proper assessment is required of the nature of the work-in-progress and its degree of completion. Management will need to be close at hand for the accurate assessment of this stock

- management should be making test counts and checking these counts to the stocksheets

- there should be no movement of stock during the count ideally, but if production is continuing, the movement of stock should be closely controlled

- when the count has finished, test checks should be made by management to ensure the accuracy of the count

- a clear record needs to be made of the last goods despatched and received prior to the stocktake.

(c)   Work to be carried out during the stocktake and the recording of work done includes:

- checks on all the procedures detailed in part (b) above

- taking some test counts, concentrating on high value items. The counts will be in both directions ie, from the stock to the stocksheets and vice versa

- record details of the counts in the audit working papers. The details will include references sufficient to identifying the stock items to the stocksheets at a later date

- if discrepancies arise between the test counts and the actual count, the stock will need to be counted again. A record should be made of the discrepancy

- if any of the stock is being counted by weighing, a check is required of the weighing procedures and test checks will be required

- some of the stock may be in unopened containers. Some of these will need to be opened to check the contents tie in with the stocksheets. A record of the checks will be made in the audit working papers

- at the end of the stocktake further test checks will be made to ensure all the stock has been counted and these tests will also be recorded

- details of the last goods issued and received prior to the stocktake are required. If possible, copies of the documents should be taken

- details of the stocksheets used should be recorded. It may be possible to have a complete copy of the sheets from the company

- the audit firm's checklist will be completed

- any relevant information should be recorded during the stocktake and a conclusion on the satisfactory nature of the count (or otherwise) should be made.

16 STOCK VALUATION

The purpose of this question is to examine students upon the audit of stocks and work in progress.

(a)   *Audit objective*   *Audit procedures*

Physical stock count

(i)	The stock is owned by the company	(i)	enquire of the company's staff as to the possibility of consignment stocks or third party stocks being on the company premises
		(ii)	observe any stock which is set aside or specially marked. This fact may indicate non-ownership
		(iii)	record any stock which is not owned by the company
(ii)	The stock count is carried out accurately and records obsolete stock for subsequent exclusion	(i)	make test counts to ensure that the recorded amounts are accurate on the stock tags and are described accurately
		(ii)	record the client's counts for subsequent recounting and testing
		(iii)	compare physical counts with stock records (if any)
		(iv)	observe whether movement of stock takes place during the count
		(v)	test for obsolete stock by enquiry of factory employees and management and being observant of damaged or physical deteriorating stock
		(vi)	ensure that obsolete stock is recorded on the stock count sheets and in the audit working papers.
(iii)	Information is obtained to ensure sales and purchases are recorded in the proper period	(i)	record the numbers of the last goods received note and last despatch note used in the accounting period for subsequent use in cut-off tests
		(ii)	check that these items have been correctly listed on the stock sheets
		(iii)	review and observe the goods received and despatch areas for any items which should be included or excluded from the stock count and record such items.

Valuation of stock

(i)	Stock items shown on the stock evaluation sheets are valid	(i)	trace stock listed on stock evaluation sheets to stock count sheets and auditors recorded test counts for existence and description
		(ii)	test stock listed on stock count sheets to stock records
(ii)	All existing stock items are correctly recorded on the stock evaluation sheets	(i)	ensure that no stock count sheets have been added to or deleted from the stock listings. Reference should be made to audit working papers recording numbers of stock sheets issued and returned
		(ii)	trace items from stock count sheets to stock evaluation sheets (reverse test of above procedure in (i)(i)).
(iii)	Stock is properly priced	(i)	perform price tests on stock items. This would include testing raw material stocks to purchase invoices, ensuring that sufficient invoices are examined to account for the quantity of stock being tested. Work in progress/finished goods would be agreed to costing records which should have been tested at the interim audit
		(ii)	perform net realisable value tests on stocks
		(iii)	agree valuation procedures are in accordance with SSAP 9.

(b)   The auditor would ordinarily obtain direct confirmation in writing from the custodian of the stock held at third parties. However if the stock is material in the context of the financial statements, then the auditor might apply the following procedures:

(i)   Review and test the client's procedures for ensuring that the third party is maintaining adequate safeguards over the stock.

(ii)   Obtain a report from the custodian's auditor on the controls exercised over the stock.

(iii)   Observe the custodian's physical inventory and obtain a copy of the relevant stock sheets.

(iv)   Obtain copies of the clients internal audit reports relating to the stock held at third parties.

(v)   Obtain a certificate from the custodian setting out the stock currently held on the clients behalf.

(vi)   Discuss with company management the nature of stock and reasons why stock is held at third parties.

(vii)   Examine any company documentation detailing amounts of stock held at third parties.

17   GOING CONCERN

The purpose of this question is to examine students on the implications of the going-concern status of a company for the auditor.

(a)   When financial statements are prepared on a going-concern basis then:

      (i)   Assets are recorded on the basis that the company will be able to realise or recover them at or above recorded amounts in the normal course of business.

      (ii)   Liabilities are recognised and recorded on the basis that they will be discharged in the normal course of business.

      SSAP 2 defines the going-concern concept as meaning that the enterprise will continue in operational existence for the foreseeable future. This means that the financial statements are prepared on the assumption that there is no intention or necessity to liquidate or curtail significantly the scale of operation.

(b)   The auditor should plan and perform procedures designed to identify material matters which might enable the auditor to form an opinion on the going-concern status of a company. These procedures should include the following:

      (i)   A review of forecast and budget information produced by a company, and the quality of the systems in place for producing this information. This would include a review of the key assumptions underlying the forecasts and budgets, and a review of the cash flow budget.

      (ii)   A review of the evidence relating to the adequacy and period of borrowing facilities. The auditor may need to obtain written information from banks or other third parties in order to be able to assess the degree of their commitment.

      (iii)   A review of the inherent risk assigned to the audit client. The sensitivity of forecasts and budgets to variable factors both within the directors' control and outside their control will be scrutinised, including relevant economic factors.

      (iv)   A review of the directors' plans for overcoming any problems their company is having or resolving any matters giving rise to doubts about the appropriateness of the going-concern basis. The auditor should consider the basis on which they have been prepared whether they are realistic and whether the plans are likely to resolve the company's problems.

      (v)   A consideration of any professional advice obtained by the directors as to the extent of the company's difficulties and the practicalities of overcoming them. It may be necessary for the directors to obtain legal advice on the consequences of the company continuing to trade while it is known by the directors not to be a going concern.

      (vi)   A review of the financial records including the order book, directors' minutes and an analytical review of the financial statements.

      The nature and scope of the auditor's procedures will depend upon the circumstances of the client. The extent of the procedures will be determined by the extent of the resources it requires to continue as a going concern.

(c)   The following are examples of factors which might cast doubt on the going-concern status of a company:

      (i)   internal matters such as loss of key management, labour difficulties or excessive dependence upon a few product lines where the market is depressed

      (ii)   external matters such as loss of key suppliers or customers or technical developments which render a key product obsolete

      (iii)   an excess of liabilities over assets

(iv)   default on terms of loan agreements

(v)   significant liquidity or cash flow problems

(vi)   major litigation in which an adverse judgement would imperil the company's continued existence

(vii)   denial of normal terms of credit by suppliers

(viii) major debt repayment falling due where refinancing is necessary to the company's continued existence.

(The above list is not exhaustive and students need only list six factors.)

(d)   The previous Auditing Guideline: 'The auditors considerations in respect of going concern (August 1985)' had a passive air about it. Where the auditor was satisfied that the financial statements had been prepared on a going-concern basis, no mention of any matters relating to the going-concern status were normally required in the audit report.

The current guidance in SAS 130 'The going concern basis in financial statements' goes somewhat further. There is now a duty on the part of the auditor to plan and perform procedures specifically designed to identify material matters which might cast doubt upon the going-concern status of the company.

It would be possible to extend the auditor's responsibilities still further. For example SAS 130 does not stipulate a time period beyond the balance sheet date over which the auditor should satisfy himself that the company will remain in operation. It would be possible for a revised SAS 130 to insist that the auditor's report specifically includes a statement that the auditor's opinion is that the company will remain in operational existence for at least the following twelve months, unless stated otherwise. This requirement would highlight the issue of going concern more than is currently the case.

18   LAMBLEY PROPERTIES PLC

Answer Plan

(a)   'Standard' contents; directors' responsibility; credit facilities; events since balance sheet date; continuing support to subsidiary; lack of grounds of claim from Eastwood.

(b)   Management evidence; other evidence

(c)   FRS 12 requirement; evidence required.

(Tutorial note: there is a movement away from the provision of standard letters of representation but the auditor will find it helpful to suggest the types of comments that are required.

Part (c) is a standard question on the audit of a particular contingent item, rather than the audit of contingencies in general ie, you are not being asked to search for other possible contingencies.)

(a)

Lambley Properties plc
Address

A Auditor & Co
Certified Accountants
Address

XX-XX-19X3

Dear Sir

We confirm to the best of our knowledge and belief, and having made appropriate enquiries of other directors and officials of the company, the following representations given to you in connection with your audit of the company's financial statements for the year ended 31 January 19X3:

(i) We acknowledge as directors our responsibility for the financial statements which have been presented to you for the purpose of your audit and all the transactions undertaken by the company have been properly reflected and recorded in the accounting records. All other records and related information, including minutes of all management and shareholders' meetings, have been made available to you.

(ii) A wholly owned subsidiary, Keyworth Builders has been incurring losses. We believe the company has a future and we expect the company to be continuing to trade at 31 January 19X4. No decisions have been made prior to 31 January 19X3 to change the level of activities of the company and thus there are no additional costs to be provided in the accounts.

(iii) There is a claim by Eastwood Manufacturing plc for £5 million for alleged cost of rectification of a defective building. We have obtained the opinion of a chartered surveyor and independent legal advice, and these parties confirm our view that there are no grounds for the claim from Eastwood Manufacturing plc. We believe that no provision should be included in the accounts for this claim.

(iv) The company has at no time during the year made any arrangement, transaction or agreement to provide credit facilities (including loans, quasi-loans or credit transactions) for directors or to guarantee or provide security for such matters.

(v) There have been no events since the balance sheet date which would necessitate revision of the figures included in the financial statements or inclusion of a note. Should further material events occur which may necessitate revision of the figures or of a note, we will advise you accordingly.

Yours faithfully

Signed on behalf of the board of directors

(b) A letter of representation is an example of 'management' evidence. Management may be tempted to distort the financial statements eg, to meet the expectations put on a company by shareholders or to hide their own fraudulent activities.

The auditor is unlikely to place the same amount of reliance on management evidence as on either his own or third party evidence because of the inherent bias.

However written evidence is more reliable than oral evidence. **S392 CA85** indicates that should management give the auditor knowingly false information, they are guilty of a criminal offence. The auditor can gain some assurance over the quality of evidence because of this statement.

The auditor would be negligent if he relied solely on the letter of representation. The statements in the letter should always be supported by other corroborative evidence.

(c) Best accounting practice (now encapsulated in FRS 12) requires that a provision should be included where an actual liability exists, rather than the possibility of a liability. So three conditions must be satisfied:

(i) a present obligation exists as a result of a past event

(ii) it is probable that a transfer of economic benefits will be required to settle the obligation, and

(iii) a reliable estimate can be made of the amount of the obligation.

The auditor will therefore need to examine the correspondence between the company and the surveyor and lawyer. This will indicate whether the view of the management is supported by this third party evidence.

He will also need to consider the reliability of the third parties to provide this evidence. The surveyor's qualifications and links with the company are particularly important in this respect.

Other legal correspondence between the company, Lambley Properties and the lawyer should be examined to see if there is any other relevant information eg, discussion of an out of court settlement.

If the auditor does not feel he can rely on the third party evidence already supplied, he can ask to discuss the matter with the advisors of the company. If he is still not satisfied he should consider obtaining further expert opinion from other persons.

19   JONES, ROBERTS, WILLIAMS, GRIFFITHS AND EVANS

(a)   **Jones Ltd**

Materiality

The amount of the loss at £30,000 represents 20% of pre-tax profit and more than 4% of debtors; it would therefore seem to be material in both income statement and balance sheet terms, although it is clearly more material in relation to profit.

Relevant accounting principles

The bankruptcy of the debtor indicates that the company has overstated profit and assets as at the year-end by £30,000. This letter provides evidence of a condition existing at the balance sheet date (SSAP 17 - 'Accounting for post balance sheet events). It should therefore be treated as an adjusting event. The prudence concept (SSAP 2 - 'Disclosure of accounting policies') would dictate that the loss should be provided for in full in the financial statements at 30 September 19X4.

Form of audit report

The management's refusal to adjust the accounts for the loss means that a disagreement exists between management and the auditor. In such a case, the auditor has to make a decision as to whether the amount of the loss is 'fundamental' or 'material but not fundamental'. Without more facts being available, it is difficult to draw conclusions satisfactorily in this area, but on the face of it an 'except for' form of audit qualification would appear appropriate as the true and fair view would not be entirely destroyed if the loss were to remain unadjusted.

(b)   **Roberts Ltd**

Materiality

The amount of £10,000 represents only 2% of the stated profit before tax of £500,000 and does not, in itself, appear to be material in terms of its impact on the financial statements. Unfortunately, however, the potential losses may be very much more significant than the figure of £10,000, since other claims are now pending, and the auditor may have to conclude that the whole legal matter is potentially material.

Relevant accounting principles

There is clearly a contingent liability in respect of potential claims arising from the product defect. Under SSAP 2, the prudence concept dictates that potential loss which is material should be accrued in the financial statements where it is probable that future events will confirm the loss and that the loss can be estimated with reasonable accuracy (except where the possibility is remote). The matter is also covered in FRS 12 - *'Provisions, contingent liabailities and contingent assets'*.

Form of audit report

There is clearly uncertainty with regard to the outcome of the pending claims and the potential liability which they represent. The auditor will have to decide whether or not the possibility of loss is likely or remote. Management has apparently chosen to ignore both the actual loss (which is not of itself material) and the potential loss (which may well be material). If the auditor can be convinced that management's view is acceptable and the disclosure in the notes is adequate, then a qualification may be completely avoidable. The auditor should be aware, however, that items which are not material when considered individually may well have a cumulative effect which is material in total. If the auditor does not believe that the management's view is acceptable, or does not think that the disclosure is adequate, then there is a disagreement as to the way in which the uncertainty has been treated. In this case, an 'except for' qualification is probably sufficient. However, if the auditor believes that the claims are likely to be successful and are likely to be substantial then it may be necessary to issue an adverse opinion.

(c)   **Williams plc**

Materiality

The loans are not bad debts and so have no effect on the reported loss. However, this sort of matter cannot have the same materiality test applied to it as in the cases previously discussed in this answer. Amounts owed by directors are required to be disclosed as a requirement of the Companies Act 1985. Materiality should, therefore, not be measured in relation to profit or loss for the year or the balance sheet position, but in relation to the requirements of the law. It would appear that the loans are not allowed and that Williams plc is materially in non-compliance with the Companies Act 1985.

Relevant accounting principles

As mentioned in the question, the loans are not allowed and disclosure should in any case be made under the Companies Act 1985. The item is required to be separately disclosed and cannot be 'hidden' as part of a figure containing other 'debtors collectable within one year'.

Form of audit report

The standard audit report requires the auditor to state specifically whether or not the financial statements comply with the Companies Act 1985. The financial statements of Williams plc do not fully comply with the requirements of the Act. The fact that Williams plc is a manufacturing concern would indicate that such loans to directors would not be made in the normal course of business, as could be argued if the company were a bank, for example. In these circumstances, the auditor is required to include details of the loans in the audit report, and to qualify the report by stating that the loans contravene the provisions of the Companies Act 1985. In view of the fact that the loans were subsequently repaid, the auditor would probably not need to qualify as to the true and fair view shown by the financial statements.

(d)   **Griffiths Ltd**

Materiality

The fall in value is clearly material. In fact, the auditor would probably have to view the matter as fundamental, because providing for the loss would have the effect of converting a net profit before tax of £250,000 into a loss of £50,000.

Relevant accounting principles

The Companies Act 1985 requires fixed assets to be written down where there has been a permanent fall in value. The Act does not allow falls in the value of one asset to be offset against increases in the value of another asset. Each asset has to be considered separately.

SSAP 2 - 'Disclosure of accounting policies' - states that the directors should ensure adequate provision is made for all known liabilities (expenses and losses). The accounting treatment adopted, offsetting known losses against unrealised profits, is unacceptable. As the company admits that a permanent fall in value has taken place, it should make full provision against the loss. Further, as the other trade investments (with reputedly high realisable values) are permanent investments not held for resale, the accounting treatment adopted is clearly not acceptable.

Form of audit report

As mentioned above, it is likely that the auditor would have to view the matter as fundamental. It is also a matter of disagreement and the auditor will probably be forced to give an adverse opinion, stating that the financial statements do not show a true and fair view.

(e)   **Evans plc**

Materiality

The £10,000 represents 10% of the reported net profit before tax, and so would appear to be material. However, the actual materiality of this item in relation to profit is, in fact, a somewhat judgemental matter.

The auditor would probably conclude that the possible error in calculating the £10,000 was not material in relation to the profit of £100,000, since the amount of any error will probably be substantially less than the full amount included in the accounts. Further since the accounting records were only destroyed for the early part of the year, the auditor would still be able to confirm the calculations for the later part of the year. In these particular circumstances, therefore, the auditor may consider that the amount of any error (which is likely to be considerably less than £10,000) is not material.

Relevant accounting principles

It is perfectly acceptable for the company to add the cost of its own labour and materials in the construction of the warehouse, since these have been used to create a capital asset. This is following the 'matching' or 'accruals' concept as set out in SSAP 2 - 'Disclosure of accounting policies' - and applied in SSAP 12 - 'Accounting for depreciation'.

Form of audit report

As the accounting treatment is generally acceptable, and the amount of any error is not likely to be considered material, the auditor will probably be able to give a standard unqualified audit report.

20   DUTY OF CARE

(Tutorial note: you would gain many marks in this question by simply presenting the facts and stating why they were relevant. Although this answer does go into a lot of detail to explain fully the trend in case law, the examiner's report states that candidates would gain good marks for presenting the facts and stating why they were relevant. A difficult question in the time available. Try to ensure that all cases are mentioned rather than going into detail about one only; a broad answer will gain many more marks than a narrow one.)

(a)   Auditor's duty of care to third parties

At present in the United Kingdom the auditor's contract is with the company he is auditing. The company can therefore sue the auditor on breach of contract if the audit is carried out incorrectly.

Until recently a third party has not been able to sue the auditor. The tests to be shown in court are that:

(i)   there was a duty of care to the third party by the auditor; and

(ii)   there was a breach of this duty; and

(iii)   the third party suffered financial loss as a result of this breach of duty.

How the auditor's liability has been extended, taking into account the above tests, is best shown by looking at some important cases in chronological order.

(i)   Candler v Crane Christmas (1951)

In this case Candler sued the accountants Crane Christmas when he lost money he had invested in a company, the accounts of which Crane Christmas had prepared. The court ruling was that although the accounts were negligently prepared, Candler could not recoup his losses from the accountants because he did not have a contract with them. There was therefore no duty of care owed to third parties.

(ii)   Hedley Byrne v Heller & Partners (1964)

Although this is a case dealing with banks, it is relevant for accountants. The plaintiff lost money when a bank reference from the defendant turned out to have been negligently produced. Basically the bank indicated that a mutual client was a good credit risk when this was not the case. The court ruled that Hedley Byrne, although they did not have a contract with the bank Heller & Partners, could recoup their losses due to the negligence and loss involved. The three tests noted above were therefore met and satisfied. However, the bank did not have to pay any damages due to a general disclaimer in its letter absolving it from any liability.

The decision affected accountants in that if a third party can show that it relied on the work of an accountant which later turned out to be wrong, it can claim damages. However, this principle was only extended to plaintiffs whom the auditor actually knew by name. Unidentified third parties would still not be able to claim against the auditor.

(iii)   **JEB Fasteners v Marks Bloom & Co (1981)**

In this case JEB Fasteners lost money when the company in which they had invested, BG Fasteners, went into liquidation. The plaintiff had used the latest set of audited accounts of BG Fasteners to assist in the investment decision and these accounts were agreed in court to have been audited negligently. The defendants considered that their defence was good because they did not know about JEB Fasteners by name at the time the audit report was signed. The auditors were therefore under Hedley Byrne not liable to the plaintiff for damages.

Woolf J also noted, however, that the defendants should have realised that BG Fasteners would accept a bidder for the business, given its loss-making state. He therefore ruled that Marks Bloom & Co were liable to JEB Fasteners on the grounds of reasonable foresight ie, that they should have realised that a company such as JEB Fasteners would be making an offer, and therefore they were liable to this company.

Damages were not awarded because JEB Fasteners could not prove sufficient reliance on the audited financial statements. Nevertheless, the principle remained that auditors were liable to third parties they should be able to reasonably foresee.

(iv)   **Re Twomax (1983)**

This Scottish case confirmed JEB Fasteners when a firm of accountants was sued successfully with no doubt as to the reliance being placed on the audited accounts.

(v)   **Lloyd Cheyham v Littlejohn de Paula (1985)**

Littlejohn de Paula successfully defended themselves against a negligence claim in this case by showing:

(1)   that they had followed the standard expected of the normal auditor ie, that in Accounting Standards and Auditing Standards;

(2)   that their working papers were good enough to show consideration of the problems raised by the plaintiff and reasonable decisions made after consideration;

(3)   that the plaintiff had not made all the reasonable enquiries one could expect when, in this case, purchasing a company eg, a review of the business was not undertaken upon investigating the purchase but only after purchase.

The judge, therefore, held that far too much reliance was placed on the accounts by the plaintiff and he awarded costs against the plaintiff to the defendant.

(vi)   **Caparo Industries v Dickman and others (1989)**

This case investigated the auditor's relationship to shareholders and third parties who purchase shares in a company and then lose money as a result of a foreseen fall in the share price - foreseeable that is by the auditor. The decision here indicates that the auditor will not be liable to potential investors or to individual shareholders but only to shareholders as a group.

Recent decisions, therefore, have attempted to extend auditor liability to third parties. As long as the auditor follows the steps in the Littlejohn case (above), it would appear to be unlikely that he will be found guilty of negligence.

(b)   **Ensuring that audit risk is minimised**

Audit risk may be minimised in two basic ways - by ensuring that planning is adequate and by following the auditing standard on Quality Control.

(i)   **Planning**

If an auditor plans an audit properly, those areas of the audit that are potentially risky will have been identified, and the auditor can ensure that resources are devoted to those areas to minimise the risk of misstatement in the financial statements.

(1)   Ensuring that the audit objectives are known eg, statutory audit only, and therefore ensure that the client accepts this by sending a signed copy of the engagement letter back to the auditor. The auditor is not looking for any immaterial fraud as this would not affect the true and fair view given by the financial statements.

(2)   Planning the audit will ensure that work is directed to cover the whole of the company's accounting systems. Thus reviewing last year's files and discussions with management will identify all the accounting systems - adequate audit programmes can then be written to cover all of these systems.

(3)   If particularly difficult or critical areas come to light, then additional resources will be devoted to these to investigate the problem fully. Thus last year's file may note a difficult stocktake; therefore an experienced senior may be sent to attend this year rather than a semi-senior or junior staff member.

The aim of planning, therefore, is to identify risk areas early in the audit and to ensure that appropriate action is taken to minimise the potential risk that they pose.

(ii)   **SAS 240 on Quality Control**

SAS 240 *Quality control for audit work* recognises that if the auditor ensures that all jobs are done to a high standard, this of itself will minimise the amount of risk involved to the auditor. A complete, well presented and referenced audit file is likely to prove of much more value in court than a shoddy and only partly referenced file.

Particular procedures to employ to ensure that audit work is of a high standard include:

(1)   observing all Auditing Standards;

(2)   before accepting any appointment, ensuring that there are no conflicts of interest between the firm's duty as auditors and other non-professional situations eg, client being a close relative;

(3)   following from (2) above, also ensuring that potential clients are of a good standing eg, not potentially insolvent;

(4)   ensuring that the firm has the skills necessary to perform the service for the client eg, detailed use of computer auditing if the client has a highly computerised accounting system;

(5)   ensuring that all staff members are properly recruited and trained to be able to audit in accordance with professional and the firm's own standards;

(6)   ensuring that consultative procedures are available to reconcile problems between staff and partners;

(7)   ensuring that full file reviews are carried out either by another auditing firm, or by another office of the same firm.

If these procedures are followed the firm should be less liable to negligence claims as noted above.

(c)   **Litigation directed at auditors or directors of company**

The directors of a company are required under S226 CA85 to prepare accounts which show a true and fair view. If therefore the financial statements do not show a true and fair view, the directors have breached their duty under the Act. The fact that at least one director signs the accounts indicates that they are aware of this requirement.

The auditor of a company then reports on the accuracy of the financial statements ie, does he concur with the directors' opinion that the financial statements show a true and fair view? In doing this he also reports on the stewardship function of the directors; the members own the company but do not run it - they employ the directors. The auditor therefore in effect reports that what the directors say is correct.

Both the directors and the auditor therefore in some way confirm the accuracy of the financial statements. It can be argued that both should share the blame if the financial statements are found to be incorrect. Unfortunately, because the auditor has insurance against being sued, it is more likely that he will be the subject of litigation because some financial benefit is seen from suing him rather than the directors who do not have insurance.

9 NEW SYLLABUS EXAMINATIONS

Section A - ALL THREE questions in this section are compulsory and MUST be attempted

21 (Question 1 of examination)

Your firm is the auditor of Southwell Engineering Limited, and you have been asked by the senior in charge to describe how you can use computer assisted audit techniques to audit the company's computerised sales and sales ledger system. Southwell Engineering will allow you to use your data on test files to check the correct operation of the accounting computer programs and to use computer audit programs to interrogate the sales ledger file. You have already satisfied yourself that controls over access to the sales ledger system are effective.

In the computerised sales system:

(a)   details of goods to be dispatched are input into the computer, and after approval by the credit controller, a dispatch note is printed in the dispatch department who send the goods to the customer

(b)   the computer prepares the sales invoice using prices from the price file. It posts the invoice to the sales ledger and the sales and VAT to the nominal ledger. The invoice is sent to the customer

(c)   cash received and discount allowed is posted to the sales ledger by the sales accounting department

(d)   the system allows posting of credit notes, adjustments (to correct errors) and writing off of bad debts

(e)   at monthly intervals, statements are sent to customers

(f)   the computer can print out at any time:

      (i)   details of transactions on any account
      (ii)   an aged analysis of sales ledger accounts
      (iii)   the total of the balances on the sales ledger
      (iv)   details of transactions posted in the month
      (v)   an analysis of sales income for the month.

The following information is required when inputting dispatch note details:

(a)   customer account number
(b)   date of dispatch (if different from the current date)
(c)   part number and quantity of each item dispatched
(d)   any special discounts allowed to the customer.

You are required to describe:

(a)   the test data you would enter into the computerised sales system to check the correct processing of dispatch notes and sales invoices

(8 marks)

(b) how a computer audit program can assist you in carrying out a debtors' circularisation, including selecting debtors to circularise

(5 marks)

(c) how you would use a computer audit program to help in verifying the year end debtors on the sales ledger.

(7 marks)

(Total: 20 marks)

Notes:

(a) in part (a) you are not required to describe how you would check the correct processing of cash, discount, credit notes and adjustments

(b) you are not required to describe in detail how you would carry out a debtors' circularisation, you are only required to consider the aspect of a debtors' circularisation required by part (b) of the question

(c) an alternative term for 'computer audit programs' is 'audit software'.

---

22   (Question 2 of examination)

Your firm is the auditor of Silverhill Potteries Limited, which is a wholesaler of pottery products (eg, cups, saucers, plates, mugs etc), and you are carrying out the audit for the year ended 30 April 1994. You have been asked by the senior in charge of the audit to identify stock which may be worth less than cost and to check that it has been valued correctly. The company has a computerised stock control system which records receipts and dispatches of stock, current stock quantities and the age of the stock. You attended a count of all the stock at the year end.

You are required to:

(a) define in detail the basis for valuing stocks in accordance with SSAP 9 *Stocks and long-term contracts* (see note below)

(4 marks)

(b) state the types of stock which may be worth less than cost, and describe the investigations you will carry out to identify this stock

(8 marks)

(c) describe the audit work you will carry out to determine the net realisable value of the stock you have found from your investigations in part (b) above.

(8 marks)

(Total: 20 marks)

Note: You should assume that:

(i)   stock quantities are correct
(ii)   the stock should be valued in accordance with SSAP 9 *Stocks and long-term contracts*; and
(iii)   there is no long-term contract work in progress.

---

23   (Question 3 of examination)

The partner in charge of the audit of Sinfin Wholesale plc is concerned about the controls in the company's computerised purchases system, and has asked for your advice. In the purchases system, invoices and credit notes are posted to the computerised purchase ledger by the purchases accounting department, and the computer automatically raises the cheque when the invoice is due for payment.

For cheque payments:

(a) for payments under £500 pre-printed cheques are used, and no further authorisation of the cheque is required, as the authorised signature is included in the printing

(b)   for payments from £500 to £5,000 an authorised person is required to initial the cheque, and

(c)   for payments over £5,000 an authorised signatory must sign the cheque.

You are required to describe the controls which should be in operation to prevent fraud and error in the company's purchases system in relation to:

(a)   controls to ensure that only authorised purchase invoices and credit notes are correctly posted to the purchase ledger

(7 marks)

(b)   controls over the addition, amendment and deletion of suppliers and ensuring that only authorised suppliers are on the standing data file

(5 marks)

(c)   controls over the cheque payments and the custody of cheques.

(8 marks)
(Total: 20 marks)

Section B - TWO questions only to be answered

24   (Question 4 of examination)

The new audit trainee of your firm of registered auditors has asked you to advise him on the reliability of the following types of third party evidence:

(i)   valuation of land and buildings by a valuer
(ii)   the replies to a debtors' circularisation
(iii)   the letter received from the bank.

You are required to:

(a)   discuss the reliability of each of the three types of third party evidence listed in (i) to (iii) above, and consider the accuracy of the valuations they provide

(9 marks)

(b)   for valuations provided by a valuer, describe the work you would carry out to check the independence, qualifications and experience of the valuer and the accuracy of the valuation

(5 marks)

(c)   for the letter received from the bank, describe the work you would perform in checking the bank reconciliations and that the balance on the bank accounts, as included in the financial statements, is correct.

(6 marks)
(Total: 20 marks)

25   (Question 5 of examination)

You are carrying out the audit of Mowbray Computers Limited for the year ended 30 April 1994. The company assembles microcomputers from components purchased from the Far East and sells them to retailers, and to individuals and businesses by mail order. In the current year, there has been a recession and strong competition which has resulted in a fall in sales and the gross profit margin. This had led to a trading loss and the company experiencing going concern problems.

You are required to:

(a)   Describe the factors which indicate that a company may not be a going concern. Your list should include all factors, and not just those which apply to Mowbray Computers Limited.

(10 marks)

(b) Consider the form of audit report (ie, qualified or unqualified) you would use on Mowbray Computer Limited's financial statements, if you conclude that the company is experiencing serious going concern problems, in the following two situations:

(i) you conclude that the financial statements give sufficient disclosure of the going concern problems

(ii) there is no disclosure of the going concern problems in the financial statements and you believe there is a serious risk that the company will fail in the foreseeable future.

(6 marks)

In each case you should say how the audit report will differ from an unqualified audit report (ie, example 1 of SAS 600 *Auditors' reports on financial statements*).

(c) State the parties who may successfully sue you as auditor for negligence, and consider the arguments you could include in your defence, when:

(i) the financial statements of Mowbray Computers Ltd for the year ended 30 April 1994:

- do not mention any going concern problems, and
- your audit report on these financial statements was unqualified, and

(ii) the company fails on 15 February 1995.

(4 marks)
(Total: 20 marks)

26   (Question 6 of examination)

You have been asked to carry out the audit of Longton University Nursery which looks after the young children of staff and students during term time.

A management committee runs the nursery, it meets monthly and minutes are prepared by the secretary. The members of the management committee are elected annually. The nursery rents its premises from the university, who send monthly invoices for the rent, rates, light and heat. Fixed assets comprise mainly equipment for use by the children and are depreciated at 20% per annum on cost. There is no fixed asset register for maintaining details of fixed assets owned by the nursery.

The treasurer records all accounting transactions in an analysed cash book and keeps vouchers relating to receipts and payments. The draft accounts, which are shown after the requirement to this question, have been prepared by the treasurer from these records.

You are required to describe:

(a) (i) the system you would expect to be in operation to control income and expenditure, and

(ii) the audit work you would carry out to verify the income and expenditure account

(11 marks)

(b) the audit work you would carry out in verifying the balance sheet, including the movement in fixed assets.

(9 marks)
(Total: 20 marks)

Longton University Nursery

Draft Income and Expenditure Account
for year ended 31 March 1994

Income	£	£
Fees		41,595
Fund raising events		7,419
Bank deposit account interest		130
		49,144
Expenditure		
Salaries	30,798	
Rent, rates, light and heat	12,530	
Telephone	558	
Insurance	753	
Refreshments	941	
Repairs to equipment	168	
Depreciation of equipment	2,883	
Honoraria to auditor	50	
Sundries	435	
		49,116
Net surplus		28

Draft Balance Sheet at 31 March 1994

	£	£
Fixed assets		6,870
Current assets		
Debtors - fees due	759	
Bank deposit account	4,528	
Bank current account	1,241	
	6,528	
Less: Current liabilities		
Auditor's honoraria	50	
		6,478
		13,348

Capital	£
At 1.4.93	13,320
Net surplus for the year	28
At 31.3.94	13,348

Movement on fixed assets

	Cost £	Dep'n £	NBV £
At 1.4.93	12,372	4,668	7,704
Additions	2,049	-	2,049
Depreciation charge	-	2,883	(2,883)
At 31.3.94	14,421	7,551	6,870

EXAMINER'S COMMENTS

General comments

The general standard of candidates' answers was disappointing. However, a small number of candidates performed well in the exam. In particular, the answers were poor in practical auditing areas, especially verification of balance sheet items. These included questions: 2 (c) in determining net realisable value; 4(c) in checking the bank reconciliation; and 6 (b) in verifying the balance sheet.

To maximise their chances of passing this exam, candidates need to: answer five questions on the paper; answer all parts of each question; answer parts of the questions in the correct order; provide an answer of adequate length, aiming for at least two pages for each question. Some candidates' handwriting was difficult to read, too small, or was written in faint blue pen. You may not gain the marks you deserve because the marker cannot read what you have written; a black pen would be preferable. In many cases candidates answered their version of the question, rather than the points asked by the question. Candidates can only be awarded marks for points relevant to the question being asked, so most candidates who provided an answer on their own version of the topic failed to achieve a pass mark.

Question 1: examined candidates' knowledge of computer assisted audit techniques.

Generally, the answers were very poor with many candidates failing to answer parts of the question, or providing very brief and superficial answers. Answers would have been much better if candidates had read the article in the February 1994 issue of the *Students' Newsletter*, 'Auditing in a Computer Environment' which provides a comprehensive study.

Part (a) required candidates to suggest the test data which should be entered into the computer to check the operation of the computer program. Many answers were weak, and some candidates described the processes in a sales system, rather than what the question was asking. Candidates should have described the input of both valid and invalid data (few mentioned invalid data). Furthermore, they should have checked the output produced from inputting this data (very few candidates considered this point). Part (b) asked how a computer could help with a debtors' circularisation. The answers to this part were better, but more candidates should have suggested using the computer to produce the letters to send to the debtors. Descriptions of statistical techniques to select the debtors were rather weak.

The answers to part (c) on the use of computer audit programs were even weaker than part (a). The sales ledger file will contain the outstanding transactions at the year end, but little information about transactions during the year. Frequently, only the last month's transactions will be retained on the file, in addition to the uncleared items. Therefore, many of the suggestions about checking the transactions posted during the year were hardly appropriate. Many candidates suggested the computer audit program could be used to check sales cut-off, but it should be easier to check this without the use of a computer audit program.

Question 2: required an explanation of stock valuation, and how stock worth less than cost should be found and its value verified.

The answers to part (a), on the valuation of stock, were disappointing. Many candidates just said that stock should be valued at the lower of cost and net realisable value, which was worth a mark. However, the question asked for a more detailed description of the valuation of stock, and most answers were quite poor. The model answer in the Question and Answer booklet shows what is required.

The answers to part (b) on finding stock which may be worth less than cost were quite good. However, some candidates failed to consider the characteristics of stock of a pottery company. For instance, they suggested it might be perishable, or they cited obsolescence in terms of computers. The answers to part (c) were very poor, and candidates should ensure they have a better understanding of this important topic in the future. The best evidence of the selling price of the stock is the price on a sales invoice issued after the year end - few candidates mentioned this point. Common suggestions included: asking management, using the auditor's judgement, using analytical review, considering the price of competitors and asking for a valuer, all of which are poor evidence compare with checking sales invoices after the year end. Most candidates gave the impression that the selling price was net realisable value, which is wrong, as net realisable value is the selling, distribution and marketing expenses. The very weak answers failed to mention selling price, and were either a continuation of part (b) or checked the cost of the stock, which is irrelevant.

Question 3: examined candidates' understanding of controls over input of purchase invoices and credit notes into a computerised purchases system; controls over changes to supplier details and over cheque payments.

Most of the answers to part (a), on input of purchase invoices and credit notes, were quite good. In part (b) some candidates missed the important points that a responsible official (eg, the chief accountant) should authorise new suppliers, deletion of suppliers and changes to supplier details, and suppliers should not be deleted when there is a balance on the account. In part (c) on controls over cheque payments, many candidates criticised the controls as being weak, and then failed to answer the question. Criticism of the controls was worth a mark, but many candidates answered the question in terms of all cheques being signed by two employees, which was not answering the question. They should have provided an answer to the situation in the question where cheques under £500 were issued with a printed signature, those between £500 and £5,000 were initialed and those over £5,000 required a signature. The situation in the question is one which is likely to occur in a large company where the auditor will have to audit the existing system and will have little influence over the system the company uses.

Question 4: examined candidates' knowledge on the reliability of various types of third party evidence.

This was the most popular question in part B. Many answers stated that 'the auditor should obtain relevant and reliable audit evidence sufficient to enable him to draw reasonably conclusions therefrom'. Then most candidates stated that documentary evidence is more reliable than oral evidence, evidence obtained from independent sources is more reliable than that secured solely from within the enterprise and that auditor-generated evidence is the most reliable form of audit evidence. Stating these points gains no marks and is wasting time, so candidates should avoid doing this. It is the application of auditing principles which is important in this exam. Part (a) of the question asked candidates to consider the accuracy of valuations provided by a valuer, the replies to a debtors' circularisation and the replies by the bank. Most of the answers concentrated on the procedures involved in obtaining this third party information. This was not what this part of the question required, but candidates did get some marks for considering these points. Regarding valuation, a good answer would suggest that it is difficult to value properties and valuations can be subject to considerable inaccuracies. The points made by candidates on the debtors' circularisation were better, as some suggested that the debtor may not be careful in providing a reply (ie, the debtor may not check their purchase ledger) and the better candidates said that confirmation of the balance did not confirm that it was collectable. With regard to the bank letter, candidates tended to concentrate on errors in bank letters, which are unusual. Few candidates said that the balance provided by the bank would not be the same as the cash book balance because of uncleared lodgements and unpresented cheques. Most of the answers to part (b) on checking the qualifications and experience of the valuer were quite good. Generally, the answers to part (c) on checking the bank reconciliation were very poor. Many candidates failed to consider the bank reconciliation at all. Few candidates checked the clearance of unpresented cheques and uncleared lodgements. Hardly any suggested that late clearing of lodgements could be a teeming and lading fraud or that late clearing of unpresented cheques could mean they were sent to creditors after the year end. Most candidates should have had experience of checking the bank reconciliation, even if it is only of their own bank account, yet few displayed a satisfactory understanding of this topic.

Question 5: examined candidates' understanding of going concern problems.

The answers to part (a) on factors indicating going concern problems were quite good. However, many candidates listed points without discussing them. If candidates included a discussion of each point, they were awarded more marks, as they demonstrated a deeper understanding of the topic. Generally, the answers to part (b) were poor. In part (i) candidates should have suggested the auditor should provide an unqualified report with an explanatory paragraph. Only a few candidates provided the correct answer. Some answers were very confused: firstly, suggesting an unqualified report should be given and then saying it should be qualified. Many candidates suggested that a 'subject to' qualification should be given, when this is not permitted by SAS 600. It was apparent that many of these candidates were unaware of SAS 600, which is an important Auditing Standard. Most attempts at writing an audit report were very poor.

The answers to part (ii) were little better. Candidates who stated a 'disclaimer of opinion' should note that this is an acceptable answer (not a good one). The correct answer was an adverse opinion, which only a few candidates suggested. Once again, some candidates suggested a 'subject to' qualification should be given, while others suggested an unqualified opinion should be given (even when they suggested the report for part (i) should be qualified!). Few marks were allocated to part (c), so a concise answer was required. The question asked candidates to suggest the Caparo case, which limits the parties who can sue the auditor to the company and shareholders as a body. Many answers considered older cases, which are less relevant, and they suggested a much wider range of parties who could sue the auditor. Surprisingly, it was apparent that many candidates were unaware of the important decision in the Caparo case. Few candidates gave a convincing answer to the arguments the auditor could use in his defence against a negligence claim. Also, many candidates incorrectly suggested that the auditor would not be liable as the failure occurred too long after the year end. I would agree it is more than 6 months after the date of the audit report, but it is still within 12 months of the company's year end.

Question 6: required candidates to describe systems to control income and expenditure and the audit work necessary to verify the balance sheet.

This was the least popular question on the paper, yet many of the answers to part (a) were quite good. The answers to part (b) were weaker. The weakness of many of the answers to part (a) was that, candidates suggested, controls and accounting systems which would be appropriate to a medium-sized company, rather than the small nursery in the question. For instance, they suggested that two people should open the post and that the organisation would keep purchase, sales and nominal ledgers. It is likely that the treasurer will keep only a cash book from which the accounts are prepared. However, there should be some controls over income and expenditure to minimise the risk of fraud and error by the treasurer. In part (ii) the largest item of income is fees, and the largest expenditure is salaries, so audit work should concentrate on these items. Candidates could have suggested more checks over completeness of income. This could be performed by test checking sales income from attendance records to the cash book and completeness of income by analytical review (eg, average number of children × annual fee). On expenditure, candidates should have checked payments to purchase invoices and verified payment of salaries by checking from cash payments to employees to details of hours worked. Some answers failed to consider salaries. Many answers suggested checking that the depreciation was in accordance with SSAP 12 (Accounting for Depreciation) but few candidates checked that the depreciation charge in the accounts was calculated correctly.

The answers to part (b) on verifying the balance sheet were disappointing. More candidates should have suggested checking the bank reconciliation for the bank accounts. Many candidates suggested carrying out a debtors' circularisation, which is inappropriate in such a small organisation. Debtors would be checked by obtaining details of the amounts outstanding at the year end and checking receipt of fees after the year end. The question specifically asked candidates to check fixed assets, but most answers were short, superficial and unconvincing. Once again, it is inappropriate to ask a valuer to value the fixed assets in such a small organisation. Hardly any candidates suggested checking for unrecorded liabilities, such as rent and other charges made by the University.

As the question contained a profit and loss account and balance sheet, candidates should have used the figures in their answers. Almost all candidates ignored them.

ANSWERS TO JUNE 1994 EXAMINATION

21   (Answer 1 of examination)

(a)   In using test data to check the operation of the company's accounting computer programs, first I would either prepare some test files or copy the client's standing data and transaction data files. Then I would print out these files, including the balances on each sales ledger account and the total of the sales ledger balances. The purpose of printing the contents of the files at this stage is to enable me to check that after input of the test data, the changes in the contents of the files are correct.

Test data comprises valid and invalid data. Valid data should be processed correctly and with invalid data either a warning should be given (for minor errors) or the data should be rejected.

First, I will input valid sales data comprising:

(i)   a valid account number
(ii)   the current day for dispatch
(iii) various items to dispatch with the part number and quantity of each item.

I will check that the computer produces a dispatch note and a sales invoice in accordance with these details, and updates the sales ledger. I will check that the correct prices have been used on the sales invoice and that the calculations on the sales invoice are correct.

Invalid data will include:

(i)   an invalid account number. If the account number is not on the standing data file, the computer should reject the data input. However, the computer will not reject an account number which is for a valid customer, so the computer should display the customer's name and address on the screen so that the user can check that it agrees with the details on the record from which data is being input

(ii)   an invalid date could be input. If it includes alphabetic letters it should be rejected. If it is for a date earlier than the current date, the computer should give a warning and allow the data to be input again. If the date is some time in the future, a warning should be given (ie, it should accept a date up to a week in the future, if it is up to a month in the future a warning should be given and if it is more than a month it should be rejected)

(iii) an incorrect part number can be input. This is similar to inputting an invalid account number, as it should be rejected if it is not on the file. The computer should display details of the part on the screen so that the user can check that it is in accordance with the part number which has been input (ie, the computer will not be able to detect an incorrect part number, which is on the standing data file). The part number may have a check digit to minimise the risk of an invalid number being input. Also, it may comprise a letter followed by five numbers, and the computer can have a format check to ensure the first character is alphabetic followed by five numeric characters - this format check can be tested by inputting invalid characters (eg, numbers where alphabetic characters are expected and vice versa)

(iv)   the computer should not accept any alphabetic characters when the quantity is input, and it should not accept zero or negative quantities. For most items it should only accept whole numbers (as one cannot have half of a car!) but for liquids and solids measured by weight or volume it may allow decimal figures. For some items, there may be a limit of the quantity the computer will accept. The test data will be designed to check these controls.

Following the input of this data, the listing of the invoices will be printed out, as well as the sales ledger accounts updated and the total of the balances on the sales ledger. I will check that the sales ledger accounts have been updated correctly and that the closing balance after inputting the data is equal to the opening balance plus the value of the invoices posted to the ledger. I will check that sales income has been recorded correctly and posted to the nominal ledger.

(b)   A computer audit program can be used to select debtors for circularisation from the sales ledger file using a random statistical sampling method. The most appropriate method to use is monetary unit sampling, where the probability of a debtor being selected is proportional to its value. A computer audit program can be used to perform this task.

The procedure for selecting debtors using monetary unit sampling is as follows. If the total of the sales ledger balances is £1 million, and 50 debtors are to be circularised, one debtor is circularised for every £20,000. First, the debtors are listed in account number order, and a random number between 0 and 20,000 is selected (say 13,199). The following example illustrates how this method is used:

| | Debtor name | Balance | Total b/fwd | Total c/fwd | Select? |
		£	£	£	
1	AGJ Ltd	4,663	0	4,663	No
2	AHG Ltd	10,925	4,663	15,588	Yes
3	AKD Ltd	13,524	15,588	29,112	No
4	APD Ltd	17,236	29,112	46,348	Yes
5	ASG Ltd	241	46,348	46,589	No

Debtor 2 is selected because its balance straddles £13,199 (ie, £13,199 straddles the b/f balance of £4,663 and the c/f balance of £15,588), and debtor 4 is selected because its balance straddles £33,199 (ie, 13,199 + 20,000).

The computer audit program can be used to check the ageing of the debtor balances (as described below), print out old outstanding balances and those over the credit limit. I will circularise a sample of these balances which look doubtful. These will include debtors where I am aware the company is in financial difficulties, and those where there are old unpaid items. In addition, I may circularise a few zero value balances and credit balances.

Using the list of debtors I have decided to circularise (arrived at from the procedures described above), the computer audit program will be used to write the letters to debtors and include the balance in the letter. Also, a copy of the statement at the year end may be included in the letter to enable the debtor to identify the reasons for the difference between his purchase ledger balance and the client's sales ledger balance. In addition, the computer can send out second letters to debtors who have not replied, analyse the results of the debtors' circularisation and produce a statistical conclusion to this test (ie, provide a quantitative measure of the accuracy of the sales ledger).

(c)   A computer audit program can be used on the sales ledger transaction file to:

(i)   add up the individual items on each sales ledger account and check that the total agrees with the total balance on that account (normally, the computer stores the individual items and the total balance on an account in separate data files)

(ii)   check the ageing of sales ledger accounts and compare this ageing with that produced by the company's normal accounting program

(iii)   add up the balances on each sales ledger account and agree it to the total of the balances on the sales ledger. The computer audit program can add up the individual ageing of each account and check it to the total ageing, and it can calculate the number of accounts with a balance and the total number of accounts on the standing data file. The total number of accounts will be checked to the number printed by the company's accounting computer program

(iv)   the computer can print out sales ledger accounts where the customer is over the credit limit or the debts are overdue. It can print out credit balances and those with unallocated cash (ie, where cash received has not been matched to sales invoices)

(v)   select debtors for a debtors' circularisation, write the letters to the debtors and analyse the results (as described in part (b) of this question).

Any differences between the figures calculated using the computer audit program and those printed out by the company's normal sales accounting computer program would be investigated.

The checks above will assist the auditor in the following audit tasks:

(i)   checking of the additions will be more comprehensive than the auditor could perform manually. Once the computer audit program is set up, it will take very little time to carry out with a consequent time saving in future years

(ii)   checking the ageing of debts provides confidence that the company's age analysis provides a reliable source of audit evidence

(iii)   the overdue debts and those over the credit limit can be investigated to see if they are doubtful debts. Credit balances often arise through errors (eg, where invoices are not posted to the sales ledger) and unallocated cash indicates weaknesses in the company's system of control (as they should contact the customer and ask which invoices are being paid and if there are any disputes).

22   (Answer 2 of examination)

(a)   Stock is valued at the lower of cost and net realisable value. SSAP 9 defines:

(i)   cost as the purchase price (including import duties, transport and handling costs and any other directly attributable costs) less trade discounts, rebates and subsidies.

For work in progress and finished goods of a manufacturer, the costs of direct labour and production overheads, based on a normal level of activity, are included in the value of stock

(ii)   net realisable value is the actual or estimated selling price (net of trade but before settlement discount) less costs to be incurred in selling, distribution and marketing (and for work in progress and raw materials, less all further costs to completion).

Normally, a FIFO (first in, first out) basis is used. Other acceptable bases include weighted average cost and standard cost (provided they are similar to actual cost). However, SSAP 9 states that the LIFO (last in, first out) basis is not an acceptable one for valuing stock.

(b)   The types of stock which may be worth less than cost include:

(i)   slow moving and obsolete stock
(ii)   damaged and seconds stock
(iii)   stock which is being sold below cost (eg, in a sales promotion).

Also, it is desirable to check that categories of stock with a high value at the year end are being sold for more than cost (if they are being sold for less than cost, they should be valued at net realisable value).

To identify such stock, I will:

(i)   obtain details of such stock as recorded on the stock sheets at the stocktake, and in my audit working papers. Slow moving stock is likely to be dusty (or the packaging dusty) and it may be stored in a different area from fast moving stock. It should be apparent if stock is damaged. Seconds stock may be put in a different area, or it may be labelled 'seconds' on the shelf where it is kept. In addition, there may be odd items of pottery (eg, some cups without saucers) or incomplete sets which may be worth less than cost (some may be worthless)

(ii)   the computerised stock records should note damaged and seconds stock (ie, they should be in a different stock category from perfect stock). I will find details of slow moving stock from the computerised stock records. Some pottery stock may be held for long periods, but I will record stock which is over six months old as it is probably slow moving. Also, I will record apparently fast moving stock (cheap sets of pottery) which has been in stock for over three months, as it may be slow moving

(iii)   I will inspect sales reports, management reports and board minutes for further evidence of stock which may be worth less than cost. These reports should mention stock lines which are being discontinued, stock which is difficult to sell or slow moving, and damage to stock. Also, they will report special offers where stock may be being sold for less than cost. I will list details of such stock which may be worth less than cost

(iv)   I will ask the appropriate management (eg, sales director, storehouse manager) and the directors if there is any stock worth less than cost and I will record details of such stock. In particular, I will ask them if any stock is being sold below cost (eg, in a sales promotion).

I will note the items of stock which I have recorded from the work described above and I will check net realisable value in the manner described in the next part of the question.

(c)   As stated in part (a) of the answer, net realisable value is:

(i)   the actual or estimated selling price; less
(ii)   costs to be incurred in selling, distribution and marketing.

As Silverhill Potteries only has goods purchased for resale, costs to completion are not relevant.

I will perform the following checks to determine the net realisable value of the items I have identified in part (b). First, I will determine the actual or estimated selling price.

If all the stock has been sold between the year end and the date of my checks, I will check the selling price to sales invoices issued after the year end (the selling price is after trade discount but before settlement discount). If most of the year end stock has been sold by the time of my check, then the selling price after the year end will be used for that stock.

If there have been few (or no) sales after the year end, I will check sales invoices selling the stock before the year end. This will be the best estimate of the price the stock will be sold for after the year end.

However, if the stock has become obsolete between the last sale before the year end and my audit check, then the selling price before the year end may be too high compared with the price the stock will be sold for after the year end. So, I will have to consider a fair price this stock will be sold for after the year end (this will be the estimated selling price).

If there have been few sales before and after the year end, the stock may have to be sold at a very low price to provide space for new stock. If the value of this stock (at cost) is significant, I will have to check the company's plans for disposing of the stock. Overall, it is probably wise to estimate a very low selling price.

Some damaged items of stock and odd items (eg, single cups without saucers) may be worth only scrap value, and I may accept that they should be included in stock at zero value.

It should be noted that it is unreliable to determine the selling price from the company's price lists, as this type of stock is probably being sold at a lower price than that shown on the price list.

I will compare my estimates of selling prices with the company's. I will discuss cases where there are significant differences between my estimates and the company's, and I will discuss with them situations where I find it difficult to estimate the selling price of the stock (eg, for incomplete sets, and very slow moving stock). Based on these discussions I will consider whether the management's estimates of the selling prices of the stock are reasonable.

These checks above will have determined the actual or estimated selling price. Net realisable value is found by deducting costs to be incurred in selling, distribution and marketing from this selling price.

Generally, selling, distribution and marketing expenses are small, so I will find the year's selling, distribution and marketing costs and total sales from the nominal ledger. I will calculate the ratio of selling, distribution and marketing costs to total sales for the year (say it is equal to 4%). Using this figure, net realisable value will be 96% of the actual or estimated selling price.

If it is apparent that some items of stock will incur larger selling, distribution or marketing costs, then the actual costs would be deducted from the selling price to determine net realisable value. For instance, if the items have to be exported then the carriage costs will be high.

From these investigations, I will determine the net realisable value of the stock. Assuming I have found the cost of the stock, I will value the stock at the lower of cost and net realisable value. Then I will compare my stock value with the company's. I will discuss any significant differences with them, and I will note any significant disagreements in my schedule of unadjusted errors.

23   (Answer 3 of examination)

(a)   Obviously, it is very important that only authorised purchase invoices and credit notes are posted to the purchase ledger as posting an unauthorised purchase invoice could result in a fraudulent payment. Also, if the invoice value posted to the purchase ledger is wrong, it could result in an overpayment and the time taken in recovering this overpayment. The controls which should be in operation to ensure that only authorised purchase invoices and credit notes are posted to the purchase ledger include:

(i)   the individual posting the purchase invoice (or credit note) should check that it is addressed to Sinfin Wholesale and has been (where appropriate):

-     initialled as agreed to a signed goods received note
-     for services, there is acknowledgement that the service has been received
-     initialled as agreed to the purchase order
-     initialled as prices agreed to the purchase order or a price list
-     initialled that computations have been checked
-     final authorisation has been made by a responsible official

(ii)   the individual who posts purchase invoices to the purchase ledger should be sufficiently independent of other functions to ensure that there is a proper division of duties for internal control purposes. For instance the individual should not have custody of stock, or cheques paying suppliers, or for ordering goods and services, or for inputting adjustments or changing supplier details on the standing data file

(iii)   purchase invoices should be input into the computer in batches, with sequential numbering by the computer. The value and number of invoices in the batch should be calculated manually and when these invoices have been posted to the purchase ledger, the totals accepted should be the same as the manual totals, and any difference should be investigated. Details of each batch of invoices should be recorded in a batch control book (eg, batch number, number of invoices and their total value) and any break in the sequence of batches should be investigated as this indicates an unauthorised input of invoices. Credit notes should be input in separate batches from purchase invoices (as this reduces the risk of a credit note being posted as an invoice and vice versa)

(iv)   when a purchase invoice (or credit note) is posted to the purchase ledger the operator should check that the supplier's name and address on the computer are the same as that on the purchase invoice. Any differences should be investigated.

(v)   ideally, only purchase invoices for authorised suppliers should be posted to the purchase ledger. If a sundry purchases account is used for paying suppliers who are not authorised by the company, there should be strong controls over its use. In particular, a responsible official (eg, the chief accountant) should inspect the transactions on this account at least once a month (and at the end of the month) to ensure they are not fraudulent. All transactions on the sundry purchases account should remain until the end of the month, so that fraudulent transactions cannot be eliminated (and thus the fraud hidden)

(vi)   periodically, the value of expenses should be checked to budget and previous years in order to detect any fraudulent input of invoices (or errors). This may be delegated to the individual departments responsible for their budgets

(vii)   suppliers' statements should be reconciled monthly to the balances on the purchase ledger by a person independent of the purchases and purchase accounting function. Any differences should be investigated.

(b)   It is important to have effective controls over the addition, amendment and deletion of suppliers, as otherwise an individual could perpetrate a fraud by creating a supplier in their own name (or that of a friend), post items to that account and obtain payment. There should be the following controls:

(i)   the company should have a standard form which authorises addition, amendment and deletion of suppliers on the purchase ledger standing data file. Before any changes to supplier details are input into the computer, this form should be authorised by a responsible official, such as the chief accountant

(ii)   changes to supplier details should be input in sequentially numbered batches which should be recorded in a batch control book. Any breaks in the batch numbers should be investigated, as they indicate unauthorised changes to supplier details. Ideally, new suppliers, changes to supplier details and deletion of suppliers should be entered in separate batches. Following input of batches, the computer should print out the accepted data, and this should be checked to the input details (eg, by one employee reading from the computer details and the other checking the details agree to the input form)

(iii)   a responsible official (eg, the chief accountant or internal auditor) should periodically test check additions, amendment and deletion of suppliers to ensure that all data input has been authorised

(iv)   the buying department manager should periodically review the list of authorised suppliers and he should recommend deletion of suppliers which are no longer used (ie, dormant accounts increase the risk of fraud). Some of these accounts will be found by looking at the purchase ledger account and seeing that there have been no transactions for some time. It may be possible for the computer to print out suppliers where there has been no transaction for, say, more than six months. This should ensure that these dormant accounts are deleted

(v)   periodically, a person independent of the purchases function should obtain a print-out of all authorised suppliers and check their details against manual records (eg, forms authorising addition or amendment of supplier details). Documentation from the supplier (eg, purchase invoices, order confirmations and correspondence from the supplier) will provide additional evidence of the existence of the supplier.

(c)   There is a serious risk in this system that unauthorised cheque payments may occur. The controls described above should ensure that only authorised transactions are posted to authorised purchase ledger accounts. However, the question says that cheques under £500 require no signature, so it could be possible for an employee to steal a cheque, type the details (ie, in their own name) and misappropriate it. The controls which should be exercised over cheques should include:

    (i)   each of the three types of cheque should be labelled:

- payment under £500
- payment £500 to £5,000
- payment over £5,000

For the cheques to £500 there should be an authorised signature printed on the cheque, and for cheques between £500 and £5,000 there should be a heading beside the space where the authorised initial is required. Cheques over £5,000 should not include a printed authorised signature, and they should indicate the number of authorised signatures required (although the question says only one authorised signatory is required, if two are required, the cheque should have two 'signatory' words beside the place where each signature should be placed)

    (ii)   when the computer prints the cheques, it should print the three value levels in separate batches, so that the appropriate cheque stationery can be loaded into the printer

    (iii)   there should be strict controls over the custody of unprinted cheques, especially those for payments under £500 and also for those for payments up to £5,000. The cheques should be kept in a safe and only taken out of the safe when they are required. Ideally, the times when the cheques are taken out of the safe should be recorded in a register, and this authorisation should be by a responsible official

    (iv)   ideally, cheques should be sequentially numbered by the computer (when they are printed) and the bank should be informed of the cheque numbers used. The cheques should be printed in a script (ie, font) which is easily identified by the bank, but is not easily copied by a fraudster. Also, it should be impossible to amend the printed sum (eg, by using indelible ink)

(v)   all spoilt cheques should be cancelled (by writing 'cancelled' across the crossing) and they should be filed to keep as evidence of not being used

(vi)   all cheques should be crossed 'A/C payee' so that they can only be paid into the stated bank account and cannot be negotiated

(vii)   a responsible official or the internal auditor should periodically inspect cheques after printing before they are sent to the creditor to ensure they are not fraudulent. This can be done by checking that the cheque is payable to an authorised supplier and that the payment is made for authorised purchase invoices which are recorded on the purchase ledger account. This check is particularly important for cheques under £500

(viii) the person initialling cheques between £500 and £5,000 should be aware that the payment is to an authorised supplier, and this check should apply to the authorised signatory signing cheques over £5,000

(ix)   following printing of the cheques, the remittance advice should be attached to the cheque, the cheque should be signed (where appropriate), the items should be put in an envelope and they should be sent to suppliers. It should be impossible for any employee concerned with the purchases and purchase accounting functions to intercept the cheque before it is put in the post to the supplier (if the cheque can be intercepted, this could allow a fraud to take place)

(x)   the cashier should check that cheques appearing on the bank statement also appear in the cash book (part of the cash book will be the record of cheque payments made by the purchase ledger system). Any apparently unauthorised cheques should be investigated immediately

(xi)   the bank reconciliation should be prepared at least monthly (probably by the cashier) and it should be checked by a responsible official, such as the chief accountant or internal auditor

(xii)   if possible, the paid cheques should be obtained from the bank and a person independent of the purchases and cash payment system should check:

-       the cheque is not negotiated (crossing the cheque 'A/C payee' should prevent negotiation of cheques). Any negotiated cheques should be investigated

-       the payee name and the value of the payment should be agreed to the purchase ledger account and the cash book on a test basis

-       the cheque has been signed correctly.

---

24   (Answer 4 of examination)

(a)   (i)   Provided the valuation comes from an independent, qualified and experienced valuer, this evidence is obtained from a well qualified and competent individual. However, valuation of land and buildings is very difficult and can be subject to considerable error (eg, the recent downward revaluation of almost £500 million to £861 million of properties of Queens Moat Houses). It is easier to value properties if there are a large number of similar properties available (eg, small industrial units and small shops), as the valuer should be aware of how much similar properties are selling for and he can use these values to estimate the value of the client's property. If the property is large or of a specialised nature the valuation may be unreliable. With a specialised property (eg, a car manufacturing plant) there is the question of whether the purchaser wants to use the property for the same use, or he may decide to demolish it to construct a building for a different purpose. If the buyer wants to demolish the property, the value of the land and buildings will be no more than the value of the land (ie, it could be worth the value of the land less the cost of demolishing the buildings).

During the recession in the UK in the early 1990s there were few sales of properties, and the selling price of the properties depended on whether there was a willing purchaser and how quickly the seller wanted to dispose of the property. Thus, a 'normal sale' will achieve a much higher price than a forced sale (eg, arising from a liquidation). An example of this is that repossessed houses sold for much lower prices than other houses where the seller was in no hurry to sell the property.

(ii)   The replies to a debtors' circularisation are moderately reliable. The limitations are that some debtors agree every reply to a debtors' circularisation, when it is apparent that there are disputed invoices. Also, some debtors may disagree the client's balance, and I, as auditor, will have to check whether the differences are validly goods and cash in transit, or whether they are disputes. Goods in transit are goods sent to the customer shortly before the year end, the invoice of which has not been posted to the customer's purchase ledger. Cash in transit is cash paid by the customer, which is not received by the client until shortly after the year end. A practical problem is that many debtors do not reply to the circularisation (many debtors never reply to any circularisation) and some debtors say they cannot confirm the balance. As the replies to debtors' circularisations are sent direct to the auditor's office by the debtor, it is impossible for the company to amend the debtor's reply.

A significant weakness of a debtors' circularisation is that it does not confirm whether the debt is good (ie, the debtor can reply agreeing the balance but he may be unable to pay the sum due). So, alternative audit procedures have to be carried out to check whether the debt is good.

As far as the quality of audit evidence is concerned, in carrying out a debtors' circularisation one is checking the customer's purchase ledger. In practice, purchase ledgers tend to be less reliable than sales ledgers, as there are often delays between receiving the goods and the purchase invoice and in checking the purchase invoice. These delays mean that most purchase ledgers have some cut-off errors (ie, goods have been received before the year end but the purchase invoice has not been posted to the purchase ledger before the year end). Sales ledgers tend to be more accurate as the dispatch of goods, preparation of the sales invoice and posting it to the sales ledger are under the client's control and they are usually carried out within a day. Also, sales ledgers have to be accurate to ensure the company receives cash from sales promptly, and thus minimise cash flow problems.

(iii)   The letter from the bank is excellent audit evidence, as banks are a very reliable source of evidence, and the letter is sent direct to the auditor, thus preventing the client from manipulating figures. These comments apply to bank letters received from UK clearing banks. With any bank, the reported overdraft should be correct, but, if the bank is in financial difficulties, the balance of cash at the bank may not be recoverable. Although it is unusual for balances of cash at the bank to be doubtful, this did arise for depositors in BCCI (ie, an example of a bank which failed).

In conclusion, the valuation from a valuer is probably the least reliable form of audit evidence because of the difficulty in valuing properties (as described in the answer). The replies to a debtors' circularisation are less reliable than the letter from the bank which is the most reliable form of third party audit evidence.

(b)   In order to check the accuracy of the valuation, I would first check the independence, qualifications and experience of the valuer. On independence, the valuer should work for (or be a partner of) a firm of valuers and he should not be an employee of the audit client or related to the directors of the audit client. On qualifications, he should be a member of a professional body, such as the Royal Institution of Chartered Surveyors. The valuer should be experienced in valuing similar properties to the client's and in the same geographical area. For instance, the valuation would be unreliable if the valuer was only experienced in valuing domestic properties and the client owned industrial properties. Also, the valuer should have experience in valuing properties in the same geographical area as the client, as, for instance, properties in London have a different value from those in Birmingham. The basis of the valuation should normally be an existing use valuation. It would not normally be appropriate to use the rebuilding cost of the property as a valuation base (except for insurance purposes).

In order to check that the value of the property is reasonable, I would inspect the property and check that its value is consistent with the value of similar properties. I may have had experience of clients buying similar properties recently, so this will give me a guide to the property's value. Also, the price properties are advertised by estate agents is a guide, although the estate agent's asking price is likely to be higher than the finally agreed sale price.

(c)   In order to check the accuracy of the cash book balance in the company's accounts, I will have to check the bank reconciliation. I will obtain a copy of the bank reconciliation from the client and:

(i)   check the additions on the bank reconciliation

(ii)   check receipts and payments from the bank statement to the cash book for the month before the year end

(iii)   note uncleared items at the year end from the cash book (and the previous month's bank reconciliation) and agree them to the bank reconciliation

(iv)   check the clearance of the items after the year end

(v)   most cheque payments should have cleared within a week of the year end. If there are a significant number of cheques uncleared two weeks after the year end, it is an indication that the cheques were not posted to creditors until after the year end. So, these payments should be reversed in the cash book and added to creditors at the year end (ie, a payment is normally treated as a payment when the cheque is sent to the creditor)

(vi)   lodgements should be cleared within two banking days of the year end. If there is a longer delay, it indicates there may be a teeming and lading fraud. To check if there is a teeming and lading fraud, I will check that yesterday's cash receipts were banked either yesterday evening or today (by checking the entry in the cash book and the date stamped by the bank on the copy of the paying-in slip). If there is a delay, I should be able to count the unbanked cheques and cash - if they are 'missing', a teeming and lading fraud is taking place.

(vii)   agree the balance per the bank on the bank reconciliation to the bank letter and the bank statement

(viii)   agree the cash book balance on the bank reconciliation to the cash book and draft accounts.

If there is more than one bank account, the reconciliation of all the bank accounts should be checked. The number of bank accounts should agree to the number in the bank letter (or if the accounts are held at more than one bank or branch, I will check them to letters received from all the banks where accounts are held). I will check the validity of all accounts opened and closed in the year, by checking the last statement for accounts closed and the first for accounts opened.

25   (Answer 5 of examination)

(a)   Most businesses fail because of liquidity problems, and the failure usually occurs when the bank calls in the loan or overdraft, or the lenders appoint an administrator, receiver or liquidator. However, going concern problems can be divided into profitability, liquidity and other problems. Frequently, these problems are inter-related. However, I will consider them in separate sections. Profitability problems include:

(i)   the company making losses or low profits. With low profits, they are insufficient to fund the replacement of fixed assets and the increase in working capital due to inflation or expansion. Losses exacerbate these problems and usually create liquidity problems

(ii)   a fall in sales due to a recession, which either reduces profitability or creates a loss

(iii)   in a recession, most companies reduce the prices of their products (to try to maintain sales), and this results in a fall in the gross profit margin with a consequent effect on net profit

(iv)   loss of a major customer, which results in a significant fall in sales. Normally it takes some time to acquire new customers. If a customer fails and it results in a bad debt, this will create an additional loss in the profit and loss account

(v)   loss of a supplier, if the product is not available from another source

(vi)   technological change which occurs more rapidly than the company can adapt. For instance, IBM's trading loss in 1993 could be attributed to an increase in sales of microcomputers with small profit margins (and more competition) and a fall in sales of large computers with large profit margins. IBM could not adapt to the change in market conditions sufficiently quickly

(vii)   the company's products may become out of date compared with its competitors, so sales will decline

(viii)   the company may not have sufficient money to fund research and development to keep up with competitors. This could have happened to Jaguar cars if it had not been taken over by Ford. Research and development costs tend to be relatively fixed, so the cost of research and development per car for Jaguar is higher than for Mercedes or BMW who produce more cars. Without sufficient research and development of products, the company's products will become out of date and they will lose sales to competitors

(ix)   foreign competition. This particularly applies to low technology products which are labour intensive to produce, so that countries with low labour costs can produce the items at a much cheaper price than manufacturers in the UK. This applies to textile products, and the assembly of components for microcomputers

(x)   a fall in the value of the £ will adversely affect importers, as the cost of the products they import will increase. They will either have to increase prices charged to customers or reduce their margins, both of which will adversely affect profitability

(xi)   an increase in the value of the £ will make it more difficult for companies to export their products, as they will either have to increase the prices charged to customers (in local currency) or reduce their margins. In this situation the cost of imported goods will fall and this will increase competition in the home market

(xii)   redundancy costs required to reduce the number of employees to achieve break-even in the future

(xiii)   a low or negative interest cover. If the interest cover is less than one, the company is making insufficient profits to pay the interest on its loans. This will tend to increase gearing and thus exacerbate the company's liquidity problems.

Liquidity problems include:

(i)   the bank overdraft over the limit, or close to it. Often, companies experiencing going concern problems regularly exceed their overdraft limit

(ii)   a gearing ratio of over 1. Normally, banks get worried when gearing (loans and short-term borrowing divided by shareholders' funds) exceeds 1. Also, they are more worried when gearing is increasing (than if it is falling). A low current ratio or acid test ratio indicates liquidity and going concern problems

(iii)   a high level of stocks, which may indicate that some of the stock is difficult to sell and thus may be worth less than cost

(iv)   a high level of debtors, which increases the risk of bad debts

(v)   a high level of creditors. If the company is experiencing liquidity problems, it will pay creditors more slowly to avoid exceeding borrowing limits, so the age of creditors will increase

(vi)   overtrading. In this situation, the company increases sales rapidly, and the increase in working capital (and fixed assets) has to be funded from borrowing and creditors as the company will not have had time to make profits to overcome the liquidity problem

(vii)   purchasing fixed assets for expansion, but there is insufficient time for the increased sales and profit to fund the loans to purchase the fixed assets

(viii)   acquiring fixed assets by hire-purchase or leasing. Although this reduces apparent liquidity problems, the fact that the company has to use this method of financing is usually because direct purchase of fixed assets would result in borrowing limits being exceeded

(ix)   factoring debtors. Although this reduces borrowing, factoring is usually carried out by companies which are already experiencing liquidity problems

(x)   expanding the business by acquiring other businesses for cash. Some notable companies did this in the UK in the 1980s and the resulting high borrowing, high interest rates and the recession precipitated their collapse. Coloroll is an example of such a company which failed in the early 1990s.

Other factors indicating going concern problems include:

(i)   poor or ineffective management. This reason is often cited by receivers and liquidators

(ii)   a low level of stock. Although this will minimise liquidity problems, customers may require items immediately which are not in stock. In the long term the company will lose sales as the customers go elsewhere because they find the company does not have the items they require

(iii)   loss of key staff, such as the sales director or production director

(iv)   a lazy or disruptive workforce.

(b)   (i)   According to SAS 600 *Auditors' reports on financial statements*, the going concern problem is fundamental uncertainty (ie, it is uncertain whether the company will continue to trade to 30 April 1995, and, if the company failed, the consequences of the failure would have a fundamental effect on the financial statements). However, the answer to the question in SAS 600 (Appendix 1) of 'Do the financial statements, including note disclosures about fundamental uncertainties give a true and fair view?' is YES. This leads to an unqualified opinion with explanatory paragraph. With this form of unqualified audit report, the audit report is the same as for an unqualified report but with an additional paragraph which is headed 'Fundamental uncertainty' (ie, example 4 in SAS 600). This paragraph will disclose the going concern problems and refer to relevant notes in the financial statements. Normally, the paragraph will say that the continuation of the business will depend on the company becoming profitable and the bank and creditors continuing to support Mowbray Computers. This paragraph ends with the statement 'Our opinion is not qualified in this respect.' This is followed by the normal 'Opinion' paragraph of an unqualified audit report.

(ii)   If there is no disclosure of the going concern problem in the financial statements, then the answer to the first question, described above, is NO. This leads to the second question 'Is the effect of the disagreement so material or pervasive that the financial statements as a whole are misleading?' to which the answer is YES. Thus, an adverse opinion must be given (ie, similar to example 10 in SAS 600). With an adverse opinion, the paragraph headed 'Opinion' is changed to 'Adverse Opinion'. The first paragraph after the heading 'Adverse Opinion' will give details of the going concern problems, and the need for the company to become profitable and obtain support from the bank and creditors to allow it to continue to trade. The second paragraph explains that because of the failure to include details of the going concern problems, the financial statements do not show a true and fair view of the company's affairs as at 30 April 1994 and of its loss for the year then ended.

(c)   SAS 130 *The going concern basis in financial statements* does not specify a fixed period of time for which directors should form a view on whether a company is a going concern, but if they choose less than a year from the date of approval of the accounts, they should consider making additional disclosure by way of explanation. Auditors are required to consider the company's ability to continue as a going concern, and any relevant disclosures in the financial statements.

As Mowbray Computers has failed within a year of 30 April 1994, and the auditor has given an unqualified report, certain parties may be able to successfully sue him for negligence. The decision in the Caparo case is that only the company and the shareholders as a body can bring a claim for negligence against the auditor (and no others). It is probable that the court will refer to SAS 130, and this indicates that the audit report for the year ended 30 April 1994 should have mentioned these going concern problems. As the auditor did not mention them, the claim for negligence could be successful. In the situation in the question, the going concern problems were apparent during the audit of the accounts for the year ended 30 April 1994, and this reduces the strength of the auditor's defence. There are a variety of arguments the auditor could make in defence against a negligence claim, but these depend on the circumstances. If Mowbray Computer's failure was precipitated by a sudden event, or one that occurred after the audit report was signed (and was not expected to occur at the time the audit report was signed), then the auditor may have a good defence against the negligence claim. These events could include a large legal claim against Mowbray Computers, a substantial loss on a contract entered into after 30 April 1994 or unexpected guarantee claims. Thus, if the failure of Mowbray Computers could not have been foreseen at the date the audit report was signed, then the auditor should be able to avoid a claim for negligence.

26	(Answer 6 of examination)

(a)   (i)   There appears to be a serious weakness in the system of internal control as the treasurer appears to be responsible for banking receipts, making payments and recording them in the cash book. Because of the weak system of internal control and the small number of transactions, it is not appropriate to rely on internal controls, so I will perform a vouching audit, checking all transactions during the year. Where possible, evidence from other sources would be found for all receipts and payments.

For fees, parents should be issued with a receipt when they pay their fee, which gives the fee paid, the name of the parent and the number of children paid for. There should be a list of children attending the nursery, and the fees received can be checked to this list. This list of children should be confirmed by a person independent of the treasurer.

For fund raising events, a person other than the treasurer should count and record the takings before handing them to the treasurer, and it should be impossible for this person to misappropriate the takings (eg, two people could be responsible for counting the takings before handing them to the treasurer with a note of the cash handed over).

For payment of salaries, each employee should submit a time sheet to the treasurer which is authorised by the supervisor. From this the treasurer can calculate the salary, and each employee should sign a sheet when receiving the salary.

For other expenses there should be an invoice from the supplier of the goods or services. Other evidence is noted in part (ii) of the answer.

There should be two cheque signatories. All cash and cheques received should be banked promptly. If payments are made by petty cash, there should be an imprest system and a voucher for each item of expenditure.

  (ii)   In auditing the income and expenditure account, I would:

- check the additions in the cash book

- vouch all receipts and payments from the bank statement to the cash book

- vouch all payments from the cash book to the cheque stubs. If the paid cheques are available, I will check that the payee agrees with the details on the cheque stub, the amount is correct, the cheque is signed by an authorised signatory and it is not negotiated (crossing cheques A/C payee will prevent them from being negotiated)

- vouch all receipts from the cash book to the paying-in book

- vouch all receipts and payments to supporting documentation (see below).

In auditing income, I will perform the following checks:

- check that fees have been received for all children attending the nursery. Details of the fees received will be checked from the copy of the receipt given to the parent to the cash book. Also, they will be checked to the list of children attending the nursery. The minutes of meetings of the management committee and the chair of the management committee should confirm that the list of children is complete

- for fund raising events, I will note these events from the management committee minutes, and I will check there is a net receipt for each event. I will enquire if there is evidence independent of the treasurer confirming the proceeds from these events. If there is such evidence, I will check it to the sum banked by the treasurer. If there is no evidence, I will report this weakness to the management committee

- the bank deposit account interest will be checked to the bank statement.

For expenditure, I will perform the following checks:

- for salaries, I will check there is a form from each employee detailing the sum claimed, and this should be authorised by the supervisor. I will check the rate per hour to the management committee minutes and check the total sum due. Then I will check that each employee has signed for receipt of their wage

- all the other expenses, other than depreciation, would be checked to purchase invoices. If there is inadequate evidence, I will ask for confirmation of the expense from the chair of the management committee. If there is a substantial payment with no external evidence, I will report it to the management committee

- the depreciation will be checked as being 20% of the cost of fixed assets (in the draft accounts the figure is correct).

The depreciation charge may be less than 20% of the cost of the fixed assets if there are some fully written down fixed assets.

Finally, I will check additions on the income and expenditure account.

(b)   For the balance sheet, I will consider fixed assets at the end of this answer. For current assets, I will:

(i)   check the fees due in the balance sheet to supporting information, and that they are received after the year end (by checking to the cash book after the year end). I will discuss any fees still due at the time of my audit with the treasurer

(ii)   check the bank deposit account balance to the bank statement

(iii)   check the reconciliation of the current account balance to the bank statement. In particular, cheques issued immediately before the year end should be cleared within a week of the year end. Also, lodgements should be cleared by the bank within two working days of the year end. If there is any delay in clearing lodgements I will have to check if there is a teeming and lading fraud

(iv)   consider if there are any other debtors outstanding at the year end. I can do this by checking receipts after the year end, and determine whether they relate to pre-year end transactions. I will consider whether there are any current liabilities. This will be done by checking payments after the year end - I will check if any of these relate to pre-year end transactions. For instance, the charge from the university for light and heat is likely to be in arrears, and if March's expense is paid in April, there should be an appropriate accrual in the balance sheet. I will obtain confirmation from the management committee that there are no other liabilities and contingent liabilities.

The system for recording fixed assets is weak, as they should maintain a fixed asset register. However, it is probably impractical to prepare a fixed asset register for these accounts (see note at the end of the answer to this part). The work I will perform on fixed assets will include:

(i)   checking the opening balance of cost and depreciation to last year's accounts

(ii)   vouching additions to invoices

(iii)   checking the depreciation charge is 20% of cost (the accounts show this is calculated correctly - if there are any fully written down fixed assets, the depreciation charge should be less than 20% of cost)

(iv)   asking the management committee whether the life of the fixed assets is about five years, and considering whether the estimated life is reasonable

(v)   asking the management committee if there have been any disposals of fixed assets. If there have been disposals, I will check the proceeds have been received (the draft accounts do not show any disposal proceeds), and an appropriate deduction should be made from the schedule of movement on fixed assets (I will consider whether this is reasonable)

(vi)   I will inspect the fixed assets and consider whether their value (ie, depreciated cost) is likely to be about £6,870. I will have to report to the management committee if I feel their value is significantly less than £6,870.

Finally, I will recommend to the management committee that they set up a fixed asset register which gives details of each year's major purchases (small purchases could be written off in the year of acquisition). From the value of the depreciation provision in the balance sheet, it appears unlikely that there are any fully depreciated fixed assets.

Based on this work, I will decide whether the balance sheet is fairly stated. I would add that there does appear to be considerable uncertainty about the value of fixed assets.

DECEMBER 1994 QUESTIONS

Section A - ALL THREE questions in this section are compulsory and MUST be attempted

27   (Question 1 of examination)

You are the auditor of FENTON ELECTRONICS LIMITED, which has recently installed a computerised bar code system to record goods received, sales and stock quantities. The company is a retailer of electrical products.

In this computerised system:

(a)   when the goods are received, the goods received department:

    (i)   either read the bar code on the box containing the product, or input the bar code number manually; and

    (ii)   manually input the number of items received (eg, a box may contain 100 video tapes).

The quantity of items received is added to the quantity of stock recorded on the computer.

(b)   when goods are sold to the customer, the bar code of the product is either read or input manually, and the computer produces the sales invoice using the selling price of the product, as recorded on the computer's standing data file. The quantity of items sold is deducted from the stock quantity recorded on the computer.

(c)   periodically, the stock is counted and these counts are compared with those on the computer. The stock quantities on the computer are amended when significant differences are found.

(d)   the system allows:

    (i)   details of new products and the selling prices of products to be added or amended;

    (ii)   stock quantities to be amended from differences found at the stock count;

    (iii)   special prices to be charged to customers (eg, where the product is damaged or discontinued).

The main products the company sells comprise:

(a)   slower moving products, such as televisions, video recorders, video cameras and audio equipment;
(b)   fast moving, low value products, such as batteries, video and audio tapes.

You are required to:

(a)   describe the edit checks which should be incorporated into the computer system to ensure that details of goods received are correctly entered into the computer;   **(4 marks)**

(b)   (i)   suggest how frequently stocktakes should be carried out, and

    (ii)   describe the procedures the company should carry out to ensure the stock quantities in the computer system are accurate;   **(6 marks)**

(c)   describe the controls which should be used to ensure that the prices of the products on the computer file and on the products in the store are correct;   **(5 marks)**

(d)   describe the controls which should be implemented to minimise the risk of break-down of the system, and to enable the system to be re-started with the minimum delay.   **(5 marks)**

(Total: 20 marks)

28   (Question 2 of examination)

Your firm is the auditor of Ravenshead Engineering Ltd, and you have been asked to suggest the audit work you will carry out in verifying trade creditors and purchase accruals at the company's year end of 30 September 1994. You attended the stocktake at the year end.

The company operates from a single site and all raw materials for production are received by the goods inwards department. When the materials are received they are checked for quantity and quality to the delivery note and purchase order, and a multi-part goods received note is made out and signed by the storekeeper. If there are any problems with the raw materials, a discrepancy note is raised which gives details of the problems (eg, incorrect quantities or faulty materials).

The purchase accounting department receive the purchase invoices, check them to the purchase order and goods received note and post them to the purchase ledger. At the end of each month, payments are made to suppliers. The purchase ledger is maintained on a microcomputer.

The main sundry creditors and accruals at the year end include:

(a)   wages accruals, PAYE and National Insurance;

(b)   VAT;

(c)   time dependent accruals, such as interest on loans and overdrafts, telephone, heat and light, and other expenses paid in arrears.

Most employees' wages are paid weekly in arrears.

You are required to describe in detail the audit work you will carry out to:

(a)   check suppliers' statements to the balances on the purchase ledger;   **(8 marks)**

(b)   verify that purchases cut-off has been correctly carried out at the year end;   **(5 marks)**

(c)   ensure that sundry creditors and accruals are correctly stated.   **(7 marks)**
                                                                                    (Total: 20 marks)

29   (Question 3 of examination)

You have been asked by the senior in charge of the audit of Bingham Manufacturing Ltd to describe certain aspects of the work you will carry out in auditing the company's wages system. Employees of Bingham Manufacturing are paid on the basis of hours worked and quantities produced. The hours worked are recorded on clock cards and the quantities produced are confirmed by the foreman. Wages are paid in cash each Friday for the previous week's work. Appointment of employees is authorised by the managing director, and the personnel department maintains employees' records and their rates of pay. The cashier is separate from the wages department.

Previous years' audits have highlighted weaknesses in internal controls in the company's wages system. This has allowed an employee in the wages department to perpetrate a fraud by creating fictitious employees on the payroll and misappropriating the wages. Thus, some of your audit tests have been designed to detect whether this fraud is still taking place.

A 'starters and leavers' test is carried out to ensure that employees are not paid before they commence employment or after they have left.

You are required to:

(a)   state the principal controls you would expect to exist in a wages system and explain their purpose;
                                                                                    (5 marks)

(b)   assuming you decide not to attend the wages pay-out, suggest other techniques you can use to check the existence of employees;

(5 marks)

(c)   describe how you will carry out a starters and leavers test;

(4 marks)

(d)   describe the analytical review techniques you can use in auditing the wages system. This should include suggesting any ratios you would calculate.

(6 marks)
(Total: 20 marks)

Section B - TWO questions ONLY to be attempted

30   (Question 4 of examination)

Auditing Standard 600 on *Auditor's reports on financial statements*, issued in May 1993, introduced the extended audit report and changes in the form of qualified reports.

Your firm is the auditor of the following two companies, and you have been asked to consider the form of qualified or unqualified audit report which should be given.

(a)   Gamston Burgers plc has a loss-making branch and it has included fixed assets relating to this branch at £710,000 after deducting a provision for permanent diminution in value of £250,000. The directors believe that if operating changes are made and economic conditions improve, there is a reasonable probability of the branch trading satisfactorily, which will result in the current value of tangible fixed assets exceeding £710,000. However, under the current circumstances, the directors consider the extent of any permanent diminution in value to be uncertain. You have obtained all the evidence you would have reasonably expected to be available.

If trading conditions do not improve, your audit investigations have concluded that the branch will have to close. If the branch closes, the tangible fixed assets will be worthless, as the property is leased and the cost of moving any tangible fixed assets will be more than their net realisable value. If the tangible fixed assets are worthless, you have concluded that the effect will be material, but it will not result in the financial statements being misleading.

(b)   Keyworth Supermarket Limited sells food to the general public and customers pay in cash or by cheque. Your audit tests reveal that controls over cash takings and custody of the stock are weak, and you have not been able to obtain sufficient evidence to quantify the effect of any misappropriation of stock or cash takings. You have concluded that:

(i)   if the uncertainty relates to all the company's sales, it could result in the financial statements being misleading, and

(ii)   if the uncertainty relates to only the sale of fresh fruit and vegetables, which comprise 10% of the company's sales, it will have a material effect on the financial statements but it will not result in them being misleading.

You are required to:

(a)   list and briefly describe the contents of an unqualified audit report;

(8 marks)

(b)   consider and describe the form of an unqualified or qualified audit report you would give in each of the following situations:

(i)   on Gamston Burgers plc's financial statements if you agree with the directors' statements about the uncertainty relating to the value of the tangible fixed assets of the branch;

(ii)   on Gamston Burgers plc's financial statements if you have come to the conclusion that trading conditions will not improve and the company will close the branch. Thus, the tangible fixed assets will be worthless;

(iii)   on Keyworth Supermarket Ltd's financial statements if the uncertainty about the misappropriation of stock and cash takings relates to *all* the company's sales;

(iv)   on Keyworth Supermarket Ltd's financial statements if the uncertainty about the misappropriation of stock and cash takings relates only to the sale of fresh fruit and vegetables which comprise 10% of the company's sales.

(12 marks)
(Total: 20 marks)

Note: in part (b) the marks are divided equally between each of the parts (i) to (iv).

---

31   (Question 5 of examination)

You are the auditor of Hatton Wholesale Ltd and you are auditing the financial statements for the year ended 31 October 1994. You have carried out an analytical review on the profit and loss account and are concerned that there has been a significant fall in the gross profit margin, as shown by the following statement (1994 figures are from the draft accounts and 1993 figures are from the audited accounts).

Year ended 31 October	1994 £'000	1993 £'000
Sales	2,514	3,126
Opening stock	441	426
Purchases	2,067	2,214
	2,508	2,640
Closing stock	412	441
Cost of goods sold	2,096	2,199
Gross profit	418	927
Gross profit %	16.6%	29.7%

You have been asked to determine whether the fall in profit is correct or due to errors in the preparation of the financial statements.

The company does not maintain book stock records, and stock quantities were found from a physical stocktake at 31 October 1994. For sales to customers:

(a)   the sales department receive orders from customers and raise a multi-copy dispatch note when the goods are available;

(b)   the credit controller authorises the dispatch note

(c)   the dispatch department send the goods to the customer and a copy of the dispatch note is sent to the sales accounting department

(d)   the sales accounting department prepare the sales invoice from the dispatch note.

The company only prepares annual accounts. Assume that the accounts for the year ended 31 October 1993 are correct.

You are required to:

(a)   suggest possible reasons for the fall in the gross profit margin;

(6 marks)

(b)   describe the work you will carry out to:

    (i)   compare the gross profit on actual sales during the year with the gross profit in the financial statements;

(3 marks)

    (ii)   highlight any uninvoiced sales or sales at incorrect prices;

(4 marks)

    (iii)   highlight any understatement of the value of closing stock.

(7 marks)
(Total: 20 marks)

32   (Question 6 of examination)

SASs 200 to 240 deals with the topics of planning, controlling and recording. You are the manager responsible for the audit of Radford Retail plc which has a number of stores which sell household products to the general public, including furniture, electrical equipment, cooking equipment and carpets.

The company has an annual turnover of about £20 million. In previous years' audits there have been problems with:

(a)   misappropriation of stock by employees and customers

(b)   slow moving and damaged stock which is worth less than cost, and

(c)   incomplete recording of sales when the customer pays in cash (these represent 55% of all sales).

The company has a small internal audit department, the staff of which visit branches and perform appropriate audit work at the head office.

You are required to:

(a)   describe the work you will carry out and the matters you will consider in planning the audit prior to the commencement of the detailed audit work, including consideration of the timetable for the audit;

(12 marks)

(b)   describe the procedures you will carry out to control the audit including reviewing the work of audit staff.

(8 marks)
(Total: 20 marks)

EXAMINER'S COMMENTS

General comments

Some candidates performed well in the exam, but many produced poor answers which displayed a very weak knowledge of the subject.

One weakness of many candidates' answers was that they did not answer parts of questions directly. Others modified the question so that they can produce an answer to a related topic they feel they understand. In either case, this is not answering the question set and the likely result is that the answer will not be awarded a pass. Answering the question which is asked is the best approach to maximising marks.

On answering the question directly, in question 1(b)(ii) the key to the answer was to count the stock, check the quantities with those on the computer and investigate differences. In question 2(a) suppliers' statements should be checked to balances on the purchase ledger and differences investigated. For these questions, many students took an approach of checking controls, when a substantive approach was required.

In questions 3(b) and (d), 5 and 6: the best approach was to suggest a wide variety of points rather than concentrate on a few topics.

As stated after the June 1994 exam, to maximise their chance of passing this exam candidates need to:

(a)   answer five questions on the paper;
(b)   answer all parts of each question;
(c)   answer parts of the question in the correct order;
(d)   provide an answer of adequate length, aiming for at least two pages for each question.

Question 1: Examined candidates on a computer system which recorded purchases and sales in a retail store.

In part (a) most candidates listed standard edit checks, rather than those which would be appropriate to reading or inputting product bar codes and quantities.

In part (b)(i) a few candidates suggested stocktakes should be carried out annually, which is probably too infrequent.

In part (b)(ii) more candidates should have answered this part directly, by carrying out a stocktake and investigating differences between the physical count and the quantity on the computer. Many candidates suggested checking systems for recording of purchases and sales, which would be time consuming and would not necessarily detect loss of stock through damage or stealing by customers or staff.

In part (c) most candidates concentrated on checking controls in changing prices on the computer and in the store. Surprisingly few candidates suggested the important point of checking prices of products on the shelves to those on the computer file.

Part (d), on minimising the risk of break-down of the system, was answered satisfactorily, although answers did not contain the number or variety of points expected.

Question 2: Examined candidates on the final audit work of checking suppliers' statements, cut-off, sundry creditors and accruals.

The answers to part (a) were disappointing, as many candidates did not consider checking balances on suppliers' statements to those on the purchase ledger, which the question required. Those who answered the question as required obtained good marks. A number of candidates suggested carrying out a creditors' circularisation, which was not answering the question.

The answers to part (b) on purchases cut-off were better, although some answers could have been clearer. An answer should not only consider receipt of goods but also posting of the purchase invoice to the purchase ledger (or including it as a purchase accrual if the goods are received before the year end).

The answers to part (c) on sundry creditors and accruals were satisfactory. The main weakness of many answers was they failed to consider time apportionment of many accruals, such as electricity, gas, telephone, interest and wages.

Question 3: Examined candidates on controls and tests in a wages system.

Generally, the answers to part (a) on principal controls in a wages system were quite good.

In part (b) the weakness of most candidates' answers was that they failed to consider a sufficient variety of ways of checking the existence of employees. Some candidates said they would attend the wages pay-out, when the question stated that a decision had been made not to attend.

Some of the answers to part (c) on performing a starters and leavers test were weak. The key to the answer was to check to the payroll that employees are not paid before they start or after they have left.

The answers on analytical review techniques in part (c) were disappointing, with some candidates suggesting very few points.

Question 4: Required an explanation of the contents of an unqualified audit report according to SAS 600, and forms of qualified or unqualified reports which would be given in a number of situations.

Many of the answers to part (a) on the contents of an unqualified audit report were good, but some candidates described the former 'short form' audit report.

Many of the answers to part (b) on which form of qualified or unqualified audit report should be used, were weak. The question said 'consider and describe', so just stating the form of qualification did not constitute a satisfactory answer.

In part (i) the correct answer was an unqualified audit report with an explanatory paragraph, but it was apparent that many candidates were not aware of this form of report, or when it should be used.

The answers to part (ii) were better, many students suggesting an 'except for' qualification. However, some candidates incorrectly said that in using 'except for', the audit report would be unqualified.

Many of the answers to part (iii) described the correct form of qualification, although a number suggested an 'except for' qualification.

In part (iv) many candidates suggested the audit report would be unqualified but answers were weak at justifying this view. A significant weakness in some candidates' answers was that they described the form of qualification, but did not justify their opinion. A few candidates said the audit report would be either qualified or unqualified but failed to describe the form of qualification.

Question 5: Required candidates to investigate a fall in a company's gross profit margin.

In part (a) the best approach was to suggest a variety of points. Some points suggested by candidates would not have affected the gross profit margin (ie, a fall in sales or bad debts).

In part (b) the suggested approach was to find the selling price of certain products from sales invoices and the purchase price from purchase invoices and compare the gross profit from these sources to the gross profit in the accounts.

The answers to part (ii) were satisfactory. To check for uninvoiced sales it should be checked that there is a sales invoice for each dispatch note, and prices on invoices can be checked to price lists.

The answers to part (iii) were less good. Once again, the best approach was to suggest a variety of points, rather than concentrate on a few possibilities.

Question 6: Examined candidates on planning (part (a)) and controlling (part (b)) an audit.

The best approach was to suggest a large number of points, rather than concentrate on a few items. Many of the candidates' answers were quite good.

In part (a) weaker candidates answered the question in terms of carrying out an audit, which was not answering the question.

The answers to part (b) were less good, with some candidates failing to suggest an acceptable number of relevant points.

ANSWERS TO DECEMBER 1994 EXAMINATION

27   (Answer 1 of examination)

(a)   The following edit checks should be performed when details of goods received are entered into the computer:

(i)   The bar code number should be entered correctly when the employee reads the code using a scanner. However, the bar code should incorporate a check digit (ie, to detect incorrect reading of the bar code) and the computer should check the product's number with the standing data file. It should give a warning if there is no product with this number on the standing data file.

(ii)   When the bar code number is input manually, there is a greater risk of it being entered incorrectly. First, the computer should check that no alphabetic characters have been entered. Then, as noted in part (i) above, the computer should check that the check digit is consistent with other numbers entered for the product, and it should check the bar code number is on the standing data file. Ideally, when the product number is entered into the computer, the product's description should be displayed on the screen of the terminal and the employee should confirm it is consistent with the product received.

(iii)   The computer should check that the quantity of goods received is reasonable. For instance, the company could receive 100 video tapes but it is unlikely to receive 100 televisions of the same type. It is unlikely that it will receive a single video or audio tape.

(b) (i)   Most of the fast moving stock should be counted each week. However, it may be counted less frequently if management believes the risk of losing the stock is less than the cost of counting it.

It is probably acceptable to count slower moving stock at monthly intervals. If significant stock differences are found (ie, between the physical count and the stock quantities recorded by the computer), more frequent counts should be performed. There should be strong controls over stock which has a high risk of being stolen (eg, video cameras and recorders). There may be more frequent stocktakes of these high value items.

(ii)   The company should count the stock periodically (at the intervals suggested in part (b)(i) above) and compare the totals of the counts with those recorded by the computer. Ideally, the counts should be performed when the store is closed as there will be no receipts or sales of products. However, it is more likely that the counts will be performed when the store is open (as this avoids paying the employees overtime), but the company should be careful to ensure there are no sales or purchases cut-off errors. Purchases cut-off errors could occur when the stock is counted:

-       between counting the stock and checking the quantity on the computer, some more products are received and entered into the computer, or

-       there are delays in inputting goods received into the computer, and the stock is counted, but the items of goods received have not been entered into the computer at the time the physically counted quantities are checked to those on the computer.

Similarly, a sales cut-off error could occur when the stock is counted, and a sale takes place after counting the stock but before the employee checks the quantity on the computer. Any significant differences found during the stock counts should be investigated. Normally, the physical stock quantity will be the same as or less than the figure shown by the computer (because of stock loss).

Where there is an apparently large stock difference, the stock should be counted again (including checking whether some of the stock is stored in a different part of the store). Where significant stock losses are detected, the company should instigate procedures to reduce the risk of this loss, such as securing the stock (eg, using a wire which sounds an alarm when it is broken), using video cameras (to find who is stealing this stock) and asking the store detective to check these items more frequently.

The computer should give a warning when stock quantities are negative (this may arise from the incorrect bar code number being entered when the goods are received, or when they are sold). Negative stock quantities should be investigated.

Very slow moving stock should be investigated to check if it still exists (eg, the actual stock quantity may be zero, but the computer may record a small stock balance, which does not exist).

After investigating any stock differences, where a significant difference is confirmed, a change of stock quantities on the computer should be authorised by the managing director, and the stock quantities on the computer should be amended to the quantity counted at the stocktake (adjusted for any goods received and sold between the stock count and the time the computer's quantities are adjusted).

As stated above, greater security should be exercised where large differences are found between the physical and computer stock quantities.

(c)   There should be a laid down procedure for authorising changes to the prices of products. A list of price changes should be prepared on a standard form, and the managing director should authorise:

(i)   addition of new products and prices
(ii)   changes in prices of existing products
(iii)   deletion of products.

The prices of the products on the shelves should be changed at the same time as the prices are changed on the computer's standing data file. Frequently, with these systems, the computer prints out labels for the shelves at the same time as the product prices are changed on the computer. Ideally, prices should be changed when the store is closed.

Periodically, an employee should record the prices of the products in the shop and compare them with the prices on the computer. This can be performed using a portable computer, which can read the bar code of the product and the employee can enter the price manually. Then, the data can be downloaded into the main computer and checked against the prices on the main computer. The main computer can list any cases where the prices are different.

There should be controls to prevent unauthorised changes to prices on the price file (eg, by the use of passwords).

The prices on the computer file should be printed out periodically and checked with manual records. If the cost of products is entered into the computer, it can list products where the gross profit is unusually high or low, and these can be investigated. Also, when recording prices of products in the store, staff can be asked to note any unexpectedly high or low prices.

The system should only allow deletion of products if the stock quantity on the computer's file is zero.

(d)   In order to minimise the risk of break-down of the system through hardware or software faults, there should be the following controls:

(i)   The hardware should come from a reputable supplier, it should be shown to be reliable, and it should be tested before it is used as part of the complete system (if it is a new system, the total system should be tested before it is used for recording the daily transactions). Where necessary, the components of the system should be serviced regularly, there should be a record of all faults and components should be replaced when they become faulty (eg, disk drives). All cables between the main computer and the terminals (including the cash check-outs) should be screened to prevent them picking up stray signals, and all power supplies should be filtered and controlled to prevent mains spikes and fluctuations in mains voltage.

(ii)   The software should be shown to be reliable before it is used (ie, another user should have confirmed it is reliable), and it should have been used by another company on the hardware purchased by Fenton Electronics. Any changes in the software should be tested before they are used by Fenton Electronics (eg, by test checking the system at a week-end when the shop is closed).

(iii)   Frequently, with this type of system, there is more than one computer, so the second computer takes over when the main computer fails.

(iv)   The company should use a non-interruptible power supply, which maintains power to the system when there is a power failure. This system may either allow the computer to operate for a short time (to allow it to be shut down without corrupting the data files) or it may have a separate power supply which will power the system for long periods.

(v)   The computer should record the tasks it is performing (ie, which terminal's data it is processing) to help to find the reason for any fault.

(vi)   Regular back-ups should be kept of all data. This should be performed at least daily, and these tapes should be kept at a separate location so they are not destroyed by a fire in the shop. In addition to keeping these regular back-ups, the system can record all transactions as they occur, which will allow the data to be updated to the time of the failure (ie, by using last night's back-up tapes and today's record of transactions).

(vii)   There should be laid down procedures which should operate following failure of the system. Periodically, these procedures should be tested so that staff are aware of their duties, and any faults in the procedure can be corrected (ie, like a fire drill).

(viii)   Periodically the system and data files should be checked for viruses. All exchangeable disks should be checked for viruses before any data is copied from or to them.

---

28   (Answer 2 of examination)

(a)   The work I will perform in checking suppliers' statements to the balances on the purchase ledger will include:

(i)   I will assess the system of control in the purchases system and its reliability. This will be based on the results of my tests of control, other investigations and my experience in previous years. Where the purchases system is reliable, I will check fewer items than if it is unreliable. If I find discrepancies in my audit tests, I will increase the sample of items I check. I will check fewer suppliers' statements to the purchase ledger balances if a member of the company's staff regularly performs these checks and corrects discrepancies.

(ii)   Generally, I will check a larger proportion of suppliers where the balances are large, or where there are a large number of transactions. Where there is no supplier's statement for one of these important accounts, I will either contact the supplier to confirm the balance, or ask for a statement at the year end (this could be sent by fax).

(iii)   Where the balance on the supplier's statement is the same as the purchase ledger balance, I will record the agreement in my audit working papers and carry out no further work on that balance.

(iv)   Where there is a difference, I will divide it into:

-    goods in transit
-    cash in transit
-    other differences.

(v)   Goods in transit are invoices on the supplier's statement which are not on the client's purchase ledger. If these differences have been included in purchase accruals, I may perform no further checks. However, for large value items, I will check the goods received note (GRN) to ensure they were received before the year end. If there is no purchase accrual, I will check the date on the GRN. If the date on the GRN is after the year end, the treatment is correct. However, if it is before the year end there is a cut-off error, and the value of these goods will have to be included in my schedule of unadjusted errors.

(vi)   For cash in transit, I could check to the next month's supplier's statement that the cheque was on the supplier's sales ledger just after the year end. An alternative is to check to the bank statement the date the cheque is cleared by the bank after the year end. If there is a significant delay in clearing the cheque (and this is common to a number of cheques issued immediately before the year end), this indicates that the cheques were sent to suppliers after the year end. If this has been happening, the value of these cheques should be deducted from the year end bank overdraft in the draft financial statements and added to creditors at the year end (as the payment did not occur until after the year end).

(vii)   For other differences, if they are small, they can be ignored. However, if they are significant I will discuss them with the client and I may ask if I can contact the supplier to confirm the reason for the difference. The year end accounts should include an appropriate provision to allow for such differences (generally, this should be the difference between the balance on the supplier's statement and that on the client's purchase ledger).

(viii)   Based on these tests, I will assess whether they provide sufficient evidence that trade creditors and purchase accruals are correctly stated at the year end. If, because of errors I have found, I believe I have not obtained sufficient reliable evidence, I will increase the number of purchase ledger balances I check against suppliers' statements.

(b)   The best place to start a purchases cut-off test is from goods received notes issued immediately before and after the year end. Generally, the test should cover a sample of items during the period two weeks before to two weeks after the year end, concentrating on larger value items. More items are likely to be selected from before the year end than after the year end, as there is a greater risk of cut-off errors with these transactions.

At the stocktake, I should have recorded the last goods received note number issued before the year end (eg, number 1462). Goods received before the year end should have a goods received note number of 1462 or less and goods received after the year end should have a goods received note number of 1463 or more.

I will select a sample of goods received notes issued before the year end, and follow through to the purchase invoice. For these goods I will check that:

(i)   either the purchase invoice has been posted to the purchase ledger before the year end or a purchase accrual (equal to the invoice value) has been included in the accounts at the year end;

(ii)   if there are book stock records, I will check that the goods have been included in the book stock records before the year end.

There will be a purchases cut-off error where either:

(i)   the purchase invoice has not been posted to the purchase ledger before the year end and there is no purchase accrual; or

(ii)   the purchase invoice has been posted to the purchase ledger before the year end and there is a purchase accrual at the year end.

For goods received after the year end, I will select a sample of goods received notes issued after the year end, and follow through to the purchase invoice. For these goods I will check that:

(i)   neither the purchase invoice has been posted to the purchase ledger before the year end nor a purchase accrual been included in the accounts at the year end;

(ii)   if there are book stock records, I will check that the items of goods received have not been included in the book stock records before the year end (they should have been included in the book stock records after the year end).

There will be a purchases cut-off error where either:

(i)   the purchase invoice has been posted to the purchase ledger before the year end, or

(ii)   there is a purchase accrual at the year end (and the purchase invoice has been posted to the purchase ledger after the year end).

(c)   I will perform the following work in checking sundry creditors and accruals:

(i)   I will assess the level of accruals, and the systems of control. I will perform less work on small accruals than material ones. If the company's system of determining accruals is good, I will perform less work than if controls are weak.

(ii)   I will compare this year's accruals with last year. I will investigate cases where there was an accrual last year, but none this year, and vice versa. Also, I will investigate any large changes in accruals.

(iii)   The wages accrual will be checked to the payroll. As 30 September 1994 is a Friday (say), the wages accrual will be the whole week's gross wages.

(iv)   The PAYE and NI accrual will be checked back to the payroll. If the payroll produces a month's summary, it should be the figure on the summary. If only each week's PAYE and NI is printed by the payroll, I will check the accrual equals the sum of September's deductions. It should be noted that the NI accrual will include both the employee's and the employer's charge. I will check to the cash book that the accrual is equal to the payment to the Inland Revenue after the year end (ie, in October).

(v)   The VAT creditor will be checked as being the VAT on sales and purchases (from the sales and purchases day books) for the months since the end of the last VAT quarter and VAT on sundry cash receipts and payments. If the year end is the end of a VAT quarter, I will check the VAT creditor at the year end is equal to the payment to Customs & Excise after the year end.

(vi)   Accrued interest on the bank loan and overdraft will be checked to the letter I have received from the bank, and it may be confirmed by the sum charged by the bank after the year end. For other loans, the accrued interest will be checked as being the product of the amount outstanding, the current interest rate and the time since the last charge.

(vii)   Other accruals will be checked to invoices received after the year end (or if no invoices have been received after the year end, then invoices received before the year end will be used). Unless there is any special reason, the charge should be apportioned on a time basis. For instance, if the electricity bill received after the year end is £2,400 for three months and there were two months electricity accrued, the accrual should be £2,400 × 2/3 = £1,600. Similar checks will be made on other significant accrued expenses (eg, gas, telephone, motor expenses, leasing charges etc).

(viii)   I will consider whether there are any circumstances which have arisen in the year which may result in new accruals, and I will check if these accruals have been included (or that the accrual is zero).

29   (Answer 3 of examination)

(a)   The principal controls in a wages system and their purpose would include:

(i)   there should be a proper division of duties in the wages system. For instance, employees who calculate wages should not be responsible for making up the wage packets, for dealing with disputes over wages or for keeping unclaimed wages. Where there is a weakness in the division of duties, there should be an effective system of internal check, whereby one person test checks the work of another;

(ii)   there is proper control over custody of cash for wages and unclaimed wages;

(iii)   wages are only paid to employees for work done;

(iv)   employees are paid at the authorised rate;

(v)   there is appropriate authorisation of such matters as appointment of new employees, dismissal of employees, changes in rates of pay, promotions and overtime;

(vi)   deductions are correctly calculated (or for voluntary deductions, are authorised by the employee) and paid promptly to the relevant authorities;

(vii)   payments are made to the correct employees;

(viii)   the transactions are correctly recorded in the books of account, including the allocation of the wages expense between sales, manufacturing, administration etc.

The purposes of these controls are implied in the points above. However, their aim is to ensure that employees are paid at authorised rates for work done (or hours worked), that the transactions are recorded accurately in the accounting records, that the employees and other authorities (eg, Inland Revenue) are paid the correct sums and that the risk of fraud and error is minimised.

(b)   In checking the existence of employees, I will start from the payroll, as an auditor should only be concerned with checking employees who are paid. The following techniques can be used for checking the existence of these employees:

(i)   the signature of the employee signing for his or her wage can be checked to the record in the personnel department. The signature of the employee in the personnel records should have been obtained when the individual started employment in the company (if this was a long time ago, the personnel department should get an updated signature). The personnel department should be sufficiently independent of the wages department to ensure that their records of individuals employed by the company are accurate. When performing this check, I will ensure the individual was employed by the company at the date of the payroll (ie, it was not before the individual started being employed or after he/she had left);

(ii)   the employee can be checked to the annual return made to the Inland Revenue (for PAYE and National Insurance purposes), and there may be notifications from the Inland Revenue of changes in the employee's tax code. If the employee has just joined the company (and had previously been employed by another organisation), there should be a notification from the former employer of the individual's tax code, gross pay and tax paid to date;

(iii)   the employee should have a National Insurance number, which should be of a valid form;

(iv)   the department manager could acknowledge a list of individuals employed in his/her department (but this could be weak audit evidence);

(v)   there may be other evidence of the existence of employees, such as piecework returns, and correspondence kept in the personnel department.

(c)   The purpose of a starters and leavers test is to ensure that employees are neither paid before they start nor after they have left the company's employment. The test can be performed for the whole of the company's year, but it is more common to perform the check for part of a year (eg, six months).

To carry out this procedure, I will select two payrolls, say six months apart, and compare the names on the payroll. Where the name appears on both payrolls, the employee has been paid for the full six month period. Where the name appears on the first payroll and not the second, this is a 'leaver', and where the name appears on the second payroll and not on the first, this is a 'starter'. I will list the names of the starters and leavers and go to the personnel department to find the dates the employees either started or left the company. Then, for starters I will check that they were not paid for the week before they started, and for leavers I will check that they were not paid for the week after they had left. As many weekly paid employees are paid a week in arrears, due allowance will have to be made when performing the check. If they are paid in arrears:

(i)   starters will not be paid the first week of their employment, and their first wage will be at the end of their second working week;

(ii)   leavers will be paid the week after they leave, but not the week after that.

Based on these tests, I will determine whether starters and leavers have been paid correctly (ie, a fraud could be carried out by paying starters before they start or leavers after they have left - the wage would be misappropriated by an employee in the wages department).

(d)   The analytical review techniques I can use in auditing the wages system will include:

(i)   the gross and net wages, the PAYE and National Insurance will be compared for each month and with the previous year (net wages will be the weekly payment in the cash book). Any unusual changes can be investigated. For employees paid weekly, there may be a large charge in the week before they go on holiday, as they will be paid for the current week and two holiday weeks;

(ii)   the average wage per employee will be calculated and any significant changes will be investigated. The ratio of income tax and National Insurance to gross wages will be checked (this should not fluctuate very much);

(iii)   the ratio of wages to sales will be calculated and compared with previous years. Any significant changes would be investigated;

(iv)   a sample of payrolls will be scrutinised and any large wages will be investigated. These wages should be agreed to information held in the personnel department;

(v)   where the system of internal control is weak (eg, where staff are involved in recording or paying their own wages), the wages of these employees will be checked. This will probably include staff in the wages department, the cashier and the managing director. This will include checking the total pay for the year for these employees;

(vi)   the returns to the Inland Revenue will be test checked to the payroll. This will include monthly PAYE and National Insurance payments, and test checks of annual returns for individual employees;

(vii)   the computations on the payroll will be test checked, including the calculation of the deductions and the sum of each employee's pay to the total. I will check that the total gross pay is equal to the total net pay plus the deductions. These checks may be very limited where the wages system is computerised and the wages programs have been shown to be reliable;

(viii)   the analysis of the wages expense (eg, sales, production, administration wages) will be test checked from the payroll to the nominal ledger and the total for the year will be compared with previous years. Any significant changes will be investigated;

(ix)   for staff paid a fixed weekly or monthly wage, the total gross wages will be checked as being the product of the number of employees paid in the year (from the personnel records) and the average annual salary (from the authorised salary rates). This check will be more difficult where employees work overtime or are paid on a piecework basis, but similar checks could be made for these employees (overtime and piecework should be related to sales);

(x)   if the payroll system is computerised, the checks are likely to be less detailed than if it is a manual system, as it is probably more difficult to fraudulently manipulate a computerised system.

30   (Answer 4 of examination)

(a)   The extended unqualified audit report includes the following matters:

(i)   it is headed 'Auditors' report to the shareholders of ABC plc', as auditors report to the shareholders (or members) of the company;

(ii)   the first paragraph states that the auditors have audited the financial statements and it gives the pages which the audit report covers (these include the financial statements, and the notes to the financial statements, but they exclude such matters as the review of operations, the chairman's statement, the directors' report and five or 10 year summaries). It then states the accounting convention used in the financial statements (usually the historical cost convention, which may be modified by revaluation of certain fixed assets) and it mentions the accounting policies and the page where they can be found;

(iii)   the second main part states the directors' and auditors' responsibilities. Usually, the directors' responsibilities are included in a separate note, outside the audit report, so the auditors' report only says that the directors are responsible for preparing the financial statements and it refers to the note in the accounts giving details of the directors' responsibilities.

It says the auditors are responsible for forming an independent opinion, based on their audit, and to give an opinion to the shareholders;

(iv)   the third main part describes the audit procedures in general terms. It includes the following matters:

- the audit is conducted in accordance with Auditing Standards

- matters are examined on a test basis (rather than every transaction being examined)

- estimates and matters of judgement are assessed

- the auditors consider whether the accounting policies are appropriate, consistently applied and adequately disclosed

- sufficient evidence is obtained to give the auditor reasonable assurance (ie, not total assurance) that there are no material mis-statements

- mis-statements include fraud, other irregularity and error

- the auditor considers whether the presentation of the financial information is adequate.

(v)   the final main paragraph is the opinion, where the auditor says that in his opinion the financial statements show a true and fair view of the state of affairs of the company (ie, the balance sheet) at the year end and the profit or loss for the year, and have been properly prepared in accordance with the Companies Act 1985. The 'old' audit report used to mention cash flow statements, but this requirement is not included in the Auditing Standard;

(vi)   at the end of the report, the auditor gives the firm's name and address, the fact that he (or she) is a registered auditor, and the date. In addition, they normally say whether they are a Certified or Chartered Accountant. The date of the audit report is usually the same as the date the directors sign the financial statements and their report. The auditors should not sign the audit report before the directors have approved and signed the financial statements.

(b)   (i)   Considering the diagram in Appendix 1 of SAS 600, in both this situation (and part (ii)) I have received all the evidence I would have reasonably expected to be available. However, the financial statements are affected by a fundamental uncertainty (ie, the value of the tangible fixed assets).

In this situation, I believe disclosure of the uncertainty relating to the tangible fixed assets is appropriate, so the financial statements do give a true and fair view. So, in these circumstances I can give an unqualified opinion with an explanatory paragraph (similar to example 4 of SAS 600). The explanatory paragraph will be headed 'Fundamental Uncertainty' and it will appear immediately before the 'Opinion'. The explanatory paragraph will explain the uncertainty of the value of the tangible fixed assets of the branch and refer to explanations given in the notes to the financial statements. It will end with the statement 'Our opinion is not qualified in this respect'. The opinion paragraph will be the same as that in an unqualified report.

(ii)   As stated above, I have received all the evidence I would have reasonably expected to be available, and the financial statements are affected by a fundamental uncertainty (ie, the value of the tangible fixed assets).

However, in this situation, the financial statements do not show a true and fair view, as the tangible fixed assets have been included at £710,000 whereas they are worthless. The question explains that the effect of the disagreement is not so material or pervasive that the financial statements as a whole are misleading, so a qualified opinion - 'except for disagreement' will be given (similar to example 7 of SAS 600). With this form of qualified audit report, the 'opinion' paragraph is replaced by a paragraph headed: 'Qualified opinion arising from disagreement about accounting treatment'. This will explain that the value of the fixed assets, included in the financial statements at £710,000, is worthless. So, a provision of £710,000 should be included against these fixed assets. The final paragraph commences with the words: 'Except for the absence of this provision . . .' and it follows by explaining that otherwise the financial statements show a true and fair view and comply with the Companies Act 1985.

(iii)   The question says that I have not received all the evidence I would have reasonably expected to be available in relation to cash takings and custody of stock, so the answer to the first question in SAS 600 Appendix 1 is NO.

The next question in Appendix 1 asks if the possible effect is so material or pervasive to the financial statements that it could, as a whole, make them misleading. The answer to this question is YES, so a qualified opinion -disclaimer - should be given (similar to example 9 of SAS 600). With this form of qualification the basis of opinion paragraph will include an explanation of the uncertainty relating to cash takings and custody of stock. The opinion paragraph is modified to 'opinion: disclaimer on view given by financial statements'. It will explain that because of the possible effect of the limitation of evidence available to the auditor, he is unable to form an opinion as to whether the financial statements give a true and fair view, but in all other respects they have been properly prepared in accordance with the Companies Act 1985. At the end of this section a similar paragraph to that given in example 9 of SAS 600 will be added, to the effect that the auditor:

-       has not received all the information and explanations that he considered necessary for the purposes of his audit, and

-       he is unable to determine whether proper accounting records have been maintained.

(iv)   In this example the first part is similar to part (iii) - I have not received all the evidence I would have reasonably expected to be available in relation to cash takings and custody of stock.

The answer to the second question 'is the possible effect so material or pervasive to the financial statements that it could, as a whole, make them misleading' is NO. This leads to a qualified opinion - except for limitation - being given (very similar to example 8 of SAS 600).

In the 'basis of opinion' part of the report the problem about cash takings and custody of stock relating to 10% of the turnover will be explained, and that there were no other satisfactory audit procedures that the auditor could adopt to confirm that these cash takings were properly recorded.

The 'opinion' heading is changed to 'qualified opinion arising from limitation in audit scope'. This will say 'except for any adjustments that might have been found to be necessary had we been able to obtain sufficient evidence concerning cash takings and custody of perishable stock, in our opinion the financial statements give a true and fair view . . . '. At the end of the opinion paragraph, the following paragraph will be added:

In relation to the limitation in our work relating to cash takings and custody of perishable stock:

-       the auditor has not received all the information and explanations that he considered necessary for the purposes of his audit, and

-       he is unable to determine whether proper accounting records have been maintained.

31   (Answer 5 of examination)

(a)   The possible reasons for the fall in the gross profit margin include:

(i)   there has been a reduction in selling prices (eg, because of competitive pressures), or the increase in selling prices has not kept pace with the increase in purchase costs or there has been a change in sales mix to lower margin products;

(ii)   sales are understated, either because some dispatches are not invoiced or sales are made at a lower than normal price. Also, the issue of credit notes for unsatisfactory products would reduce the gross profit margin (ie, if the stock was not returned, but the credit note was issued as an allowance to the customer). Returns by customers could adversely affect the gross profit margin, if subsequently this stock had to be sold at less than the normal selling price;

(iii)   closing stock is understated, either because not all the stock has been counted, or too low a price per unit has been put on the stock. Write-down of closing stock (because it is worth less than cost) could reduce the gross profit margin;

(iv)   there are sales or purchases cut-off errors, particularly:

-       goods dispatched in October have not been included in sales until November

-       goods received in November have been included in October's purchases;

(v)   purchases are overstated, probably because there has not been proper checking of goods received (ie, that the full sum has been paid for short deliveries). As stated in part (i) above, purchases could be larger than expected if suppliers are either charging a higher than expected price, or overcharging on their purchase invoices (which the company accepts);

(vi)   there could be misappropriation of stock, probably by employees. Is it worthwhile for employees to steal the stock, and are the procedures over custody of stock effective (eg, video recorders would be attractive for employees to steal);

(vii)   has a significant amount of stock been written down or written off in the year. Such stock may be obsolete, damaged or slow moving;

(viii)   as the question says that the 1993 accounts are correct, no error can arise from this source. However, if there is doubt about the accuracy of 1993's accounts, overstatement of the value of the closing stock and cut-off errors in 1993 could result in an understatement of gross profit in 1994s accounts.

(b)   (i)   To determine the weighted gross profit margin from actual sales, I will check the gross profit achieved on actual sales by selecting some large value sales invoices in the year. I will find the gross profit on these sales noting the selling price on the sales invoice and the purchase price from the purchase invoice. From these investigations I will calculate a weighted gross profit margin.

If the weighted gross profit margin is similar to the year's gross profit margin of 16.6%, this shows the reason for the low gross profit margin. If I find this is happening, I will increase my sample size to confirm it and provide more reliable evidence to present to the directors.

If this test shows a gross profit margin of about 30%, then there is another reason for the low gross profit in the year to 31 October 1994 (such as those described in part (a)). so, I will have to carry out other tests to determine the reason.

(ii)   To check any uninvoiced sales, I will check that a sales invoice is raised for each dispatch of goods. First, I will check that dispatch notes are sequentially numbered. If they are not sequentially numbered, it is probably impossible to check that all dispatches have been invoiced, and I will report this weakness to the directors. I will go to the dispatch department and ask the staff if they raise a dispatch note for every dispatch of goods (if this is not happening, this is part of the cause of the problem, and I will assess the loss in sales revenue). If a dispatch note is raised for each dispatch, I will check for a sample of dispatch notes that a sales invoice is raised and posted to the sales ledger, and I will note any cases where no sales invoice is raised. I will check the sequence of a sample of dispatch notes and investigate any missing ones.

To check if sales are being made at incorrect prices, I will select a sample of sales invoices, concentrating on larger value ones and check that the prices charged are the prices shown on the company's price list. I will note any low prices charged or large trade discounts given. In addition, I will find if there are any zero value invoices and I will quantify the loss in value from such sales. It is difficult to identify understated sales, because if too low a price is charged, an understatement of sales will result in a low value invoice, and it is probable that these low value invoices will be a small percentage of the total number of low value invoices in the year (thus making them difficult to detect). Also, it is unlikely that a customer will complain if a lower than normal price is charged for a product.

(iii)   To check whether the stock quantities counted at the stocktake are understated, I will look at my notes when I attended the stocktake, and I will ask the stocktakers and the company's management the procedures undertaken when the stocktake was carried out. In particular, there should be no movement of stock during the stocktake (ie, it is best to carry out the stocktake at a week-end when there are no purchases or sales) as movement of stock may result in stock being counted twice or not at all. Stock should be marked when counted and the management should select items randomly at the end of the count to ensure they appear on the stock sheets. The stock sheet numbers used in the count should be recorded and all the stock sheets should be used when valuing stock.

The stock may be undervalued because too low a price per unit has been used, or stock has been written down to net realisable value. I will ask the appropriate manager which stock has been written down to net realisable value, and I will determine the reduction in value of this stock below cost (this will affect the reported gross profit margin). It will be quite difficult to identify stock which has been underpriced as it is unlikely that I will be aware of which stock may be of high value. So, I will ask the appropriate manager which stock is of high value, I will locate this on the stock sheets and check to purchase invoices that it has been valued at cost. Also, I will locate high value stock at 31 October 1993 and find this stock at 31 October 1994. The price used to value this stock at 31 October 1994 should be similar to the price at 31 October 1993. If it is significantly less at 31 October 1994 I will check it is correct by checking to the appropriate purchase invoice. In addition, I will select a sample of large value purchase invoices posted to the purchase ledger in the year and check that the stock has been valued at the same price as the purchase invoice.

For large value lines of stock, I will attempt to reconcile the quantities of opening and closing stock, purchases and sales in order to see if there is any stock loss or uninvoiced sales. In terms of quantity:

closing stock = opening stock + purchases - sales.

The stock quantities will be found from the stock sheets, and purchases and sales will be found from purchases and sales invoices. I will note any discrepancies I find and quantify the value of the 'lost stock'.

I will compare stock turnover with previous years, and I will ask the management if they consider that the current year's stock turnover and value are reasonable. The stock turnover in 1994 is 2.35 months and in 1993 it was 2.41 months. However, the fall in sales in 1994 (19.6%) could suggest that the age of stock should have increased, as many companies do not reduce purchases immediately sales fall, so one would expect the age of stock in 1994 to be higher than in 1993.

---

32   (Answer 6 of examination)

(a)   In planning the audit prior to the commencement of detailed audit work, I will consider the following matters:

(i)   the timetable for the audit will be considered. For a public company the starting point is usually the date of the AGM. The timetable will be worked back from this point, so the dates of the following stages will be considered:

-    the date when the financial statements are posted to the shareholders (this must be at least 21 days before the AGM)

-    the date when the financial statements are signed by the directors and the partner signs the audit report (there should be adequate time for printing and checking the proofs of the annual accounts)

-    the date when the detailed audit work is completed. There must be sufficient time between this date and when the audit report is signed to allow for review of the audit work, carrying out additional work (where audit tests provide insufficient evidence) and making final adjustments to the accounts

- the period when the final audit takes place. The start of the final audit should be at a time when valuable audit work can be carried out, but it may be before the full accounts have been prepared. If the accounts are only available part way through the final audit, there should be sufficient time to audit them before the period allowed for detailed audit testing ends. Ideally, there should be some slack in the time budget to allow for delays and resolving problems experienced in the audit. If the timetable is very tight, it may be appropriate to carry out certain procedures at the interim audit (eg, the debtors' circularisation) or immediately after the year end before the detailed audit work commences (eg, the bank reconciliation)

- the dates of the stocktakes are important and the extent to which the company's internal audit department will assist in this work. As there are a number of shops, I will have to consider which shops the internal auditor and my staff should visit and which will not be visited for the stocktake

- the date of the interim audit visit and the work which should be carried out at this stage. As stated above, if there are time pressures at the final audit, some work related to the final audit can be undertaken at this stage

(ii)   I will visit the company prior to the detailed audit work and meet the directors. This will make me aware of developments since last year's audit, and I will discuss the timetable (described in part (i) above) and agree the extent to which the company's staff will assist in the audit work. This assistance will include help by the internal audit department and the schedules the company's staff will prepare for my staff (eg, bank reconciliations, suppliers' statement reconciliations, assessment of doubtful debts, movements on fixed assets).

(iii)   I will ask the company's management if there have been any changes in the company's staff, management structure and accounting systems which will affect my work (eg, a new computerised accounting system will probably require more audit work). I will inspect the management accounts and board minutes.

(iv)   I will consider the extent to which problems experienced in last year's audit have been resolved this year. More time will have to be allocated to the three problems mentioned in the question: misappropriation of stock, stock worth less than cost and incomplete recording of cash sales.

(v)   I will consider the effect on the audit of the introduction of new accounting and auditing standards and other legislation since last year's audit.

(vi)   I will assess the level of audit risk, which will affect the amount of audit work which should be carried out.

(vii)   A fee will be agreed with the client, which may be increased if major problems are experienced during the audit. This fee will be a significant factor in deciding the staff time available to perform the audit (also, the reverse should apply as the minimum fee should be based on the minimum acceptable time to perform the audit commensurate with an acceptable level of audit risk).

(viii) I will consider the level of experience required for the audit staff. I will check that the appropriate staff are available, and the audit work will be divided between them so that the work each member performs is within their abilities and experience. Ideally, the same staff should undertake the interim and final audit work and there will be a saving of learning time if staff have been on the audit of Radford Retail in previous years. I will prepare a budget of the time allocation for each aspect of the audit and the sequence in which the work should be performed.

(ix)   I will specify the materiality level for the audit, and the value when errors and uncertainties should be recorded (this could be as small as one tenth of the level of materiality, and it may be even smaller for individual shops). Although no fixed figure for materiality can be specified with the limited information provided in the question, a turnover of £20 million would suggest a profit before tax of £2 million (at a net profit margin of 10%), and materiality of 10% of profit before tax would result in a materiality level of £200,000. Errors over £20,000 would be noted if it was decided that all errors over 10% of the materiality level should be recorded.

(x)   I will prepare an audit planning memorandum, which will include many of the matters discussed above. The question says that there have been problems with cash, stock loss and valuation in previous years, so these points will be included in the memorandum and more time will be allocated in the budget to these areas.

(xi)   I will discuss my findings from this work with the partner and ask him to make any amendments to my audit planning memorandum and plans for the audit.

(b)   To some extent the controlling of audit work overlaps with planning. Before staff start the detailed audit work they should be given the audit planning memorandum, and, after they have read it, I will discuss the audit with them and the particular problems they may experience. If the staff are unfamiliar with the audit of retailers, I will describe their particular problems and the areas of highest audit risk. As in all other audits, staff should be told to report any significant problems to the senior in charge of the audit, who should report them to me if they cannot be resolved. Any areas where material errors or uncertainties are found should be recorded and reported to me through the senior in charge of the audit.

All audit work should be recorded in the audit working papers, which will include a record of the work done, the matters considered and the conclusions reached. Standard schedules should be completed by the audit staff (eg, stocktaking, Companies Acts and audit completion checklists), audit staff should initial each page of their working papers, and, if there is an audit programme, staff should initial the sections of the work they have completed.

The senior in charge of the audit should report to me (on at least a weekly basis) the progress of work on the audit, including:

-     the time spent to date
-     the progress made
-     any significant problems
-     if the audit is going to take more time than budgeted
-     any delays which may result in late completion of the audit.

Staff should be allocated work according to their abilities and experience. Generally, this should be done by the senior in charge of the audit, but I will review his plans, decide the allocation of work which minimises audit risk and make any amendments. All audit work should be reviewed by more senior staff. The senior in charge of the audit should review the work of the other staff employed on the audit, and I will review all the working papers of the audit staff. This review should occur while the audit is taking place, so that problems can be highlighted and corrected with the minimum waste of time and delay. I will be careful to ensure that there has been adequate audit work on the three problem areas noted in the question, namely the misappropriation of stock, problems with stock being worth less than cost and the full recording of cash sales. The degree to which the audit partner reviews the detailed audit work will depend on the audit firm's policy and his assessment of the risk of the audit. The audit working papers should be made available to the partner so that he can look at the audit work connected with his investigations. The audit working papers should include a section which records significant errors and uncertainties detected in the financial statements and any major problems experienced by the audit staff.

It is generally agreed that care should be exercised at the final stages of the audit, as pressures during this period are greatest, which increases the risk of error. In particular, all significant final adjustments to the financial statements should be properly audited and details of this work should be recorded in the audit working papers.

Immediately prior to the partner reviewing the audit work, a memorandum should be prepared for him to consider. Its contents will include:

(i)   a summary of the financial statements, including calculation of appropriate ratios and justification of the figures based on business conditions during the year;

(ii)   a summary of audit work done, particularly on material items in the financial statements and in areas of highest risk (eg, custody of cash, misappropriation and valuation problems with stock);

(iii)   a list of all significant errors and uncertainties revealed during the audit and a summary of the total errors and uncertainties in the financial statements;

(iv)   a list of matters to discuss with the company's directors, and a suggestion of the adjustments which should be made to enable an unqualified audit report to be given.

JUNE 1995 QUESTIONS

Section A – ALL THREE questions are compulsory and MUST be attempted

33   (Question 1 of examination)

Your firm is the auditor of Oxton Pumps Ltd and you have been asked to check the valuation of the company's stock at cost at its year end of 30 April 1995.

Oxton Pumps manufactures a range of domestic central heating pumps. These pumps comprise an electric motor, impeller (to pump the water) and casing. There are sundry parts, including pipe fittings, nuts and bolts, and electrical connections. The pumps are assembled from components bought by Oxton Pumps (the company does not manufacture any parts).

You attended the stocktake at the year end and you are satisfied that the stock was counted accurately and that there are no sales or purchases cut-off errors.

The company does not use a standard costing system, and work in progress and finished goods are valued as follows:

(1)   Material costs are determined from the product specification, which lists the components required to make a pump.

(2)   The company produces a range of pumps. Employees record the hours spent on assembling each type of pump; this information is input into the payroll system which prints the total hours spent each week assembling each type of pump. All employees assembling pumps are paid at the same rate and there is no overtime.

(3)   Overheads are added to the stock value in accordance with SSAP 9 *Stocks and long-term contracts*. The financial accounting records are used to determine the overhead cost, and this is applied as a percentage based on the direct labour cost.

The company carries out monthly stocktakes when all the stock is counted. The value of stock in these stocktakes is used in preparing the monthly management accounts.

The production records show the quantity of each pump produced each month. Production quantities are derived from the quantity transferred to the finished goods store and the change in work in progress each month. For direct labour costs, you have agreed that the labour expended for a unit in work in progress is half that of a completed unit.

The draft accounts show the following materials and direct labour costs in stock:

	Raw materials £	Work in progress £	Finished goods £
Materials	74,786	85,692	152,693
Direct labour		13,072	46,584

The costs incurred in April, as recorded in the financial accounting records, were:

	£
Direct labour	61,320
Selling costs	43,550
Depreciation and finance costs of production machines	4,490
Distribution costs	6,570
Factory manager's wage	2,560
Other production overheads	24,820
Purchasing and accounting costs relating to production	5,450
Other accounting costs	7,130
Other administration overheads	24,770

For your calculations assume that all work in progress and finished goods were produced in April 1995 and that the company was operating at a normal level of activity.

Required

In relation to the information given above:

(a)   Describe the audit work you would carry out to verify for *finished goods*:

   (i)   the material cost;
   (ii)   the direct labour cost.

                                                                        (7 marks)

(b)   (i)   Describe the matters you would consider and the audit work you would carry out to determine whether the company is operating at a normal level of activity.

   (ii)   Explain which direct labour and overhead costs should be included and which should be excluded, if the company is operating at a lower than normal level of activity.   **(8 marks)**

(c)   Calculate the value of overheads which should be added to work in progress and finished goods in accordance with SSAP 9 *Stocks and long-term contracts*.   **(5 marks)**
                                                                        (Total 20 marks)

(*Note:* in part (c) you should include details and a description of your workings and all figures should be calculated to the nearest £.)

---

34   (Question 2 of examination)

Your firm is the auditor of Daybrook Insurance Brokers Ltd which operates from a number of branches and provides insurance for the general public and businesses. The company obtains insurance from large insurance companies, and takes a commission for its services. You have been asked to audit certain aspects of the company's fixed assets for the year ended 31 March 1995.

The company's main fixed assets comprise:

(1)   freehold land and buildings;
(2)   microcomputers, printers and related equipment which are used by staff;
(3)   cars which are provided to directors and salespeople who visit customers.

The company has been operating for a number of years, and it maintains details of its office equipment and cars on a computerised fixed asset register. The company uses the following depreciation rates:

(1)   buildings   2% per annum on cost
(2)   office equipment (including computers)   10% per annum on cost
(3)   motor vehicles (ie, cars)   25% per annum on cost

You are concerned that the depreciation rate for the computers may be inadequate.

On 1 April 1994 Daybrook Insurance Brokers purchased a competitor's trade for £500,000. This comprised the competitor's customers and trade name but it did not include any other assets or liabilities. In the financial statements for the year ended 31 March 1995 the goodwill has been included in the balance sheet and it is being amortised over a period of 10 years.

Required

(a)   Describe how you would verify the ownership of:

      (i)   freehold land and buildings;

      (ii)   computers and cars.   **(5 marks)**

(b)   (i)   Describe the investigations you would carry out to determine whether the depreciation rate of the computers is adequate.

      (ii)   Describe the factors you would consider when deciding whether to qualify your audit report on the understatement of the depreciation of the computers.

Assuming you decide to qualify your audit report on the understatement of depreciation on the office equipment, you should describe the form of qualified audit report you would use.

(8 marks)

(c)   Describe the audit work you would carry out to determine whether the goodwill on purchase of the competitor's trade is worth £450,000 at 31 March 1995 and that the amortisation charge of £50,000 is reasonable.

(7 marks)
(Total 20 marks)

---

35   (Question 3 of examination)

Your firm is the auditor of Lenton Textiles Ltd and you have been asked to suggest the audit work which should be carried out on the sales system.

Lenton Textiles Ltd sells textile products to shops. Most of its sales are made on credit, but very small customers who do not have a sales ledger account can collect their purchases and pay in cash. For these cash sales:

(1)   the customer orders the items from the sales department, which raises a pre-numbered multi-copy advice note;

(2)·   the dispatch department make up the order and give it to the customer with a copy of the advice note;

(3)   the customer gives the advice note to the cashier who prepares a hand-written sales invoice;

(4)   the customer pays the cashier for the goods by cheque or in cash;

(5)   the cashier records and banks the cash.

For credit sales, cheques and cash are received in the post. The post is opened by two people, who record cash and cheques received. The cheques and cash are given to the cashier who records them in the cash book and pays them into the bank. The cashier reports the cheques and cash received to the sales accounting department which posts the items to the sales ledger.

Credit notes must be authorised before they are sent to customers and posted to the sales ledger.

Required

(a)   (i)   State the weaknesses in the cash sales system.

      (ii)   Describe the systems based tests you would carry out to check there is no material fraud or error in this system.   **(7 marks)**

(b)   (i)   Briefly explain why two people should open the mail which contains cheques and cash from customers.

      (ii)   Describe the audit work you would carry out when you attend the opening of the mail and follow through the process to banking of the cheques.   **(6 marks)**

(c)   (i)   List the reasons why credit notes may be issued.

        (ii)   Describe the audit work you would perform to check that all credit notes have been authorised and issued for a valid reason.
                                                                        (7 marks)
                                                                        (Total 20 marks)

Section B – TWO questions ONLY to be attempted

| 36 | **(Question 4 of examination)** |

The directors of Melton Manufacturing Ltd have asked your firm to act as their auditors for the year ended 30 September 1995. They will be asking their existing auditors to resign as they say they do not provide a cost effective service.

Required

(a)   Describe the investigations you would carry out and the statutory and ethical matters you would consider before you can:

        (i)   accept the appointment as the company's auditor; and
        (ii)   be appointed the company's auditor.   **(11 marks)**

(b)   (i)   Explain why it is important that an auditor should send a letter of engagement to the client prior to undertaking the audit.

        (ii)   Briefly describe the main contents of a letter of engagement which you would send to the directors of Melton Manufacturing Ltd.
                                                                        (9 marks)
                                                                        (Total 20 marks)

| 37 | **(Question 5 of examination)** |

You are auditing the financial statements of Eastwood Engineering plc for the year ended 31 March 1995, and the partner in charge of the audit has asked you to consider the audit work you would carry out on closure costs and capital commitments.

You are aware that the company plans to close one of its factories and make the employees redundant, and you have been asked to consider how this closure should be disclosed in the financial statements for the year ended 31 March 1995. You should assume that the effect of this closure is material.

The loss arising from the closure will include:

(1)   costs of making employees redundant;

(2)   the loss on disposal of fixed assets, which comprise freehold land and buildings, fixtures and fittings, plant, computer equipment and motor vehicles;

(3)   loss in the value of stock, which will be surplus to requirements when the factory is closed.

Required

(a)   Describe the audit work you would carry out to determine whether the closure of the factory should be treated as an adjusting or a non-adjusting post balance sheet event.

                                                                        (5 marks)

(b)   Assuming you decide the closure is an adjusting post balance sheet event, describe the audit work you would carry out to check the loss arising from the closure in the financial statements.   **(10 marks)** (c)　(i)　　State how capital commitments should be disclosed in the financial statements in accordance with the Companies Act 1985.

　　(ii)　　Describe the audit work you would carry out to verify the value of capital commitments in the financial statements.　　　　　　　　　　　　　　　**(5 marks)**
　　　　　　　　　　　　　　　　　　　　　　　　　　　　　　　　　　(Total 20 marks)

(*Note:* you should answer the question in accordance with SSAP 17 *Accounting for post balance sheet events*.)

38　(Question 6 of examination)

'The decision in the **Caparo** case has led many informed commentators to believe that auditors have no liability to third parties for negligence, which has led to a deterioration in the quality of audit work.'

You are required to discuss this statement, and in particular:

(a)　explain the decision in the **Caparo** case and state the parties who may successfully sue the auditor for negligence;　　　　　　　　　　　　　　　　　　　　　　　　　　**(3 marks)**

(b)　discuss the reasons why the **Caparo** judgment may lead to a deterioration in the quality of auditors' work;　　　　　　　　　　　　　　　　　　　　　　　　　　　　　**(6 marks)**

(c)　describe the measures which have been introduced and the factors which have led to an increase in the independence of auditors and an improvement in the quality of their work.
　　　　　　　　　　　　　　　　　　　　　　　　　　　　　　(11 marks)
　　　　　　　　　　　　　　　　　　　　　　　　　　　　　　(Total 20 marks)

(*Note:* the Caparo case is **Caparo Industries plc v Dickman and others** – House of Lords judgment.)

ANSWERS TO JUNE 1995 EXAMINATION

33   (Answer 1 of examination)

Examiner's comments and marking guide

Question 1: examined candidates on auditing raw materials, labour and overheads to be included in stock.

In part (a)(i) most candidates correctly checked the material cost to the purchase invoice. Answers on checking the direct labour cost were less good. Careful reading of the question, and a verbal description of how the calculation would have been checked, would have produced a good answer. The labour cost of a unit in stock is the labour cost for the month (from the payroll) divided by the number of units produced (from the production records).

The answers to part (b) were weak. A logical approach would have produced a good answer, eg, compare sales with budget and previous years, ask management to consider if there is any idle time, and consider stock levels.

The answers to part (b)(ii) on which overheads should or should not be included in stock were usually either non-existent or very poor.

Many candidates did not answer the computation in part (c). Candidates should have been able to list the production overheads from the question, but only a minority of candidates identified them correctly. Some candidates incorrectly thought that selling and distribution costs were part of production overheads, and others included direct labour in overheads. Very few candidates obtained the correct answer.

Although candidates performed poorly in parts (b) and (c), they examine very important aspects of the audit of stock. A calculation like that in part (c) should not be unexpected, as Auditing is concerned with verifying amounts in financial statements, and it may involve performing calculations or checking the client's computations.

			Marks
(a)	(i)	Check of material costs	
	(ii)	Check of direct labour costs	
		Generally 1 mark a point up to a maximum of	7
(b)	(i)	Check if company is operating at a normal level	
	(ii)	If lower than normal, which labour and overheads should be included	
		Generally 1 mark a point up to a maximum of	8
(c)		Calculation of overheads	
		Up to a maximum of	5
Total			20

Note: In part (a) you may decide to allocate your marks 4 and 3 marks to parts (i) and (ii)
In part (b) you may decide to allocate your marks 5 and 3 marks to parts (i) and (ii)

Step by step answer plan

Step 1   Read the question again and make sure that you focus on precisely what is required.

Step 2   This looks like a conventional question on the valuation of stock, requiring some knowledge of SSAP 9. The company does not manufacture any parts itself, so all parts will be bought in from external suppliers who will send purchase invoices showing the cost of the parts supplied. The company does not use a standard costing system, so all valuations will be based on actual costs (per the purchase invoices) rather than any calculated standard costs. You are told that the company is operating at a normal level of activity, so there is no need to write off the cost of any unused production capacity, as would have been required by SSAP 9.

Step 3 Part (b) tests the implications in practice if the company is operating at a lower than normal level of activity. Put yourself in the auditor's position. How would you test whether or not the company's present level of activity is the normal level of activity? Reference to the previous accounting period is an obvious first step.

Step 4 Part (c) tests your application of the principles of SSAP 9.

Step 5 Only when you are confident that you are about to answer the question that has been set, should you start writing.

The examiner's answer

(a)   (i)   I would perform the following work in checking the cost of materials in a pump. First, I would obtain details of the pumps in finished goods stock and I would select a sample of pumps which each have a high value (either because they are individually expensive, or there are a larger number of lower value pumps). I would obtain the specification for each of these pumps. For each specification I would inspect an actual pump to check that the components required for the pump are consistent with the specification. Then I would check the cost of the major components to purchase invoices (I would probably have to ask the company's staff the name of the supplier of the individual parts). As stated in the question, the main components would be the electric motor, the body of the pump and the impeller. For small parts, such as nuts and bolts, electrical connections and pipe fittings I would consider whether their cost is reasonable. If their cost appears to be wrong, I would check it to purchase invoices. If prices of components are rising (or falling), the valuation should normally be on a FIFO (first in, first out) basis, so the latest purchases would be in raw materials, the next in work in progress and the earliest in finished goods.

I would check that the finished goods were produced recently and that April's purchases are similar to previous months.

I would check the additions of the cost of individual items to the total. I would record any errors I find in the valuation of the pumps. The total value of the finished goods would be checked as the product of the quantity of each pump and the cost per unit.

(ii)   For direct labour cost I would obtain the production records, and for a sample of large value pumps I would calculate the direct labour time to produce each pump. The labour hours to produce a single unit of one type of pump would be found by determining the hours to produce the pumps in April (which would be found from the payroll and the break-down of hours for each type of pump) and dividing it by the quantity produced, which would be found from the production records. The rate per hour for the employees would be found from April's payroll, and the labour cost per pump would be the product of the hours to produce a pump and the direct labour rate. The direct labour rate may include employer's national insurance, pension, sickness and other benefits. I would check that April's wages are similar to previous months and that the finished goods were produced recently. I would quantify any errors I find in these calculations, and if they are significant, I would record them in my schedule of unadjusted errors.

An alternative method of calculating the labour hours to produce a pump is to use the costing records. However, these hours may be unreliable, because there is no indication that the hours in the costing records are compared with the actual hours the employees take to produce each type of pump. As these hours are unreliable, checking the cost of labour in this way will be unreliable.

Did you answer the question?

Note that in part (a) no discussion is required of the valuation of work in progress.

(b)   (i)   The investigations I would carry out and the matters I would consider in determining whether the company is operating at a normal level of activity would include:

– I would compare the level of production with previous years. If it is similar to previous years, and in previous years the company was operating at a normal level of activity, then it is operating at a normal level of activity this year. It may be difficult to assess the level of production activity, so, if there is no significant change in stock during the year, the value of sales would be a close approximation to production activity

- I would compare production (or sales) with budget. If sales are similar to budget, the company is probably operating at a normal level. If sales are significantly less than budget, the company is probably operating at a lower than normal level

- I would look at the amount of overtime being worked by production staff (the question says no overtime is being worked, but I will check to the payroll and ask staff if overtime is being worked). If the overtime being worked is similar to previous years, then the company is probably operating at a normal level. If no overtime is being worked (and overtime was being worked in previous years) there is a risk that activity is less than the normal level. The main matter to consider is whether there is idle time. I would ask the company's directors, the production director (or manager), and the employees and check the payroll to see if there has been idle time in April. If there is idle time, then the company is working at a lower than normal level

- I would ask management if there have been any changes in production in the year, and, if I was on the audit last year, I should be able to assess whether there have been any changes. Also, minutes of management meetings and board minutes should record any changes. If there has been new machinery or an increase in the production capacity (eg, by an increase in the production area) then it would probably not be appropriate to compare this year's production with last year, as this year's production should be higher. If there has been an increase in production capacity but no increase in sales, it is probable that the company is operating at a lower than normal level of activity.

Based on this work, I would decide whether the company has been operating at a lower than normal level of activity.

(ii)   Stock should be valued at the cost of production when the company is operating at a normal level of activity. So, any inefficiencies which arise through the company operating at a lower than normal level of activity should be charged to the profit and loss account. So, if the company is operating at a lower than normal level of activity, the direct labour and overheads in stock should:

- only include fixed overheads relating to a normal level
- exclude any direct labour costs which are classed as idle time.

For instance, if the company is operating at 80% of its normal level, only 80% of the fixed overheads should be included in the stock value. Fixed overheads would include rent and rates of the factory. Provided variable overheads are entirely variable, all these overheads can be included in the value of stock.

If direct labour is paid entirely on the amount produced, all the direct labour cost can be included in the value of stock. However, if 10% of the labour cost represents idle time (or is used to increase the employees' wage to a minimum level), only 90% of the direct labour cost should be included in the value of stock.

Did you answer the question?

Note that the examiner has listed several different methods for determining whether the company is operating at a normal level of activity. This is much better than a lengthy description of just one method.

(c)

	Raw materials £	Work in progress £	Finished goods £
Materials	74,786	85,692	152,693
Direct labour		13,072	46,584

Analysis of April 1995 data into production and other overheads:

	Total costs £	Production overheads £	Other overheads £
Direct labour	61,320		
Selling costs	43,550		43,550
Depreciation and finance costs of production machines	4,490	4,490	
Distribution costs	6,570		6,570
Factory manager's wage	2,560	2,560	
Other production overheads	24,820	24,820	
Purchasing and accounting costs relating to production	5,450	5,450	
Other accounting costs	7,130		7,130
Other administration overheads	24,770		24,770
	180,660	37,320	82,020

Direct labour cost   £61,320

Production overhead rate $\dfrac{37,320}{61,320} \times 100\% = 60.86\%$

Answer	Raw materials £	Work in progress £	Finished goods £	Total £
Materials	74,786	85,692	152,693	313,171
Direct labour		13,072	46,584	59,656
Production overheads (at 60.86% of direct labour cost)		7,956	28,351	36,307
	74,786	106,720	227,628	409,134

34 (Answer 2 of examination)

Examiner's comments and marking guide

Question 2: examined candidates on verifying certain fixed assets, considering whether depreciation of computers was adequate, and auditing goodwill.

The answers to part (a) on verifying the ownership of freehold land and buildings, computers and cars were satisfactory. In part (a)(i) more candidates should have suggested inspecting the land registry certificate. Some answers tended to concentrate on verifying the *existence of* the fixed assets, rather than their ownership, limiting the number of marks which could be awarded.

Part (b) was designed for candidates to argue that a 10 year life for computers was excessive. More candidates should have been critical of the company's policy. Answers on whether to qualify the audit report were weak. Most candidates correctly suggested using an 'except for' qualification, but a few still suggested using the 'subject to' qualification, which is no longer permitted since the introduction of SAS 600.

Some candidates failed to answer part (c) on the amortisation of the goodwill. Candidates should have asked themselves 'is the life of the goodwill as long as 10 years' (this seems unlikely) and 'is it worth £450,000 at the year end'. Generally, the answers were weak. Many candidates spent too much time on checking the ownership of the goodwill, rather than verifying its value at the year end and the amortisation charge for the year.

		Marks
(a)	Verifying ownership of land and cars	
	Generally 1 mark a point up to a maximum of	5
(b)	Checking depreciation rate of computers and effect on audit report	
	Generally 1 mark a point up to a maximum of	8
(c)	Checking value of the goodwill and amortisation	
	Generally 1 mark a point up to a maximum of	7
Total		20

Step by step answer plan

Step 1   Read the question again and make sure that you focus on precisely what is required.

Step 2   Part (a) is a standard check on the ownership assertion. A land registry certificate can confirm the ownership of nearly all land in the UK. The purchase invoice would be the first document to look for to prove the ownership of computers and cars.

Step 3   The essence of part (b) is that 10 years seems a bit long as the assumed working life of computers. In practice they are replaced typically every four or five years or so.

Step 4   Part (c) is testing whether 10 years is an appropriate life for the goodwill which has been purchased. The auditor must determine what intangible has been acquired for the goodwill payment: if it is an existing trained workforce but they are all on the point of leaving, 10 years would be too long.

Step 5   Only when you are confident that you are about to answer the question that has been set, should you start writing.

The examiner's answer

(a)   (i)   The ownership of freehold land and buildings would be verified by:

–   checking the latest conveyance, which should be in the name of the company;

–   checking the land registry certificate, which should give a plan of the plot and building (ie, the offices) and state that it is owned by the company;

–   contacting the land registry to confirm the ownership of the land (eg, the company's records could be photocopies, and this check would confirm the ownership of the building and land).

The plan of the land and buildings would be checked as being consistent with the company's premises and land.

(ii)   The document which confirms the ownership of the computers and cars is the purchase invoice, which should describe the item accurately (including stating its serial number, and, for a car, its registration number) and it should be addressed to the company. However, if the item had been bought a number of years ago, the purchase invoice may not be available, so it may not be possible to perform this check. However, the company does maintain a fixed asset register, and all material items should have been vouched from the purchase invoice to the fixed asset register. So, by checking the fixed asset to the fixed asset register, the ownership of the fixed asset would probably have been confirmed (as the invoice for the fixed asset would have been vouched to the fixed asset register when it was bought, so all material items in the fixed asset register would have been vouched to a purchase invoice in the year of purchase). As the fixed asset register is computerised it would not be possible to find the auditor's original check of the purchase invoice to the fixed asset register. However, provided the closing balance of the previous year has been agreed to the opening balance of the following year, this provides good evidence that items in the fixed asset register have originally been vouched to a purchase invoice.

Did you answer the question?

Note that the examiner has only dealt with the ownership assertion in his answer. Don't waste time by discussing other assertions such as existence or valuation.

(b)   (i)   The depreciation rate of 10% on cost seems very low for computers, as it indicates a life of 10 years. To assess the life of the computers, I would suggest the following:

–   Ask management their policy for renewal and upgrading of computers. If they plan to replace the computers in the near future, then a depreciation rate of 10% per annum appears to be too low. If they plan to defer purchase of new computers, I would consider whether this is realistic. Software developments are likely to make their existing computers unusable, unless they are all very new. Also, the speed and storage capacity of their existing computers are likely to become inadequate in the future.

–   Look at disposals of computers (or scrapping), and check if there is a profit or loss on disposal. If there is a loss on disposal the depreciation rate is too low, and if there is a profit on disposal, the depreciation rate is too high (which seems unlikely). If there are a large number of computers which are fully written off, it indicates the depreciation rate is too high (this seems very unlikely).

–   Look round the offices and check if there are any unused computers. It is probable that they are obsolete, and I would ask management's views on whether they would be used again (I would be suspicious if they believe they would be used again). If these obsolete computers are hidden, I should be able to find them by selecting old computers from the fixed asset register and checking their existence (they may be kept in a store room). In order to confirm they exist, management would have to show them to me. These obsolete computers would probably have a very low value, and it may be appropriate to assume they are worthless.

–   Consider the age of existing computers which are being used, and the effect of hardware and software developments which would make them obsolete. For instance, many computers purchased five years ago cannot run 'Windows' and are excessively slow at running sophisticated word processing packages. So, these computers would be obsolete now if these packages are being used, or they would become obsolete when the company starts to use them. On IBM PC type computers, those computers with 80386 processors are slow, 80486 processors are the 'norm', and Pentium processors are being used for the fastest machines. Any computers with earlier processors are probably obsolete.

(Tutorial note: this was the situation in mid-1995. By 1999 it is probably fair to say that Pentium processors are now the 'norm' and any earlier processors would be thought of as slow.*)*

Based on these investigations, I would decide the life of the computers and estimate the understatement of the depreciation charge and the overstatement of the value of the computers. I believe that a depreciation rate of 20% to 25% on cost should be used for computers, giving a life (to zero value) of four to five years.

(ii)   As stated in part (b)(i) above, I would quantify the amount of the understatement of the depreciation charge and the overstatement of the value of the computers and consider whether this error is material.

It would appear to be too 'tight' a requirement that the depreciation charge and the value of the computers should be within 10% of their 'true' value. If a material error is taken as 10% of the profit before tax, then if the understated depreciation charge affects the profit before tax by more than 10%, then its effect is material and the audit report should be qualified. Also, if the effect of this error together with other errors overstates profit before tax by more than 10%, the audit report should be qualified. However, it seems unlikely that the error in the depreciation charge would affect the profit before tax by more than 10%.

For the value of the computers in the balance sheet, it is more difficult to say how much a material error would be. It could be taken as 10% of the net book value of fixed assets (which may be considered to be too large an acceptable error), or it may be 10% of the value of plant and machinery (which may include motor vehicles and fixtures and fittings).

Concerning qualification of the audit report, looking at the diagram in Appendix 1 of SAS 600 *Auditors' reports on financial statements*:

− I have seen all the evidence I would have reasonably expected to be available.

− The financial statements are prepared in accordance with GAAP.

− The understated depreciation is not a fundamental uncertainty.

− The financial statements do not give a true and fair view.

− The effect of the disagreement is not sufficient to make the financial statements misleading.

So, the form of qualified audit report is a qualified opinion 'except for disagreement' which is similar to example 7 in the Auditing Standard.

(c)   The audit work I would perform to determine whether the goodwill is worth at least £450,000 at 31 March 1995 would include the following:

(i)   I would obtain the purchase agreement, and check that Daybrook Insurance Brokers has acquired the trade, and has legal title to it. I would check to the cash book that payment has been made to the business which has sold its trade.

(ii)   I would obtain details of the trade which has been purchased (this will comprise customers and may include staff of the old business).

(iii)   I would check that the trade was worth £500,000. This would include checking the profitability of the business before it was purchased and comparing the cost with the cost of purchasing similar businesses. If these investigations suggest that Daybrook Insurance Brokers had paid too high a price, I would recommend that the goodwill in the balance sheet should be reduced to the normal cost of purchasing such a trade (and the difference written off).

(iv)   I would ask the company to provide a schedule of the trade and commission earned from this business. I would check that the business on the schedule relates to what has been acquired (ie, it should be renewal of premiums from customers of the old business, and not customers of Daybrook Insurance Brokers or new customers since the acquisition).

(v)   I would ask the company to provide an estimate of the profitability of the business acquired. The gross income would be the commission from the insurance premiums, and the costs would relate to employees' wages and overheads incurred in carrying out that business. It may be possible to identify the employees, if they are in a separate department or building. Otherwise, it is probably acceptable to apportion overheads on the basis of the premium income received in the purchased and existing business. I would test check the income from premiums and the overheads, and the calculation of the net profit of the business acquired.

(vi)   I would consider whether the profitability of the business acquired is consistent with the amount paid for it. The return on the investment should be greater than the cost of borrowing money to finance the investment. If the return is quite high, then the value of £450,000 for the goodwill is probably acceptable.

The amortisation period of 10 years seems long. If the business acquired is being operated as a separate branch, it would be easier to check the value of the goodwill and its amortisation period, than if the new business has been incorporated into the existing business. One would expect the goodwill to relate to the business's customers when it was purchased on 1 April 1994, and that it would not relate to any customers acquired after 1 April 1994. I would look at the rate at which existing customers are lost, by asking the company's management. To check this, I would select a sample of customers of the business when it was acquired at 1 April 1994 and check the proportion who renew their premiums. If at least 90% of the customers renew their premiums, then the amortisation period is reasonable, but if it is only 50%, the goodwill should be written off more rapidly.

Based on these investigations, I would decide whether the value of the goodwill in the balance sheet at 31 March 1995 and the amortisation of £50,000 in the profit and loss account are reasonable.

Did you answer the question?

Note how the examiner has given at least 7 points in his answer to earn the 7 marks available. Did your answer contain at least 7 separate points?

---

35 (Answer 3 of examination)

Examiner's comments and marking guide

Question 3: examined candidates on controls and tests in a sales system.

Most of the answers to part (a) on the weaknesses in the cash sales system were good, although the suggestions of the audit tests were weaker.

The answers to part (b) on opening the mail and banking the cheques were quite good.

The answers to part (c) were weaker. A number of candidates did not know what credit notes are.

Most candidates limited the number of reasons for issuing credit notes to three or less, so their audit work in part (c)(ii) was rather limited.

		Marks
(a)	Weaknesses in cash sales system and audit checks Generally 1 mark a point up to a maximum of	7
(b)	Why two people should open the mail and audit checks Generally 1 mark a point up to a maximum of	6
(c)	Reason for issue of credit notes and audit checks Generally 1 mark a point up to a maximum of	7
Total		20

Step by step answer plan

Step 1   Read the question again and make sure that you focus on precisely what is required.

Step 2   This looks like an easy question on the sales and cash systems. The key point in any cash system is to ensure proper division of duties; the cashier should not also be involved in raising documents in the sales system, for example. Division of duties will lessen the possibility of theft and fraud.

Step 3   Each part of the question is worth roughly equal marks, so must be given equal time to be answered. Don't write too much on parts (a) and (b) and leave not enough time for a proper answer to part (c).

Step 4   Only when you are confident that you are about to answer the question that has been set, should you start writing.

The examiner's answer

(a)   (i)   The weaknesses in the cash sales system include the following:

– The question does not mention that sales invoices are sequentially numbered (if they are not pre-numbered, they should be, to ensure there are no missing items).

– When the dispatch department give the customer the goods there is no control to ensure he pays for them. He should not be given the goods until he returns with an invoice which has been receipted by the cashier.

– The sales invoice should not be raised by the cashier, as he could perpetrate a fraud by issuing a full-cost invoice and getting the cash from the customer. Subsequently, he could issue a lower value invoice, destroy the original invoice and misappropriate the difference.

– As the cashier raises the sales invoice there is no control to correct any errors he makes. Also, he may not use the correct prices when preparing the sales invoice (as he may not have an up-to-date price list).

– There is no control to ensure that the cashier banks the cash for each sales invoice. Another member of staff should check this is happening.

– There would be a significant improvement in the controls in the system if the sales department raised the sales invoice (rather than the cashier), and, as stated above, the customer was not allowed to collect the goods until he had paid for them. As a further control, the sales department could post the sales invoice to a sundry sales account in the sales ledger, and the cashier could post the cash. The balance on this account would show invoices raised where no cash has been received, and they should be investigated.

(ii)   The audit work I would perform on the cash sales system would include the following:

– I would record the system and perform a walk-through test to confirm my flowchart is correct.

– I would evaluate the controls and note the weaknesses (these have been described in part (i) above).

– I would test the system by starting from a sample of advice notes raised by the sales department. These advice notes should be sequentially numbered. I would check a sample of advice notes (eg, four sets of 50 sequentially numbered advice notes spread throughout the year) and investigate any that are missing from the sequence. Then, for a smaller sample of advice notes, I would check the following for each advice note.

– I would check that a copy of the advice note is in the dispatch department, that there is evidence of the goods being dispatched (either by a change in the stock records or acknowledgement by the storekeeper on the advice note), and that the customer has signed for the goods.

– I would follow through to the cashier and I would check that he has raised a sales invoice and that its value has been recorded in the cash book. I would check that the sales invoice is sequentially numbered (if it is not, I would note the fact in my management letter), that it refers to the advice note, that the details agree with the advice note, that the prices per unit are correct and the calculations on the invoice are correct.

– For a large sample of advice notes, I would check that a sales invoice has been raised and the cash has been entered in the cash book. I would investigate cases where there is an advice note and no cash has been banked for this sale.

– I would check the bank reconciliation to ensure that these cash sales are banked promptly (or I could check that the most recent cash sales have been banked promptly).

— Based on this work, I would decide whether the system is operating accurately. There are many serious weaknesses in the system, as noted in part (i) above, and these would be reported in my management letter, together with any problems I have found in my tests. If I find a lot of problems, I would check more items and I would report them to the chief accountant, financial director or managing director.

(b)   (i)   The reason why two people should open the mail is that this transaction involves custody of the asset (ie, cheques) and recording the transaction (ie, recording cash received). If opening of the mail was carried out by a single person, there would be no division of duties between these two transactions, so there would be a weakness in the system of internal control which could allow a fraud to take place (or an error to be undetected). By having two people open the mail, one checks the work of the other (ie, a system of internal check), and provided there is no collusion, this should prevent fraud and error taking place. Ideally, neither of these two people should be the cashier.

       (ii)   The audit work I would perform in checking from the opening of the mail to banking of the cheques would include:

— I would attend the opening of the mail as a surprise. Two people, independent of the cashier and sales accounting department should open the mail. The cheques received should be listed and the total calculated. A copy of the list and the cheques should be handed to the cashier, and the second copy of the list should be filed (separately from the cashier).

— I would obtain a copy of this list and check that the cheques are entered in the cash book and subsequently banked by the cashier.

— There should be evidence that a responsible official periodically test checks the lists of cheques received to the cash book.

— The total of the cash received for the day as recorded in the cash book should be entered on the paying-in slip, and the paying-in slip should be stamped by the bank on the same day or the day after the cheques have been received. I would check to the bank statement that this sum has been credited to the bank statement on either the same day as the cheques were paid in or shortly afterwards (ie, within two banking days). If there are any delays in banking the cash, it indicates there may be a teeming and lading fraud, which I would have to investigate.

— I would check a further sample of days' cash received, starting from the list of cheques received to the entry in the cash book and the date stamped by the bank on the paying-in slip. This sample would be spread throughout the company's year. A check of the bank reconciliation at a recent month end should ensure that no teeming and lading fraud is taking place (ie, cash received on the last day of the month should be credited by the bank within two or three banking days).

(c)   (i)   The reasons why credit notes are issued include the following:

— When the goods are returned.

— When there is a 'short delivery' (all the goods on the invoice are not received by the customer). Credit is given for the goods not delivered.

— When the invoice charges the goods at too high a price. Credit is given for the difference.

— Any other errors on the sales invoice (eg, incorrect VAT charged, or computation errors)

— Where the goods are faulty. Sometimes this may result in the goods being returned, but in other cases an allowance may be given to compensate the customer for the goods not being perfect.

— Additional charges made on the invoice which should not have been made or are more than agreed (eg, charges for carriage when there should be no carriage charge).

(ii) In checking the authorisation of credit notes and ensuring they are issued for valid reasons, I would:

- ascertain and record the system. I would expect all credit notes to be authorised, as described in the question. There should be sufficient controls in the system to prevent fraudulent or unauthorised credit notes from being issued;

- select a sample of credit notes from a number of places in the system. The credit notes should cover the company's financial year and a greater proportion of large value credit notes would be checked. The credit notes would be selected from:

    - the sales ledger (with a computerised sales ledger this would be from entries on customers' statements);

    - the note acknowledging return of goods by the customer, which is raised by the department receiving these goods (it may be the dispatch department). This check would ensure that credit is given for all goods returned;

    - a sample of credit notes which are filed in sequential number order;

    - a sample of credit notes listed in the sales day book.

For all these credit notes, I would check that they have been authorised by an appropriate responsible official, as described in the question. For the return of goods, I would follow through from the goods returned note to the credit note and check that the quantities on the credit note agree with the goods returned, and the price per unit agrees with the original sales invoice (or is less than the sales invoice figure if the customer returns the goods damaged). I would note any returns of goods where no credit note has been issued (as a provision should be included in the accounts if the credit note has not been issued before the year end). Also, if there is a long delay between the return of goods and issue of the credit note, there could be cut-off errors at the year end (this point would be included in the audit working papers for consideration at the final audit).

For most of the other items, I would check the company's records of correspondence with the customer. Ideally, there should be a letter from the customer as this would provide good audit evidence. If there are only written notes by the company's staff, this is weaker evidence and it could be fraudulent (eg, the company could raise a credit note for a valid debt, and an employee misappropriate cash received from the customer). This evidence would be more reliable if it comes from more than one member of the company's staff (eg, a member of the sales staff and the credit controller).

Considering the points raised in part (c)(i) of this answer, the evidence I would expect to see would comprise:

- where there is a short delivery, there should be a letter from the customer and evidence that not all the goods were received. The stock records may indicate that not all the goods were sent, and a claim should be made against the carrier if that company has lost some of the goods;

- where the charge is at too high a price, I would check the correct price to the company's authorised price list;

- where there is an error on the invoice, I would inspect it and consider whether it is reasonable;

- where the goods are faulty, there should be a letter from the customer, and there may be a report from an employee of Lenton Textiles which confirms that the goods are faulty or damaged;

- where there are unauthorised charges on the invoice, I would check that they should not have been made.

Based on this work I would assess the strengths of the system for issuing credit notes. I would report any weaknesses to management.

Did you answer the question?

Note that the examiner's answer to part (c) is much longer than you would be expected to produce in the exam. The important point is to list at least 5 or 6 reasons why credit notes might be issued, and to list at least 4 or 5 audit steps in part (ii).

---

36 (Answer 4 of examination)

Examiner's comments and marking guide

Question 4: examined candidates on matters for an auditor to consider before being appointed a company's auditor, and the letter of engagement. Most answers to this question were good.

In part (a), on being appointed an auditor, many candidates listed a large number of 'auditor independence' issues, but they failed to consider other matters. Candidates gain more marks by considering a wide range of points.

The answers to part (b), on the letter of engagement, were quite good. Some candidates wrote out a letter of engagement when the question only asked them for the main contents of the letter. Candidates were not penalised for this, but it would have taken more time and may have restricted the time they had available to answer the other questions.

			Marks
(a)		Matters to consider before accepting audit appointment and statutory and ethical matters	
		Generally 1 mark a point up to a maximum of	11
(b)	(i)	Why an auditor should send a letter of engagement	
	(ii)	Contents of letter of engagement	
		Generally 1 mark a point up to a maximum of	9
Total			20

Step by step answer plan

Step 1 Read the question again and make sure that you focus on precisely what is required.

Step 2 This is a standard question on appointment of an auditor and engagement letters. It is important to deal with all the aspects in the question in part (a): investigations, statutory matters, ethical matters. The purpose of an engagement letter is principally to avoid misunderstandings between the client and auditor. Knowledge of the example letter at the end of SAS 140 would be useful in part (b).

Step 3 Only when you are confident that you are about to answer the question that has been set, should you start writing.

The examiner's answer

(a) The matters I would consider before accepting appointment as the company's auditor would include:

   (i) I assume that I am a member of the Association of Chartered Certified Accountants, I hold a practising certificate and am a registered auditor. Also, I should have adequate professional indemnity insurance cover. If this applies, I have the basic qualifications to be auditor of Melton Manufacturing Ltd.

   (ii) I would try to determine the reason for the change in auditor. The question says that the directors believe they do not receive a cost effective service from the existing auditor. However, there may be problems with the level of the audit fee and the existing auditor may want to qualify his audit report (which the directors are trying to prevent).

(iii)   I would obtain copies of previous years' audited accounts. If the audit report is qualified, it indicates that the audit has a higher than normal risk. From these accounts I would assess whether the company is having going concern problems (by calculating appropriate ratios, such as the gearing ratio) and if there could be weaknesses in the system of internal control (because the company is small or has a dominant proprietor). With a manufacturing company there are likely to be more problems with the valuation of stock, but there would be less risks over sales and purchases as they are likely to be on credit. There could be problems with obsolete plant and machinery.

(iv)   I would consider the size of the audit client and the fee compared with my other clients. The Guide to Professional Ethics says that an auditor's independence may be compromised if the fee from a single client exceeds 15% of the total practice income (10% for listed and other public interest companies).

(v)   This is not a public company, but for a public company the auditor should not normally both prepare and audit the financial statements. For other companies, if the auditor both prepares and audits the financial statements, it is desirable that these are carried out by different staff.

(vi)   I would consider whether I am sufficiently independent of the client. In particular, I should not hold shares in the client company (if I do hold shares, I should dispose of them before I become auditor). Also, I should not be an employee or a director of the client company, I must not have any close family relationship with any directors of the company (eg, being a brother/sister, mother/father or son/daughter of any of the directors), and I must not have any close business relationships with the company or its directors (eg, I must not be in partnership with any of the directors of the company, or own a business jointly with them).

(vii)   I would check that no conflict of interest arises through me accepting appointment as auditor of Melton Manufacturing.

(viii)   I would consider the level of fee I would charge. It should be sufficient to provide an acceptable return, as an inadequate fee could result in insufficient audit work being carried out and thus increase the audit risk.

(ix)   I would consider whether I have the experience to audit the company, and staff to perform the detailed audit work. If I do not audit any manufacturing companies, I may not have the skills to audit the stock satisfactorily. Thus, I would have to refuse the audit appointment.

(x)   I would consider whether I would require staff with special skills or external specialists to carry out certain aspects of the audit.

Some of the statutory and ethical matters have been considered above. However, the additional ethical matters I would have to consider include:

(i)   I would ask the client if I can communicate with the retiring auditor. If the client refuses, I should refuse the audit appointment.

(ii)   I would contact the retiring auditor and ask if there are any matters he wants to bring to my attention which would influence my decision on whether to accept appointment as auditor.

(iii)   If the company has not paid the retiring auditor's fees, I can still accept appointment as auditor. However, this indicates that the company is a 'bad payer', so I may decide not to accept the appointment.

Concerning the statutory responsibilities, the additional matters would include:

(i)   The company must give special notice (at least 21 days) to hold a meeting at which an ordinary resolution is proposed to appoint me as auditor. Only a 50% majority is required to pass this resolution. The company must send a notice of the meeting and a copy of the resolution to the retiring auditor, who has a right to attend and speak at the meeting.

(ii)   I must ensure that this resolution has been passed by the meeting before I start my audit work.

On these points about statutory appointment of the auditor, it is apparent that I would have already agreed to act as auditor before the meeting (subject to the meeting agreeing my appointment).

Did you answer the question?

Note the large number of investigations listed by the examiner in his answer to part (a). With 11 marks on offer you should be aiming to list at least that number of points in your answer.

(b)   (i)   The main reason why it is important that an auditor should send a letter of engagement to the client is that it explains the duties of the auditor and the contract which exists between the auditor and the client. If no letter of engagement is sent, disputes and misunderstandings may arise about the auditor's duties.

The letter of engagement explains that the auditor's duties are governed by the Companies Act 1985, and cannot be limited by the company. Also, the auditor reports to the shareholders (and not the directors) whether the financial statements show a true and fair view.

Further, it explains the directors' responsibilities, particularly that they are responsible for preparing the financial statements (although the auditor can prepare the financial statements for the directors, if requested) and for ensuring there are proper systems of internal control to prevent or detect errors, irregularities and fraud.

The auditors are only responsible for giving an opinion on the financial statements. They are not responsible for detecting small errors and fraud, but their audit procedures should have a reasonable expectation of detecting material errors and fraud.

Finally, the engagement letter explains that the fee is based on the time spent by partners and staff in carrying out the audit.

It is important that the auditor obtains the directors' agreement of the letter of engagement and that a revised letter is sent when there are significant changes to the terms of the existing letter.

(ii)   The main matters in a letter of engagement include:

–   The letter is written on the auditor's headed paper and is addressed to the directors of Melton Manufacturing Ltd.

–   It states the directors' responsibilities for keeping proper accounting records and for preparing financial statements which show a true and fair view. The directors must make available to the auditor all the records he may reasonably require, and provide answers to the auditor's questions.

–   The auditor has a statutory duty to report on whether the financial statements show a true and fair view and comply with the Companies Act 1985.

–   Normally, the auditor would report if the financial statements do not comply in any material respect with accounting standards (SSAPs and FRSs).

–   The audit is conducted in accordance with Auditing Standards.

–   Oral or written representations may be asked from the directors concerning various matters in the financial statements.

–   The directors are responsible for preventing and detecting irregularities and fraud. The audit procedures would be designed so there is a reasonable expectation of detecting material misstatements in the financial statements. However, the audit should not be relied upon for detecting all irregularities and fraud which may exist.

–   As auditor, we may provide additional services, such as:

- preparing financial statements;
- lodging returns with the Registrar of Companies;
- investigating irregularities and fraud;
- providing taxation services.

- Fees are based on the time spent by partners and staff and on the levels of skill and responsibility involved.

The letter ends by saying that it remains effective until it is replaced. and it asks the directors to agree the terms of the letter in writing.

Did you answer the question?

Note that the examiner has not reproduced an example letter of engagement in part (b) (ii); the question asks only for a brief description of the contents of such a letter.

---

37   (Answer 5 of examination)

Examiner's comments and marking guide

Question 5: required candidates to consider the accounting treatment of the closure of a factory, and the audit of capital commitments. This was the least popular question on the paper, and most of the answers to this question were poor.

The answers to part (a) on whether the closure was an adjusting or non adjusting event were often weak, and the results imply that candidates have a limited knowledge of the auditing aspects of this accounting standard.

The answers to part (b) on auditing the closure cost were slightly better, although many were very short. Stronger candidates gained credit for referring to certain FRS 3 aspects of the closure, namely, including trading relating to the closure under 'discontinued operations' in the profit and loss account.

The answers to part (c), on capital commitments, were very poor. Only a very small number of candidates knew what capital commitments are. Although this is not a central matter in published accounts, it does appear in all full sets of company accounts. Also, it indicates the capital expenditure plans of the company.

		Marks
(a)	Closure of factory - adjusting or non-adjusting?	
	Generally 1 mark a point up to a maximum of	5
(b)	Audit of cost of closure of factory	
	Generally 1 mark a point up to a maximum of	10
(c)	(i) Disclosure of contingencies	1
	(ii) Audit of contingencies	
	Generally 1 mark a point up to a maximum of	4
Total		20

Step by step answer plan

Step 1   Read the question again and make sure that you focus on precisely what is required.

Step 2   This question requires knowledge of the distinction in SSAP 17 between adjusting and non-adjusting post balance sheet events.

Step 3   Part (b) is worth 10 marks so deserves close attention. The question tells you the three items that make up the loss arising from the closure, so the approach in your answer should be to discuss each of these items in turn.

Step 4 Part (c) demonstrates more overlap between this syllabus and the accounting syllabus. This is not surprising since the auditor has to give an opinion on whether the financial statements comply with the Companies Act 1985.

Step 5 Only when you are confident that you are about to answer the question that has been set, should you start writing.

The examiner's answer

(a) The Appendix of SSAP 17 *Accounting for post balance sheet events* says that closing a significant part of the trading activities is a non-adjusting event if this was not anticipated at the year end. However, it does not provide any guidance in defining the word 'anticipated'.

I would look at the following documents and consider the following matters to decide whether this item should be treated as an adjusting or a non-adjusting post balance sheet event:

(i) I would discuss the matter with the directors and senior management. This will include considering the principal points required to come to a conclusion as to whether the item should be an adjusting or a non-adjusting post balance sheet event (ie, was the closure anticipated before the year end).

(ii) I would inspect the board minutes. If the closure decision has been made before the year end, it is an adjusting event. However, if this decision was made after the year end I would have to perform more work.

(iii) I would look at management reports. If they suggest the decision to close the factory was made before the year end, then it is probably an adjusting event.

(iv) I would look at the monthly accounts of the factory. If it has been making a loss for some time before the year end, and the situation does not change significantly after the year end, then it is probably an adjusting event.

(v) If the change from profits to losses occurred after the year end, then it is probably a non-adjusting event.

(vi) If there has been the loss of a major customer after the year end, which makes the factory non viable, then this is probably a non-adjusting event.

Based on these investigations, I would decide whether the item should be treated as an adjusting or a non-adjusting event. As there is a relatively short time between the year end and my audit, it is probable that this item is an adjusting event. If I come to the conclusion that the item is an adjusting event, but the company has included it as a non-adjusting event, I would ask the directors to amend the financial statements and if they refuse I would have to qualify my audit report (with an 'except for' qualification similar to example 7 of SAS 600 *Auditors' reports on financial statements*).

Did you answer the question?
Note how the examiner's answer to part (a) concentrates on listing audit steps (ie, answering the question) rather than spending a long time discussing aspects of SSAP 17.

(b) I would obtain a schedule from the company of the costs of closure included in the financial statements. Then I would look at each of the three costs listed in the question.

For redundancy costs, I would:

(i) identify the employees who are being made redundant, and confirm this to any other supporting information. For instance, if all the employees at the factory are to be made redundant, then the names of the employees would be agreed to the factory's payroll (or personnel records). I would obtain evidence if any of the employees are to be transferred to another part of the business, when they should not be part of the redundancy cost;

(ii)   determine the basis on which the redundancy payment is to be made. Normally, this is based on the number of years' service and the final gross pay. I would ask about the progress of negotiations on the basis for determining the redundancy pay, and I would consider whether the company's proposals are likely to be accepted by the employees;

(iii)   test check the calculation of the redundancy costs, by checking the employee's gross pay to the payroll (or personnel records) and the length of service to the personnel records. If some employees have been made redundant at the time of my check, I would check that the amount paid to them agrees with the amount on the company's schedule;

(iv)   check if any of the employees being made redundant have a contract with the company, which would increase their redundancy payment. If this is happening, I would check that the redundancy cost in my schedule is correct.

For the loss on fixed assets, I would ask the company for a schedule of the items which would be sold or scrapped, and the associated costs. No amount would be included in the provision where there is likely to be a profit on disposal. It is not clear from the Accounting Standards whether anticipated profits can be offset against expected losses, but I would consider whether the total loss on disposal of the fixed assets is reasonable. For the land and buildings:

(i)   if they have been sold by the time of my investigations, I would be able to calculate the profit or loss exactly, as the disposal proceeds and costs would be known;

(ii)   if they are not yet sold, I would obtain details of the land and buildings and their balance sheet value;

(iii)   then, I would obtain the estimated disposal proceeds. These estimates are likely to be more reliable if they are by an independent valuer, rather than the directors of Eastwood Engineering;

(iv)   from this information, and my experience with other clients, I would consider whether the estimated sale proceeds are reasonable (this would be after selling costs);

(v)   I would check the calculation of the profit or loss on disposal, and note any significant difference in my schedule of unadjusted errors.

For the fixtures and fittings, plant and machinery, and computers, I would obtain a schedule of their balance sheet value and their estimated disposal proceeds. The fixtures and fittings would either be sold as part of the building, when the loss would have been determined as described above for land and buildings. Otherwise, the fixtures and fittings would probably have a low value, and, provided the company's estimate is prudent, I would consider the figure to be reasonable (the fixtures and fittings may have no value).

If plant and machinery is specialised, it would probably be worth only scrap value, so the company's schedule should have a low value. Where the estimated disposal proceeds of the plant are significant, I would ask the company for evidence of its value. If any plant has been sold at the date of my investigations, I would check the sale proceeds to the figure on the company's schedule. Similar checks would be made for computers. Most computer equipment which is more than a few years old probably has negligible value. From these investigations I would check the profit or loss on disposal and compare it with my estimates.

For the motor cars, I would obtain details of them (ie, the model, its age, mileage and condition) and test check the estimated proceeds to Glass's Guide or similar publication (which gives the value of second-hand cars). For other motor vehicles I may be able to check their value to similar documents, or to advertisements in local newspapers. If any of the vehicles have been sold by the time of my investigations, I would check the actual proceeds to the company's estimates. From these investigations I would check the profit or loss on disposal and compare it with my estimates.

For the loss on the value of stock, I would obtain a schedule from the company of the stock which is likely to be sold for less than cost. From sales of this stock since 31 March 1995, I would check that the estimate of the sale proceeds is reasonable. For much of this stock, its value would be very small (ie, close to scrap value). Where a high value is attributed to an item of stock I would discuss this with the company's management and consider whether their representations are reasonable. In addition to these checks, I would look at all the factory's stock at 31 March 1995, and consider whether any stock has been omitted from the company's schedule of obsolete stock. I would concentrate my investigations on high value stock, and check that this stock is either likely to be sold or has been included in the list of stock which would be scrapped.

Based on these investigations, I would consider whether the company's estimate of the closure provision is reasonable (and not materially misstated).

(c) (i) The Companies Act 1985 Schedule 4, para 50(3) requires companies to disclose in their financial statements the aggregate amount or estimated amount of contracts for capital expenditure so far as not provided for.

   (Tutorial note: until 1996, in respect of capital commitments a company had to disclose both

- the amount of contracts for capital expenditure, so far as not provided for, and

- the amount of capital expenditure authorised by the directors which has not been contracted for.

   However the second requirement was deleted by Statutory Instrument SI 1996/189, so now only the first amount has to be disclosed.*)*

(ii) The audit work I will carry out in verifying capital commitments will include the following:

- I will obtain a schedule of capital commitments from the company.

- I will check the authorisations for capital expenditure in the board minutes before the year end to the schedule, and I will note any items authorised in the board minutes which are not included in capital commitments.

- I will check purchase orders for capital equipment issued before the year end and check that they are included in items contracted for and that they are included at the correct value. Where the fixed asset has been received before the year end, it will not be included in capital commitments.

- Some items of capital expenditure may be in progress at the year end (eg, building a new factory). In this case, I will check that the amount included in capital commitments is the total amount authorised less the amount included in fixed assets at the year end.

- I will compare this year's capital commitments with last year and consider whether the change is reasonable, and that the same basis was used. The value of capital commitments is likely to fluctuate, as it will be affected by the general level of capital expenditure and any major projects (eg, construction of new buildings).

   Based on this work, I will decide whether capital commitments are fairly stated in the financial statements.

38   (Answer 6 of examination)

Examiner's comments and marking guide

Question 6: examined candidates on the Caparo case and its implications for audit quality.

The answers to part (a) were quite good. However, a number of candidates seem unaware of this important case. Some candidates used this part to demonstrate their knowledge of the historical development of auditors' liability. However, they gained very little credit for this, as the question was asking about the Caparo case in particular.

The answers to part (b) were weak, and many answers included points which should have been in part (c) of their answer. Ignoring other factors, it is probable that auditors' work would deteriorate as the Caparo judgement reduces auditors' risk compared with what existed before the case was decided. Many candidates were reluctant to suggest that auditors' standards may deteriorate, but economic theory would suggest that this would happen.

The answers to part (c) were better, and the question gave the better candidates the opportunity to list a large number of points.

		Marks
(a)	Decision in the *Caparo* case Generally 1 mark a point up to a maximum of	3
(b)	Will *Caparo* result in a deterioration of audit standards? Generally 1 mark a point up to a maximum of	6
(c)	Factors which will improve audit standards Generally 1 mark a point up to a maximum of	11
	Total	20

Step by step answer plan

Step 1   Read the question again and make sure that you focus on precisely what is required.

Step 2   The Caparo case is central to any discussion of auditor liability in the UK. Part (b) invites discussion of quality; SAS 240 will help you here and in part (c), which combines independence and quality.

Step 3   Only when you are confident that you are about to answer the question that has been set, should you start writing.

The examiner's answer

(a)   The **Caparo** decision limits the persons who can sue the auditor for negligence to the company and the shareholders as a body. No other person can successfully sue the auditor – this includes potential shareholders who decided to buy shares on the basis of the audited accounts, existing shareholders who purchased additional shares, banks and other suppliers, customers, employees etc. The company would sue the auditor under the law of contract, but the shareholders would sue the auditor under the law of tort.

Essentially, only persons who have paid the auditor a fee can sue him for negligence. The company pays the audit fee, and the shareholders as a body can be considered to represent the company, and thus they are able to sue the auditor. Also, the auditor reports to the shareholders as a class and not individually.

> **Did you answer the question?**
>
> Note that part (a) only offers 3 marks, so don't write a long essay wasting time.

(b)   The **Caparo** decision may lead to a deterioration in the quality of audit work, as it reduces the auditor's risk of being sued for negligence. From an economic point of view, it could be argued that auditors balance risk against reward. If auditors reduced their risk to zero, they would have to check a very large proportion of transactions, the audit cost would be enormous and the auditor would make a loss. At the other extreme, if the auditor did no work, the profit (before negligence claims) would be large, but the risk of a negligence claim would be very large. So, an auditor should carry out sufficient work to reduce the risk of a negligence claim to an acceptable minimum. Economic theory would suggest that an auditor would stop performing more work when the cost of an additional hour's work is greater than the reduction in the potential negligence claims against the auditor. However, it appears that auditors tend to be risk averse and perform more work than this optimum position. Two factors tend to mean that auditors perform more work than economic considerations would suggest. First, the auditor would need to check all material items in the financial statements to come to an opinion on the financial statements, and the amount of work needed to do this is probably more than pure economic considerations would suggest. Secondly, negligence claims adversely affect the auditor's reputation, so the auditor would want to minimise the risk of these happening. The negligence claims may lead to a loss of work and the auditor being unsuccessful in obtaining new work, and these would adversely affect the profitability of the audit firm. As a further point, negligence claims result in considerable time being spent by partners and senior staff in defending their position, which is both time-consuming and reduces the time partners can spend on existing business, developing the practice and obtaining new clients.

Nevertheless, if the auditor perceives that the risk of a legal claim is reduced (because of the limitations of the parties who can sue, which resulted from the **Caparo** decision), then it is probable that he would reduce the audit work until the risk of being sued returns to its former level.

So, I would agree with the contention that the **Caparo** decision (on its own) is likely to lead to a reduction in the quality of auditors' work.

(c)   However, there are a number of recent developments, and other measures which are likely to mean that the quality of audit work is improving. These include:

(i)   The Companies Act 1989 introduced Recognised Supervisory Bodies (RSBs) and registration of auditors. The monitoring units of the RSBs are required to visit registered auditors and check their work. The Association of Chartered Certified Accountants is a RSB and its monitoring unit aims to visit every registered auditor within a period of five years. These visits are likely to increase the standard of audit work, and unsatisfactory work can lead to disciplinary action including withdrawal of the practising certificate.

(ii)   Auditing Standards provide a measure for acceptable standards of auditing and assist the auditor in deciding which matters should be considered when performing a particular task (eg, composing a letter of engagement, preparing an audit report). It seems probable that Auditing Standards improve the quality of audit work.

(iii)   The extended audit report introduced in SAS 600 provides the user of accounts with more information about the audit process and the responsibilities of the directors and auditors. It has probably led to a reduction in the audit expectation gap.

(iv)   The Companies Act specifies requirements concerning the independence and qualifications of a statutory auditor. Also, there are ethical rules issued by the Association of Chartered Certified Accountants (ACCA), which are tighter than those specified by the Companies Act. For instance, auditors should not beneficially hold shares in clients and the audit fee should not be more than 15% of the practice income (10% for listed and public interest companies).

(v)   The Cadbury Report and its recommendation that all listed companies should have an audit committee comprising non-executive directors should assist in the independence of the auditor and contribute to an improvement in the quality of audit work.

(vi)   The ACCA requires registered auditors to undertake a specified number of hours of continued professional education each year, in order to keep up to date.

(vii)   Auditors try to minimise legal claims. This is for a number of reasons. First, legal claims bring bad publicity to the audit practice which damages its reputation and can lead to a loss of existing and potential new clients. Claims against professional indemnity insurance (PII) are likely to lead to increased premiums in the future. Claims against the firm result in considerable time being spent by partners in ascertaining facts relating to the claim (eg, inspecting audit working papers, interviewing staff and obtaining legal advice) and then in defending themselves against the negligence claim. This reduces the time available for partners to service clients, to obtain new clients and to develop the business.

(viii)   Firms are introducing and refining their quality control procedures. This is to reduce the risk of claims against them. Good planning and documentation of audit work reduces the risk of material errors and fraud being undetected, and thus improves the quality of the audit.

(ix)   It appears that the public's expectations of auditors are increasing, and there is greater publicity of examples of material errors being undetected by auditors (eg, BCCI, Maxwell, Barlow Clowes and Polly Peck). Auditors want to avoid such adverse publicity, and this would result in an improvement in the standard of their work. Serious problems revealed in the examples above would make auditors more careful in similar situations. For instance, after Polly Peck auditors would be more careful to consider whether bank balances are recoverable, and the problems with Robert Maxwell would make auditors more careful when there is a dominant chief executive.

(x)   In the UK there has been publicity about the increased number and value of claims against the 'big six' firms of auditors. Auditors will perceive they have an increased risk of being sued, so they will take measures to improve the quality of their work to reduce the risk of being sued.

Did you answer the question?

Note that the examiner has listed 10 separate points in his answer to part (c). You should aim for 10 or 11 separate points to earn the 11 marks on offer.

DECEMBER 1995 QUESTIONS

Section A - ALL THREE questions are compulsory and MUST be attempted

39   (Question 1 of examination)

You are carrying out the audit of Ruddington plc for the year ended 30 September 1995, which is a wholesaler of microcomputers, accessories and software used with microcomputers. The accessories include printers, scanners, and additional disk drives. You have been asked by the senior in charge of the audit to identify stock which may be worth less than cost and check it is valued in accordance with SSAP 9 *Stocks and long-term contracts*.

You are concerned about the value of one of the company's products, Alpha, and you have obtained the following information on purchases and sales of the product around the year end:

Alpha Date	Purchases units	Purchase price per unit £	Sales units	Selling price per unit £
2. 9.95	100	500	60	530
16. 9.95	60	503	80	528
30. 9.95	70	506	50	526
14.10.95	50	509	70	524
28.10.95	80	512	50	522
11.11.95	40	515	40	520
Stock at 30.9.95	150 units			

The purchases and sales are for the two weeks ended on each of the above dates (ie, 70 units were purchased in the two weeks ended 30 September and 50 units were sold in the same period). You should assume that all sales and purchases in each two week period were at the same price per unit.

Your investigations have revealed the following relationship of expenses to sales:

(a)   selling and marketing costs comprise 3% of sales value in total
(b)   distribution costs are 2% of sales value
(c)   administration expenses are 7% of sales value.

Stock is valued in accordance with SSAP 9 *Stocks and long-term contracts* at the lower of cost and net realisable value on a first-in, first-out basis.

You are required to:

(a)   Calculate, to the nearest £, the value of Alpha at 30 September 1995:

    (i)   at cost
    (ii)   at net realisable value
    (iii)   the value to be included in the financial statements in accordance with SSAP 9.

(5 marks)

(b)   Describe the audit work you will carry out to identify stock which may be worth less than cost.

(8 marks)

(c)   Describe the audit work you will carry out to check that the company's estimate of net realisable value has been determined correctly for the stock identified in part (b) above.

(7 marks)
(Total: 20 marks)

Note: You should assume:

(a)   stock quantities have been counted accurately at the stocktake
(b)   there are no purchases or sales cut-off errors
(c)   there is no long-term contract work in progress.

---

40   (Question 2 of examination)

Your firm is the auditor of Motor Components plc, which manufactures electrical components which it sells to car manufacturers and retailers. It has a number of factories, at different geographical locations, which manufacture the components, and all accounting information is kept on a mainframe computer at the head office. Access to the computer is through terminals at head office and factories. Information from the factories is transmitted to the computer at head office through the national telephone system, and the factories can retrieve information from the head office computer through the national telephone system (eg, British Telecom in the UK).

You have been asked by the partner in charge of the audit to consider the controls which should be used to permit only authorised input and retrieval of data from the main computer by staff at head office and at the factories.

In part (b) of the question:

(1)   retrieval of information involves inspecting data on files without amending them

(2)   input of transaction data involves input of invoices and credit notes to update the purchase ledger, or hours worked to calculate employees' wages and deductions

(3)   standing data files contain details which are changed infrequently, such as details of suppliers, and employee names and wage rates.

You are required to:

(a)   Describe the controls which can be used to control access to the main computer from terminals at head office and consider the effectiveness of each of them.

(6 marks)

(b)   Consider and contrast the controls which should be exercised over:

(i)   the purchases system, and
(ii)   the wages system, for:

-    retrieval of information
-    input of transaction data
-    changes to standing data files.

(8 marks)

(c)   Consider the additional controls which should be instigated (in addition to those described in part (a) above) to prevent unauthorised access to the computer through the national telephone system.

(6 marks)
(Total: 20 marks)

Note: in part (b), 4 marks are allocated to part (i) and 4 marks to part (ii).

---

41   (Question 3 of examination)

You have been asked by the manager in charge of the audit of Spondon plc to consider and describe various aspects of carrying out a debtors' circularisation at its year end of 31 October 1995. The company sells all its products on credit, and the draft accounts show an annual turnover of £25 million and year end debtors of £5.3 million. Your tests of control on the sales system have shown that there is a satisfactory division of duties in the sales system and only minor errors were found in the tests of control.

You are required to:

(a)   Consider the reliability of a debtors' circularisation in providing audit evidence and in verifying the value of year end debtors.   **(7 marks)**

(b)   Describe the work you will carry out in auditing the replies to the debtors' circularisation where:

   (i)   the debtor disagrees the balance and provides a different balance   **(6 marks)**

   (ii)   the debtor does not reply to the circularisation. In answering this part you should consider

      -   the techniques you would use to verify the existence of the debtor

      -   the investigations you would carry out to check the recoverability of the debt on the sales ledger.   **(7 marks)**
      (Total: 20 marks)

Section B - TWO questions ONLY to be attempted

42   (Question 4 of examination)

The following equation can be used to determine audit risk:

$$AR = IR \times CR \times DR$$

where: AR   =   Audit risk
   IR   =   Inherent risk
   CR   =   Control risk
   DR   =   Detection risk

The partner in charge of the audit of Calverton Wholesale Ltd has asked you to consider the effect of audit risk on your audit approach to compliance and substantive tests.

He has asked you to consider whether it is more efficient in terms of audit time to perform compliance and substantive tests or substantive tests alone. He has supplied you with the following information for audit tests of the purchases system of Calverton Wholesale Ltd:

Required level of audit risk:

AR = 5%

Inherent risk:

IR = 90%

If no compliance tests are performed:
CR = 100%

If compliance tests are performed:
CR = 30%.

To achieve the required level of audit risk, it is necessary to check the following number of items in the compliance and substantive tests, and find no errors:

	No compliance tests	Compliance tests
Compliance tests	0	40
Substantive tests	130	45

The partner estimates the following times (in hours) are required to perform the tests:

	Compliance tests	Substantive tests
Fixed time	2.5	1.5
Variable time per item	0.3	0.25

You are required to:

(a)   Provide a definition and explanation of the terms:

    (i)   Audit risk
    (ii)   Inherent risk
    (iii)   Control risk
    (iv)   Detection risk.   **(6 marks)**

(b)   Calculate the time required to audit the purchases system:

    (i)   using both compliance and substantive tests
    (ii)   using only substantive tests

    and state which procedure is more time efficient   **(3 marks)**

(c)   Consider the circumstances when it is appropriate to use only a substantive approach in an audit and when a combination of compliance and substantive tests should be used.

    (4 marks)

(d)   Discuss the advantages and limitations of using the risk based approach when auditing the financial statements of companies.   **(7 marks)**
    (Total: 20 marks)

Note: in Statements of Auditing Standards (SASs), Compliance Tests are called Tests of Control, and Substantive Tests are called Substantive Procedures.

43   (Question 5 of examination)

A Statement of Auditing Standards has been issued on 'Quality control for audit work'. The partner in charge of your audit firm has asked how the overall quality of the work carried out within the firm can best be monitored and maintained.

You are required to:

(a)   Explain the reasons why it is important for audit firms to maintain a high quality of audit work.   **(4 marks)**

(b)   Describe the quality control procedures which should be implemented by the audit firm over:

    (i)   standardisation of audit working papers, and
    (ii)   recruitment and training of audit staff.   **(9 marks)**

(c)   Explain how 'cold reviews' can be carried out, and describe how these reviews can enhance the quality of audit work.   **(7 marks)**
    (Total: 20 marks)

Note: 'Cold reviews' are periodic reviews of a sample of the firm's audit files by independent reviewers from within the firm.

---

44   (Question 6 of examination)

Your firm is the auditor of Burton Housing Ltd which is a small charity and housing association. Its principal asset is a large freehold building which contains a restaurant, accommodation for 50 young people, and recreational facilities.

The charity is controlled by a management committee which comprises the voluntary chairman and treasurer, and other voluntary members elected annually. However, day-to-day management is by a chief executive who manages the full-time staff who perform accounting, cleaning, maintenance, housing management and other functions.

You are auditing the company's financial statements for the year ended 31 October 1995. Draft accounts have been prepared by the treasurer from accounting records kept on a microcomputer by the bookkeeper. The partner in charge of the audit has asked you to consider the audit work you would perform on income from rents, and the income and expenditure account of the restaurant.

For income from rents:

(a)   the housing manager allocates rooms to individuals, and this information is sent to the bookkeeper

(b)   each week the bookkeeper posts the rents to each resident's account on the sales ledger. All rooms are let at the same rent

(c)   rents are received from residents by reception staff who are independent of the housing manager and bookkeeper. Reception staff give the rents to the bookkeeper

(d)   the bookkeeper posts cash received for rents to the sales ledger, enters them in the cash book and pays them into the bank

(e)   the housing manager reports voids (ie, rooms unlet) to the management committee.

The restaurant comprises the manager and four staff, who prepare and sell food to residents and other individuals.

Cash takings from the restaurant are recorded on a till, and each day's takings are given to the bookkeeper who records and pays them into the bank. Details of cash takings are recorded on the till roll.

The system for purchasing food comprises:

(a)   the restaurant manager orders the food by sending an order to the supplier

(b)   food received is checked by the restaurant manager

(c)   the restaurant manager authorises purchase invoices, confirming the food has been received

(d)   the bookkeeper posts the purchase invoices to the purchase ledger

(e)   the bookkeeper makes out the cheques to pay the suppliers, which the chief executive signs. The cheques are posted to the purchase ledger and cash book.

The bookkeeper is responsible for paying the wages of staff in the restaurant. The restaurant manager notifies the bookkeeper of any absences of staff.

You should assume that the income and expenditure account of the restaurant includes only:

(1)   income from customers who purchase food
(2)   expenditure on purchasing food and wages of restaurant staff.

You are required to consider the controls which should be in operation and the audit work you will carry out to verify:

(a)   for rents received:

      (i)   recording of rental income on the sales ledger

      (ii)   receipt and recording of rents received from residents

      (iii)   posting of adjustments, credit notes and write off of bad debts on the sales ledger.

(11 marks)

(b)   the income and expenditure account of the restaurant.

(9 marks)

(Total: 20 marks)

ANSWERS TO DECEMBER 1995 EXAMINATION

39 (Answer 1 of examination)

Examiner's comments and marking guide

Question 1: asked candidates to calculate cost and net realisable value in part (a). Part (b) was concerned with finding stock which might be worth less than cost and part (c) asked candidates to describe evidence they would seek to determine net realisable value.

In part (a), many candidates made no attempt at the calculations and many calculated wrong answers. This is very disappointing, as an auditor would not be able to audit a figure in the financial statements if they could not calculate it.

The answers to part (b) were quite good, although more candidates should have related their answer to the business in the question.

Most of the answers to part (c) were weak, if answered at all. Very few candidates provided a satisfactory explanation of how net realisable value of stock would be found.

The topic of auditing the value of stock, particularly determining net realisable value, is very important, and it was very disappointing that there were so few good answers. This question usefully illustrates how stock worth less than cost is found and valued, and candidates should study the model answer. Many candidates did not understand that cost is determined from purchases before the year end, and net realisable value from sales after the year end.

				Marks
(a)	For calculation of cost, NRV and SSAP 9 value			
	(i)	cost	1.5	
	(ii)	net realisable value	3	
	(iii)	lower of cost and NRV	0.5	
			—	5
(b)	Finding stock which may be worth less than cost			
	Generally 1 mark a point up to a maximum of			8
(c)	Estimating and checking net realisable value			
	Generally 1 mark a point up to a maximum of			7
Total				—
				20

Note: in part (a) you should award ½ mark for each item which contributes to cost, and 1 mark to each item which contributes to NRV. If the student gets the total value correct he/she should be given the full mark for that part.

Step by step answer plan

Step 1 Read the question again and make sure that you focus on precisely what is required.

Step 2 This is a standard question on the practical application of SSAP 9. Computer equipment is an example of an area of business where falling prices mean that cost is likely to exceed NRV for some lines of stock.

Step 3 With 8 marks available for part (b), one must list at least 8 audit tests, preferably 10 or 12, to gain all the marks. These tests must refer to the question ie, concern computer equipment, rather than be a general discussion.

Step 4 Part (c) requires an accurate knowledge of the definition of NRV contained in SSAP 9.

Step 5 Only when you are confident that you are about to answer the question that has been set, should you start writing.

The examiner's answer

(a)   **Alpha**

(i)   Stock at cost on a FIFO basis:

Date purchased	Quantity	Price/unit £	Total value £
30.9.95	70	506	35,420
16.9.95	60	503	30,180
2.9.95	20	500	10,000
	150		75,600

(ii)   Net realisable value is the selling price less selling, distribution and marketing expenses. Selling and marketing expenses are 3% of sales value and distribution costs are 2% of sales value, so net realisable value is 95% of the selling price.

Date sold	Quantity	Selling price £	NRV/unit £	NRV £
14.10.95	70	524	497.80	34,846
28.10.95	50	522	495.90	24,795
11.11.95	30	520	494.00	14,820
	150			74,461

(iii)   The valuation according to SSAP 9 is at the lower of cost and net realisable value. As net realisable value is less than cost, the stock will be valued at net realisable value ie, £74,461.

(b)   To find stock which may be worth less than cost, I will:

(i)   obtain a schedule from the company of stock which is worth less than cost and discuss this with the company's management

(ii)   look at last year's audit file and note any items of stock which were thought to be worth less than cost last year (or where I was concerned about their value). If the items are still in stock, and there have been few sales, they will probably have a very low value

(iii)   record stock which is damaged, sub-standard and slow moving (ie, it will be dusty or soiled) at the stocktake. I will ensure that staff counting the stock record such details on the stock sheets. They should produce a more comprehensive list than mine, and, after the stocktake, this stock can be found from the stock sheets

(iv)   inspect the stock records and note items which have been in stock a long time. This period depends on the company's turnover of stock. If the average stock age is 1.5 months, I would note items which have been in stock for more than three months

(v)   ask the company's staff if there is any stock which is slow moving or will be sold at less than cost. Those questioned will include the stores staff and sales staff

(vi)   inspect management reports, sales reports and board minutes and note any stock which is slow moving or may be sold for less than cost

(vii)   consider technical developments and reports in the technical press which comment on products which are becoming obsolete or are having to be sold at a substantial discount. For instance, with IBM compatible computers, most of the sales will be '486' and 'Pentium' processor machines. Computers with '386' processors and slower '486' computers will have to be sold for low prices, which may be less than cost. If '386' computers are being sold at a loss, then '386' related products will be difficult to sell, such as '386' motherboards and maths co-processors. Certain components of computers may have very few sales, such as low capacity hard disk drives (when customers require high capacity ones), low definition video cards and monitors. I will list these items and check whether they will have to be sold for less than cost

(viii)   ask if there are any products where a new model has been introduced. This information can come from management and the technical press. A new, improved, product will make the old product difficult to sell, so it may have to be sold for less than cost. For instance, a new printer may produce a higher definition image and customers will be reluctant to buy the old, inferior, printer. In 1994-95 there has been price competition with the prices of most computers falling (particularly the 'high-end' ones), and there have been substantial reductions in the price of flat-bed scanners

(ix)   ask if there are problems with reliability of any of the products, which will depress sales and lead to high repair claims (these may be covered by the manufacturer's warranty). Inspection of records of repairs will indicate unreliable products

(x)   note any products which are damaged, or have been returned by customers because they are faulty (and the customer has asked for a refund or a replacement product)

(xi)   check sales after the year end to see if any items are being sold at a low price or substantial discounts are being given on products. By inspecting monthly sales figures after the year end, I may highlight stock which is difficult to sell and thus may be worth less than cost

(xii)   as an 'insurance measure', I will check if high value lines of stock are being sold for less than cost after the year end, by checking sales invoices issued after the year end. If sales are at less than cost, there will be a substantial over-valuation if this stock is valued at cost.

(c)   As described in part (a) of the question, net realisable value is the actual or estimated selling price less selling, distribution and marketing expenses. As selling, distribution and marketing expenses are likely to be small, I will check the selling price against cost, and if it is similar to or less than cost, I will determine net realisable value and value the stock at the lower of cost and net realisable value.

The most accurate value of the selling price is the price on the sales invoice which sells the stock after the year end. So, I will note the selling price on sales invoices issued after the year end which sell the stock noted in part (b) above - this will be the actual selling price of this stock.

If some of the year end stock is unsold at the time of my audit checks, I will consider whether the remaining year end stock will be sold at a similar price. Future sales are likely to be at a similar price if sales before and after the year end have been at a reasonable level, but the remaining stock may have to be sold at a lower price if there have been few sales since the year end.

If there have been no sales since the year end, I will look at the selling price on sales invoices before the year end. This will be a guide to the selling price after the year end. However, if the product has been superseded by an improved one around the year end, the selling price after the year end is likely to be lower than the selling price before the year end. As it is apparent that sales of these products are slow, it is probable that there will need to be a price reduction to sell the remaining stock. I will discuss the matter with the company's management, and consider whether their estimate of the selling price after the year end is reasonable. For instance, a 10% to 20% reduction in the selling price would be reasonable, but it would not be realistic to estimate the selling price after the year end at 10% more than the pre year end selling price.

If there have been no recent sales (ie, no sales since some time before the year end), I will ask management their estimate of the product's selling price. I will consider whether it is reasonable. The price this stock will eventually be sold for will probably be very low.

From these investigations I will have obtained the actual or estimated selling price. To determine net realisable value, I will deduct selling, distribution and marketing expenses. If sales are 'normal', I will calculate the ratio of selling, distribution and marketing expenses to sales value. If these costs are 5% of sales value, then the net realisable value of the stock will be 95% of the actual or estimated selling price. I will consider whether any of these items of stock will require additional selling, marketing or distribution expenses, in which case I will deduct the actual costs from the selling price to find net realisable value.

Finally, I will ensure that, for each product, stock is valued at the lower of cost and net realisable value. If I find any significant errors, I will record them on my schedule of unadjusted errors. If there are any significant uncertainties about the stock value, I will include them in my audit file under the heading 'notes for consideration by the manager or partner'.

Did you answer the question?

Note the examiner's approach in parts (b) and (c) to list a large number of separate audit procedures, each with a brief description, rather than to describe a few procedures in detail.

---

40   (Answer 2 of examination)

Examiner's comments and marking guide

Question 2: asked candidates to describe controls over access to computers in part (a). Part (b) asked about controls in purchases and wages systems, and part (c) asked about controls over access to the computer through the national telephone system.

The answers to part (a) were satisfactory. Many candidates would have gained more marks if they had suggested a larger number of controls. Most candidates failed to 'consider the effectiveness of the controls', which the question also required.

The answers to part (b) were varied in standard. In part (i) many candidates suggested much tighter controls over retrieval of information from purchases systems than are necessary. The better answers suggested who should be authorised to access the information or update the files. A number of candidates appeared to be confused about what constituted 'retrieval of information', 'input of transaction data' and 'changes to standing data files'.

Most of the answers to part (c) were very weak. Candidates should look at the model answer to see the variety of points which could be mentioned.

Many of the answers to this question were disappointing, particularly as it uses knowledge they should have gained in studying for paper 5.

			Marks
(a)	Controls over access to computer system from terminals		
	Generally, for each point, ½ mark for the point		
	and ½ mark for the discussion up to a maximum of		6
(b)	(i)	Controls over access to purchases system	
		Generally 1 mark a point up to a maximum of	4
	(ii)	Controls over access to wages system	
		Generally 1 mark a point up to a maximum of	4
(c)	Controls over access through the national telephone system		
	Generally, for each point, ½ mark for the point and		
	½ mark for the discussion up to a maximum of		6
Total			20

Step by step answer plan

Step 1   Read the question again and make sure that you focus on precisely what is required.

Step 2   Part (a) requires a description of controls **and** their effectiveness. Both aspects must be answered. With 6 marks available, we should aim to discuss at least 6 separate controls.

Step 3 The question reminds you what is meant by retrieval, transaction data and standing data for part (b) in case you have forgotten from your Paper 5 studies and suggests the 6 separate aspects to consider ie, retrieval, transaction data and standing data for each of the purchases and the wages system.

Step 4 Part (c) calls for controls in addition to those that you mentioned in part (a), so don't go overboard and list everything that you know on the subject in part (a) and leave yourself nothing to say in part (c). It is in questions like this that the importance of planning before you start writing becomes evident.

Step 5 Only when you are confident that you are about to answer the question that has been set, should you start writing.

The examiner's answer

(a)   The controls which can be used to control access to the main computer include:

(i)   locking the room containing the terminals with a key or code number. The weakness of this control is that anyone with a key or code number could have access to any system on the computer (if there were no other controls). It is unusual to keep terminals in separate rooms, as in most businesses they are kept on the employee's desk

(ii)   locking the terminal. This has a similar weakness to (i) above, but if each terminal has a unique key, the number of people with a key will be restricted, and this will limit the chance of an employee obtaining an unauthorised key. However, many terminals (or keyboards) have the same key, which would negate the effectiveness of this control

(iii)   using a password. With most modern computer systems each employee has a unique password, and the computer looks up a table to check the password is correct, and the table in the computer limits the systems the employee can use. Employees should not leave a note of their password near their terminal, they should not let other employees use their password, and passwords should be changed periodically to reduce the risk of them becoming known to other employees

(iv)   a number of passwords can be used, with the first password allowing the employee access to the main computer system, and additional passwords being required to allow access to each application (eg, the payroll system). The greater the number of passwords, the less is the risk of an unauthorised person accessing the system

(v)   for particular systems, the computer can limit the terminals which can access the system. For instance, in the purchases system, the computer can restrict input of data and changes to standing data files to terminals in the purchases accounting department. However, the system will allow relatively unrestricted access to employees obtaining details of purchase ledger balances. This control will prevent people in departments obtaining information on some matters which are confidential (eg, payroll data) or in areas where they have no need for the information (ie, the goods received department will be prevented access to sales information)

(vi)   the computer should record which terminals and employees are using each system, and this log should be checked periodically by a responsible official (eg, the head of the computer department). The responsible official should investigate cases where access to systems is being made from unauthorised terminals or by unauthorised employees

(vii)   there should be strong controls to prevent any changes to the computer programs used to process accounting data. Only a senior authorised person (eg, the data processing manager) should be allowed to authorise replacement of accounting computer programs. Changes to these programs should occur only when the authorised person uses his/her password to access the system and inputs a secret code to instigate replacement of the accounting computer program. If a department within the company writes the computer programs, it should not be allowed to change the programs used for processing accounting data. Before any changes are made to the computer programs, they should be tested by a separate department to ensure they are free from errors (ie, bugs), and only the data processing manager should authorise changes to the accounting computer programs. If controls over changes to computer programs are weak, it could allow fraudulent changes to be made, or untested changes could occur which corrupt the accounting records

(viii)   access to the system can be limited to the normal working hours of the business. Access to the system outside these hours may either be prohibited or only permitted with authorisation by a senior responsible official (using his/her password). Access to computer systems outside normal working hours may be for an unauthorised purpose.

(b)   (i)   The controls over access to the purchases system will depend on the company's perception of the confidentiality of this information. Considering each of the items in the question:

- Information about purchase ledger balances is relatively unconfidential, so a large range of employees will be allowed to access this information.

- For input of invoices and credit notes, the system should restrict input of this data to the purchases accounting department, by both restricting its input to terminals in the purchases accounting department and only allowing staff in the purchases accounting department to input this data (by only allowing staff with the appropriate password to input this data). Data should be entered into the computer in batches and the total value of invoices input into the computer should be the same as the batch total. Any differences should be investigated. Also, only authorised purchase invoices and credit notes should be entered into the computer. This will require each purchase invoice to be agreed to the purchase order, to the goods received note and be authorised by a responsible official. The computer should sequentially number each batch of data and the purchases accounting department should record batch details in a manual register (ie, batch number, number of items, total value, opening purchase ledger balance and closing purchase ledger balance). In this way it will be possible to detect unauthorised input of transaction data.

- There should be even stronger controls over changes to standing data files containing suppliers' names and addresses. This should be restricted to the purchases accounting department, but, ideally, it should require authorisation by a senior responsible official, such as the purchasing manager. This will apply to addition of new suppliers, amendment of supplier details and deletion of suppliers. Once again, each batch of data should be sequentially numbered, and the computer should print out what has been entered. Ideally, this should be checked before the standing data files are updated. Periodically, the standing data files should be checked with the manual records of suppliers. Suppliers which are no longer used should be deleted, but the system should not allow a supplier to be deleted where there is an outstanding balance on the account.

(ii)   With the wages system the information is much more confidential than with the purchases system. Considering input of each of the types of data:

- There should be much stricter controls over retrieval of information (eg, employees' names and wage rates). Normally, this should be limited to the wages and personnel departments, and there may be even stricter controls over obtaining details of senior employees' salaries. The controls will be by means of passwords for individuals, and only terminals in the personnel and wages department will be permitted to access this data. In addition, it may be decided that senior staff in the accounting department and directors will be allowed to access this information, and department managers may be allowed to obtain details of the salaries or wages of their staff.

- Input of transaction data (ie, the weekly or monthly details for calculating employees' wages) will be restricted to the wages department, by means of passwords and only allowing this function to be performed on wages department terminals.

- The wages department may be allowed to change information on standing data files, but this could create a weakness in the system of internal control, so this may be limited to the manager of the wages department. More junior staff in the wages department may be allowed to change deductions and employees' tax codes, but there should be stricter control over addition of new employees and deletion of employees who have left. Input of details of starters and leavers may be restricted to appropriate staff in the personnel department. Periodically the standing data files of employees' details should be printed out and checked with the appropriate records. These checks should be performed by a member of staff independent of the wages department (and possibly the personnel department, as well). As there are likely to be weaknesses in the division of duties in the wages department, it is important that details on the computer of employees in the wages department should be checked on each occasion (as well as test checking other employees).

Did you answer the question?

Note the structure of the examiner's answer to part (b), precisely following the requirements of the question.

(c)   The additional controls which should be instigated to prevent unauthorised access to the computer through the national telephone system include:

   (i)   ideally, the telephone numbers which gain access to the main computer should be ex-directory to deter 'hackers' from gaining access to the system

   (ii)   private lines can be used to transfer data between the main computer and the factories. These should be more secure than general telephone lines. These lines would be owned by the telephone operator (eg, British Telecom in the UK), but they would only allow transmission of data between the head office and factories

   (iii)   a call-back system can be used. In this system, the individual at the remote site gets the terminal to ring the main computer. The terminal identifies itself to the main computer, and then the line is disconnected. The main computer looks up the user's telephone number on its file and rings that telephone number, and so connects the terminal. If the attempt at access is from an unauthorised source, the computer will not ring that telephone number (as it will not be on its file)

   (iv)   if the data is confidential, it can be encrypted before it is sent to the main computer, and the main computer will translate it to make it meaningful again

   (v)   the central computer may have a number of telephone numbers which can be used for access, and some of these telephone numbers may restrict the systems which can be accessed. For instance, if customers are allowed to access the main computer to obtain stock details and place orders, only those functions may be allowed to be performed using that telephone number

   (vi)   the telephone number of the main computer may be ex-directory and staff at factories will not know the number. Staff at factories will access the main computer using specialised software. Embedded in the software will be the telephone number of the main computer, so the software will not connect to the main computer until the authenticity of the employee has been verified. The software will connect the user to the main computer, using the confidential telephone number. In this way, staff will not know the main computer's telephone number, and it will prevent them gaining access from home, or another unauthorised source

   (vii)   other procedures which are described in the answer to part (a) should also be instigated, including the use of passwords and independent checks of the computer logs (eg, by the data processing manager).

---

41   (Answer 3 of examination)

Examiner's comments and marking guide

Question 3: was concerned with debtors' circularisations.

In part (a) the important word was 'reliability' (of a debtors' circularisation). Many candidates described the procedures for carrying out a debtors' circularisation, which was not what the question required. Some of the answers to this part were quite good.

Most of the answers to part (b)(i) were weak, as candidates failed to divide the difference into 'cash in transit', 'goods in transit' and 'other differences'. Many candidates who did consider these points failed to look into each difference in sufficient depth. The model answer shows what is required. Many candidates suggested asking the client or debtor to find the difference, and a number of candidates incorrectly suggested the audit report should be qualified.

The answers to part (b)(ii) were better, with many candidates making good suggestions to verify the existence of the debtor. The answers on investigating the recoverability of the debt were less good.

This is an important topic in auditing and candidates should ensure that they have a thorough understanding of this topic. Most of the answers to this question were too superficial.

		Marks
(a)	Reliability of debtors' circularisation as audit evidence Generally 1 mark a point up to a maximum of	7
(b)	Audit work in checking replies to a debtors' circularisation:	
	(i) where the balance is disagreed Generally 1 mark a point up to a maximum of	6
	(ii) where the debtor does not reply Up to 4 marks for verifying existence of debtor and up to 3 marks for checking collectability of debtor Generally 1 mark a point up to a maximum of	7
Total		20

Step by step answer plan

Step 1   Read the question again and make sure that you focus on precisely what is required.

Step 2   Part (a) hinges around the word 'reliability'. SAS 400 contains a number of relevant points as to how the reliability of evidence can be assessed; relating these points to a debtors circularisation could offer a way to answer this question.

Step 3   The actual performance of follow up work to a debtors circularisation is standard bookwork. The best way to assess the recoverability of a year end debt is to look at subsequent cash receipts. There is no doubt about debts which have paid up by the time of the audit work.

Step 4   Only when you are confident that you are about to answer the question that has been set, should you start writing.

The examiner's answer

(a)   There are two types of debtors' circularisation. The most common is the positive circularisation, where the auditor writes a letter to the debtor, on the client's headed paper, asking the debtor to reply direct to the auditor whether the debtor agrees, disagrees or cannot confirm the balance on the client's sales ledger. The debtor is asked to reply under all circumstances.

With a negative circularisation, a similar procedure is carried out, but the debtor is asked to reply only if he disagrees the balance.

Frequently, with positive circularisations of debtors the percentage of debtors who reply is low. With a negative circularisation, the percentage who reply is even lower. However, with a negative circularisation only those who disagree with the balance reply to the circularisation, so it is assumed that those who do not reply agree the balance. This is an invalid conclusion, as many debtors never reply to any circularisation, and some of these debtors will disagree the balance. So, a negative circularisation, by itself, provides weak evidence of the reliability of debtors on the sales ledger, as many debtors who do not reply may disagree with the balance.

From this stage, we will consider positive circularisations only, as the weakness of the negative circularisation has been discussed in the paragraph above. With a positive circularisation it is common for most of the debtors circularised not to reply, so in these cases the auditor obtains no evidence from the circularisation and additional procedures have to be carried out (see the answer to part (b)(ii) of the question). When a reply is received, this provides good evidence of the existence of the debtor, as the debtor replies direct to the audit firm's office and the reply cannot be intercepted by the client. The debtor could have close relationships with the audit client (eg, the companies may have common ownership, or the owners or directors could be related), but this is unusual. However, these close relationships could affect the reliability of the reply from the debtor (ie, the client could ask the debtor to reply agreeing the balance, when it is not agreed, or is fictitious).

Where the client and debtor are independent of each other, the replies to the circularisation are quite good audit evidence. However, there are some limitations in the reliability of the evidence:

(i) some debtors reply agreeing the balance for every circularisation, even when there is a difference. In some cases they sign the reply as agreeing the balance without checking their purchase ledger. If the reply is from a junior member of the debtor's staff it is less reliable than that from a senior member such as the chief accountant.

(ii) sometimes the debtor disagrees the balance when the balance on the client's sales ledger is correct. Usually, this arises through cash and goods in transit (see the answer to part (b)(i) below). In most businesses the sales ledger is more reliable than the purchase ledger, as the sales invoice is posted to the sales ledger at the same time as the goods are dispatched to the customer (or within a day) and cash is posted to the sales ledger when it is received (or within a day). However, with purchase ledgers, there may be a considerable delay between receiving the goods and posting the invoice to the purchase ledger, as there may be a delay in receiving the purchase invoice, and there will be delays in checking the invoice to the goods received note and purchase order and getting it approved before it is posted to the purchase ledger. These delays can be variable, and create cut-off errors. Also, some customers post the cash to their purchase ledger at the same time as the cheque is written out, but they delay sending the cheque to the creditor (ie, to the supplier of the goods), in order to improve their cash flow and minimise overdraft interest charges. This creates further inaccuracies in the customer's purchase ledger

(iii) some debtors reply saying they cannot confirm the balance because of the accounting records they keep. With this type of reply, only the existence of the debtor is confirmed

(iv) agreement of the balance by the debtor does not confirm that it is recoverable. For instance, the debtor may confirm the balance, but, because of cash flow problems, he is unable to pay it and it becomes a bad debt. However, many debtors who are experiencing cash flow or going concern problems will not reply to the circularisation. Nevertheless, this is a serious weakness of a debtors' circularisation. Checking cash received after the year end is the best way of verifying the recoverability of the debt

(v) although the great advantage of a debtors' circularisation is that it confirms the existence of the debtor, it is time-consuming to carry out, and, because of the limitations described above, it is a less efficient way of verifying debtors than other techniques, such as looking at aged debtors at the year end and checking cash received after the year end (but this may be less effective at confirming the existence of the debtor)

(vi) a further problem of a debtors' circularisation is that it is carried out on only a sample of debtors, which is often a very small percentage of the number of debtors and a small percentage of debtors by value (usually much less than 50% by value). So, there is the problem of sampling risk (ie, that the auditor's sample may show that sales ledger balances are agreed by debtors, but this is unrepresentative of the whole population of the company's debtors).

Did you answer the question?

Note how audit evidence can be obtained for several assertions from a single test eg, a debtors circularisation can provide evidence of existence and valuation.

(b) (i) Where the debtor disagrees the balance and provides a lower agreed balance, the difference will comprise:

- goods in transit
- cash in transit
- other differences.

The auditor should reconcile the balance agreed by the debtor with the balance on the sales ledger dividing the difference into the three items described above. If there are problems in reconciling these balances, the auditor should contact the debtor and obtain details of the make-up of the balance on the customer's purchase ledger (frequently, debtors' circularisations ask debtors to provide the make-up of their purchase ledger balance when there is a disagreement). Ideally, the 'other differences' should be zero, or kept to a small value.

Goods in transit are invoices on the client's sales ledger which are not on the customer's purchase ledger. If the invoices are for goods dispatched shortly before the year end, I will check to the dispatch note that they were dispatched before the year end. If they were dispatched after the year end there is a sales cut-off error and the items should be removed from debtors and added to stock. If they were dispatched near the year end, the difference probably arises because of the delays in the customer posting the invoice to his purchase ledger. If the dispatch was some time before the year end, it is probably a disputed item, so I would ask the credit controller about the invoice and inspect correspondence with the debtor. From this I would assess whether the debt is recoverable. If the value of the invoice is significant, I may ask for permission to contact the debtor so that I can discuss the problem. If this is refused, this is likely to be a disputed item (or even a fictitious item) and I will probably assess that a substantial provision should be made against this item (if this is refused, I will put it in my schedule of unadjusted errors).

Cash in transit is cash on the customer's purchase ledger which is not on the client's sales ledger. If this cash is on the customer's purchase ledger shortly before the year end and is in the client's cash book and sales ledger shortly after the year end, then it is probably cash in transit, and the sales ledger balance will be correct. However, if there is a substantial delay it could be either because the customer delays sending cheques to their suppliers, or there is a teeming and lading fraud. The entry of the cheque in the client's cash book and sales ledger after the year end can be checked. To check whether a teeming and lading fraud is being carried out, I will check that today's cheques received in the post are either banked today or tomorrow. With most teeming and lading frauds the cash received is entered in the cash book on the correct day (ie, when it is received), but it is apparently banked a few days later. This can be detected by checking the bank reconciliation and noting that lodgements into the bank are credited promptly by the bank (if there is a substantial delay there is probably a teeming and lading fraud).

If the other differences are small, I will perform limited checks on them, as they will probably be immaterial. If they are large, I will try to quantify them (eg, they may be discounts taken by the customer, or debit notes posted to the customer's purchase ledger). I will discuss them with the credit controller, and inspect correspondence with the debtor. In addition, I may contact the debtor to discuss these differences. From these investigations I will assess whether a provision should be included for these items.

(ii)   Where the debtor does not reply to the circularisation, a number of techniques can be used to confirm the debtor's existence:

- evidence generated by the company is weak, so checking sales invoices, dispatch notes and order confirmations provides weak evidence of the existence of the debtor

- the best evidence of the existence of the debtor which is available within the company is correspondence from the debtor, such as orders from the debtor on that debtor's headed paper, and correspondence from the debtor which can be found in the sales department and with the credit controller

- cheques received are further evidence of the existence of the debtors. Only the most recent (unbanked) cheques will be available for the auditor to inspect, but there should be remittance advices from customers showing the invoices which each cheque pays. The name of the customer on the paying-in slip is evidence of the debtor, although this is evidence generated by the company

- other evidence can be obtained from trade directories and telephone directories. This confirms the existence of the business on the client's sales ledger, but it does not confirm that the business is a debtor of the client (ie, the debtor balance on the sales ledger could be made up of either fictitious sales invoices or invoices posted to the wrong account)

- a further letter could be sent to the debtor to confirm that he receives goods from the client, but, as the debtor did not reply to the circularisation, no reply may be received to this letter

- finally, the debtor can be telephoned and asked if he purchases goods from the client (eg, by asking the debtor's purchasing manager). In using the telephone, one must be careful the call is not intercepted by the client, as occurred in the Equity Funding fraud.

To check the recoverability of the debt at the year end, I will check its ageing. Also, I will check cash received between the year end and the time of my audit check. Any year end invoices cleared by cash received since the year end can be considered good, as it is unusual for debtors to request repayment. If the sum paid since the year end is large, one should check that the cheque has cleared (and has not 'bounced'), particularly for debtors whose year end balance is very old. The date of this exam is just under 1-5 months after the year end, yet year end debtors are about 2-5 months, so many of the year end debts will be uncleared at the time of my investigation. I will look at the year end debts which are still outstanding and consider whether they are recoverable. If the year end debt is being paid by the debtor in a regular manner (eg, it is up to three months old at the year end and one month's invoices have been paid in November), it is probable that the outstanding balance is recoverable. However, old outstanding items are probably doubtful as there is likely to be a dispute with them. These could be August or earlier invoices which are still unpaid in December. I will discuss them with the client, inspect correspondence with the debtor and consider whether a doubtful debt provision should be made against them. The other problems will be with very old debts where the debtor is having going concern problems. The risk will be lower where they are being repaid at regular intervals (eg, monthly) and the customer's cheques do not 'bounce'. I will discuss these debtors with the credit controller, inspect correspondence and consider whether a doubtful debt provision should be made against these debts.

Based on these investigations, I will determine whether these debts will be recoverable and estimate the value of any doubtful debt provision which should be made against them.

Did you answer the question?

Note that the examiner's answer to part (b) is longer than a student would be expected to produce in the time available. You should aim to make the same number of points, but in rather less depth.

42 (Answer 4 of examination)

Examiner's comments and marking guide

Question 4: asked candidates to define the elements of audit risk in part (a). Part (b) required a calculation of audit time. Part (c) asked candidates to consider alternatives of compliance and substantive tests, and part (d) asked them to consider the advantages and limitations of the risk based approach to auditing.

Many of the answers to this question were weak and showed little understanding of this important aspect of modern auditing.

In part (a), very few candidates mentioned the word 'material' in their definitions. Auditors are not concerned with all fraud and error, they are concerned only with material fraud and error in the financial statements. Although most candidates understood each of the risk elements, some had little understanding, while others were confused about control risk and detection risk.

The calculations in part (b) were poorly attempted. Candidates should have known how to produce the correct answer from their studies of basic cost accounting. Although many of the answers to part (c) were brief, most candidates provided a satisfactory answer. A few candidates incorrectly said that if controls are strong no compliance tests will be carried out, and if controls are weak, compliance tests will be carried out. This showed a serious weakness in their understanding.

The answers to part (d) were very short, and, as expected, most considered only the advantages of the risk based approach to auditing (and not the disadvantages). Answers should have stated that the risk based approach directs the auditor to perform more work in high risk areas and less work in low risk areas. This approach should lead to either a reduction in audit risk or in the time to complete the audit.

		Marks
(a)	Definition of elements of audit risk ½ mark for definition and 1 mark for explanation of each item, thus Up to 1.5 marks each item up to a maximum of	6
(b)	Calculation of audit time 1 mark for each audit time and 1 mark for decision Up to a maximum of	3
(c)	Discussion of compliance v substantive approach Generally 1 mark a point up to a maximum of	4
(d)	Discussion of advantages and limitations of using the audit risk model Generally 1 mark a point up to a maximum of	7

Total   20

Step by step answer plan

Step 1 Read the question again and make sure that you focus on precisely what is required.

Step 2 Parts (a) and (c) are standard bookwork and offer easy marks to the well-prepared student

Step 3 Part (b) looks unusual, but is only worth 3 marks. Some knowledge of the behaviour of fixed and variable items is required (ie, costing knowledge), but don't spend more time on this than 3 marks deserves.

Step 4 The risk-based approach to audit is the modern approach, investing time to investigate the categories of audit risk so that more time can be spent on risky areas and less on safer areas. Both the advantages **and** limitations of such an approach must be discussed.

Step 5 Only when you are confident that you are about to answer the question that has been set, should you start writing.

The examiner's answer

(a) (i) *Audit risk* is the risk that the auditor will come to an inappropriate audit opinion on financial statements. That is, the auditor will provide an unqualified report when there are material errors in the financial statements or will give a qualified report when there are no material errors.

(ii) *Inherent risk* is the risk of material errors in the financial statements before taking into account the effectiveness of internal controls. In most organisations the inherent risk is 100% or close to 100%. It is related to the type of business of the company. Companies with a high inherent risk include those where a large number of the transactions are in cash (eg, retailers), those where there is rapid technical change (eg, computer manufacturers), companies subject to high political risk (eg, where they may be taken over by the government, or there are severe exchange and other controls), companies with going concern problems and companies with a dominant chief executive.

(iii) *Control risk* is the risk that controls in the company's accounting systems will fail to prevent or detect material errors or fraud. In small businesses the control risk is likely to be high, as there will be too few staff to have an effective division of duties for internal control purposes, so in these businesses it is not appropriate to carry out tests of control. Where there is an effective system of internal control, which is confirmed by audit tests, then the control risk will be low and this allows fewer substantive procedures to be performed.

(iv) *Detection risk* is the risk that audit tests (ie, substantive tests and analytical review) fail to detect material errors. Detection risk is reduced by performing substantive checks on a larger sample of items.

In the definitions above, the word 'errors' includes irregularities, fraud and uncertainties.

	Did you answer the question?

Note that definitions do not have to be word-for-word accurate from SASs. Any wording will earn the marks as long as it clearly explains the principles.

(b)   The total audit time is as follows:

	Compliance tests	No compliance tests
Compliance tests:		
Fixed time	2.5	0.0
Variable time	12.0	0.0
Substantive tests:		
Fixed time	1.5	1.5
Variable time	11.25	32.5
	27.25	34.0

From these calculations, it is more time-efficient to perform a combination of compliance and substantive tests.

(c)   From the calculation in part (b) above, it can be seen that it is more appropriate to use a combination of compliance and substantive tests as it results in an overall saving in audit time. Generally, this occurs when there are sufficient staff to allow an effective system of internal control to operate (usually with a division of duties which will prevent or detect fraud and error) and there are a large number of transactions. In this situation, using an entirely substantive approach would require a large number of transactions to be checked, whereas checking the system of internal control will produce a lower control risk and allow the detection risk to be raised, thus allowing fewer substantive tests to be performed.

It is not appropriate to check internal controls when they are weak, as checking these controls will confirm that control risk is high, so performing compliance tests will be a waste of time. Internal controls will be weak in small organisations where there are too few staff for a proper division of duties. Also, in small organisations the proprietor will operate the system of internal check, but usually there is no control over his actions, and this will create a weak system of control.

In very small organisations it is not appropriate to perform compliance tests, as it is quicker to check all, or a substantial proportion, of the transactions during the year. Performing compliance tests does involve a fixed time (ie, to ascertain and record the systems and evaluate the controls) and this fixed time cannot be recovered in the relatively short time required to substantively check all transactions. Also, in these organisations there will be few staff (all accounting functions may be performed by a single person) so checking controls is inappropriate, as they do not exist (or hardly exist).

In large audits, auditors usually rely heavily on internal controls which allows them to perform limited substantive tests. This reduces the audit time, compared with undertaking only substantive tests, and thus it results in a cost effective audit.

(d)   The advantages of using the risk based approach are that it provides a framework for the conduct of the audit, it focuses auditors' attention on risk, it allows development of efficient and effective audit programs and it develops an enquiring attitude of mind. In addition, the risk based approach links into the concept of materiality, and the techniques of statistical sampling.

The audit risk approach is helpful in identifying the areas of the audit where most work should be performed. It allows the auditor to spend more time in the areas of highest risk and less time in low risk areas, thus either reducing the overall time for the audit or reducing overall audit risk. It avoids excessive time being spent on low risk areas. For instance, in many businesses petty cash expenditure is small. Although the risk of errors and fraud in petty cash systems are relatively high, it is most unlikely that they will be material (as total petty cash expenditure will hardly be material), so audit work in this area can be limited.

Where internal controls are weak, the control risk will be high, which will require a lower detection risk in order to achieve the required level of audit risk. This means that more substantive checks will have to be performed in that area.

Using the risk based approach to auditing, the auditor will be able to examine each area of the profit and loss account and balance sheet and assess the inherent and control risks for these areas. The control risk will be confirmed by compliance tests. From this, a required level of detection risk will be determined, as:

$$DR = AR /(IR \times CR)$$

A low detection risk will require a large number of items to be checked and a high detection risk will allow the auditor to check a small sample of items.

Essentially, by examining each significant item in the profit and loss account and balance sheet (ie, in terms of materiality and inherent and control risks), the auditor will be able to assess the amount of work required in that area. For instance, with a capital intensive company the depreciation charge will be large so checking its accuracy will be important. Where there are rapid changes in technology and risk of obsolescence, this will increase the inherent risk and require more detailed audit work. In many businesses the value of stock is material, and it has a high inherent and control risk, as there may have been counting errors, and there is a high risk of errors in the valuation of each item of stock, thus giving a high risk that the value of stock is materially misstated. Where there is a perpetual inventory system, stock quantities should be more accurate (as counts can be compared with the stock records), which reduces the control risk. Thus the risk of errors in stock quantities is reduced, so a higher detection risk can be permitted, which allows the auditor to carry out fewer checks.

With cash sales businesses, there is a high risk of misappropriation of cash, thus creating a high inherent risk. So, to ensure a low audit risk, it is necessary for the control risk to be determined by the auditor by checking that the systems for controlling and recording cash are reliable. If the control risk is high, the auditor will have to perform extensive substantive checks.

As explained above, in very small audits, it is hardly appropriate to calculate audit risk, because of the time taken to assess each element of risk. However, it is worthwhile to consider audit risk from a qualitative point of view, as it is likely to highlight areas of highest audit risk and thus indicate where the auditor should concentrate his audit work.

There are a number of problems with the audit risk model. Frequently, it is impossible to estimate the values of inherent risk, and, to a lesser extent, control risk with any degree of certainty. If these elements cannot be determined accurately, then one cannot accurately determine the value of detection risk which is required to achieve the overall level of audit risk.

A further problem is that auditors consider audit risk for each system - sales, purchases, stock, fixed assets, nominal ledger, cash, wages etc. The auditor may decide an overall audit risk of 5% is acceptable. However, if an AR = 5% is used for each of the systems above, then the overall audit risk will be much higher than 5% (ie, allowing 5% risk to sales/debtors, 5% to purchases/creditors, 5% to fixed assets/depreciation would give an overall audit risk of substantially more than 5%). So, there is a need to allocate audit risk between each system in a flexible manner so that a higher level of audit risk is permitted in higher risk areas and a lower level of audit risk is allocated to low risk areas. So, for many systems, the acceptable level of audit risk could be as low as 1%.

Finally, there is the question of whether the audit risk equation given in the question is correct. Analytical review is used in many audits, and analytical review risk (ARR) should be included in the equation:

$$AR = IR \times CR \times ARR \times DR$$

As ARR will be less than 1, this will allow a higher value of detection risk (DR) and thus allow fewer audit checks to be performed so as to achieve the required level of audit risk. Once again, assessing ARR is likely to be subject to considerable error, as it is quite possible for analytical review to indicate no problems when there are material errors, uncertainties or fraud. Also, analytical review may indicate problems, when there are no material errors in the financial statements (eg, an increase in debtors' age indicates that there may be more bad debts, but these have been adjusted for in the financial statements).

A further problem is that the auditor may assume that his assessment of control risk may apply to the whole system (eg, a sales system). However, there may be little or no controls over some parts of accounting systems, so the control risk for these aspects of the system could be 100%. This could apply in the following circumstances:

(i)   adjustments made to the financial statements by the accountant for accruals and prepayments, and correction of other errors

(ii)   in the valuation of the year end stock and determining the doubtful debt provision, which may be carried out by one person.

If there is no internal check over these items, it will mean the control risk is high, so the auditor should perform more checks to reduce the level of detection risk and hence achieve the required level of audit risk.

From the discussion above, it can be seen that the audit risk approach is helpful in achieving an efficient and low risk audit. However, it is difficult to quantify accurately each of the risk elements in the equation, and thus the equation will provide a less quantitative guide to audit work than may be apparent from the simple equation.

Did you answer the question?

Note that although there is far more in the above answer to part (d) than would be expected in the time available, this is a key topic and so deserves close study

---

43   (Answer 5 of examination)

(Examiner's comments and marking guide)

Question 5: was concerned with quality control in audit work. Part (a) asked candidates to consider why quality is important to auditors. Part (b) considered standardisation of working papers, and recruitment procedures. Part (c) was concerned with 'cold reviews'.

In part (a) candidates should have said that auditors should have a high quality of work so as to minimise the risk of negligence claims. Also, high quality work should assist in attracting new audit customers and retaining existing ones. A variety of other points on quality control were mentioned by candidates, but these are less important than minimising exposure to negligence claims.

Most of the answers to part (b)(i) on standardisation of working papers were too brief. If working papers are standardised, the audit staff will have a formal procedure for recording their audit work. Managers and Partners will be able to review the audit work more easily and ensure a comprehensive audit has been carried out. Most of the answers to part (b)(ii) on recruitment and training of staff were weak. Recruitment procedures should ensure that high quality staff are appointed, and training should ensure they are kept up to date and their knowledge developed.

Many candidates appeared to be unaware of 'cold reviews'. The feedback procedures of 'cold reviews' should ensure that errors or weaknesses in audit work are highlighted and overcome in the future. The risk of audit work being subject to a 'cold review' should ensure the standard of audit work is maintained.

Most of the answers to this question were rather brief.

		Marks
(a)	Explanation of importance of quality control Generally 1 mark a point up to a maximum of	4
(b)	Advantages of standardising audit working papers and training of staff Generally 1 mark a point up to a maximum of	9
(c)	How cold reviews can enhance the quality of audit work Generally 1 mark a point up to a maximum of	7
Total		20

Step by step answer plan

Step 1   Read the question again and make sure that you focus on precisely what is required.

Step 2   Focus your mind on SAS 240 and apply your common sense. Without high quality, existing clients will be dissatisfied and will not reappoint you, and you may face claims for damages for negligent work.

Step 3   The discussion of cold reviews in part (c) is worth 7 marks and should therefore be reasonably long. Even if you've never heard of the term before, it is defined for you in the question so you should be able to write about the concept.

Step 4   Only when you are confident that you are about to answer the question that has been set, should you start writing.

The examiner's answer

(a)   The reasons why quality is important to audit firms include:

(i)   a high quality audit ensures there is the minimum risk of the auditor coming to an inappropriate audit opinion (ie, giving an unqualified audit report when there are material errors in the financial statements, and vice versa)

(ii)   it should ensure that an appropriate length of time is spent on each aspect of the audit, more time being spent on higher risk and material areas and less time on lower risk areas and low value items

(iii) the reduction in audit risk will reduce the risk of the audit firm being sued for negligence. The costs of defending claims for negligence and of paying any damages can be substantial

(iv)   providing a high quality service will improve customer satisfaction and the reputation of the audit firm. This should increase the growth of the firm and its profitability (as the firm will be able to charge a larger fee for a service of perceived higher quality).

(b)   (i)   It is important that each audit firm has a standard system of recording audit work. For instance, all current year audit work on sales and debtors will be filed under the letter 'D', with final audit work on pages 1-99, and interim audit work on pages 100-199. Also, details of sales and debtors accounting systems will be included in the permanent file under the letter 'D' (ie, flowcharts of the accounting systems, and evaluation of controls). In this way, any member of staff can pick up any audit file, and immediately find the audit work on sales and debtors. Standardised ways of recording audit work, including flow chart symbols, and noting conclusions to audit tests, should ensure that the audit work is carried out to a consistently high standard.

Other parts of the audit file will include the draft financial statements, which will be referenced to schedules of the detailed audit work. There should be a section to notify the manager and partner of problems encountered in the audit, and the manager or partner should record the actions taken on these problems. This section will include problems encountered when the manager and partner reviewed the audit file.

It is important that all audit work is recorded, as verbal evidence is very weak, particularly as it may be recollection of events which had taken place many months earlier. Written evidence is much stronger, particularly in a court of law.

By standardising audit working papers, records of audit work can be kept in a logical and orderly sequence. This should help to ensure that all aspects of the audit work are covered by staff, and that an effective review of the work is carried out by managers and partners. Thus the quality of the audit and review should be enhanced.

(ii)   Selection and training of staff is important in order to maintain the quality of audit work. Ideally, the audit firm should appoint the highest quality staff it can obtain for the salary it is offering. Past academic performance, qualifications and experience should be considered before appointing staff.

Many audit firms use aptitude tests on numerical and verbal skills to assess the abilities of potential new staff. Also, recruitment staff are trained in interview techniques and on identifying the characteristics of applicants which will make them effective in their work for the professional firm. New student accountants will probably have only academic qualifications, but qualified staff should also have appropriate experience. The firm should have training procedures for new staff to make them aware of the firm's audit procedures (ie, types of audit procedure carried out and systems of recording audit work). The performance of staff on audits can be monitored by means of assessment of their work on each audit, under a number of specified criteria. The staff rating system could range from 'A' for excellent, through 'C' for satisfactory to 'E' for unsatisfactory. There should be procedures for acting on unsatisfactory reports, and counselling staff to improve their performance in weak areas. For training of student accountants, there should be a progressive system of courses to enhance their knowledge of auditing techniques, ranging from a basic course on the firm's audit procedures and carrying out basic audit work, through more advanced aspects, such as auditing stock, to advanced aspects of controlling an audit. For all staff there should be training courses to keep them up to date with current developments (eg, the introduction of new Accounting and Auditing Standards and changes in legislation, including taxation), and to make them aware of common problems found on audits, and how to overcome these problems.

The work given to staff should be related to their experience and abilities. For instance, it would be inappropriate to ask a new trainee to audit the valuation of the stock of a manufacturer, but that member of staff could audit various aspects of checking stock quantities and sales and purchases cut-off.

By providing appropriate training to audit staff, and allocating them work which is within their capabilities, this ensures that the quality of audit work is maintained, and thus audit risk is minimised. Having poorly trained staff, or giving them work which is beyond their current experience and abilities will result in a poor quality audit and a significant increase in audit risk.

Did you answer the question?

Note that your answers to parts (i) and (ii) should be roughly of equal length, unless the question indicates otherwise. Is your answer balanced in this way?

(c)   It is common for medium-sized and large audit firms to carry out 'cold reviews'. These take place some time after the audit has been completed and after the audit report has been signed. The staff carrying out the 'cold reviews' are normally from another office of the firm and they have not been involved in any aspect of the audits being reviewed.

The reviewers select a sample of audits, and for each one they look through the audit files and question the partner and manager in charge of each assignment. The reviewers look at each aspect of the audit, and check that sufficient audit work has been carried out, it is properly recorded and appropriate conclusions have been reached. Correspondence with the client will be inspected, and any problems following the audit will be noted (eg, material errors which were not detected in the audit, and any allegations by the client or third parties that the audit has been carried out negligently). Any apparent weaknesses in the audit will be discussed with the partner and manager. At the end of the procedure, the reviewing panel will prepare a written report which summarises their conclusions and notes any serious weaknesses highlighted by the review. This report will be made available to all relevant managers and partners, including the senior partner of the office. If the review highlights common weaknesses in audit procedures, or serious errors, the appropriate staff will be told, training procedures may be modified, and these problems may be noted in a staff newsletter.

The reason why 'cold reviews' should enhance the quality of audit work will include:

(i)   if staff are aware that these reviews are carried out, it will make them more careful in their work. This may have little effect on the work of junior staff, as their work will be reviewed by the manager and partner before the audit report is signed, thus they should always be careful in their work. However, it will have a more significant effect on the work of more senior staff

(ii)   an independent review is another person looking at the audit. They may uncover important points, which the manager and partner in charge of the audit may have overlooked

(iii) the independent review should provide a feedback system, whereby managers and partners are informed of weaknesses in their audit procedures. More serious weaknesses will be reported to other staff, and, if this is a common weakness, it should be reported in a staff newsletter. In this way, the weakness should be highlighted and staff will ensure that audit procedures are modified so as to prevent this weakness from recurring.

44 (Answer 6 of examination)

Examiner's comments and marking guide

Question 6: was concerned with auditing and checking controls over rent received and the income and expenditure account of a restaurant.

Although this question was less popular than the other two optional questions, it was generally well answered. Candidates had the opportunity to make a considerable number of points, and thus obtain a good mark.

In part (a) answers tended to concentrate on a criticism of the existing controls, with few points on the audit procedures which would be carried out. In part (iii) some candidates suggested goods should be checked as being returned before a credit note is issued. In renting a room, there are no physical goods to return!

In part (b) candidates' answers tended to concentrate on criticising the controls. Only a few candidates included a significant number of points on checking the income and expenditure account.

Candidates would have obtained more marks if they had described the audit work they would carry out in part (a), and the checks they would perform on the income and expenditure account in part (b).

		Marks
(a)	Audit tests on rent received	
	(i) input of rental income	
	(ii) cash received from residents	
	(iii) posting of adjustments, credit notes and write-offs	
	Generally 1 mark a point up to a maximum of	11
(b)	Checks of income and expenditure of restaurant	
	Generally 1 mark a point up to a maximum of	9
Total		20

Step by step answer plan

Step 1 Read the question again and make sure that you focus on precisely what is required.

Step 2 Many candidates would be nervous about selecting an optional question on this topic (auditing aspects of a charity), since their studies would have concentrated on the audit of trading companies which buy and sell physical goods. But decent marks are available on this question if you choose to select it for answer.

Step 3 Part (a) asks for controls **and** audit work to carry out on each of three aspects of rents received, so the format of your answer must deal with these six areas.

Step 4 Similarly, in part (b) you must consider controls **and** state the audit work you will carry out.

Step 5 Only when you are confident that you are about to answer the question that has been set, should you start writing.

The examiner's answer

(a)   (i)   There are serious weaknesses in the system of recording rents on the sales ledger, as it appears that no one checks the bookkeeper's work, so there appears to be no control over fraud or error by the bookkeeper.

- I will ascertain the system for recording usage of rooms and posting invoices to the sales ledger, and check that it is operating in the manner described in the question.

- There are a number of potential weaknesses in internal controls in the accounting system. The bookkeeper performs a number of functions, including posting invoices and cash to the sales ledger, and handling rents. Thus, there is a serious weakness in the system of internal control, which should be overcome by checks of the bookkeeper's work by an independent person. An independent person should check that rents posted to the sales ledger each month (or week) are consistent with the net income (ie, gross income less rent lost due to voids). An independent person should authorise write off of bad debts on the sales ledger (eg, the chief executive, and not the housing manager). Where the weakness is not overcome by a system of internal check, I will perform more checks in that area, and suggest in my management letter additional checks the management should perform.

- I will check that the rent income each month is similar to previous periods and to budget. I will use analytical review to check the level of voids and bad debts. For instance:

  Occupancy (%) = (actual rent income/theoretical rent income) × 100%

  where theoretical rent income is the product of the number of accommodation units (ie, 50) and the annual (or monthly) rent per room.

  Voids (%) = 100 − Occupancy (%)

  The level of voids should be similar to previous periods and to the previous year. The report of voids by the housing manager will provide evidence to support (or otherwise) the level of voids. I will investigate matters if I find the level of voids recorded by the accounting system is significantly different from those reported by the housing manager.

- I will test check that rents are correctly posted to the sales ledger. I will use the information provided by the housing manager, and check that the correct value of invoice is posted to the appropriate account. The risk is that an invoice is not posted to the sales ledger, so I will have to check that an invoice has been posted to the sales ledger for each room let for a sample of weeks during the year. Analytical review, as described above, is probably the most effective way of checking that an invoice has been posted to the sales ledger for each room let (but it does not check that the invoice has been posted to the correct sales ledger account, which the test in this part of the question does).

- it is important to check adjustments and credit notes posted to the sales ledger and write off of bad debts, which is covered in part (iii) of this answer.

       (ii)   The controls over receipt and recording of rents received should include:

- The reception staff should issue a receipt when they receive rent from a resident. A copy of the receipt should be retained by the reception staff. When the member of reception staff goes off duty, they should count the cash and the receipts, and give them to the bookkeeper. Reception should keep a copy of the amount of cash handed to the bookkeeper. Any differences between cash and receipts should be investigated.

- An independent member of staff (eg, the chief executive) should check that the rents cash posted to the sales ledger and banked is the same as that received from reception.

- An independent person should deal with any complaints from residents that they have paid their rent, but it has not been recorded as having been received.

In auditing the system:

- I will record the system, and perform a walk through test to check it is operating in the manner I have recorded.

- I may check the system of recording receipt of rents from residents, by observing reception staff performing this task.

- I will select a sample of days transactions during the year to check. I will check that the total of cash received has been posted to the sales ledger, and that it has been recorded in the cash book and banked. I will check to the bank statement that it has been banked promptly (if there is a delay, there could be a teeming and lading fraud).

- I will check the posting to the sales ledger of a sample of rents received.

- I will check that an independent person deals with disputes about rents received.

- I will investigate any problems I find, and note any serious weaknesses in my letter to management.

(iii) The posting of adjustments, credit notes and write off of bad debts are ways of hiding a fraud in the system. I would expect all these items to be authorised by the chief executive, and, if they are large, I would expect them to be reported to the management committee, and approved by them.

I will select a sample of adjustments, credit notes and write off of bad debts from the sales ledger, the sales day book and the original documents. I will check that the correct value of the item has been posted to the sales ledger, and I will extract the original document.

As explained above, I will check that the original document has been authorised by the chief executive, and record any cases when this has not happened. I will check the authenticity of the transaction to other supporting documentation. Adjustments are likely to be to correct errors, so I will look at the original transaction, and check that the adjustment corrects the error. Credit notes can be used to correct errors, and for correcting a charge when the resident had left. I will check to the housing manager's records that the resident had been charged for the period he/she used the accommodation (and not for more or less than that period).

For write off of bad debts, I will check that the debt has been outstanding for some time and that the resident has left (to the housing manager's records). I will check that the chief executive has authorised the write off, and, if it is large, that the write off has been authorised by the management committee. There should be evidence that Burton Housing 'chases' slow payers, and takes appropriate procedures to recover doubtful debts.

As a further check, I will look at the sales ledger for rents and its ageing. Although credit balances may indicate overpayment by residents, they could arise from not posting rent invoices to the sales ledger, thus indicating a weakness in this part of the system. So, I will investigate credit balances on the sales ledger. I will investigate old debts to see if any should be written off. The accounts department may avoid writing off bad debts, but this will be highlighted by old items on the sales ledger. A risk with old debts is that they have arisen from misappropriation of cash received from residents. Thus, old debts need to be scrutinised by the chief executive and the management committee.

(b) I would perform the following work in checking income and expenditure of the restaurant:

(i) I would carry out analytical review of the draft accounts. In particular, I would calculate the ratio of food costs to sales and compare them for each period and with the previous year. Any significant changes would be investigated. In addition, I would compare the ratio of wages costs to sales and other expenses to sales and investigate any significant changes. The actual wages cost each month would be extracted, and any significant changes would be investigated. Wages costs should remain relatively unchanged, provided the number of employees remains about the same

(ii)   I would attempt to calculate the ratio of food costs to sales for a sample of products the restaurant sells. The costs of food can be found from purchase invoices and the quantities used can be found from the restaurant manager. I will consider whether the quantities used are reasonable - I may check this by having a meal! The difference between the gross profit in the accounts and the theoretical gross profit, based on the selling price and the cost of the food, will be the wastage/loss. I will consider whether this is reasonable. It should be similar to previous periods and previous years, and to other restaurants I audit

(iii)   the question says the restaurant has a till. Each item of food sold should be recorded on the till and these details and the cash received from the customer should be recorded on the till roll. Till rolls for the year under review should be retained by the housing association until the financial statements have been approved at the annual general meeting. For the till rolls, I will test check that the amount banked is equal to the total at the end of each day's till roll. Small discrepancies will be allowed, but I would investigate large differences. There should be controls over inputting credits on the till. While an item is being entered, it would be acceptable to cancel the transaction, but this should not be possible after the total button has been pressed. Any credits entered on the till should require authorisation by the restaurant manager and the copy of the receipt of the transaction being cancelled should be retained (the cancelled receipt could be initialled by the customer and the restaurant manager and retained with the till roll). Checking till rolls is not a wholly reliable way of checking completeness of sales income, as staff may not record all takings on the till (they could misappropriate the unrecorded takings at the end of the day). I will consider whether the controls in the system are effective at preventing this from happening. Controls can include supervision by the restaurant manager and the use of video cameras on the till

(iv)   starting from invoices for food purchases posted to the purchase ledger, I will follow them back and check that the restaurant has acknowledged that the food has been received, and there is a purchase order. Also, I will check that the food purchased is used in sales to customers. For instance, if the purchase is of chocolate confectionery, but the restaurant does not sell these items, then this is part of a fraud. It should be noted that there is a weakness in the system of internal control in the purchases system, as the restaurant manager both orders the food and authorises the purchase invoice before it is posted to the purchase ledger. To overcome this weakness, the order should be authorised by the chief executive, and the bookkeeper should report to the chief executive any cases where a fraud is suspected

(v)   I will test check that the employees on the payroll charged to the restaurant actually work for the restaurant. This can be done by checking the current week's payroll and asking the restaurant manager to point out each employee. The rates of pay of the employees can be checked to the personnel records and the hours worked to clock cards (or attendance sheets). Any overtime should have been authorised by the restaurant manager or more senior employee (eg, the chief executive). The existence of the employee can be confirmed to the personnel records and the signature of the employee receiving his or her wage packet

(vi)   I will check the closing stock of food to previous periods and consider whether it is reasonable. The age of the stock should be less than a month (possibly only a week) as some of it will be perishable. The frequency of deliveries will be an indication of the age of the stock, the more frequent the deliveries, the shorter should be the stock age

(vii)   I will check the value of purchases and wages are reasonable. I will compare them with previous periods and the previous year and investigate any significant changes. I will check large costs to purchase invoices, or other supporting documentation.

Based on these investigations, I will consider whether the accounts of the restaurant are reliable. One of the important checks is of the ratio of food cost to sales value for actual portions sold by the restaurant and comparison of this ratio with the ratio in the financial statements. If there appears to be a significant wastage or loss of food (or understatement of sales income), I will report my concerns to the chief executive of the housing association and the management committee, and I may have to qualify my audit report on this matter (if the sums involved are material). A material error for the housing association may be smaller than one for profit making businesses, as the general public has a greater expectation that a charity is run properly and that there is no fraud.

Did you answer the question?

Note how part (b) covers all aspects of income and expenditure expected in the restaurant, not just the buying and selling of food.

JUNE 1996 QUESTIONS

Section A - ALL THREE questions are compulsory and MUST be attempted

45 (Question 1 of examination)

You are commencing the audit of the sales system of Ilkeston Products plc, which is a new client.

Ilkeston Products plc operates from a single site and it has a computerised sales system. The company is quite large, and there is proper division of duties within the sales system. So, the audit approach will be to assess the audit risk and carry out compliance tests on the controls, followed by substantive procedures.

The audit partner has asked you to describe the audit work you will carry out in auditing the sales system, under each of the headings listed below.

You are required to describe the work you will carry out in auditing the sales system:

(a)   in ascertaining, recording and confirming the system. You should consider the advantages and limitations of using flowcharts and narrative notes to record the system.

(6 marks)

(b)   in evaluating controls in the system. For internal control questionnaires (ICQ's) and internal control evaluation forms (ICE's) you should:

  (i)   give examples of one question commonly found in an ICQ and one in an ICE;
  (ii)   explain the general form of questions and answers for an ICQ and ICE; and
  (iii)   consider the relative advantages and limitations of ICQ's and ICE's.

(7 marks)

(c)   in performing compliance tests on the system. Your answer should consider:

  (i)   the basis you should use to select items for testing;
  (ii)   the number of items you should test;
  (iii)   the action you would take if you find errors in your tests.

(7 marks)
(Total: 20 marks)

Notes:

(a)   In Statements of Auditing Standards, 'Compliance Tests' are called 'Tests of Control'.
(b)   In part (c) (ii) you are not required to calculate the number of items you should test.
(c)   You are not required to consider the use of computer assisted audit techniques.

46 (Question 2 of examination)

Heanor Manufacturing plc is planning to purchase a new sales accounting system for use with its minicomputer. The managing director has asked for your advice on certain matters relating to the new computerised sales system.

The old system used the computer to produce sales invoices from handwritten dispatch notes, post them to the sales ledger, record cash received and produce an aged analysis of debtors. The main weaknesses of the old system were that many documents were either handwritten, typed (eg, order confirmations) or were produced irregularly (eg, order confirmations). Also, it was possible to dispatch goods to customers which were a bad credit risk, thus creating unacceptable debt collection costs and a high level of bad debts.

With the new computerised sales system, it is proposed that:

(a)   the order confirmation should be produced by the computer;

(b)   the dispatch note should be produced by the computer when the goods are ready for dispatch, and at the date required by the customer;

(c)   the sales invoice will be produced by the computer at the same time as the dispatch note, using information from the dispatch note and prices per unit from a standard data file. When the computer produces the sales invoice, it posts it to the sales ledger;

(d)   receipt of cash from customers will be recorded on the sales ledger and in the cash book in a similar way to the old system.

Access to the system will be from terminals. Controls over access to the system will be by passwords and restricting the terminals from which certain tasks can be performed.

In view of the large number of dispatches of goods to customers, the managing director wants credit checks on customers to be performed by the computer with the minimum intervention by the credit controller. The credit checks by the computer will use data input into the system by the credit controller, and information on the sales ledger. When the computer's criteria decide that goods should not be dispatched to a poor creditworthy customer, the system will have provision to allow the credit controller to override the computer's decision and authorise dispatch of goods to the customer.

For the new computerised sales system **you are required to**:

(a)   describe the controls the computer system should incorporate before it:

      (i)   issues an order confirmation to a customer;
      (ii)   raises a dispatch note and authorises dispatch of goods to the customer.

                    (6 marks)

(b)   describe the controls which should be exercised over:

      (i)   changing customer details including adding new customers, amending their details and deleting customers;

      (ii)   changing customer credit limits;

      (iii)   changing the selling prices of products.

                    (10 marks)

(c)   describe:

      (i)   the credit control criteria the computer system should use to decide whether to prevent dispatch of goods to customers;

      (ii)   the manual procedures which should be exercised before the system allows goods to be dispatched to a company where the computer's criteria reject dispatch of the goods.

                    (4 marks)
               (Total: 20 marks)

---

47   (Question 3 of examination)

You are the senior in charge of the audit of Tollerton Limited, and you are auditing the company's trade creditors at 30 April 1996.

A junior member of the audit team has been checking suppliers' statements to the balances on the purchase ledger. He is unable to reconcile a material balance, relating to Carlton Limited, and has asked for your assistance, and your suggestions on the audit work which should be carried out on the differences.

The balance of Carlton Ltd on Tollerton Ltd's purchase ledger, is shown below:

Purchase ledger

Supplier: Carlton Limited

Date	Type	Reference	Status	Dr	Cr	Balance
10.2	Invoice	6004	Paid 1		2,130	
18.2	Invoice	6042	Paid 1		1,525	
23.2	Invoice	6057	Paid 1		2,634	
4.3	Invoice	6080	Paid 2		3,572	
15.3	Invoice	6107	Paid 2		1,632	
26.3	Invoice	6154	Paid 2		924	
31.3	Payment	Cheque	Alloc 1	6,163		
	Discount		Alloc 1	126		
14.4	Invoice	6285			2,156	
21.4	Invoice	6328			3,824	
30.4	Payment	Cheque	Alloc 2	6,005		
	Discount		Alloc 2	123		
30.4	Balance					5,980

Carlton Ltd's supplier's statement shows:

Customer: Tollerton Limited

Date	Type	Reference	Status	Dr	Cr	Balance
7.2	Invoice	6004		2,130		
16.2	Invoice	6042		1,525		
22.2	Invoice	6057		2,634		
2.3	Invoice	6080		3,752		
13.3	Invoice	6107		1,632		
22.3	Invoice	6154		924		
10.4	Receipt	Cheque			6,163	
4.4	Invoice	6210		4,735		
12.4	Invoice	6285		2,156		
18.4	Invoice	6328		3,824		
28.4	Invoice	6355		6,298		
30.4	Balance					23,447

Carlton's terms of trade with Tollerton allow a 2% cash discount on invoices where Carlton receives a cheque from the customer by the end of the month following the date of the invoice (ie, a 2% discount will be given on March invoices paid by 30 April).

On Tollerton's purchase ledger, under 'Status' the cash and discount marked 'Alloc 1' pay invoices marked 'Paid 1' (similarly for 'Alloc 2' and 'Paid 2').

Tollerton's goods received department check the goods when they arrive and issue a goods received note (GRN). A copy of the GRN and the supplier's advice note is sent to the purchases accounting department.

You are required to:

(a)   Prepare a statement reconciling the balance on Tollerton's purchase ledger to the balance on Carlton's suppliers statement.

(4 marks)

(b)   Describe the audit work you will carry out on each of the reconciling items you have determined in your answer to part (a) above, in order to determine the balance which should be included in the financial statements.

(10 marks)

(c)   In relation to verifying trade creditors:

   (i)   consider the basis you will use for selecting suppliers' statements to check to the balances on the purchase ledger;

   (ii)   describe what action you will take if you find there is no supplier's statement for a material balance on the purchase ledger.

(6 marks)
(Total: 20 marks)

Section B - TWO questions ONLY to be attempted

48   (Question 4 of examination)

The partner in charge of your audit firm has asked your advice on frauds which have been detected in recent audits.

(a)   The audited financial statements of Lambley Trading Ltd were approved by the shareholders at the AGM on 3 June 1996. On 7 June 1996 the managing director of Lambley Trading Ltd discovered a petty cash fraud by the cashier. Investigation of this fraud has revealed that it has been carried out over a period of a year. It involved the cashier making out, signing and claiming petty cash expenses which were charged to motor expenses. No receipts were attached to the petty cash vouchers. The managing director signs all cheques for reimbursing the petty cash float. Lambley Trading has a turnover of about £2 million and the profit before tax is about £150,000. The cashier has prepared the draft financial statements for audit.

The partner in charge of the audit decided that no audit work should be carried out on petty cash. He considered that petty cash expenditure was small, so the risk of a material error or fraud was small.

You are required to:

   (i)   briefly state the auditor's responsibilities for detecting fraud and error in financial statements;

   (ii)   consider whether your firm is negligent if the fraud amounted to £5,000;

   (iii)   consider whether your firm is negligent if the fraud amounted to £20,000.

(9 marks)

(b)   The audit of directors' remuneration at Colwick Enterprises plc has confirmed that the managing director's salary is £450,000, and that he is the highest paid director. However, a junior member of the audit team asked you to look at some purchase invoices paid by the company. Your investigations have revealed that the managing director has had work amounting to £200,000 carried out on his home, which has been paid by Colwick Enterprises. The managing director has authorised payment of these invoices and there is no record of authorisation of this work in the board minutes. The managing director has refused to include the £200,000 in his remuneration for the year, and to change the financial statements. If you insist on qualifying your audit report on this matter, the managing director says he will get a new firm to audit the current year's financial statements. The company's profit before tax for the year is £91 million.

Assuming the managing director refuses to amend the financial statements, **you are required** to:

   (i)   consider whether the undisclosed remuneration is a material item in the financial statements;

   (ii)   describe the matters you will consider and the action you will take:

      -    to avoid being replaced as auditor; and
      -    if you are replaced as auditor;

   assuming the managing director owns 60% of the issued shares of Colwick Enterprises.

(iii)   describe the matters you will consider and the action you will take to avoid being replaced as auditor, assuming Colwick Enterprises is a listed company with an audit committee, and the managing director owns less than 1% of the issued shares.

(11 marks)
(Total: 20 marks)

49   (Question 5 of examination)

Tutorial note

Question 5 of the June 1996 exam is not included here since it dealt with the topic of audit exemption reports, which are now obsolete. At the time of the exam companies with turnover less than £90,000 were exempt from audit, those with turnover in excess of £350,000 were required to have a full audit, while those with turnover between these limits were exempt from audit as long as a reporting accountant prepared an audit exemption report.

These rules were changed by Statutory Instrument in 1997. Companies with turnover less than £350,000 are now exempt from audit, so the requirement for an audit exemption report no longer exists.

50   (Question 6 of examination)

Your firm is the auditor of Hyson Computers Limited. You have been asked by the audit manager to audit capitalised development expenditure at the company's year end of 30 April 1996.

Hyson Computers Ltd is a company which writes software and develops microcomputer systems. It sells the software to retailers or direct to small businesses. In 1994, the managing director felt there would be a market for combining a microcomputer, printer and scanner to produce a system for small businesses. Work on developing this system started in May 1995. The expenditure incurred comprised:

(a)   purchase of computers, scanners, modems and printers to develop the system;

(b)   purchase of standard software for performing various tasks;

(c)   writing special software to allow the following functions to be performed, often at the same time:

(i)   normal operation of the computer for accounting and other functions;
(ii)   use of the scanner to send faxes by telephone, and use of the printer to print faxes received by the business;
(iii)   use of the scanner and printer as a photocopier;
(iv)   use of the scanner to input images into the computer, and software to convert written images into text.

At the company's year end of 30 April 1996, £500,000 has been spent on developing the system. The managing director says:

(a)   the system is almost ready for selling to customers;

(b)   there has been a lot of interest from customers; and

(c)   a few selected customers have been given test systems to see if it meets their needs and report any problems.

In the draft financial statements for the year ended 30 April 1996, this development expenditure has been capitalised at £500,000.

The audit manager has explained to you that any research and development expenditure capitalised in the company's financial statements must comply with the conditions of SSAP 13 (Accounting for Research and Development). He has summarised these conditions as:

(a) there is a clearly defined project;
(b) the expenditure must be separately identifiable;
(c) the project must be technically feasible and commercially viable;
(d) the total deferred development costs are expected to be exceeded by future sales less associated costs;
(e) the company has adequate resources to complete development and sell the product.

You are required to:

(a) describe the audit work you will carry out to verify the expenditure of £500,000 on development of the software and hardware system, described above.

(8 marks)

(b) describe the matters you will consider and the investigations you will carry out in deciding whether development expenditure of £500,000 can be capitalised in the financial statements.

(8 marks)

(c) consider and describe the form of qualified or unqualified audit report you will give, in **each of** the two situations below, if the directors refuse to amend the financial statements, and you come to the conclusion:

(i) there is a risk that the £500,000 capitalised development expenditure will not be recoverable;

(ii) that it is not possible for the company to develop a commercially viable product, so there will be no sales, and the £500,000 capitalised development expenditure is worthless.

(4 marks)
(Total: 20 marks)

Note: In part (c) you should assume that the £500,000 deferred development expenditure is material, but that if it is valueless, it will not create going concern problems.

ANSWERS TO JUNE 1996 ANSWERS

The model answers to the questions are longer and frequently more detailed than would be expected from a candidate in the examinations. However, the model answer may not include all valid points mentioned by candidates - credit will be given to candidates mentioning these points.

The model answers may be used as a guide to the form and standard of answers candidates should try to achieve. However, the answers may not be as detailed as one would find in text books on the subject.

45   (Answer 1 of examination)

Examiner's comments and marking guide

Question 1: was concerned with the steps in auditing a sales system.

Many of the answers to part (a) on ascertaining, recording and confirming the system were good, although some candidates (wrongly) restricted their answers to flowcharts and narrative notes. Some candidates said that flowcharts were better at recording complex systems, while others said narrative notes were superior. Flowcharts are better at showing division of duties and avoid the ambiguities which are common with narrative notes.

The answers to part (b) on ICQs and ICEs were not as good. Most candidates were able to identify an ICQ, although some though it was an ICE. However, most candidates were unable to suggest an appropriate ICE question (many of the suggestions were ICQ questions). Frequently, the answers to part (iii) were weak.

The answers to part (c) on selecting items for testing were satisfactory, but they were not as good on part (iii) which asked candidates to suggest the actions they would take if they found errors. If the numbers of errors is small, the auditor would increase the sample of items he/she tests. If there are a large number of errors, the auditor will have to report the matter to management and consider whether other controls will prevent material errors from taking place.

		Marks
(a)	Ascertaining, recording and confirming the system Generally 1 mark a point up to a maximum of	6
(b)	Evaluating controls Generally 1 mark a point up to a maximum of	7
(c)	Performing compliance tests Generally 1 mark a point up to a maximum of	7
Total		20

Note: in part (b) (i) you should give 1 mark for an appropriate ICQ question and 1 mark for an appropriate ICE question. The remaining 5 marks should be allocated to parts (ii) and (iii)

Step by step answer plan

Step 1   Read the question again and make sure that you focus on precisely what is required.

Step 2   Part (a) can be split up into ascertaining (eg, ask or observe staff), recording (including flowcharts and narrative notes) and confirming (eg, by a walkthrough test). There's quite a lot to say for 6 marks.

Step 3   Part (b) is standard bookwork on the difference between an ICQ and an ICE.

Step 4   Part (c) involves tests of control on the sales system. Always try and apply statistical sampling methods where they are appropriate rather than any other basis of sampling.

Step 5   Only when you are confident that you are about to answer the question that has been set, should you start writing.

The examiner's answer

(a)   To ascertain the system, I will:

    (i)   ask if the company has a description of the sales system. If they have, I will put a copy in my permanent file

    (ii)   ask staff how sales are processed by the system

    (iii)   obtain sample documents used in the system, such as order confirmations, dispatch notes, sales invoices and customer statements.

From this information, I will either produce a narrative description of the system or a flowchart. Except for small systems, using a narrative description is unsatisfactory, as:

    (i)   it can be incomplete (some operations have not been described)
    (ii)   it can be vague or misleading
    (iii)   often it is not written in a logical order or consistent manner.

Using a flowchart is better, as it clearly shows the system. In a flowchart, processing of transactions goes down the paper and different departments have columns allocated to them across the page. The pictorial representation of the system avoids ambiguities and it is effective at indicating division of duties. The audit firm should use a standard set of flowchart symbols.

It is common to supplement the flowchart with brief notes of each operation (eg, the sales manager authorises the order confirmation).

Normally, flowcharts show how transactions are processed when there are no problems. Narrative notes or brief flowcharts should be prepared for actions taken on problems. For instance, the following should be recorded:

    (i)   what happens when the credit controller does not authorise dispatch of the goods because of credit problems

    (ii)   procedure over return of goods and issuing credit notes.

Some of the larger audit firms use microcomputers to produce flowcharts. It is apparent from the question that this is a new audit client with a computerised sales system, so the auditor will have to record this system in the manner described above. However, in future years, if there is little or no change to the accounting system, the auditor will perform a walk-through test and make any changes to the flowchart.

To confirm the system, the auditor will check a small sample of transactions through the system. This test will check whether the system operates in the manner laid down in the flowchart. Any differences found between the flowchart and checking transactions through the system will be investigated, and, if the flowchart is shown to be incorrect, it will be modified.

Sometimes this walk-through test is performed after recording the system, and sometimes after evaluating the controls. It is better to perform the test after recording the system, as controls will be evaluated on the system which actually exists (rather than the system which the auditor has been told exists).

Did you answer the question?

Note that this is a new client, so the auditor has no previous experience of the system. Note also the advantages of flowcharts over narrative notes in recording a system.

(b)   (i)   Normally, controls are evaluated either by using an internal control questionnaire (ICQ) or an internal control evaluation form (ICE).

An example of a question in an ICQ is:

'Does the credit controller check the creditworthiness of the customer, and give his/her authorisation before the goods are dispatched to the customer.'

An ICE asks key control questions, such as:

'Can goods be dispatched to a customer who is a poor credit risk.'

(ii)   An ICQ contains standard questions for each major accounting system.

If the answer to the question is 'Yes' the control exists, and if it is 'No' there is a weakness. The questions in the ICQ should be designed in this manner so that a 'Yes' answer is satisfactory and a 'No' answer is unsatisfactory. In this way, the manager or partner can look down the answers to the ICQ and consider the effects of the 'No' answer.

Also, the audit staff can consider whether the apparent weaknesses indicated by 'No' answers are overcome by other controls in the system.

An ICE asks key control questions, as illustrated in the example above. An answer must be provided which describes the controls in the system to prevent this happening. It can be quite difficult to decide the controls which would prevent this happening, so these questions have to be answered by more senior staff with more experience of auditing accounting systems.

(iii)   The limitations of an ICQ are they are a standard set of questions which may not apply to the particular system being audited. In particular, the questions are likely to be too detailed for sales systems in small companies but may be inadequate for large complex systems. However, the questions are relatively easy to answer, so they can be completed by less senior staff than an ICE. Also, as ICQ's have a comprehensive list of questions, it should highlight most weaknesses in the system.

With an ICE, there may be no question in the auditor's standard set of questions which asks about and thus highlights a weakness in the system.

Currently, most firms who audit large companies use ICE's for evaluating controls, and the use of ICQ's has become less common. This is probably because the questions in the ICE ask the auditor to describe the controls necessary to minimise the risk of fraud and error (ie, one of the principal aims in auditing a sales system is to ensure that goods are not dispatched to customers who are a poor credit risk). Also, the answers to the questions in the ICE will be related to the client's sales system rather than some generalised system, which the ICQ assumes. The answers to the ICE can be used to decide the controls to check in compliance tests. One of the weaknesses of the ICQ is that the questions about controls may not ensure that the sales system is effective at preventing fraud and error (ie, the ICQ may not ask questions on all controls required to minimise the risk of fraud and error).

Following evaluation of the controls by the ICE or ICQ, the auditor will consider the effectiveness of the controls. Where controls are strong, the auditor will perform limited compliance tests. Where there appear to be weaknesses in controls, more extensive compliance tests will be carried out to check whether the weakness has led to error or fraud. Where controls are generally weak, the auditor may decide not to carry out compliance tests, but rely entirely on substantive procedures.

Did you answer the question?

Note the clear differences between an ICQ and an ICE. Check these differences if you are not sure.

(c)   (i)   Normally, items for compliance tests should be selected on a random basis.

This technique could be used to select sequentially numbered dispatch notes using random number tables (or computer generated random numbers). The level of confidence an auditor may require could be that at a confidence level of 95%, the error rate is 8% or less (ie, there is a 5% risk that the maximum number of errors in the population is 8 items in every 100). The confidence level and maximum error rate will be determined by the auditor so as to achieve the overall level of audit risk.

If the auditor considers the value of the item or the error is important, then some form of monetary sampling should be used, in which the probability of the item being selected is proportional to its value. Using this technique in auditing a sales system, sales invoices would be selected according to their value, with large value sales invoices having a proportionately higher probability of being selected.

Other methods may be used to select items in compliance tests. Sometimes a sequence of transactions may be checked, because it is convenient, or the audit test may be used to check there is no break in the sequence. Alternatively, the auditor may check every 50th dispatch note, say starting at number 6027, then 6077, 6127 and so on.

Finally, the auditor may use his judgement to select items, although this may be criticised for not being random. For instance, the auditor may deliberately select items which have a high risk of having problems, or he may avoid items with a high risk of problems to produce a favourable result to the test.

(ii)   Where controls are strong, the auditor will carry out limited compliance tests on the controls. This means that a small sample of the year's transactions will be checked. The number of items checked will:

-       depend on the level of control risk the auditor wishes to achieve, the lower the control risk, the larger will be the sample of items checked

-       probably be specified in the audit firm's manual, or, if microcomputers are used on the audit, the microcomputer will suggest the number of items to check.

The number of items selected should have a statistical basis. As indicated above, the auditor may decide that he/she requires a confidence level of 95% that the error rate is 8% or less. A statistical table, the audit manual or a microcomputer will indicate the number of items the auditor should test. For apparently weak areas of the system, the auditor would increase the sample of items he/she checks.

(iii)   If errors are found, the auditor will have to increase the sample of items he/she checks, in order to achieve the required value of control risk.

If a large number of errors are found, the auditor would report the matter to the company's management. If the weakness is considered to be serious, it will be reported to management in the management letter (or letter of weakness). The auditor will have to consider the effect of the weaknesses on substantive procedures and the audit report. A high incidence of errors found in compliance tests will result in a high control risk, which will require a lower detection risk so that the auditor achieves the required level of audit risk. Thus, the auditor will have to carry out more extensive substantive procedures (ie, on a larger sample of items). If the weaknesses revealed in the compliance tests are very serious, the auditor may have to qualify his audit report.

---

46   (Answer 2 of examination)

(**Examiner's comments and marking guide**)

Question 2: asked about controls in a computerised sales system.

In part (a) on controls over accepting orders and dispatching goods, many candidates did not realise that some of the points made in part (i) could be repeated in part (ii), such as checking whether the customer was over the credit limit, or there were old, outstanding debts.

In part (b) on controls over changing standing data, many candidates would have scored more marks if they had considered each of the points (i) to (iii) separately. Also, part (i) has three aspects, adding new customers, amending customer details and deleting customers, which should have been considered separately.

The answers to part (c) were not as good as expected. In part (i) the computer should look at old unpaid debts as well as customers being over their credit limit.

		Marks
(a)	Controls over issuing order confirmation and dispatch note	
	Generally 1 mark a point up to a maximum of	6
(b)	Controls over changing customer details, credit limits and selling prices	
	Generally 1 mark a point up to a maximum of	10
(c)	Credit check controls and overriding them	
	Generally 1 mark a point up to a maximum of	4
Total		**20**

Note: in part (c) many of the points may be short, when you should give ½ mark a point.

Step by step answer plan

Step 1 Read the question again and make sure that you focus on precisely what is required.

Step 2 This is a question about controls in a computerised sales system. With 6 marks available in part (a), you must describe at least three (say, four to be on the safe side) controls in each of part (a) (i) and (ii). You'll get a better mark for a short description of several controls rather than a lengthy description of few controls.

Step 3 A similar approach is required for part (b). Describe three or four controls for each of (b) (i), (ii) and (iii) by reading through the question and deciding on controls that are relevant to the required area.

Step 4 Part (c) centres around credit limits and the aged analysis of debtors that the computer can produce.

Step 5 Only when you are confident that you are about to answer the question that has been set, should you start writing.

The examiner's answer

(a)   (i)   The controls the computer system should incorporate before it issues an order confirmation to the customer will include:

- the customer should be checked as being one on the standing data file

- the computer should check the customer's current sales ledger balance. If dispatch of the goods would make the customer exceed its credit limit, a warning should be given. If this happens, the company may decide that the authorisation of the credit controller should be given (using a password before the order confirmation is issued). Also, the order confirmation could include a note saying that dispatch of the goods would exceed the customer's credit limit, so some payment by the customer is requested before the goods can be sent

- the system should check that the goods being ordered are available (they should not be a discontinued line) and that they are likely to be in stock by the dispatch date (this could be found from current stock levels, plus planned production, less committed sales)

- the order should either confirm the standard selling prices for the items ordered, or, if special prices are to be charged, they should be authorised by the sales director or sales manager before the order confirmation is issued.

(ii)   There should be the following controls before the computer raises a dispatch note and authorises dispatch of goods:

- the customer should be authorised, and should have an account on the sales ledger

- the computer should check that there is an order confirmation relating to the goods being dispatched, and that the quantity of goods being dispatched does not exceed the quantity on the order confirmation

- the computer should check to the book stock records that the goods are in stock and available for dispatch

- the creditworthiness of the customer should be checked. Normally, the system should not raise a dispatch note and invoice which would result in the customer going over the credit limit. The system may prevent deliveries to customers who have unpaid invoices older than a certain period (eg, four months). Also, there should be a system whereby the credit controller can stop deliveries to customers (eg, where the customer is unacceptably slow at clearing outstanding debts). Provided the credit limit is not being exceeded and the customer is not on 'stop', the system should allow processing of the dispatch note. The system should allow dispatch notes to be issued where the customer is over the credit limit or on 'stop', where this is authorised by the credit controller, or other authorised person. Ideally, the system should record the person who has given the authorisation.

Did you answer the question?

Note the format of the examiner's answer. When asked for a set of computer controls, the answer is in the form: The computer should check X, Y and Z before P, Q and R are initiated.

(b)   (i)   The controls over amending customer details will be less tight than for adding new customers and deleting customers. Where there is a small change to customer details, such as a change of address, this may be allowed by staff in the sales accounting department or the sales department. Changes should be authorised either by the sales director or chief accountant on a standard form, and the computer should record details of these changes and produce a sequentially numbered print-out when details of the changes are made. There should be a standard procedure for authorising new customers. New customers should apply on a standard form, giving references, details of their bank and recent audited accounts. Heanor Manufacturing should obtain the references, obtain credit reference reports (eg, from Dun and Bradstreet), look at the account and consider the information. The credit controller should recommend terms of trade and a credit limit for the customer, which should be authorised by the sales director and financial director.

Customers should be deleted from the file where Heanor Manufacturing:

- does not expect any more orders, or

- the customer has a poor record (eg, where it is a bad payer, or frequently disputes deliveries, cancels orders or returns goods), or

- the customer has ceased trading.

The sales director should authorise deletion of customers, but the system should not allow deletion of a customer where there is a debt outstanding.

Recommendations on deleting customers may come from a number of sources, including the credit controller, the sales department and the accounts department.

Periodically, a senior member of staff should review the print-out of customer names and addresses, test check details to the company's records and recommend deletion of any customers who have not traded with the company for some time.

(ii)   In general, only the credit controller should be authorised to change credit limits of customers. The system can exercise this control by requiring the change to be made from the credit controller's terminal using the credit controller's password. As a further control, the system may require the credit controller to input a special code before the customers' credit limits are changed. Before asking the credit controller to input the code, the system should list the credit limits which are to be changed, either on the terminal's screen (with both the old and new credit limit being displayed), or, if it cannot be shown on a single screen, either the credit limits should be printed out, or the credit controller should authorise the change one screen at a time.

Matters relating to credit limits for new customers have been described in part (b)(i) above. Periodically, the computer should print out details of customers who have exceeded their credit limit, or have old unpaid debts. Also, the sales department should request any changes in customers' credit limits on a standard form. This information should be used as a basis for changing customers' credit limits. Credit limits may be reduced where the debtor is slow at paying outstanding invoices. Credit limits may be increased where the customer exceeds the credit limit, but pays within the credit period, or where the sales department requests an increase. The credit controller should consider these changes, and, for customers with large credit limits, approval may be required by the chief accountant or finance director. Periodically, the chief accountant or finance director should review credit limits, old debts and customers who exceed their credit limits to check that the credit limits are reasonable.

There may be controls in the computer system which prevent the credit controller from increasing credit limits of customers who are slow payers. In this situation, the system may require authorisation by the chief accountant or finance director as well as the credit controller.

(iii)   Staff in the sales, accounting and costing departments should suggest selling prices for new products, and changes in selling prices of existing products. Details of these changes should be input into the computer, but the change should only be allowed after authorisation by the sales director (eg, using his/her password and a secret code). The system may be designed to increase prices from a particular date (eg, 1 January), the change may be authorised before that date, but the system will continue to use the old prices until 1 January. If it is found that there are errors in selling prices, and the sales director is unavailable, another authorised individual (eg, the chief accountant) may be allowed to authorise the change.

The computer system should sequentially number the batches of all changes to selling prices, and print out details when each change is authorised. The system should retain details of all changes to selling prices for the past year, so that details of any change can be listed at any time. The company should keep the print-outs of all price changes and check that the batch number for the new batch of changes is one more than the last one in the file. If there is a missing batch number, details of the missing changes should be printed out and checked that they are correct and authorised.

Periodically, the prices of all the company's products should be printed out and checked by the sales staff to authorised price lists. Also, the system should print out any products with a low, or negative gross profit margin so that the prices of these products can be reviewed. Details of slow-moving products may be printed out, and the prices of these products may be reduced (with authorisation) to increase sales or sell discontinued lines.

(c)   (i)   The computer system should not allow the dispatch note to be printed where:

-       the invoice for the dispatch would put the customer over the credit limit (or the customer is already over the credit limit)

-       the customer has been put on 'stop' by the credit controller

-       there are items on the customer's account which are still unpaid after a particular period (eg, where there are invoices which are over four months old).

(ii)   If the sales staff want the goods to be dispatched, they should request authorisation by the credit controller. If the credit controller believes the goods should be dispatched to the customer, he/she will input a secret code which will initiate printing of the dispatch note, production of the sales invoice and posting of the sales invoice to the sales ledger.

47 (Answer 3 of examination)

Examiner's comments and marking guide

Question 3: was concerned with checking suppliers' statements to the balances on the purchase ledger.

Although part (a) on reconciling the supplier's statement to the purchase ledger balance was unexpected, many candidates produced the correct answer. In some cases, the presentation of the candidate's answer could have been improved.

In part (b) the best approach was to consider each of the reconciling items identified in part (a). It was less satisfactory to consider the two 'goods in transit' items together, as invoice 6210 is likely to be either in dispute, lost or the goods were never received. With invoice 6355 it is more likely there could be a cut-off error. Candidates who considered checking suppliers' statements generally did poorly and were awarded a low mark.

In part (c)(i) most candidates suggested selecting suppliers' statements on the basis of the value of the purchase ledger balance. Very few candidates considered the weakness of this approach, as it would have a low chance of selecting suppliers with a small balance on the purchase ledger, but a large balance on the supplier's statement, like the creditor in part (a) of the question. The answer to part (ii) was either to ask the supplier for a statement, or to ask the supplier to confirm the balance on the client's purchase ledger.

		Marks
(a)	Reconciliation of supplier's statement to purchase ledger balance	
	½ mark for each correct item and 1 mark for getting the total correct	4
(b)	Work in checking reconciling items, the suggested marking is:	
	(i) disallowed discount - up to 2 marks	
	(ii) transposition error - up to 1 mark	
	(iii) disputed invoice 6210 - up to 2 marks	
	(iv) invoice 6355 - cut-off error - up to 2 marks	
	(v) cash in transit - up to 2 marks	
	(vi) disallowed discount - up to 1 mark	
	Overall, generally 1 mark a point up to	10
(c)	(i) basis of selecting suppliers' statements - up to 3 marks	
	(ii) action if no supplier's statement - up to 3 marks	
	Overall, generally 1 mark a point up to	6
Total		20

Note: in part (a) in order to allocate ½ mark the candidate must identify the item and get the correct adjustment to profit. In part (b) you may allocate marks based on 1 mark a point.

Step by step answer plan

Step 1 Read the question again and make sure that you focus on precisely what is required.

Step 2 Part (a) should offer easy marks for the preparation of a creditors account reconciliation to the supplier's statement.

Step 3 Part (b) tells you what to do for the 10 marks: deal with each of the reconciling items from part (a) in turn.

Step 4 For part (c), don't just recommend that emphasis should be paid to those accounts with large balances in the purchase ledger. The whole point of the question is to recognise that there are accounts, like Carlton Ltd in the question, which have a low balance in the purchase ledger but to whom a large amount might be payable. The numbers in the questions are not chosen randomly; they are there to illustrate some point.

Step 5 Only when you are confident that you are about to answer the question that has been set, should you start writing.

The examiner's answer

(a) Reconciliation of purchase ledger balance to balance on supplier's statement:

				£	£
Balance per purchase ledger					5,980
Differences:					
(i)	31.3	Discount not allowed by supplier	126		
(ii)	4.3	Transposition error invoice 6080	180		
(iii)	4.4	Invoice 6210 not on purchase ledger	4,735		
(iv)	28.4	Invoice 6355 not on purchase ledger	6,298		
(v)	30.4	Cash in transit	6,005		
(vi)		Discount not allowed?	123		
				17,467	
Balance per supplier's statement					23,447

Did you answer the question?

Note that it is not important whether your reconciliation starts with the £5,980 and reconciles it to the £23,447, or vice versa. Either is acceptable, though it seems easier to start with the first balance given in the question (the £5,980) and reconcile it to the balance given second in the question.

(b) Looking at each of the items above:

(i) As the difference due to the disallowed discount is very small, I may perform very little work on this item, and record it as an unadjusted error. However, if detailed checks were considered necessary, they would be as described below.

From the date of the cash received which pays the February invoices, it appears that Carlton may not have received the cheque until after 31 March, so it would not be entitled to the cash discount of 2%. The date the cheque for £6,163 was received by Carlton can be found by looking at Tollerton's bank statement and checking the date it was cleared by the bank. If this is about 10 April, it indicates that Tollerton delayed sending the cheque to Carlton. If it is earlier than 10 April, Carlton may have been slow at posting cheques to its sales ledger. I will look at Tollerton's bank statement, and see if cheques issued on 31 March were slow at being cleared by the bank. If the delay is a week or more, this indicates that Tollerton delays sending cheques to most creditors. If most of these cheques are cleared within a week, it indicates that Carlton is slow at paying customers' cheques into the bank.

In addition to these checks, I will ask Tollerton's purchase ledger controller about this item, and inspect correspondence with Carlton. If Tollerton usually pays this disallowed discount to Carlton, this disallowed discount should be added to the purchase ledger balance. If Carlton eventually allows the discount, there is no need to add the discount to the balance.

(ii) The apparent transposition error on invoice 6080 would be checked by inspecting the invoice. If the invoice shows £3,752, then an additional creditor of £180 should be added at the year end to correct this error. No adjustment will be necessary if Tollerton's figure is correct.

(iii) It appears that invoice 6210 for £4,735 has not been included on Tollerton's purchase ledger. As this invoice is dated some time before the year end, the first question to ask is whether the goods have been received. I will check whether the goods have been received by looking for the appropriate goods received note (I may have to ask Carlton for details of this item, if no invoice can be found at Tollerton). If the goods have been received, I will check if there is a purchase invoice. If there is a purchase invoice, I will ask the purchases department why the invoice has not been posted to the purchase ledger. This will probably be because of a dispute, normally either an incorrect price, the wrong quantity or some faults with the goods. If the goods relating to this invoice are in stock (or have been sold) a purchase accrual should be made for this item. If an excessive price has been charged for the items, a lower price can be used, provided the same price is used to value the stock. If there is a short delivery, the purchase accrual would be for the actual goods received, rather than for those on the invoice.

I will inspect correspondence on this item with Carlton to assess what will be finally agreed. If there is no evidence of the goods being received by Tollerton, I will ask Carlton for details confirming that Tollerton has received the goods (this may be via Tollerton's purchasing department). If there is no evidence that Tollerton has received the goods, then no purchase accrual for this invoice is necessary.

(iv)   For invoice 6355, the question is whether Tollerton received the goods before the year end. I will check if Tollerton received the goods before the year end by looking at the date on the goods received note. If the date is before the year end, then Tollerton should include a purchase accrual at the year end for this invoice. If Tollerton received the goods after the year end, no purchase accrual is required. A further check that the goods were received is to look at the quantities of the items in stock at the year end. If the quantities in stock at the year end are about the same as, or more than, those on the invoice, there is strong evidence that the goods were received before the year end.

(v)   The cheque on 30 April appears to be cash in transit. I will check the date the cheque is cleared by the bank after the year end. If this is within a week, and most other cheques are cleared within a week, then this is validly cash in transit. If most cheques issued immediately before the year end take more than a week to clear, it indicates they were sent to suppliers after the year end, in which case they should be deducted from payments before the year end and added to creditors (as these were payments made after the year end).

(vi)   If, as appears likely, the cheque for £6,005 is not received by Carlton until some time after the year end, then the discount of £123 will be disallowed by Carlton. If this discount is disallowed, it should be added to creditors at the year end. Checks on this item are similar to those for item (i) above.

(c)   (i)   The suppliers' statements I will select for checking to the purchase ledger balances will concentrate on:

-             creditors with large balances, and

-             creditors who are large suppliers to the business (ie, those who have a large volume of transactions with Tollerton).

A sample of smaller value creditors will be selected, to check that the purchase ledger is accurate for processing lower value creditors and purchase invoices. A statistical basis could be used for randomly selecting creditors, such as monetary unit sampling, but it is unusual for auditors to use this method. A weakness of using monetary unit sampling is that it would have a low chance of selecting creditors with a small balance on the purchase ledger, but where the actual balance owing is large (like the one illustrated in part (a) of the question). The second basis of selecting creditors (ie, selecting large suppliers to the business) would have a greater chance of selecting such creditors.

(ii)   If there is no supplier's statement for a large balance on the purchase ledger, I will ask the purchase accounting department if such a statement exists. If no statement exists at 30 April, I will ask if there is a statement at 31 May. If there is a statement at 31 May, I will use it to check the balance on the purchase ledger at 30 April. If there is no statement on the client's premises, I will contact the supplier (with the client's permission) and ask them either to send me a copy of the statement, or confirm the balance on the client's purchase ledger. If it is not possible to contact the client, I will consider whether the client's system is reliable at processing purchase invoices. I will look at the balance on the purchase ledger and consider whether it is reasonable - the value of April's purchase invoices should be similar to March's. Also I will look at correspondence with the supplier, and check if there are any invoices on 'hold' which have not been posted to the purchase ledger. I will see if any goods were received immediately before the year end, and check that they have either been posted to the purchase ledger or included as a purchase accrual. Based on these investigations, I will decide whether the purchase ledger balance is correct.

48 (Answer 4 of examination)

Examiner's comments and marking guide

Question 4: was concerned with the auditor's responsibility when either fraud is not detected by the auditor, or when he/she identifies it.

In part (a)(i) most candidates said it is the directors' responsibility to detect fraud and error, but the question did not ask for this! Most candidates said either:

(i)   the auditor is not responsible for detecting fraud (ie, it is the directors' responsibility); or

(ii)   the auditor is responsible for detecting all fraud.

Neither of these are correct. The Auditing Standards say the auditor should design his/her audit procedures so that he/she has a reasonable expectation of detecting material fraud and error. The word 'material' is most important and was seldom mentioned by candidates.

The answers to parts (a) (ii) and (a) (iii) were quite good, as most candidates said item (ii) was not material and item (iii) was material, based on a material error being more than 10% of profit before tax and an immaterial error being less than 5% of profit before tax. Few candidates considered more complex aspects, such as the auditor's responsibility if he/she had been asked by the management to audit petty cash, or other error, combined with item (ii), making the total error material.

The answers to part (b) were not as good. In part (i) most candidates said the error was not material based on it being less than 5% of profit before tax. However, few candidates said that sensitivity over directors' remuneration, and the requirements of the Companies Acts made the error in the director's remuneration material. Most of the answers to part (ii) and (iii) were weak, with many candidates thinking the answers to the two parts would be identical. In part (ii) the auditor's position is very weak, as the Managing Director has the power to appoint a new auditor. In part (iii) many candidates did not understand 'audit committees', and the Managing Director's powers are very weak, as he owns less than 1% of the company's shares.

		Marks
(a)	Consideration of item (a): Generally 1 mark a point up to a maximum of	9
(b)	Consideration of item (b): Generally 1 mark a point up to a maximum of	11
Total		20

Step by step answer plan

Step 1   Read the question again and make sure that you focus on precisely what is required.

Step 2   This is a standard question on the auditor's responsibility to detect fraud. Knowledge of SAS 110 would be useful, and some reference to the word 'material' is critical. Auditors must have a reasonable expectation of detecting material misstatements in the financial statements arising from error or fraud. The meaning of material is discussed in SAS 220. For example, an extra £200,000 of directors' emoluments is certainly material compared to the current total of £450,000 for the managing director.

Step 3   Only when you are confident that you are about to answer the question that has been set, should you start writing.

The examiner's answer

(a)   (i)   SAS 110 (Fraud and Error) says that auditors should design their audit procedures so as to have a reasonable expectation of detecting material fraud and error in the financial statements. So, an auditor is probably liable if he fails to detect material fraud and error. However, the auditor may not be liable if the fraud is difficult to detect (ie, the fraud had been concealed and it is unreasonable to expect the auditor to have detected the fraud).

For immaterial fraud and error, a claim for negligence against the auditor for not detecting immaterial fraud or error would be unsuccessful (except in the circumstances described in the next section). An auditor may be negligent if he:

- finds an immaterial fraud while carrying out his normal procedures and does not report it to the company's management (but he may not be negligent if the evidence to support a suspected fraud is weak)

- carries out audit procedures on immaterial items, of which the company's management is aware, and these procedures are not carried out satisfactorily, so failing to detect an immaterial fraud. For instance, there may be a teeming and lading fraud, and the auditor may check receipts from sales are correctly recorded in the cash book and sales ledger, but fail to check that the cash from these sales is banked promptly

- carries out audit procedures on immaterial items at the specific request of the company's management, and the auditor failed to detect an immaterial fraud due to negligent work. The management would have a good case to claim damages for negligence against the auditor.

(ii)   The fraud of £5,000 is 3.3% of the company's profit before tax, so it is immaterial. As the auditor has carried out no work in this area, and is not responsible for detecting immaterial fraud, it is probable that he is not negligent. It could be argued that the other audit procedures should have detected an apparent irregularity, such as analytical review. This might have indicated an increase in motor expenses compared with the previous year and budget, or the auditor could have looked at petty cash expenditure, which would show an increase compared with the previous year. Also, it could be argued that the auditor should have looked at the absolute level of petty cash expenditure in order to decide whether to carry out work on the petty cash system. However, these arguments against the auditor are relatively weak, and it is unlikely that a claim for negligence would be successful. However, not detecting the fraud is likely to lead to a deterioration of the client's confidence in the auditor.

(iii)   The fraud of £20,000 is 13.3% of the company's profit before tax, so it is material. It appears that the auditor is negligent in not carrying out any audit work on petty cash, as he/she has contravened the advice given in SAS 110 (Fraud and Error). SAS 110 says the auditor should design audit procedures so as to have a reasonable expectation of detecting material fraud or error, so as he/she performed no work on petty cash there is no chance of him/her detecting the fraud. As a minimum, the auditor should have looked at the level of petty cash expenditure, comparing it with the previous year and the budget. This should have highlighted the increase in expenditure and led to the auditor carrying out further investigations. As this is a petty cash fraud, it could be difficult to detect, but the cashier writing out and signing the petty cash vouchers, with no receipt attached, should have led the auditor to suspect the fraud.

It could be argued that the company has some responsibility for allowing the fraud to take place, as there was a serious weakness in the system of internal control (ie, the cashier recorded and made petty cash payments, and appeared to be able to authorise petty cash vouchers). So, some employee (eg, the managing director) should have checked the cashier's work. Also, the managing director would have signed cheques which reimburse the petty cash, and he should have been aware that these had increased and investigated the reasons for the increase.

Did you answer the question?

Note that in questions involving materiality, the usual assumption is that differences of less than 5% are not material, differences of more than 10% are material, and differences between these limits may be material depending on the circumstances.

(b)　(i)　In terms of profit before tax, the sum of £200,000 is immaterial. Normally a material item, in terms of profit before tax is an error which exceeds either 5% of the profit before tax (ie, £4.55m) or 10% of the profit before tax (ie, £9.1m), so £200,000 is very small. However, in terms of the director's remuneration, the £200,000 is 44% of the managing director's annual salary of £450,000. As the Companies Act 1985 (Sch 5, part V, ss 22(3) and 35(3)) requires the managing director's emoluments to be disclosed in the financial statements, and the emoluments include non cash benefits, so there is a material misstatement of his emoluments in the draft accounts. If the directors refuse to give the correct figure of the managing director's emoluments in the financial statements, the Companies Act 1985 (s 237(4)) requires the auditor to give the correct figure of the emoluments in the audit report. Directors' remuneration is a very important item in financial statements, both as far as Companies Act requirements are concerned, and to the readers of accounts. Recent press reports and public interest in the remuneration of directors of public companies in the UK (particularly the privatised utilities) has confirmed the importance of this figure in financial statements. The company is proposing that the financial statements should show only 69% of the managing director's remuneration, so the understatement is very material.

(ii)　If the managing director refused to change the financial statements, I would have to qualify my audit report and state his total emoluments are £650,000. However, it seems probable that he will try to dismiss me as auditor before I am able to give an audit report on the financial statements. In order to change the auditor, he must:

-　　find another auditor who is prepared to replace me as auditor, and

-　　call an extraordinary general meeting to vote on the change of auditor, and

-　　give special notice (at least 28 days) of the meeting and notify the shareholders, the new auditor, and myself, as retiring auditor.

I have the right to make representations to the shareholders, which can either be sent to the shareholders before the meeting, and/or I can make the representations at the meeting when it is proposed that I am replaced.

Although these representations are likely to have little effect on the change of auditor (as the managing director owns 60% of the shares, and only a 50% vote is required to change the auditor), it would alert the other shareholders to the action of the managing director and concealment of information.

As a further point, provided the new auditors are a member of the ACCA or one of the chartered bodies, the ethical rules require the new auditor to write to me asking if there are any matters I ought to bring to their attention to enable them to decide whether or not they are prepared to accept the audit appointment. I will reply to their letter, saying that the managing director has had £200,000 of benefits-in-kind, which he refuses to allow to be disclosed in the financial statements. I have explained to the managing director that I would have to qualify my audit report if these emoluments are not disclosed, and this is the reason why he is proposing that I should be replaced as auditor. If the proposed new auditors have the expected amount of integrity, they should discuss this point with the managing director, and point out that they will have to qualify their audit report if the benefits of £200,000 are not included in his remuneration in the financial statements.

If the new auditors take over the appointment and give an unqualified report, I will take legal advice. The action I could take would include:

-　　disclosing information about the director's remuneration to the new auditor's professional body, and the fact that the audit report has not been qualified

-　　notifying Companies House of the alleged understatement of the managing director's remuneration

-　　disclosing the benefit to the Inland Revenue (as it may not have been subject to income tax)

-　　disclosing the benefit to the police.

(iii)   If the managing director owned less than 1% of the issued shares, my position as auditor would be much stronger than in the situation in part (ii) above. If the managing director refused to increase his remuneration in the draft accounts, I would explain that I would have to contact the audit committee. If he still refused to change the remuneration, I would contact the chairman of the audit committee and arrange a meeting with its members. I would explain that I would have to qualify my audit report, unless the remuneration was increased to £650,000. Also, it is likely that either the company or the managing director is committing an offence by not disclosing this benefit to the Inland Revenue. It seems probable that this meeting will decide to incorporate the benefit in the financial statements.

However if the audit committee believes the financial statements should not be changed, I will have to insist on qualifying my audit report. If, at this stage, the directors decide to replace me as auditor, they will have to convene an extraordinary general meeting and give 28 days notice. I will be able to make representations in writing to the shareholders, and/or make those representations at the extraordinary general meeting.

As Colwick Enterprises plc is a listed company, this information is likely to be picked up by the press and financial institutions, and result in adverse publicity for the company. In addition, it will make shareholders suspicious of the honesty of the managing director and the other directors.

It seems probable that the directors would realise the problems of adverse publicity if they try to replace me as auditor, and this will prevent them from proposing the change of auditor. So, it seems probable that the other directors will insist that the full remuneration of the managing director should be shown in the financial statements.

49   (Answer 5 of examination)

(This answer is not enclosed. See tutorial note at Question 5 of the June 1996 exam.)

50   (Answer 6 of examination)

Examiner's comments and marking guide

Question 6: was concerned with auditing research and development.

Although the division between parts (a) and (b) of the question was clear, many candidates included points in part (a) which were relevant to part (b) and vice versa. However, markers were instructed to award marks for valid points, even if they were included in the wrong part.

In part (a) on verifying expenditure, most candidates did not consider a sufficient variety of types of expenditure, and how each of these items would be checked.

In part (b) on considering whether the expenditure could be capitalised, most candidates recited the points (a) to (e) above the required part, but included very little discussion and description of the audit work which should be performed.

The answers to part (c) were surprisingly poor. Part (i) is an unqualified report with an explanatory paragraph - few candidates suggested this answer. Many candidates suggested using a 'subject to' qualification, which is no longer valid under SAS 600 (which applies to financial statements ending on or after 30 September 1993). In part (ii) an 'except for' qualification should be used, but many candidates incorrectly suggested the more serious 'adverse' or 'disclaimer' qualification.

Marks

(a) Audit work to verify development expenditure of £500,000
Generally 1 mark a point up to a maximum of 8

(b) Audit work to determine whether development
expenditure of £500,000 can be capitalised
Generally 1 mark a point up to a maximum of 8

(c) Audit report:
    (i)   unqualified report with explanatory paragraph - up to   2
    (ii)   qualified report - except for disagreement - up to   2
    ——
    4
    ——

Total   20
    ——

Step by step answer plan

Step 1   Read the question again and make sure that you focus on precisely what is required.

Step 2   Part (a) requires a list of audit tests to be carried out on the components of the £500,000 described in the question. With 8 marks available, you should aim at describing at least 10 audit tests.

Step 3   The 5 conditions that must hold before development costs can be capitalised in accordance with SSAP 13 are given in the question, so part (b) can be answered by dealing with these conditions in turn.

Step 4   Part (c) is standard bookwork on SAS 600.

Step 5   Only when you are confident that you are about to answer the question that has been set, should you start writing.

The examiner's answer

(a)   I would perform the following work in auditing the development expenditure of £500,000:

    (i)   it is clear from the question that this is development expenditure which can be capitalised under SSAP 13 (Accounting for Research and Development), provided the conditions of SSAP 13 are met. It can be seen that it is the 'use of scientific or technical knowledge in order to produce new... products' so it qualifies as development expenditure

    (ii)   I will obtain from the company a schedule detailing expenditure on developing the system. SSAP 13 says that the development expenditure must be separately identifiable if it is to be allowed to be capitalised. Normally this will involve development expenditure being posted to a separate account in the nominal ledger. I will check that the expenditure relates to developing the system described in the question as follows:

    (iii)   any tangible fixed assets (computers, printers, scanners) purchased for developing the system will normally be included as tangible fixed assets, rather than development expenditure. Depreciation should be charged on these fixed assets so as to write them down from cost to disposal value over the development period. As the time to develop this system is quite short, it is probable that the depreciation charge will be quite high, as the equipment will be bought new and sold second-hand. The depreciation charge can be capitalised as development expenditure, provided the fixed assets have been used only for developing the new system. If they are used for other purposes, only the proportion of the depreciation charge relating to developing the system will be debited to development expenditure

    (iv)   purchases of software and other items for development of the software will be checked to purchase invoices. I will test check large purchase invoices and a smaller proportion of smaller ones to check that they relate to development of the software described in the question

(v)   labour costs incurred in developing software will be checked to the payroll. I will check that the employees charging development expenditure either work wholly on this development, or they have recorded their hours on time sheets and that the cost of these hours has been charged to development expenditure. To confirm the validity of this expenditure, I may ask the employees if they have been working on the project

(vi)   I will check that direct overheads relating to these wages costs have been correctly added to development expenditure. Direct overheads will include employer's National Insurance, pension contributions and holiday pay credit

(vii)   I will check that other overheads added to development expenditure are reasonable. Although SSAP 13 does not specify how these overheads should be calculated, they will probably be similar to production overheads, as described in SSAP 9 (Stocks and Long-term Contracts). They will probably include the costs of office accommodation for development staff and a proportion of management costs

(viii)   I will check other expenses charged to development expenditure. These will probably include travelling costs, telephone, stationery and use of any computer time for developing the system (eg, use of a minicomputer)

(ix)   further costs, such as marketing and advertising the product will be checked to purchase invoices, and I will consider whether it is appropriate to add these costs to development expenditure.

Based on this work, I will decide whether £500,000 has been spent on developing the software for this system.

Did you answer the question?

Note that as with other auditing questions involving SSAPs or FRSs, the marks are available for describing audit procedures, not for showing a deep knowledge of the accounting standard. Don't be tempted here to write down all that you know about SSAP 13; it won't earn many marks.

(b)   The conditions to allow the development expenditure of £500,000 to be capitalised are given in the question. The first matter I will consider is whether the system will operate as intended, and reliably. In assessing this, I will:

(i)   get a member of the company's staff to demonstrate the system. They should be able to show that the system can perform more than one task at the same time (eg, copying, while processing accounting data, or receiving a fax while performing a word-processing task)

(ii)   inspect reports from pilot users to check that they are satisfied with the system, and that it operates reliably (ie, it does not crash, or lose data). I will discuss any of the users problems with the development staff, and assess whether they can be overcome. I will ask for a demonstration of new versions of the software which overcome problems experienced by users.

Based on this work, I will decide whether the system will prove reliable, and whether it will prove attractive to potential users.

Then, I will ask management for their predictions of sales, selling prices and the cost of producing the product. In auditing this item, I will:

(i)   test check their calculation of future net revenues, based on predicted sales, selling prices and costs

(ii)   consider whether their sales estimates are realistic, optimistic or pessimistic. I will look at enquiries the company has received about this software, and the number of these enquiries compared with the publicity undertaken by the company. I will check the percentage of enquiries which become actual sales for previous products developed by the company. I will consider whether the product is likely to be successful (this seems likely, as it should be a cheaper alternative than buying separate faxes and photocopiers). I will consider whether a competitor may produce a similar product, which will lead to a loss of sales. I will ask the company's management if they are aware of any competitors developing a similar product, and I will look at magazines and journals to check their representations.

During 1995, printer manufacturers have started selling fax machines which can be connected to computers to provide printing, copying and image reading facilities. I will consider whether this new product will supersede the product being developed by the company. Based on these investigations, I will consider whether the sales estimate is realistic

(iii)   check that the selling price of the product is realistic, based on the selling price of similar products. There is likely to be a structure of selling prices, with a higher price for sales of single items and progressively lower prices for larger quantity sales to customers (eg, £500 a unit for sales of 1-9 units, £400 a unit for sales of 10-99 units and £350 a unit for sales of over 100 units). I will consider whether the mix of sales (in terms of small, medium and large orders) is realistic, based on previous experience and the company's plans for selling this product

(iv)   I will check that the costs of producing and selling the software are realistic. These costs will include the cost of disks, copying the software onto the disks, and preparing and printing the manuals and boxes containing the product. In addition, I will check that the costs of marketing and advertising the product are realistic. These costs will be checked to purchase invoices, and compared with the cost of producing and marketing past products, with an allowance for the size of the product (ie, its development costs, selling prices and potential sales.)

Based on this work, I will decide whether the company's estimates of profits from future sales of the product are realistic. Currently, it appears that there is a lot of price competition and discounting of software products, and I will have to take this into account when estimating future selling prices and sales (ie, the future selling price may be lower than for past products because of price-cutting).

The next matter to consider is whether the company can stay in business for sufficiently long to sell the product. So, I will check future profit and cash flow forecasts of the company and consider whether they are realistic. If development of this project is a very large item for the company, the most adverse cash flow is likely to be at the start of sales to customers. When sales commence, cash flow from sales should exceed costs (probably by a substantial margin).

Based on these investigations, I will decide whether the £500,000 of development expenditure can be recovered against profits from future sales. If I am confident that this expenditure can be recovered against future sales, I will give an unqualified audit report. If I have reservations about the recoverability of the development expenditure, examples of the forms of audit report I could use are given in part (c) of this answer.

(c)   (i)   If I have some uncertainties about the recoverability of the development expenditure, I will ask the directors to explain the capitalised development expenditure in the financial statements. My audit report will have a section headed 'Fundamental uncertainty' which will refer to the uncertainty about the development expenditure. This paragraph will end by saying 'our opinion is not qualified in this respect'. Following this, it will have a section headed 'Opinion' which will be the same as for an unqualified audit report. If the risk of the development expenditure being worth less than £500,000 is very small, I may give an unqualified audit report. However, in view of the levels of litigation against auditors, many auditors would give an unqualified audit report with an explanatory paragraph, as described earlier in this paragraph. This form of audit report is similar to example 4 in SAS 600 (Auditors' Reports on Financial Statements).

    (ii)   If my view is that it is not possible for the company to produce a commercially viable product, then I will qualify my audit report. The opinion paragraph will be headed 'Qualified opinion arising from disagreement about accounting treatment'. It will describe the £500,000 development expenditure, and explain that 'in our opinion the capitalised development expenditure is worthless, so it should be charged as an expense in the profit and loss account, reducing profit and net assets by £500,000'. The next paragraph will say that 'except for not writing off the development expenditure' the financial statements show a true and fair view. This will be an 'except for disagreement' type of qualified audit report, similar to example 7 in SAS 600 (Auditors' Reports on Financial Statements).

Did you answer the question?

Note that an audit report detailing a fundamental uncertainty in a separate paragraph is still an unqualified audit report, though it probably offers auditors better protection against actions for negligence.

DECEMBER 1996 QUESTIONS

Section A - ALL THREE questions are compulsory and MUST be attempted

51   (Question 1 of examination)

Newark plc has a large Computing and Data Processing Department. Recently, the company has used its Data Processing Department to develop a new computerised sales and sales ledger system which is integrated with the stock control system.

Prior to the system being developed, your audit firm discussed developing the system with Newark plc. It was agreed that the system should be developed in the following stages:

(a)   feasibility study - deciding the basic specification for the system, the tasks it should perform, how much it will cost to develop and the benefits which will accrue;

(b)   specifying the system - providing a detailed specification of the system;

(c)   obtaining cost and time estimates, and ascertaining the benefits - a more detailed study of the costs and benefits, and producing a time and cost budget;

(d)   designing the system, programming and documentation - writing the computer programs and the documentation for users;

(e)   system and program testing - testing the computer programs and the system to check they are operating correctly and reliably;

(f)   training the staff to use the system - using test files and the draft documentation;

(g)   file conversion - transferring the data files from the old system, setting up new files. Ensuring the files are accurate before current transactions are entered into the system;

(h)   acceptance and authorisation - senior management checking the system will operate reliably, and the documentation is satisfactory. When they are satisfied, they should accept the system and provide their written authorisation.

The reasons for developing the new system are:

(a)   the old system will not have the capacity to store and process sales data for the company's large and expanding number of customers;

(b)   the old system did not provide the reports required to run the business effectively. The new system will incorporate these features.

The partner in charge of the audit has asked you to audit items (e), (g) and (h) above, as he believes they are the most important stages in developing the new computerised sales system.

Also, the partner has said it may be necessary to use Computer Assisted Audit Techniques to audit the new sales system.

You are required

(a)   for each of the items (e), (g) and (h) above, to describe:

(i)   the controls which should be in operation, and
(ii)   the audit tests you will perform to verify the procedures have been carried out correctly.

(9 marks)

(b) (i)   to describe the main Computer Assisted Audit Techniques which are used by auditors

(5 marks)

(ii)   to describe tests you could perform using computer audit programs on Newark's year end sales ledger file.

(6 marks)

(Total: 20 marks)

Note: An alternative term for 'computer audit programs' is 'audit software'

---

52   (Question 2 of examination)

You are carrying out the audit of the purchases system of Spondon Furniture Limited. The company has a turnover of about £10 million, and all the shares are owned by Mrs Fisher and her husband who are non-executive directors, and are not involved in the day to day running of the business. The Managing Director is responsible for running the business, but does not own any of the company's shares.

The book-keeper maintains all the accounting records and prepares the annual financial statements.

A microcomputer is used to maintain the accounting records including those of the purchases system. Standard accounting software is used, which was purchased from an independent supplier. For the purchases system, a purchase ledger is maintained to which invoices, credits, adjustments, cash and discount are posted. When purchase invoices and credits are input into the computer, the value of the invoice or credit is posted to the purchase ledger, and the expense analysis and VAT are posted to the nominal ledger.

You have determined that the documents and individuals involved in the purchases system are:

(a)   when materials are required for production, the production manager sends a hand written note to the buying manager. For orders of other items, the department manager or Managing Director send hand written notes to the buying manager. The buying manager finds a suitable supplier and raises a purchase order. The purchase order is signed by the Managing Director. You are aware that purchase orders are not issued for all goods and services received by the company;

(b)   materials for production are received by the goods received department, who issue a goods received note (GRN), and send a copy to the book-keeper. There is no system for recording receipt of other goods and services;

(c)   the book-keeper receives the purchase invoice, matches it with the goods received note and purchase order (if available). The Managing Director authorises the invoice for posting to the purchase ledger;

(d)   the book-keeper analyses the invoice and posts it to the purchase ledger;

(e)   at the end of each month, the book-keeper prepares a list of creditors to be paid. This is approved by the Managing Director;

(f)   the book-keeper prepares the cheques and remittances, and posts the cheques to the purchase ledger and cash book;

(g)   the Managing Director signs the cheques, and the book-keeper sends the cheques and remittances to the creditors.

Mr and Mrs Fisher, the two shareholders of Spondon Furniture Ltd, are aware there may be weaknesses in the internal controls in the purchases system and have suggested that an internal auditor should be appointed who reports to them.

You are required to

(a)   Identify the weaknesses in controls in Spondon Furniture's purchases system and suggest how these weaknesses can be corrected.

(10 marks)

(b)   Suggest the work an internal auditor of Spondon Furniture could carry out to check procedures in the purchases system and minimise the risk of fraud and error.

(5 marks)

(c)   Assuming Spondon Furniture does not have an internal auditor, consider whether the *external auditor* has a greater responsibility for detecting fraud and error, than would be the case if all the company's shares were owned by an executive Managing Director.

(5 marks)

(Total: 20 marks)

---

53   (Question 3 of examination)

Your firm is the auditor of Textile Wholesalers Limited, which buys textile products (e.g. clothing) from manufacturers and sells them to retailers. You attended the stocktake at the company's year end of Thursday 31 October 1996. The company does not maintain book stock records, and previous years' audits have revealed problems with purchases cut-off.

Your audit tests on purchases cut-off, which started from the goods received note (GRN), have revealed the following results:

No	Date of GRN	GRN No	Supplier's Invoice No	Invoice value (£)	On purchase ledger before year end	In purchase accruals at year end
1	28.10.96	1324	6254	4,642	Yes	No
2	29.10.96	1327	1372	5,164	Yes	Yes
3	30.10.96	1331	9515	7,893	No	Yes
4	31.10.96	1335	4763	9,624	No	No
5	1.11.96	1340	5624	8,243	Yes	No
6	4.11.96	1345	9695	6,389	No	Yes
7	5.11.96	1350	2865	7,124	No	No

Assume that goods received before the year end are in stock at the year end, and goods received after the year end are not in stock at the year end.

A purchase accrual is included in creditors at the year end for goods received before the year end when the purchase invoice has not been posted to the purchase ledger before the year end.

You are required

(a)   at the stock take:

   (i)   to describe the procedures the company's staff should carry out to ensure that stock is counted accurately and cut-off details are recorded; and

   (ii)   to describe the tests you would carry out and the matters you would record in your working papers.

(11 marks)

(b)   from the results of your purchases cut-off test, described in the question:

   (i)   to identify the cut-off errors and produce a schedule of the adjustments which should be made to the reported profit, purchases and creditors in the financial statements to correct the errors;   **(5 marks)**

   (ii)   to comment on the results of your test, and to state what further action you would take.

(4 marks)

(Total: 20 marks)

Note: Ignore Value Added Tax (VAT)

Section B - TWO questions ONLY to be attempted

---

54 (Question 4 of examination)

An auditor's independence may be compromised by the provision of other non audit services.

(a) Many audit firms provide additional services to their audit clients. These services include:

    (i) calculating the company's corporation tax liability and the directors' income tax liability, and negotiating with the Inland Revenue;

    (ii) preparing the company's financial statements for audit, from the accounting records;

    (iii) advising on systems of internal control.

You are required to consider, for each of the services listed in (i) to (iii) above:

    (i) the effect on the auditor's independence of providing these services

    (ii) the benefits provision of these services may provide to the client, and

    (iii) the procedures the audit firm should instigate to minimise the risk of providing them affecting their independence. **(10 marks)**

(b) 'Research has shown that the fees charged to listed UK companies by audit firms for non-audit work are, on average, about equal to the audit fee. It is alleged that:

    (i) audit firms are charging low audit fees in order to obtain lucrative non-audit work;

    (ii) with large fees from non-audit work, auditors will be reluctant to qualify their audit report because of the risk of losing both the audit and non-audit fees;

    (iii) auditors' reluctance to qualify their audit report compromises their independence.

If these allegations are correct, then auditors of listed companies should be prevented from providing other services to client companies'.

You are required to discuss this statement, consider each of the matters raised, and come to a conclusion on whether external auditors should be allowed to provide other services to the listed companies they audit.

(10 marks)
(Total: 20 marks)

---

55 (Question 5 of examination)

You are commencing the final audit of Hyson Computers Limited, which purchases computers and associated equipment from North America and the Far East and sells them to small computer suppliers.

You have been presented with the summarised draft financial statements for the year ended 30 September 1996 together with the audited figures for 1995:

Profit and Loss Account

	1996 £'000	1995 £'000
Sales	22,650	25,150
Cost of sales	17,650	17,605
Gross profit	5,000	7,545
Overheads	(3,950)	(3,900)
Interest	(700)	(450)
Net profit before tax	350	3,195
Corporation tax	(100)	(1,000)
Profit after tax	250	2,195
Dividends	(500)	(1,150)
Retained profit/(loss)	(250)	1,045

Balance sheet

	1996 £'000	1995 £'000
Tangible fixed assets	10,400	8,100
Current Assets		
Stock	6,400	4,300
Debtors	4,500	6,300
	10,900	10,600
Creditors - amounts due within a year		
Creditors	2,650	3,800
Bank overdraft	4,130	625
Taxation	20	875
Dividend	-	650
	6,800	5,950
Net current assets	4,100	4,650
Total assets less current liabilities	14,500	12,750
Bank loans	(6,000)	(4,000)
	8,500	8,750

	1996 £'000	1995 £'000
Capital and Reserves		
Called up share capital	5,000	5,000
Profit and loss account	3,500	3,750
	8,500	8,750

The following ratios have been produced:

		1996	*1995*
(a)	Gross profit margin	22.1%	30.0%
(b)	Net profit margin	1.55%	12.7%
(c)	Return on capital employed	4.12%	36.5%
(d)	Overheads (excluding interest) to sales	17.4%	15.5%
(e)	Dividend (% of shareholders funds)	5.88%	13.14%
(f)	Interest cover (times)	1.50	8.10
(g)	Dividend cover (times)	0.50	1.91
(h)	Current ratio	1.60	1.78
(i)	Acid test ratio (or quick ratio)	0.66	1.06
(j)	Gearing (bank overdraft included with loans)	1.19	0.53
(k)	Stock age (months)	4.35	2.93
(l)	Debtors age (months)	2.38	3.01
(m)	Creditors age (months)	1.80	2.59

The company's Financial Director has explained:

(a)   trading has been difficult in 1996, as there has been severe competition. The company has had to reduce its prices in an attempt to maintain sales;

(b)   the issued share capital is 5,000,000 ordinary shares of £1 each, and it has been the company's policy to pay an interim dividend of 10p a share on 1st May. The final dividend is determined so that total dividends for the year is about 50% of the profit after tax. In view of the low profits in 1996, no final dividend will be paid;

(c)   there are long term contracts for the purchase of computers and equipment from North America and the Far East. The company must specify these purchases six months in advance, and they must be paid in the overseas currency two months after they are received into the UK. The discount given by suppliers on these purchases increases with an increase in the quantity ordered. Currently, the company is planning to reduce purchases of this equipment as stocks are high and sales are falling;

(d)   the company has had a number of bad debts due to customers going out of business.

You are required

(a)   to comment on the company's performance in 1996, compared with 1995, based on the ratios and the information provided in the question.   **(6 marks)**

(b)   to describe the matters you will investigate in your audit, as a result of your review of the company's financial statements.   **(7 marks)**

(c)   to consider whether Hyson Computers Ltd is a going concern.

Your answer should:

(i)   consider the information provided in the financial statements;

(ii)   consider the effect on future profits and cash flows of the company's prediction that there will be a reduction in sales in the coming year; and

(iii)   describe the further investigations you will carry out and additional matters you will consider to decide whether the company is a going concern.   **(7 marks)**
      (Total: 20 marks)

Note: (a)   You should assume the ratios given in the question are calculated correctly

(b)   In the ratios given in the question:

Return on capital employed = net profit before tax/shareholders' funds × 100%
Gearing = (loans + bank overdraft)/shareholders' funds
Debtors age is based on sales
Creditors age and stock age are based on cost of sales

56   (Question 6 of examination)

Your firm is the auditor of Jane Stafford's Charity for Pensioners. The charity was formed many years ago from a large gift by Jane Stafford, the income from which is used to pay pensions to needy individuals. The original gift has been invested in fixed interest stock and shares in listed companies. The trustees manage the charity, and the full-time administrator keeps the accounting and other records and pays the pensions.

The draft summarised Income and Expenditure Account for the year ended 30 September 1996 and an extract from the balance sheet, is given below, together with the audited figures for 1995.

Income and Expenditure Account for year ended 30 September

	1996 £	1995 £
Income		
from fixed interest investments	44,200	41,900
from shares in listed companies	123,900	123,500
	168,100	165,400
Expenditure		
Payments to pensioners	141,300	144,300
Administration costs	21,600	20,500
Audit and accountancy	4,700	4,500
Sundry expenses	2,800	2,600
	170,400	171,900
Net (deficit) for the year	(2,300)	(6,500)

Extract from Balance Sheet at 30 September

	1996 £	1995 £
Cost of investments		
Fixed interest investments	511,200	511,200
Shares in listed companies	1,445,600	1,262,700
	1,956,800	1,773,900

The following information has been provided:

(a)   during the year some shares were sold at a profit of £182,900 and the proceeds were re-invested in shares of other companies;

(b)   there were no purchases or sales of fixed interest investments in the year ended 30 September 1996. In the year ended 30 September 1995 some of the fixed interest investments were sold and others purchased using the proceeds of sale;

(c)   the charity is managed by voluntary trustees who meet four times a year, and the administrator keeps the minutes of the meetings;

(d)   the trustees receive applications for pensions, and approve them if they are suitable and there is sufficient income from investments;

(e)   the administrator keeps the accounting records and pays the pensions (by cheque);

(f)   as auditor of the charity, you prepare the financial statements from the accounting records kept by the administrator, and audit those financial statements. Your audit report is addressed to the trustees of the charity.

You are required to describe the audit work you would carry out:

(a)   to verify that pensions are paid to authorised pensioners. You should consider how you would verify the existence of pensioners.   **(6 marks)**

(b)   to verify income from investments. Your audit tests should verify that all the income from the investments has been received by the Charity and included in the financial statements, including dividends from the shares in listed investments bought and sold during the year.   **(10 marks)**

(c)   to verify the ownership of the fixed interest investments and shares in listed companies.   **(4 marks)**
                                                                                                  (Total: 20 marks)

ANSWERS TO DECEMBER 1996 EXAMINATION

The model answers to the questions are longer and frequently more detailed than would be expected from a candidate in the examinations. However, the model answer may not include all valid points mentioned by candidates - credit will be given to candidates mentioning these points.

The model answers may be used as a guide to the form and standard of answer candidates should try to achieve. However, the answers may not be as detailed as one would find in text books on the subject.

51   (Answer 1 of examination)

(Examiner's comments and marking guide)

Question 1: was concerned with the procedures in developing a new computer system (part (a)) and computer assisted audit techniques (part (b)).

In part (a) many candidates did not answer the question which was asked, but described tests on a computerised sales system or wrote about general and application controls. Such answers gained very few marks.

In item (e) it is important to state that testing the programs should be carried out by different staff from those who wrote the programs.

In part (b) (i) candidates' knowledge of the different computer assisted audit techniques was weak. Many mentioned only computer audit programs and test data. Frequently, their descriptions of the techniques were too short and unclear. In part (b) (ii) on using computer audit programs on the sales ledger file, many candidates were confused between test data and computer audit programs and thus gave answers which described procedures using test data. Also, many answers suggested checking transactions during the year when computer audit programs are more likely to be used to interrogate the year end sales ledger file. Candidates should ensure that they understand this topic and the difference between test data and computer audit programs.

			Marks
(a)		Description and audit of procedures in developing a sales system and controls exercised by the company	
		Generally 1 mark a point up to a maximum of	9
(b)	(i)	Main CAAT's used by auditors, including description	
		Generally 1 mark for each item up to a maximum of	5
	(ii)	Examples of the use of a computer audit program on the year end sales ledger file	
		Generally 1 mark a point up to a maximum of	6
Total			20

Note: in part (b) (i) you may give more than 1 mark for longer points

(Step by step answer plan)

Step 1   Read the question again and make sure that you focus on precisely what is required.

Step 2   The structure for answering part (a) is clear: for each of items (e), (g) and (h) one must describe (i) the controls, and (ii) suitable audit tests. These six separate aspects will earn the 9 available marks.

Step 3   Part (b) (i) is standard bookwork. Computer audit programs are one common example of CAAT which you should be familiar with.

Step 4   Only when you are confident that you are about to answer the question that has been set, should you start writing.

The examiner's answer

(a)   Considering each of the points listed in the question: For item (e):

(i)   The staff who test the system should be independent of the systems analysts and programmers who wrote the system. This provides a system of internal check. If the staff who write the programs also test them, they will be less effective at detecting errors and they could incorporate fraudulent aspects in the programs. The results of testing should be documented. If errors are found at this stage, the system should be sent back to the programmers for rectification. The staff testing the programs should perform their tests again on the amended system to ensure the errors have been corrected.

(ii)   As auditor, I will inspect documentation relating to testing the computer programs. I will check that the tests performed by the testers are realistic and include all the major aspects of operating the system. When errors are found, I will check that they have been corrected by the programmers, and subsequently checked by the testers to verify that the error no longer occurs. At the end of the process, the testers should give their authorisation that the system is reliable and suitable for use as the company's main sales accounting system.

For item (g):

(i)   The existing sales ledger files will be converted so that they can operate on the new system. Ideally, this should occur at the year end. A computer program should be developed to convert the files from the old format to the new format (for this new sales system). The files on the new system should be printed out and test checked to ensure there are no errors in the transfer. In particular, the number of accounts, the total ageing of the debts and the total value of debtors should be the same on the new system as the old one. This transfer should be attempted before the planned transfer date to ensure there are no problems (if problems are encountered, these can be overcome before the planned transfer date).

If the transfer of files is done manually from the old to new system, there should be more detailed checks to ensure there are no errors.

(ii)   As auditor, I will check that the correct procedures have been followed and that a reasonable number of checks between the old and new files have been made by the company's staff. I will check to print-outs from the old and new systems that a sample of customer balances agree, the total of the aged debts agree and the total debtors on the sales ledger is the same. I will note any differences and investigate them with the company's staff.

For item (h):

(i)   The new sales system should be authorised for use as the new sales system. Then computer programs will be made 'production' programs which cannot be changed, unless authorised by the data processing manager. The data processing manager will only authorise changes to the programs when the amended programs have been properly tested and shown to correct the error (or overcome the problem).

(ii)   As auditor, I will check authorisation of the system by the Data Processing Manager and the Board of Directors (if the latter is required). There should be evidence that the person authorising the system has checked the system has been authorised at each stage of development, that there is evidence that the system has been set up correctly and will operate reliably, and that appropriate documentation and instruction manuals have been prepared.

(b)   (i)   The main computer assisted audit techniques are:

-   computer audit programs (or audit software). These are computer programs written by or for the auditor which interrogate data files. High level languages have been developed to enable auditors to write these programs quickly and with very few instructions. These languages allow auditors to write the programs when they are relatively inexperienced in writing computer programs. Examples of their use are given in part (b)(ii) of this answer. The main aim of computer audit programs is to check the company's accounting software produces accurate reports from the accounting data on the computer's files (eg, that the ageing of debtors on the sales ledger is correct). Also, computer audit programs can be used to re-calculate certain items (eg, interest on a bank deposit account), to select items for further investigation (eg, old debts on the sales ledger) and to produce analyses not produced by the normal accounting software.

- test data is used to check the correct processing of data. The test data will include valid data, which should be processed correctly, and invalid data which should either be rejected or a warning given. Using test data is more effective than looking at the results of processing. This is because looking at the results of processing would not detect a situation where invalid data is processed and no warning given. Using test data would highlight this problem with the accounting system.

- with an integrated test facility, a dummy unit is set up within the client's accounting system. The auditor's test data is processed to this dummy unit at the same time as the company inputs normal transactions in the system.

- with an embedded audit facility, additional instructions and criteria are included with the normal accounting software. These instructions can check that edit criteria in the accounting software operates correctly. Also, selected transactions (based on specified criteria) can be 'tagged' for subsequent audit testing and review. The progress of these transactions through the system can be recorded on an auditor's file, which the auditor will check at a later date. The transactions can be selected on specified criteria (eg, items over a particular value) or they may be selected on a random or other basis (eg, one item out of every 100 processed).

(ii)   The computer audit program will be used on the company's year end sales ledger file to:

- add up the individual items on each account and check the total agrees with the balance on that account (in most sales ledger systems, the total balance on the account is stored separately from the individual transactions)

- add up the balances on each account and agree them to the total of the balances on the sales ledger

- check the number of accounts with balances is the same as that printed by the company's sales ledger system

- check the ageing of accounts with that produced by the company's sales ledger system. Any differences would be printed out for further investigation

- print out accounts where the balance is over the credit limit or where there are items older than a specified age (e.g. over 3 months old). This can be used to audit the doubtful debt provision

- print out accounts with a zero balance, those where there has been no movement for a specified period (e.g. 3 or 6 months), and those which include journal entries or non cash credit entries above a specified amount

- print out accounts which have a credit balance. Often there is a problem with these accounts, such as a credit note being posted twice, or an invoice not being posted to the sales ledger

- the computer audit program can be used to select items for a debtors' circularisation. The program can select items using a basis such as monetary unit sampling, and customers where there is a significant risk of a bad debt.

Did you answer the question?

Note that the question in part (b) (ii) was asking about tests to perform on the year end sales ledger file, not on the file during the year.

52 (Answer 2 of examination)

Examiner's comments and marking guide

Question 2: this question asked about controls in a purchases system.

The answers to part (a) on describing weaknesses in the purchases system were generally good. More candidates could have highlighted the powers of the Managing Director and emphasised the resulting serious internal control weaknesses.

The answers to part (b) were varied. However, many candidates suggested the tests the internal auditor could perform, and thus gained good marks. The model answer suggests concentrating on the weaknesses in internal control, particularly the strong powers of the Managing Director, bookkeeper and buying manager. Few candidates answered the question in this way, but they were not penalised for taking a different, but acceptable approach.

The answers to part (c) were very weak. Most answers concentrated on the directors' and auditors' responsibility for detecting fraud and error. However, very few candidates considered the reliance placed by the shareholders on the auditor's work if the Managing Director is not a shareholder, and the consequences of the Caparo case.

		Marks
(a)	Identifying weaknesses in the purchases system Generally 1 mark a point up to	10
(b)	Suggesting work of internal auditor in checking purchases system Generally 1 mark a point up to	5
(c)	Is the external auditor more liable for negligence with Spondon Furniture than when MD owns all shares? Generally 1 mark a point up to	5
Total		20

Note: in part (a) you should give ½ mark for the point and ½ mark for the explanation

Step by step answer plan

Step 1 Read the question again and make sure that you focus on precisely what is required.

Step 2 The best approach to part (a) is simply to work through the question line by line and both identify **and** suggest solutions to the weaknesses in the system. With 10 marks available you should be looking for at least 7 or 8 different weaknesses.

Step 3 The internal auditor in part (b) could counter-balance the dominant position of the managing director, for example by carrying out reconciliations of purchase ledger balances to suppliers statements and investigating reconciling items. The important point is to relate your answer to the scenario in the question, rather than writing in general about the work of an internal auditor.

Step 4 When the company's shares are all owned by non-executives, there is a separation of ownership and control, and the auditor should be aware of the need to test for material misstatements. Following Caparo, the auditor is less at risk if all the company's shares are owned by an executive managing director, because third parties could not sue the auditor successfully for negligence, and the MD himself is unlikely to sue for a fraud and error for which he was responsible.

Step 5 Only when you are confident that you are about to answer the question that has been set, should you start writing.

(a)   It is apparent that the Managing Director and book-keeper are responsible for a significant number of actions in the purchases system, which result in serious weaknesses in the system of internal control. Looking at each of the stages in the system:

(i)   purchase orders. It appears, from the question, that only hand written orders for purchases are made to the buying manager from user departments. There should be a system whereby user departments raise pre-numbered purchase requisitions, signed by the department manager, and send them to the buying manager. The duties of the buying manager over obtaining suitable suppliers are not clear. The buying manager should obtain the best quotation in terms of price, delivery date and quality. These quotations need to be checked by a responsible official before the order is sent to the supplier. The buying manager should sign the purchase order as well as the Managing Director. The Managing Director can ask for goods or services to be supplied and approve purchase orders, which is a weakness in the system of internal control. In addition, the Managing Director authorises purchase orders, purchase invoices and signs the cheques paying suppliers. There needs to be a system to overcome these serious weaknesses in the system of internal control. However, this is difficult to achieve without an internal auditor, as all staff will eventually report to the Managing Director, so he will be able to ensure his requests are carried out. A control could be exercised by appointing an internal auditor who reports to the non-executive directors. The question says that orders are not raised for all goods and services received by the company - they should be raised for all these items. All purchase orders should be sequentially numbered

(ii)   goods received notes - the system for checking goods received appears to be satisfactory. However, the goods received notes should be sequentially numbered, and signed by the storekeeper. Where goods are not in accordance with the advice note, a discrepancy note should be produced, a copy of which should be sent to the book-keeper and buying manager. There should be a system for recording receipts of other goods and services. Ideally, the goods received department should have copies of purchase orders and it should refuse receipt of goods where there is no purchase order

(iii)   the system should ensure there is a goods received note and purchase order for every purchase invoice where goods and services are received (orders and GRN's will not be required for provision of such services as gas, electricity, rates, telephone and insurance). Ideally, the purchase order should include the price of the item being ordered, so this can be checked to the purchase invoice. The purchase invoice should include a slip:

-    where the book-keeper acknowledges it has been checked to the order and GRN, and calculations on the invoice have been checked

-    where the invoice expense is analysed

There is a weakness in the system of internal control, as the Managing Director both authorises the purchase order and the purchase invoice. To overcome this weakness, I would suggest that the user department signs the slip acknowledging the goods or services have been received. Where this would be the Managing Director, another member of staff should perform this function. Then, the Managing Director can be the second person who authorises posting the invoice to the purchase ledger

(iv)   there is no check over the book-keeper posting invoices and cash to the purchase ledger. This should be checked on a test basis by the internal auditor (see part (b) below)

(v)   the Managing Director should sign the list authorising payments to creditors, before the book-keeper processes these transactions

(vi)   the system should prevent anyone, other than the Managing Director, from signing cheques, so only payments for authorised purchases should be made. However, there is little control over the Managing Director's actions, and he could make fraudulent payments to suppliers, as he can order goods and he approves posting of the invoices to the purchase ledger. Also, the question does not say whether any evidence is presented to the Managing Director when he signs the cheques. For normal suppliers (e.g. British Telecom for payment of telephone costs) it seems probable that no evidence is necessary, apart from the remittance which shows the invoices being paid. However, for little known suppliers the Managing Director should request and inspect the invoices being paid. Also, for larger value cheques, a second signatory could be required. The non-executive directors could be shown a list of payments, prepared by the book-keeper, at the periodic Board Meetings

(vii)   there is no evidence from the question of a purchase ledger control account being maintained. This can be prepared by the book-keeper, but should be checked by an independent person (not the Managing Director). Also, the purchase ledger cash payments should be agreed to the cash book, and the bank reconciliation checked by an independent person. The cash balance in the nominal ledger should be checked as agreeing to the cash book each month

(viii)   there should be a check of the month's expense in the nominal ledger to the budget and previous periods and any significant differences should be investigated

(b)   The internal auditor should highlight the weaknesses, as described above, and suggest amendments to improve controls in the system. In particular, a system of purchase requisitions should be instigated, which are prepared by the user department (and not the Managing Director). These should be sent to the buying manager to prepare the purchase order, which will be authorised by the Managing Director. A second person, in addition to the Managing Director, should authorise purchase invoices before they are posted to the purchase ledger (eg, the buying manager).

The internal auditor should perform the following checks on a test basis:

(i)   check there is a properly authorised purchase order and goods received note for each invoice posted to the purchase ledger. The internal auditor should verify that the checks in part (a)(iii) above have been performed on the purchase invoice. He should check the expense analysis on the invoice is appropriate and that it has been correctly posted to the purchase ledger and nominal ledger. The internal auditor should record cases where there is no purchase order or no GRN for an invoice, so that the system can be made to cover receipt of all goods and services. The internal auditor should consider whether the expense is for the benefit of the company, and record cases where a fraud is suspected

(ii)   check that purchase ledger payments relate to invoices posted to the purchase ledger, and that they are correctly recorded in the cash book

(iii)   check the reconciliation of the purchase ledger control account to the balances on the purchase ledger each month (and prepare this statement if it is not done by another member of staff). The purchase ledger payments in the month (from the purchases day book) should be checked as agreeing with the total of the payments in the cash book

(iv)   suppliers' statements should be reconciled to the balances on the purchase ledger. Any differences should be explained (e.g. cash or goods in transit) and corrected the following month. The internal auditor should test check these reconciliations

(v)   the internal auditor should scrutinise the list of payments to suppliers and investigate any which appear to be unusual

(vi)   the internal auditor should investigate any debit balances on the purchase ledger (usually they are for payments where no invoice has been posted to the purchase ledger).

(c)   Essentially, the Caparo decision limits the people who can sue an auditor for negligence to the company and the shareholders as a body. SAS 110 on Fraud and Error essentially says that auditors are not responsible for detecting immaterial frauds or error. However, they should design their audit tests so that they have a reasonable expectation of detecting material fraud and error. So, the auditor could only be liable for failing to detect material fraud and error.

As the ownership of Spondon is divorced from its management and two people own all the shares, it seems probable that the two shareholders could take action against the auditor if he failed to detect a material fraud (this is much more difficult if there are a larger number of shareholders). These two shareholders are then acting as 'shareholders as a body'. Also, it appears that the two shareholders are placing some reliance on the external auditor to detect any material fraud and error when the audit is carried out. It seems probable that the external auditor will only be able to allocate a small amount of responsibility for negligence to the Managing Director, as the Managing Director does not own any shares in the company. However, as a Director, the Managing Director is responsible for instigating a system of internal control which detects fraud and error.

If the main shareholders had asked the auditor to carry out work to detect material fraud or error, then the auditor's liability for negligence will increase (provided the auditor has agreed to this additional responsibility).

A different situation arises if the Managing Director owns all the shares. If the Managing Director is carrying out the fraud, the auditor's liability for negligence should be reduced (because of contributory negligence). Also, it seems probable that the Managing Director will have tried to conceal the fraud and may have made false representations to the auditor (which contravenes the Companies Act). In this situation, it is unlikely that the Managing Director will take legal action against the auditor. If the fraud has been perpetrated by an employee, the Managing Director should take some responsibility for not detecting the fraud (contributory negligence), and this will reduce the auditor's negligence.

So, in conclusion, I would agree that the auditor has a greater responsibility for detecting error and fraud in Spondon Furniture than would be the case if all the shares were owned by the Managing Director.

Note: Candidates may produce different arguments, and come to different conclusions. They will be awarded marks based on the quality of the points they make, their discussion and the conclusions they reach.

Did you answer the question?

Note how the examiner has introduced Caparo into his solution. Any discussion of the auditor's duty of care can usefully involve a reference to the Caparo case.

---

53 (Answer 3 of examination)

(**Examiner's comments and marking guide**)

Question 3: was concerned with attending a stocktake and checking purchases cut-off.

Many of the answers to part (a) on attending the stocktake were good. However, some candidates concentrated on cut-off aspects of the stocktake, which is a minor (but important) aspect of attending the stocktake. Candidates failed to achieve a pass if they just considered cut-off. Some candidates thought the auditor would be responsible for counting and recording the stock, which is not correct.

Some candidates gave the correct answer to part (b) (i) on identifying cut-off errors. However, most candidates' answers were weak and their presentation of the answer was either very unclear or confused.

Most of the answers to part (b) (ii) on what action should be taken as a result of finding the cut-off errors in (b) (i) were weak. The auditor should perform more checks or ask the company to check more items (and the auditor would check the company's work) and probably report the problems to the company in the management letter. Also, the auditor could check suppliers' statements, but this was mentioned by hardly any candidates.

				Marks
(a)	(i)	procedures to check at the stocktake		
	(ii)	audit tests and matters to record		
		Generally ½ mark a point up to a maximum of		11
(b)	(i)	Identifying and quantifying cut-off errors		
		½ mark for identifying the correct item and		
		½ mark for correctly stating effect on profit	4	
		1 mark for getting correct total adjustment to profit (ie, £10,172)	1	
				5
	(ii)	follow-up procedures		
		Generally 1 mark a point up to a maximum of		4
Total				20

Note: in part (a) you may give 1 mark for longer points, and in part (b)(ii) you should give ½ mark for short points

Step by step answer plan

Step 1 Read the question again and make sure that you focus on precisely what is required.

Step 2 This looks like a standard question on stocktaking and cut-off. The question states that there were purchases cut-off errors in previous years, so you should be expecting to identify further errors from the data in the question.

Step 3 In part (b) (ii), a standard test on year-end creditors balances is to reconcile those balances to suppliers statements. A creditors circularisation is unusual and should not be routinely recommended.

Step 4 Only when you are confident that you are about to answer the question that has been set, should you start writing.

The examiner's answer

(a)   (i)   The company should ensure the following procedures are carried out at the stocktake:

- ideally, there should be no movement of stock during the stocktake, as this creates the risk that stock may be counted twice or not at all. Any movement of stock during the stocktake should be minimised and strictly controlled

- staff counting the stock should be issued pre-numbered stock sheets and an individual should record which sheets have been issued to each pair of counters

- the area where the stocktake is taking place should be tidy, and there should be no movement of stock during the stocktake. Any items which are difficult to identify should be identified

- the counters should be allocated areas to count stock, so that all stock is counted and none missed

- ideally, staff who are responsible for stock should not count the stock (as this would result in a weakness in internal control). However, the counters should be competent to identify the stock which is being counted

- staff should count the stock in pairs, with one member of staff counting the stock and the other recording it on the stock sheets

- stock should be counted systematically, probably from left to right along shelves

- stock should be marked when it is counted so that it is not missed or counted twice

- details of stock counted should be written on the stock sheets in ball point pen. Any alterations on the stock sheets should be initialed by the stocktaker. The bottom of the stock sheet should be signed by the employees who have counted the stock

- details of the items counted should include:

    - a description of the item
    - its part number
    - the quantity

- the stock sheets should record details of any stock which may be worth less than cost. This will include damaged, seconds and slow moving stock

- management should perform test counts and check them to the stocktakers' counts. Any differences should be investigated (eg, by recounting the stock)

- any incomplete stock sheets should be ruled off so that no items can be added

- at the end of the count, the stock sheets should be collected, and a member of staff should check they are all returned. Details of stock sheet numbers used should be recorded

- at the end of the count, management should ask staff the areas where they have counted the stock. They should randomly select areas of the factory and ask the stocktakers who has counted stock in that area. Then they can test check stock has been counted by selecting items of stock and checking they appear on the stock sheets

- management should record the numbers of the last goods received note and last dispatch note issued before the stocktake

(ii)   As auditor, I will record details of the checks I have performed on the items above. In addition, I will:

- ensure the company's staff carry out the stocktaking in accordance with the stocktaking instructions

- perform test counts of the stock. This should be performed in two ways. I will select items from the stock sheets and count the stock (this ensures stock on the stock sheets exists). I will select items of stock, count them, and check they appear on the stock sheets (this ensures that stock which exists has been recorded on the stock sheets). If my count is different from the company's, I will count the stock again, with the employees present, and ensure the correct quantity appears on the stock sheets. I will record details of my counts, and the stock sheet numbers where the items appear, so that they can be followed up at the final audit

- record the numbers of the stock sheets used in the count

- record the last numbers of documents before the year end for recording:
  - receipt of goods from suppliers (i.e. last GRN number)
  - dispatch of goods to customers (i.e. last dispatch note number)
  - return of goods to suppliers
  - return of goods from customers

- photocopy a sample of stocksheets at the end of the stocktake. They will be checked to ensure they have not been altered at a later date

- inspect a sample of stocksheets to ensure they have been signed by the staff counting the stock

- note any stock which may be worth less than cost (e.g. obsolete stock) and check that details have been recorded on the stocksheets

---

Did you answer the question?

Note that the auditor does not count the stock at a stocktake. The client's staff count the stock, while the auditor observes and may make limited test counts of his own.

(b)   (i)   In the list of items given in the question, purchases cut-off is correct for items 1, 3 and 7. So the adjustments to profit are:

Item	Reason	Adjustment (£)
	Goods received before the year end:	
2	invoice included on purchase ledger and in purchase accruals	5,164
4	invoice not included on purchase ledger or in purchase accruals	(9,624)
	Goods received after the year end:	
5	invoice included on purchase ledger	8,243
6	invoice included as purchase accrual	6,389
	net increase in profit	10,172

This will result in:

net decrease in purchases	10,172
net decrease in creditors	10,172

(ii)   The test has highlighted four errors in a sample of 7 items, an error rate of 57%, which is very high. Only a relatively small sample of goods received notes have been selected (from the sample of GRN's covered, it appears to be between 20% and 25%). With the high error rate, there is evidence of serious purchases cut-off errors, and to quantify the potential error, a larger sample of items should be selected. covering a longer period. It is suggested the period should cover two weeks before the year end to two weeks after the year end, and a greater proportion of GRN's should be selected. If there are cut-off errors at the end of these periods (i.e. two weeks before the year end and two weeks after the year end), the period for checking cut-off should be extended. In addition, the company's management should be notified of the problem. They could help by checking cut-off and giving me a schedule of the items they have checked and the errors they have found.

As further checks of purchases cut-off, I would check purchase accruals at the year end. They should be for goods received before the year end which have not been included on the purchase ledger before the year end (i.e. item 3 in the question). A purchase accrual should not be included where:

-    goods are received before the year end and the purchase invoice has been posted to the purchase ledger before the year end (item 2), or

-    goods are received after the year end (item 6)

If the company uses the date on the purchase invoice when posting purchase invoices to the purchase ledger, I would check that no invoices have been posted to the purchase ledger before the year end which have a date after the year end (i.e. none are dated 1.11.96 or later). Also, I would check that invoices posted to the purchase ledger after the year end, which have a date before the year end, are either included in purchase accruals, or the goods have been received after the year end (by checking the date on the GRN).

(iii)   As a further check of purchases cut-off, I would check the reconciliation of suppliers' statements to the balances on the purchase ledger, and investigate any differences. For instance, if there are invoices on the supplier's statement which are not on the client's purchase ledger, I will check the goods were received after the year end (if they were received before the year end, and were not included in purchase accruals, there would be a purchases cut-off error). This work should quantify the total purchases cut-off error, which should be included in the summary of unadjusted errors in my audit working papers.

54 (Answer 4 of examination)

Question 4: was concerned with the auditor providing other services to clients.

Most of the answers to part (a) were weak. On preparing the financial statements for audit, many candidates correctly said that the preparation of the financial statements should be carried out by different staff from those auditing the financial statements. It would have been helpful if they had explained why there is a problem when the same person prepares and audits the financial statements. Very few candidates referred to the Rules of Professional Conduct which state that an auditor should not normally prepare and audit the financial statements of listed and other public interest companies. On advising on internal controls, few candidates discriminated between advice on internal controls (which is acceptable) and recommending controls for a whole system (which would not normally be acceptable).

Most of the answers to part (b) were short and very weak. Some candidates correctly said that low fees could result in a reduction in audit work and the auditor coming to an incorrect opinion. Also, they said that loss of the audit fee could pressurise the auditor into giving an unqualified report when it should be qualified. However, few candidates said the risk of negligence claims should persuade the auditor to give an honest opinion. There was very little consideration of the importance of the audit report of listed companies in providing confidence in the accuracy of the financial statements. Few of the answers provided much evidence to support their final conclusion.

The topics of this question are important. Candidates should understand the issues involving considerations for and against the auditor providing additional services.

		Marks
(a)	Effect on auditors independence of providing non-audit services of taxation, preparing accounts and advising on internal controls	
	Generally 1 mark a point up to a maximum of	10
(b)	Discussion of statement in the question about provision of non-audit services for listed companies	
	Generally 1 mark a point up to a maximum of	10
Total		20

Note: For part (b) it may be more appropriate to give a subjective mark based on the quality of the candidate's answer. A marking scheme based on degree grade classifications is suggested, with a pass mark of 50%.

Step by step answer plan

Step 1   Read the question again and make sure that you focus on precisely what is required.

Step 2   Part (a) lists three services, each of which requires three aspects to be considered ie, 9 points to be covered for the 10 marks.

Step 3   Don't worry in part (b) whether your conclusion is positive or negative: there is no 'correct' answer to this problem, the marks being available to discuss the statement rather than for coming to a particular conclusion.

Step 4   Only when you are confident that you are about to answer the question that has been set, should you start writing.

The examiner's answer

(a)   Considering each of the matters listed in the question:

       (i)   Generally, there should be little effect on the auditor's independence in providing taxation services to the client. Most audit firms will have staff with specialised skills in taxation, so they should provide a good service. Also, there should be a cost saving compared with employing another firm for this service, as some of the procedures in preparing and auditing financial statements are helpful in calculating the corporation tax liability (eg, fixed asset schedules, analysis of entertainment and some other expenses). Frequently, audit firms will have different staff responsible for audit work and taxation computations, and this will tend to increase independence. The auditor's independence may be slightly compromised if a dispute arises between the company and the Inland Revenue, or if the auditor has made a material mistake in the Corporation Tax computation.

The risks with preparing and negotiating directors' tax liability with the Inland Revenue are slightly greater. A director may not have declared all benefits in kind, or the auditor may not have given the correct advice on a technical matter, or a dispute may arise with the Inland Revenue. These problems are likely to create a deterioration in the relationship with the director, so the auditor may 'back down' on a contentious issue in the financial statements in order to maintain good relations with the directors and thus continue as auditor. Ideally, the taxation computations should be performed by staff independent of the audit staff, and then checked by the audit staff.

(ii)   Many small companies do not have staff with the skills to prepare the financial statements. The auditor has these skills, and there is likely to be a time (and cost) saving if the audit firm both prepares and audits the financial statements.

However, if the same staff both prepare the financial statements and audit them, there is a greater risk that material errors will not be detected, as one is poor at detecting one's own mistakes. Also, staff may feel the item has been audited when preparing the financial statements, and this could lead to aspects of the financial statements not being audited satisfactorily. So, it is desirable (and recommended) that different staff should prepare the financial statements from those who audit them. Even in this situation, there is likely to be a cost saving, as the staff preparing the financial statements should prepare schedules which will help in the audit (e.g. schedules of additions and disposals of fixed assets, and calculation of accruals and prepayments).

If the audit firm prepares the financial statements, the letter of engagement for this work should point out that the client should accept that the accounting records are the responsibility of the company, and that the financial statements are based on the company's records and explanations received from employees and the directors.

The ACCA's ethical rules say that the auditor should not prepare the financial statements of listed and other public interest companies, except in emergency situations.

In conclusion, the provision of accounting services is unlikely to have any significantly adverse effect on the auditor's independence.

(iii)   The auditor may be quite good at advising on internal control systems, as this is an important aspect of audit work. However, if the auditor's recommendations are implemented and the system proves to have weaknesses (which may result in serious errors or fraud), the auditor may be reluctant to criticise the system (as he would be criticising himself), so his independence would be compromised. For this reason, auditors should not say how internal control systems should be set up in client companies.

However, as a result of audit work, auditors can become aware of weaknesses in internal controls in accounting systems. They should point out these weaknesses to the client, and any errors or fraud which have taken place. In addition, they can suggest how the systems can be modified to improve controls. The auditor can suggest changes to parts of systems, but they should not say how a whole system should be set up (e.g. a purchases system).

Did you answer the question?

Note the very real benefits that the auditor can offer the client in the above areas. It is in everybody's interest for some theoretical loss of independence to be suffered, for the advantages that are on offer. Don't be modest about listing the benefits that the auditor's work can bring.

(b)   Considering the points raised in the statement:

(i)   the statement that non-audit fees charged by auditors of UK listed companies are similar to audit fees is accepted.

(ii)   there is some evidence that audit fees charged to listed companies may be reduced because of fees the auditor will receive for other services. However, it is very difficult to prove this is happening. If non-audit work is very profitable, then an audit firm may charge a lower audit fee. This is because the auditor has a greater chance of obtaining non-audit work from the listed company (ie, audit firms tend to have a higher proportion of non-audit consultancy work than those firms which are not the company's auditor). So, if more 'high profit' work is available, the auditor may be prepared to reduce the audit fee to increase the chances of obtaining the non-audit work.

The reason why it is difficult to prove that audit firms are reducing audit fees is that one cannot quantify the audit fee required for a particular audit assignment. A replacement auditor may charge a lower audit fee, but this could be because the audit is carried out more efficiently, or the previous auditor had carried out more work than was necessary.

(iii)   There does seem to be a greater risk that the auditor will compromise his independence if he obtains fees from both audit and non-audit work, than if he obtains fees exclusively from audit work. If the audit firm is replaced as auditor, the audit fee and most of the fees for non-audit work will be lost. As non-audit work is likely to be more profitable than audit work, the 'pain' to the auditor of losing the audit will be even greater, as he will lose the high profit non-audit work and the relatively low profit audit work.

Risks to the audit firm of being replaced as auditor are often as a result of qualifying the audit report. The client may accept some 'technical' forms of qualification (eg, not depreciating freehold buildings), but the client will not want the audit report to contain other forms of qualification (or even an explanatory paragraph in an unqualified report indicating going concern problems). So, there is a risk that the auditor will be replaced if he qualifies his audit report. Because of the substantial loss of fees, the auditor may back down and give an unqualified audit report.

If there is a serious risk that the auditor will be sued for not qualifying the audit report, he will probably not 'back down' to pressure by the company. The auditor will want to avoid negligence claims, as they involve a lot of staff time in defending them, it adversely affects the auditor's reputation, and there will be damages to pay if the auditor loses the case (or settles out of court). Although the auditor should be covered by professional indemnity insurance (PII) for legal costs and the sum paid in damages, he may have to pay an excess (eg, the first £25,000 or £100,000 of the claim), and it is likely that future premiums for PII will increase following a claim.

(iv)   Statement (iii) is logical, as a reluctance to qualify the audit report is the outward evidence that the auditor's independence has been compromised.

The provision of other services by audit firms is likely to benefit both the client and the audit firm. This is because the fee charged is likely to be lower, as the audit firm already knows the client firm and does not have to spend time getting to know the company's business, its employees and systems. With the close relationship between the audit firm and the company, the company's staff should have a good appreciation of the strengths of the audit firm and be able to use these strengths in non-audit consultancy work. The higher profitability of non-audit work, and the better chance of obtaining this work, because you are the auditor, means that obtaining a client with a considerable amount of non-audit work is very attractive to the audit firm.

However, from the discussion above, it appears that the provision of non-audit work could adversely affect the independence of the audit firm in carrying out the audit. Technically, the audit firm is appointed by the shareholders, and the auditor reports to the shareholders. It does seem that the provision of other work creates a conflict of interest in the auditor's relationship with the shareholders. If the auditor is reluctant to qualify his audit report, the auditor is not acting in the best interests of the shareholders (and other users who rely on the financial statements).

The arguments for and against allowing auditors to carry out non-audit services for clients are finely balanced. However, listed companies have a large number of shareholders and their financial statements are relied upon by a large number of organisations. Thus, auditors of listed companies have enormous responsibilities when reporting on the financial statements. It is against the interest of these people that the auditor's independence could be compromised by the provision of non-audit services. So, on balance, it appears that the final statement of the quotation, that 'auditors of listed companies should be prevented from providing other services to client companies' should apply.

Note: As stated above, the argument for and against auditors providing non-audit services are finely balanced. Candidates will not be penalised if they come to different conclusions, based on a suitably argued case.

55   (Answer 5 of examination)

Examiner's comments and marking guide

Question 5: this question was concerned with the financial statements of a computer company. Candidates were asked to analyse the draft financial statements and consider the effects on the audit and going concern of the company.

The answers to part (a) were quite good with most candidates correctly highlighting the profitability and liquidity/borrowing problems in 1996. Many candidates failed to identify the increase in fixed assets and some missed the increase in stocks.

The answers to part (b) were satisfactory, a good answer to part (a) generally producing a good answer to this part. The matters to consider in the balance sheet are the increase in fixed assets and stock, and whether bad debts are more than has been included in the financial statements. Many answers concentrated on the profit and loss account, when the balance sheet is normally more important to the auditor. The answers to part (c) were less good and lacked depth, particularly in part (ii). Many candidates correctly identified that the company had a high risk of failing in the coming year.

		Marks
(a)	Comment on the company's performance in 1996 compared with 1995	
	Generally 1 mark a point up to a maximum of	6
(b)	Audit matters to investigate	
	Generally 1 mark a point up to a maximum of	7
(c)	Is the company a going concern?	
	Generally 1 mark a point up to a maximum of	7
Total		20

Step by step answer plan

Step 1   Read the question again and make sure that you focus on precisely what is required.

Step 2   Part (a) only offers 6 marks, so don't spend too long on this. A line-by-line analysis shows that both profitability and liquidity have worsened, while fixed assets and stocks have increased, for example.

Step 3   The increase in stock is a particular worry; computer equipment may quickly become obsolete and a provision may be required. Remember to relate the figures in the question with the trade that you are told that you are dealing with.

Step 4   The large increase in bank overdraft and reduction in sales suggests that the risk of failure is high. What evidence is available for the bank's opinion on continuing the overdraft?

Step 5   Only when you are confident that you are about to answer the question that has been set, should you start writing.

The examiner's answer

(a)   In 1995 the company's performance is good. Its profitability is very good, with a return on capital employed of 36.5% and a net profit margin of 12.7%. The liquidity ratios are normal and satisfactory (ie, gearing, current ratio and acid test ratio). The stock, debtors and creditors age are reasonable. Interest cover is excellent at 8.1, and dividend cover at 1.91 is at the required level (as indicated in the question).

In 1996, there has been a 10% fall in sales and the gross profit margin has reduced from 30% to 22.1%, thus confirming the Financial Director's assertion that trading has been difficult. Fixed assets have increased by £2.3 million (28% increase) which indicates that the company was expecting to increase sales, but sales have fallen by 10%. The increase in fixed assets appears to have been financed by the £2 million increase in the long term loan. Stock has increased by £2.1 million (49%) and its age has increased from 2.93 months to 4.35 months. The increase in stock is the main reason for the increase in the bank overdraft of £3.5 million. The gearing ratio (including bank overdraft) has increased from 0.53 to 1.19. A gearing ratio of over 1 usually indicates serious liquidity problems, as banks are reluctant to lend more money than the company holds as shareholders funds. Thus, there could be going concern problems. The interest cover of 1.5 is low, and the dividend paid is twice the profit after tax (ie, only half of the dividend has been paid out of this year's profit).

The current ratio is satisfactory. However, the acid test ratio has fallen from a reasonable 1.06 to a low 0.66, which indicates liquidity problems (for most businesses buying and selling on credit, the acid test ratio should be about 1.0). The debtors age has fallen slightly, probably because of the reduction in sales. Similarly, creditors age has fallen from a reasonable 2.59 months to 1.8 months, as a result of a fall in purchases. The fall in creditors age indicates that the company has stopped purchasing materials for production, because of the fall in sales. Thus, the company is acting correctly to the fall in sales.

(b)   The particular matters I would consider as a result of the review of financial statements, and other matters raised in the question are:

(i)   the increase in fixed assets. I would verify additions to fixed assets by vouching them to purchase invoices. In view of the reduction in the fixed asset turnover, I would consider whether the company requires all the fixed assets it has purchased, and whether some of them are surplus to requirements or obsolete and will have to be sold at a loss.

(ii)   the increase in stock. In view of the trading conditions, can all this stock be sold for more than cost, or will it have to be sold below cost? If it is sold for less than cost, it will have to be valued at net realisable value.

(iii)   the company's borrowings. With current gearing of 1.19 (ie, over 1.0), is it possible to reduce borrowing? What is the current bank overdraft limit, is it being exceeded? If it is not exceeded, how much additional finance from the bank is available?

(iv)   what are the future commitments for purchasing equipment from North America and the Far East? Is this greater than planned sales after the year end? Will prices have to be reduced further to reduce stock levels, and will this result in further losses? Reducing the level of future purchases will increase the price of items purchased (as quantity discounts will be smaller), thus further eroding the future gross profit margin. Is there an exchange risk relating to currency movements between the UK, North America and the Far East? Has this currency risk been hedged? What do other similar businesses do about currency risk (we are more at risk if they hedge future exchange rates and we do not).

(v)   debtors age and creditors age seem reasonable, so the normal audit work would be performed. However, I will have to check that the bad debt provision is reasonable, as the Financial Director has said there have been a lot of bad debts in the year (so there may be more after the year end).

(vi)   the bank overdraft and bank loans should be verified in the normal way (e.g. by obtaining a bank letter and checking the bank reconciliation). I will have to find out how close the company is to its borrowing limit. There will be a limit imposed by the bank to the overdraft and the Articles of Association may define a limit. If the company is close to, or exceeding its borrowing limits, there is a risk the company may not be a going concern.

(vii)   in view of the fall in sales, is the company planning to make some of its staff redundant? If so, a provision for the redundancy costs should be made in the financial statements (assuming the company had decided before the year end to make the employees redundant).

Did you answer the question?

Note how the answer to part (b) is rather longer than the answer to part (a), reflecting the marks available, despite the temptation to write too much for part (a).

(c)   There appears to be a serious risk that Hyson Computers may fail during the next year. The going concern problem is highlighted by:

(i)   gearing of over 1.0 - the bank may refuse to provide further borrowings to the company

(ii)   the low profitability in 1996. If the decline in profitability has been progressive for the last year, it is probable that the company is currently making losses

(iii)   if sales have continued to fall during 1996, it is probable that current sales are significantly less than 90% of 1995's monthly sales ·

(iv)   there is an exchange risk in purchasing parts for computers from the Far East and North America

(v)   the proposed reduction in purchases will increase the purchase price (due to a reduction in the quantity discount) and thus increase the cost of the computers and other equipment

(vi)   falling sales will probably mean that the company will have to reduce the selling price of its products (to maintain sales)

(vii)   the combination of increasing costs of purchasing computers from suppliers, and falling sales and selling prices will probably lead to the company making losses in 1997. This is likely to have an adverse effect on liquidity

The main matters I will consider in deciding whether the company is a going concern are:

(i)   I will ask the client for a profit and cash flow forecast for at least the year to 30 September 1997

(ii)   with the client's permission, I will ask the bank their limit on the company's borrowings, and consider whether it is adequate for future trading

(iii)   I will consider whether future sales are realistic, both in terms of the quantity of equipment sold and the selling price. It appears that it will not be possible to increase prices unless a new product is to be launched (eg, a computer with a new microprocessor)

(iv)   I will consider whether the cost of purchasing materials both from the UK and overseas is realistic. The effect of any exchange risk will have to be considered

(v)   I will consider whether overheads are realistic, and whether the profit and cash flow forecasts are realistic

Based on these investigations, I will decide whether there is a significant risk that Hyson Computers will fail. If the forecast shows that Hyson Computers will make a loss, there is a serious risk that Hyson Computers may fail. If the forecast shows Hyson Computers will be profitable, and this is realistic, then the risk of Hyson Computers failing is low, and it should be possible to give an unqualified audit report.

56   (Answer 6 of examination)

Examiner's comments and marking guide

Question 6: was concerned with auditing certain aspects of a charity. Part (a) checked the payment of pensioners. Part (b) checked investment income and part (c) checked the ownership of the investments.

The answers to part (a) were satisfactory. However, more candidates should have checked the existence of pensioners, normally by a positive circularisation, although telephoning or visiting the pensioners are acceptable alternatives.

In parts (b) and (c) most candidates were very confused about the difference between checking investment income and checking the ownership of the investments. In many answers to part (b) many candidates just checked the ownership of the investments (which is the subject of part (c)). Few candidates realised that there would be dividend and interest vouchers. Even fewer suggested checking dividends to the financial statements of Extel, or checking the interest received to the interest rate of the loan and the nominal value held. Hardly any candidates considered:

(a)   the effects on dividends of selling the shares cum or ex dividend;

(b)   the taxation consequences of receiving interest after deduction of tax and reclaiming this tax.

The answers to part (c) were weak, often because they had given the answer to this part in their answer to part (b). However, it was surprising that few candidates mentioned share certificates. Few candidates considered the sale of shares.

		Marks
(a)	Verifying payment of pensions to pensioners	
	Generally 1 mark a point up to a maximum of	6
(b)	Verifying income from investments	
	Generally 1 mark a point up to a maximum of	10
(c)	Verifying ownership of investments	
	Generally 1 mark a point up to a maximum of	4
Total		20

Step by step answer plan

Step 1 Read the question again and make sure that you focus on precisely what is required.

Step 2 Checking the existence of pensioners is similar to checking the existence of debtors: measures such as circularisation, personal visit, telephone call, etc are all possible.

Step 3 Investment income should be capable of independent checking. For fixed interest investments, the coupon rate times the nominal value should equal the annual income eg, 7% £100,000 stock should yield £7,000 pa. For shares in listed companies, the dividend rates are published publicly and can be checked.

Step 4 The principal means of verifying ownership of investments is to inspect a share certificate or report from nominees.

Step 5 Only when you are confident that you are about to answer the question that has been set, should you start writing.

The examiner's answer

(a)   The trustees should have approved a list of pensioners at some time during the year. The minutes of trustees' meetings should record new pensioners and when people cease to be pensioners (by death or ineligibility). To verify that the correct pensioners are paid, I will:

   (i)   test check payments from the cash book to the authorised list. The amount paid should agree with the amount on the authorised list

   (ii)   ideally, the paid cheques should be obtained from the bank, and I will check that they are made out to the pensioner and that they have not been negotiated. I will investigate any cases where the cheque is made out to another person or is negotiated. To confirm the authorisation of payments to pensioners, I will inspect minutes of the trustees' meetings and appropriate correspondence. If this information is not available from these sources, I will ask the trustees to confirm the payments are correct

   (iii)   I will check the procedures for identifying cases where pensioners are ineligible (because of death or change in circumstances) and consider whether they are acceptable and reliable. Ideally, a person, independent of the administrator, should visit the pensioners and report to the trustees

   (iv)   I will check for a sample of new pensioners that they are not paid before the trustees confirm they are pensioners. Payment will be checked to the cash book and authorisation by the trustees checked to the minutes of trustees' meetings. Also, I will check that individuals who become ineligible are not subsequently paid a pension (e.g. a pensioner is not paid after she has died)

   (v)   I will perform analytical review on the total pension payments. The total payment should be the product of the average pension paid and the average number of pensioners during the year. Also, it should be equal to pensions paid last year, less reductions for pensioners who have died (or are otherwise ineligible) plus payments to new pensioners and any changes to pensions of existing pensioners

   (vi)   I will check the application forms of new pensioners to ensure they qualify to be pensioners according to the trust deed of the charity. I will perform this test on a sample of individuals who have remained pensioners during the year

   (vii)   as further confirmation of the existence of the pensioners, I will write to a sample of the pensioners and ask them to reply direct to me, providing a specimen signature. I will check the signature to the charity's records. I will investigate cases where I do not receive a reply from the pensioners.

Did you answer the question?

Note how the examiner has listed 7 separate audit procedures, reflecting the 6 marks available.

(b)   I will obtain a schedule of the fixed interest investments and shares held during the year and the purchases and sales of shares in the year.

For the fixed interest investments, the total investment income received per the financial statements will be checked to the cash book. The cash book figure is likely to be different from the figure in the financial statements because of tax to be reclaimed from the Inland Revenue. The opening debtor for tax will be checked to the amount received from the Inland Revenue during the year and the closing debtor will be checked to the claim made to the Inland Revenue (and the amount received from the Inland Revenue, if it has been received by the time of the audit). For individual investments, the interest received will be checked as being the product of nominal value and the interest rate. In the UK, the interest has traditionally been received net of tax (though note that since April 1998 a stockholder has been able to apply to receive interest gross). However, as I am auditing a charity, any tax that has been deducted will be recoverable from the Inland Revenue. Some of the tax in the year may have been received from the Inland Revenue, and any amount not received by the year end should be included in debtors in the financial statements. The gross income would be included in the financial statements. If the charity owns £10,000 nominal of 8% Government Stock, the interest to be included in the financial statements should be £800. The interest received would be test checked to the cash book, and there should be a voucher received from the Government detailing the net interest received and tax deducted. This voucher will show the nominal holding of the Government Stock, which is further confirmation of the trust's holding of the Stock.

For the ordinary shares, I will ask for a schedule of dividends received. I will perform the following checks on dividends received:

(i)   check the entries in the cash book to the financial statements. The total of investment income in the cash book should reconcile to the income in the financial statements.

(ii)   for dividends received, I will inspect the dividend vouchers. This will confirm it is the correct dividend, and it provides good evidence that the charity holds the shares

(iii)   check dividends received to Extel or similar publication (which lists all dividends paid by listed companies). I will be able to use Extel to check that all dividends due have been received by the charity

(iv)   until 6 April 1999, charities are allowed to reclaim the tax credits on their dividend income. Thus the dividend in the income and expenditure account should be the grossed up figure (ie, 125% of the cash dividend received). But note that from 6 April 1999, charities are no longer entitled to repayment of these tax credits, though the Revenue is offering five year transitional relief to cushion the impact of the change.

(v)   dividends can be checked to the previous year. Most companies pay dividends twice a year, so for most of the investments there should be two dividends received at a similar date to the previous year. Some companies may stop paying dividends because of profitability problems, while others may pay them more frequently (e.g. four times a year). Where there is no dividend, this can be checked to Extel, as described above. The amount of dividends can be checked to the companies' annual financial statements, but, because of timing problems, the companies' financial statements may not show all dividends received during the charity's financial year

(vi)   for shares sold in the year, I will check that the last dividend has been received. This can be checked to Extel, or it can be indicated by the Broker's note which gives details of the sale of the shares. If the shares are sold ex dividend, a dividend should be received after they are sold. If they are sold cum dividend, the last dividend will be received before they are sold

(vii)   for shares purchased in the year, I will check that the first dividend has been received. This can be checked to Extel, or it can be indicated by the Broker's note which gives details of the purchase of the shares. If the shares are purchased cum dividend, the charity will receive the first dividend after the shares are purchased. If they are purchased ex dividend, the first dividend after they are purchased will be paid to the former shareholder, and the charity will receive the second dividend after the shares were purchased.

(viii) I will compare the dividends and interest received with the previous year, and consider whether the change is reasonable. The figures in the draft financial statements look reasonable

---

Did you answer the question?

Note how part (b) is worth 10 marks, so deserves close attention. You want to describe at least 8 audit procedures to hope to earn all the marks available.

(c)   I would check the ownership of the government securities by inspecting the certificates (which should be held securely). They should be in the name of the charity (if the charity is a company, otherwise they should be in at least two trustees' names), and the details of the interest rate, repayment date and the nominal value held should agree with the charity's records and the financial statements. As there has been no purchase or sale of these securities in the year, the cost in the balance sheet will be unchanged. I will check the ownership of the shares in a similar way to the government securities, by inspecting the share certificates. They should look genuine (i.e. they should have the company's seal impressed on them), they should be in the name of the charity (or at least two trustees) and the number of shares should agree with the charity's records and the financial statements. Only certificates for shares held at the time of my audit will be available. Hopefully, they should be for all those shares held at the year end. Receipt of interest or dividends is further evidence of ownership of the government securities and shares. The vouchers received with the interest and dividend cheques will state the holder of the stock or shares, and the nominal value or number of shares held.

JUNE 1997 QUESTIONS

Section A - ALL THREE questions are compulsory and MUST be attempted

57   (Question 1 of examination)

Your firm is the external auditor of Lenton Electrical Limited, which is a retailer of electrical products (televisions, video recorders, audio equipment and audio and video tapes). The company's year end is Wednesday 30 April 1997.

The company has a computerised stock control system which records stock quantities and is not integrated with the purchase ledger. After investigating the stock system and related controls, the senior in charge of the audit has decided that the approach to auditing stock quantities at the year end should be to:

(a)   test the operating effectiveness of controls by attending one of the periodic stocktakes on 14 April to check that the stock is counted accurately and the computerised stock records are updated correctly for differences found at the stocktake, and

(b)   substantively test the stock quantities on the computer system at 30 April 1997. These stock quantities will be used to value stock at the year end.

In the stock control system:

(a)   each product has a unique bar code

(b)   when goods are received the goods received department scans the bar code and enters the quantity. The computer adds the items to stock. When the scanner cannot read the bar code, the bar code number is input manually.

(c)   the goods received department make out a pre-numbered goods received note (GRN). They retain a copy of the GRN and attach the second copy of the GRN to the advice note and send it to the purchases accounting department.

(d)   the purchases accounting department receive the purchase invoice. They check it to the advice note, GRN and purchase order. If these checks are satisfactory, the purchase invoice is approved by the managing director. Then it is posted to the purchase ledger and the purchases account in the nominal ledger. The purchase invoices are filed in alphabetical order by supplier name.

(e)   when goods are sold to customers, the bar code is scanned. The computer deducts the items from stock and the customer's bill is produced using the prices of products on the computer's standing data file. All customers pay by cash, cheque or credit card (charge card).

(f)   a full stock count at the year end is not carried out. A stocktake is carried out every two weeks when about a quarter of the stock is counted and the quantities are compared with the quantities on the computer. All stock is counted within an eight week period.

(g)   adjustments to computer stock quantities for differences found at the stock count are input into the system and authorised by the managing director.

(h)   the stock control system can print out the quantity of any item of stock and details of receipts and sales of stock, including the date and time the stock was received or sold.

You attended one of the periodic stocktakes, which was carried out on Monday 14 April 1997 from 6pm to 8pm. About 25% by value of the stock was counted during the stocktake. The store was closed during the stocktake to avoid sales cut-off errors and minimise purchases cut-off errors.

You are required:

(a)   at the stocktake on 14th April 1997, to describe the procedures the company should instigate to ensure the computerised stock records are only amended for differences found at the stocktake and that no adjustment is made to the stock records when the difference is due to a counting error.

(6 marks)

(b)   to describe the audit procedures to check purchases cut-off at 30 April 1997.

(6 marks)

(c)   in verifying the accuracy of the computer stock quantities at 30 April 1997, to:

   (i)   describe the checks you will carry out to verify that all the stock is counted within eight weeks of the year end.

   (ii)   consider the size and frequency of the errors in computer stock quantities found at the periodic stocktakes and the effect of these errors on the accuracy of the computer stock quantities at the year end. Your answer should also consider cases when the computer system shows a negative stock balance.

(8 marks)
(Total: 20 marks)

Note: you should consider only the verification of stock quantities. You are not required to describe the work you would carry out in verifying the price per unit of stock and the total stock value.

---

58   (Question 2 of examination)

Your firm is the external auditor of Bingham Wholesale plc, and you have been assigned to the audit of the sales system. Bingham Wholesale purchases textile products (eg, clothes) from manufacturers and sells them to retailers.

An initial review of the sales system has shown that control risk is likely to be low with sufficient staff to achieve a proper division of duties. Thus, the audit manager has decided that the audit approach should be to record, evaluate and perform extensive tests of controls. If these confirm controls are effective, control risk will be low, so only restricted substantive procedures will be carried out.

You have been asked to carry out audit work on the sales system to satisfy two questions in the audit firm's Internal Control Evaluation Questionnaire (ICE) (given in (a) and (b) below).

The company has a computerised accounting system which records purchases and sales transactions and maintains records of debtors, creditors and stock (both quantity and value). Access to the computer for retrieval of information and input of data is through terminals.

The narrative description of the sales system is:

(i)   all sales are made on credit

(ii)   orders are received by the sales department staff who input details of the goods to be dispatched into the computer

(iii)   the computer calculates the invoice value, and, provided the customer is not exceeding the credit criteria, the computer prints a dispatch note set on the printer in the dispatch department

(iv)   the dispatch department staff prepare the goods and send them to the customer

(v)   the dispatch department staff record on the computer when the goods are dispatched. The computer prints the sales invoice and posts it to the sales ledger. The sales invoice is sent to the customer. The computer deducts the quantity of stock dispatched from the stock records

(vi)   the credit criteria in (iii) above comprise checking whether:

-     the invoice puts the customer over the credit limit

-     there are significant old, unpaid invoices on the sales ledger

-     the credit controller has put the customer on 'stop' (ie, no dispatches of goods are allowed to the customer)

At the request of the sales department, the credit controller can over-ride the computer's control.

Two questions in your audit firm's Internal Control Evaluation Questionnaire (ICE) for a sales system are:

(a)   Can goods be dispatched to a customer who is a poor credit risk?

(b)   Can goods be dispatched but not invoiced?

The audit manager has suggested that:

(a)   in answering ICE question (a) you should identify and check controls over:

  (i)   accepting new customers and setting their credit limits

  (ii)   amending the credit limits of existing customers

  (iii)   stopping goods being dispatched to customers who are a poor credit risk

  (iv)   collecting debts from customers

(b)   in answering ICE question (b) you should consider how goods could be dispatched but not invoiced, and suggest tests of controls and substantive procedures which could be used to detect whether this is happening.

You are required:

(a)   in relation to answering ICE question (a) - Can goods be dispatched to a customer who is a poor credit risk? - to describe the controls you would expect to see in operation

                                                                                          (13 marks)

(b)   to describe the tests of control and substantive procedures you would perform to satisfy ICE question (b) - Can goods be dispatched but not invoiced?

                                                                                          (7 marks)
                                                                                    (Total: 20 marks)

---

59   (Question 3 of examination)

Your firm is auditing the financial statements of Newthorpe Manufacturing Limited for the year ended 31 March 1997. You have been assigned to the audit of the company's fixed assets, which comprise:

(a)   freehold land and buildings
(b)   plant and machinery
(c)   fixtures and fittings
(d)   motor vehicles

The freehold land and buildings were purchased in April 1987 for £2 million. At the date of purchase a valuer estimated the value of the land at £1 million and £1 million for the buildings. Since 1987, depreciation has been charged on the building at 2% per annum on cost. At 31 March 1997 the accumulated depreciation is £200,000 before the revaluation.

A qualified valuer, who is not an employee of the company, has recently valued the land and buildings at £5 million, comprising:

(a)　　land at £2.9 million
(b)　　buildings at £2.1 million

These values will be incorporated into the financial statements at 31 March 1997.

The partner in charge of the audit is concerned at the large increase in the value of the land and buildings since they were purchased in 1987, and has asked you to check the reliability and accuracy of the valuation. He has suggested that SAS 520 'Other Specialists' could assist you in carrying out this work.

In addition, you have been asked to verify the existence and completeness of plant and machinery which is recorded in the company's computerised fixed asset register. The fixed asset register records the description of each fixed asset, the original cost, depreciation charge and accumulated depreciation. The company's accounting policy on fixed assets is to only capitalise items over £500.

You are required to:

(a)　　describe the audit work you will carry out to check whether the valuer has provided an accurate and independent valuation of the land and buildings

(9 marks)

(b)　　describe the audit work you will carry out to check the existence and completeness of plant and machinery, as recorded in the company's fixed asset register

(5 marks)

(c)　　describe the audit work you will perform to verify that:

　　　(i)　　only capital items are included in additions to fixed assets, and

　　　(ii)　　material items of capital expenditure are not charged as an expense in the year

(6 marks)
(Total: 20 marks)

Section B - TWO questions ONLY to be attempted

60　　(Question 4 of examination)

You are auditing the financial statements of Newthorpe Engineering plc for the year ended 30 April 1997.

(a)　　In March 1997 the Board decided to close one of the company's factories on 30 April 1997. The plant and equipment and stock will be sold. The employees will either be transferred to another factory or made redundant.

At the time of your audit in June 1997, you are aware that:

　　　(i)　　some of the plant and equipment has been sold

　　　(ii)　　most of the stock has been sold

　　　(iii)　　all the employees have either been made redundant or transferred to another factory

The company has provided you with a schedule of the closure costs, the realisable values of the assets in (i) and (ii) above and the redundancy cost.

Details of the plant and machinery are maintained in a fixed asset register.

A full stocktake was carried out at 30 April 1997. Audit tests have confirmed that the stock counts are accurate and there are no purchases or sales cut-off errors.

You are aware the redundancy payments are based on the number of years service of the employee and their annual salary (or wage). Most employees were given redundancy of one week's pay for each year's service. A few employees have a service contract with the company and were paid the amount stated in their service contract, which will be more than the redundancy pay offered to other employees. Employees who are transferred to another factory were not paid any redundancy.

As part of the audit of the closure cost, you have been asked to carry out the audit work described below.

You are required, for the factory being closed, to describe the audit work you will carry out to verify the company's estimates of:

(i)   the net realisable value of:

-     plant and equipment
-     stock

(7 marks)

(ii)   the redundancy cost

(4 marks)

Note:

(i)   in auditing stock, you are required only to verify that the price per unit is correctly determined

(ii)   for the redundancy cost, you should ignore any national statutory rules for determining redundancy procedures and minimum redundancy pay.

(b)   In February 1997 the directors of Newthorpe Engineering plc suspended the Managing Director. At a disciplinary hearing held by the company on 17 March 1997 the Managing Director was dismissed for gross misconduct, and it was decided the Managing Director's salary should stop from that date and no redundancy or compensation payments should be made.

The Managing Director has claimed unfair dismissal and is taking legal action against the company to obtain compensation for loss of his employment. The Managing Director says he has a service contract with the company, which would entitle him to two years' salary at the date of dismissal.

The financial statements for the year ended 30 April 1997 record the resignation of the director. However, they do not mention his dismissal and no provision for any damages has been included in the financial statements.

You are required to:

(i)   state how contingent losses should be disclosed in financial statements according to FRS 12 *Provisions, contingent liabilities and contingent assets.*

(3 marks)

(ii)   describe the audit work you will carry out to determine:

-     whether the company will have to pay damages to the director for unfair dismissal, and

-     the amount of damages and costs which should be included in the financial statements

(6 marks)
(Total: 20 marks)

Note: assume the amounts you are auditing are material.

61   (Question 5 of examination)

The senior partner of your firm of external auditors is proposing that portable PC's (ie, microcomputers) should be available on audits. He is aware that the speed and storage capacity of PC's has increased dramatically in recent years and that PC's can be connected to the clients' computers.

In view of your recent studies for Paper 5 *Information Analysis* and Paper 6 *Audit Framework*, the senior partner has asked you to write a memorandum on the use of PC's in audit work.

The following areas have been suggested as suitable applications of PC's to audit work:

(a)   spreadsheets

(b)   statistical packages

(c)   using computer assisted audit techniques (CAAT's) to test the computerised accounting systems and controls over access to the computer

(d)   word processing and similar packages to record audit work

Your firm audits companies which use PC's and minicomputers in processing and recording their accounting information. In the larger and more modern systems, data is input into the system through terminals in the relevant departments.

You are required to write a memorandum to the senior partner of your audit firm on the application and use of PC's in the work of external auditors. You should include topics (a) to (d) above and any others you consider relevant.

(20 marks)

62   (Question 6 of examination)

You are the partner in charge of a four partner firm of Certified Accountants. Your firm has been invited to tender for the audit of Phones Anywhere Limited for the year ended 31 December 1997.

Phones Anywhere Ltd was established two years ago, and it provides a mobile phone service for individuals and businesses. The system being established by the company comprises:

(a)   small portable mobile phones, which allow subscribers (users) to contact or be contacted by any other telephone

(b)   the mobile phones can be used within range of a local relay station, which receives calls from and sends calls to the mobile phones

(c)   the local relay stations are linked to a central computer which connects the calls to other users. Frequently, this is through a competitor's telephone network

(d)   currently, the local relay stations cover one large city with a population of about 1,000,000. Within the next year the system will cover all large cities in the UK with a population of over 250,000. By the year 2000, the system will cover all motorways and cities with a population of over 100,000. Extending the coverage of the system will involve considerable capital expenditure on new relay stations and require additional borrowings

(e)   the cost of the relay stations and central computer are capitalised and are written off over six years

(f)   the mobile phones are manufactured by other companies and sold through retailers. Phones Anywhere does not sell the phones, but it pays £200 to the retailer for each phone sold and subscription signed by the customer to Phones Anywhere. This payment is capitalised in the financial statements of Phones Anywhere and written off over four years

(g)   subscribers are invoiced monthly with a fixed line rental and a variable call charge. Other operators are charged for the time spent by their customers contacting Phones Anywhere's subscribers (customers). These charges are logged and calculated by the company's main computer

(h)   all the shares are owned by three wealthy individuals who are non-executive directors. They will receive a fixed salary. They do not plan to make any further investment in the company

(i)   establishing the network of relay stations and subscribers will result in the company making losses for at least three years. Current borrowings are about 20% of shareholders' funds. Because of the substantial capital expenditure and trading losses, it is expected the company will be highly geared by the year 2000.

(j)   as the company will not be profitable, the non-executive directors have decided that executive directors should receive a basic salary and a bonus based on the number of subscribers to the system

(k)   the owners plan to float the company on the London Stock exchange in the year 2000. The flotation will involve:

     (i)   issuing new shares to the general public to provide funds for the company, and

     (ii)   the three non-executive directors selling some of their shares

You are aware that Phones Anywhere has a number of very large competitors, each of which has a large number of users and comprehensive coverage (ie, over 90% of the population are within range of a relay station).

You are required, in relation to the audit of Phones Anywhere Limited, to:

(a)   consider the risks associated with the audit

(8 marks)

(b)   describe the ethical matters you should consider in deciding whether your audit firm should accept the audit. This should include considering whether your firm has the technical and logistical ability to carry out the audit

(8 marks)

(c)   come to a conclusion on whether you would advise your firm to accept or decline the audit, giving your principal reasons for coming to this decision

(4 marks)
(Total: 20 marks)

ANSWERS TO JUNE 1997 EXAMINATION

The model answers to the questions are longer and frequently more detailed than would be expected from a candidate in the examinations. However, the model answer may not include all valid points mentioned by candidates - credit will be given to candidates mentioning these points.

The model answers may be used as a guide to the form and standard of answer candidates should try to achieve. However, the answers may not be as detailed as one would find in text books on the subject.

57   (Answer 1 of examination)

Examiner's comments and marking guide

Question 1: was concerned with checking the accuracy of computer stock records and purchases cut-off. Most candidates' answers were poor, and many failed to answer the question which was asked in parts (a) and (c).

In part (a) most candidates concentrated on stocktaking procedures rather than amending the computer stock records, which the question was requesting. Candidates were given limited credit for mentioning stocktaking procedures and full credit for considering procedures over amending the computer stock records.

The answers to part (b) on purchases cut-off were of a lower standard than expected. Few candidates considered both transactions in the stock records and posting the invoice to purchases and the purchase ledger. Few candidates checked any transactions after the year end. Some candidates considered both purchases and sales cut-off when the question only asked for purchases cut-off.

The answers to part (c) were weak. It caused candidates considerable problems, yet a reasoned and logical approach could have produced a good answer. In part (i) the auditor should select some items of stock and check that they were counted in one of the stocktakes within 8 weeks of the year end. The direction of this test is important, as it is ineffective to check from the stock sheets to the stock records. In part (ii) it should have been apparent that if a considerable number of errors were found at the stocktakes, then the computer stock records would not be a reliable basis to use for valuing the year end stock. Most candidates could not understand how negative computer stock quantities could arise. Also, many candidates suggested that differences between the computer and physical quantities were due to faults in the computer stock programs, whereas it is more likely to be due to stealing of stock and other damage and loss of stock.

		Marks
(a)	Procedures over amending computer stock records	
	Generally 1 mark a point up to a maximum of:	6
(b)	Check of purchase cut-off	
	Generally 1 mark a point up to a maximum of:	6
(c)	Verifying stock quantities at the year end	
	(i) check stock is counted at stated frequency	
	(ii) considering frequency of errors found at stocktake	
	Generally 1 mark a point up to a maximum of:	8
Total		20

Step by step answer plan

Step 1   Read the question again and make sure that you focus on precisely what is required.

Step 2   Part (a) asks for procedures for amending the computerised stock records following the stocktake; don't waste time describing actions to be taken during a stocktake. Clearly any large differences should be confirmed by recounting the stock before the stock records are amended.

Step 3 Part (b) is standard bookwork, but must be tailored to the scenario given in the question.

Step 4 Part (c) is worth 8 marks, so must be given more attention than (a) or (b). To verify that all stock has been counted, one must select items of stock and then confirm when they were counted. In part (iii), the larger the size and frequency of errors in the periodic stocktakes, the less confident one will be that the year-end quantity will be accurate.

Step 5 Only when you are confident that you are about to answer the question that has been set, should you start writing.

The examiner's answer

(a)   Before checking the stock counts to the computer stock quantities, I will check purchases cut-off. The stock counts should be checked to the computer stock quantity after goods received on 14 April have been entered into the computer system. I will test check from goods received notes that goods received up to 14 April have been recorded on the computer system with a date of 14 April or earlier. This check will be more reliable if the date recorded on the computer system is the same as the date the goods were received. A limited check on sales cut-off at 14 April would be performed. However, it is probable that there are few, if any, sales cut-off errors, as the system deducts items from stock when the sale is made to the customer.

In comparing the physical and computer stock quantities at 14 April:

(i)   if the quantities are the same, no further work is required

(ii)   if the value of the difference is small (eg, 3 video tapes at £2.50 each) there is no need to change the stock quantities on the computer

(iii)   if the difference is large in terms of quantity or value, further investigations should be carried out

For larger differences, the company should count the stock again (ideally when the store is closed). If the difference still exists, then the stock quantities on the computer should be amended. If there is no difference between the current physical count and computer stock quantities, the quantity of stock on the computer should not be changed. Most of the differences will highlight the physical quantities being less than those shown on the computer, so there will have been a loss of stock. This could be for a number of reasons, including stock being stolen by employees or customers. If the value of this lost stock is significant, the company's management should instigate procedures to minimise its loss (eg, by using a security guard or using a video camera to record what is happening to the stock).

There should be a laid down procedure for amending stock quantities on the computer:

(i)   this should be permitted only after authorisation by the managing director. The computer system should only allow these adjustments to be processed after the managing director has authorised it using his/her password and a secret code

(ii)   there should be a record of the procedures undertaken to verify that the difference is valid (eg, re-counting of the stock)

(iii)   there should be a print-out of changes of the stock quantities, which should be filed. The computer system should have the facility to print out details of adjustments

(iv)   further procedures may be undertaken if the value of the stock loss is significant, such as increased security

(b)   To check purchases cut-off at 30 April 1997, I will select a sample of goods received before and after the year end from the goods received notes (GRN's) in the goods received department.

For goods received before the year end, I will:

(i)   find the advice note and purchase invoice in the purchases accounting department which relate to the GRN

(ii)   check the goods on the invoice were entered in the computer stock records before the year end, and

(iii)   check the purchase invoice was either posted to the purchase ledger before the year end or included in purchase accruals at the year end

For goods received after the year end, I will:

(i)   find the advice note and purchase invoice in the purchases accounting department which relate to the goods received

(ii)   check the goods on the invoice were entered in the computer stock records after the year end (and not before the year end), and

(iii)   check the purchase invoice was neither posted to the purchase ledger before the year end nor included in purchase accruals at the year end

---

Did you answer the question?

Note that cut-off tests must cover both goods received before the year-end and goods received after the year-end.

(c)   (i)   To check that all stock has been counted within 8 weeks of the year end, I will select a sample of stock from the computer records and check to the stock count records that the items have been counted within eight weeks of the year end (actually, at one of the stocktakes on 17 or 31 March or 14 or 28 April). If I find some of the stock is counted less frequently, I will have to extend my investigation to cover the period when all stock has been counted. I may ask the company to perform these additional checks and then check their work. If I find this is a serious problem, I will:

-    report the problem to the directors and include it in my management letter, and

-    have to consider the potential error in stock quantities at the year end based on errors found at stocktakes over the period when all the stock has been counted (which will exceed 8 weeks)

(ii)   I will look at the size and frequency of errors in quantities found at the stocktakes before and after the year end.

To check the frequency of changes to the computer stock records as a result of the stocktake, I will ask for a print-out of adjustments made after a sample of stocktakes. If there are only a small number of adjustments to computer stock quantities as a result of the stocktakes, the computer stock records at the year end will be accurate. However, if there are a large number of adjustments because of differences between the physical counts and the computer stock records, there could be material differences between the computer stock record and the actual stock quantities at the year end. I will have to determine whether these differences have a material effect on the stock value at the year end. If the error is likely to be significant, an adjustment may have to be made to the stock value for the estimated value of stock lost between the stocktakes and the year end.

The test above only checks adjustments made to the computer stock quantities. I will check that all differences between stock counts and the computer stock records result in a change to the computer stock records. I will select a sample of stock counts from the stock sheets, and compare the quantities with the computer stock records. Where there are differences, I will check that the computer stock quantities have been amended. Also, I will select a sample of adjustments to the computer stock records and check they are as a result of differences found at the stock count. If they are for other reasons, I will check to supporting evidence they are valid.

I will look at a sample of stocktakes after the year end to determine the quality of the computer stock quantities at the year end. For instance, if the stock is corrected at the stocktake on 31 March 1997 and at the next stocktake on 26 May 1997 the actual quantities are found to be 10 less than those recorded on the computer. Then, assuming the stock loss is time dependent, the actual stock quantity at 30 April 1997 will be about 5 items less than the computer stock quantity. If the computer stock quantity were used for valuing stock, it would be overstated by 5 items.

My attendance at the stocktake on 14th April should have helped to determine whether the stock counts were accurate and whether they confirmed the accuracy of the computer stock records. I will have followed through my test counts to the computer stock records to determine whether the computer records are accurate, and any amendments to computer stock quantities have been made correctly.

Negative computer stock quantities indicate errors in recording transactions in the computer stock system. So, I will have to investigate significant negative quantities of stock. Negative stock quantities can arise from inputting the wrong part number when either receiving or selling the stock. The risk is greater when the bar code number is input manually by the storekeeper (for purchases) or the employee selling the stock (for sales). These items will be easier to detect if the computer records when bar code numbers are entered manually. Most bar code numbers include a check digit, and an edit check by the computer should ensure the correct bar code number is entered. In addition, the computer should check there is a valid bar code number on the standing data file, and reject the data when there is no such part number on the standing data file. If the computer allows bar code numbers to be entered when there is no entry on the standing data file, it is probable there will be some stock with no description on the computer's file. I will have to ensure such stock is valid and correctly treated at the year end.

Negative stock quantities could occur when incorrect quantities are entered when the items are received into stock. For instance, one unit could have been entered when 10 were received. Recent records of receipts of the stock would be checked to determine whether the quantities are reasonable. For instance, it is unlikely that 1 box of video tapes would be received. The advice note or purchase invoice would be checked to verify the actual quantity received.

I will investigate other cases where there are negative computer stock quantities and check the company has treated them correctly. Ideally, negative stock quantities should not be included in the stock valuation (they should be zero), but I will have to ensure these negative stock quantities are not as a result of other stock quantities being overstated (ie, the total stock quantity may be the positive quantity in the computer stock records less a negative quantity). In this situation, if negative quantities are ignored, it will overstate the quantity of stock.

Did you answer the question?

Note that negative stock quantities always indicate that some error has arisen in the stock system, so should always be investigated, especially if a material amount is involved.

---

58   (Answer 2 of examination)

Examiner's comments and marking guide

Question 2: asked about controls which were necessary in a sales system to satisfy two ICE questions.

In part (a), candidates who followed the suggestions of the audit manager (given in the question) usually produced an answer which achieved a pass.

The answers to part (b) on checking whether goods which are dispatched are invoiced were much weaker. Once again, the direction of the test is important, as the auditor must check from the dispatch note to the invoice. It is ineffective to check from the invoice to the dispatch note, as this might detect invoices which are raised but no goods dispatched (which was not what the question was asking) but it would not detect goods dispatched where there is no invoice. The term 'substantive procedures' in the question caused many problems, and many of the candidates suggestions of substantive procedures were actually tests of controls. Very few valid substantive procedures were suggested by candidates. The best candidates realised it was possible to dispatch goods without a sales invoice being raised (by the dispatch department forgetting to record the dispatch on the computer). Goods being dispatched without an invoice being raised would create differences between the physical and computer stock quantities and would result in a fall in the gross profit margin.

		Marks
(a)	Controls to prevent goods being sent to a poor credit risk	
	Generally 1 mark a point up to a maximum of:	13
(b)	Controls to ensure goods dispatched are invoiced	
	Generally 1 mark a point up to a maximum of:	7

Total   20

Step by step answer plan

Step 1   Read the question again and make sure that you focus on precisely what is required.

Step 2   The question tells you how to approach part (a): follow the advice of the audit manager given in the question.

Step 3   Part (b) asks for both tests of control and substantive procedures; make it clear to the marker that you know the difference and that you have covered both aspects. An example test of control is to select a sample of dispatch notes, and check that an invoice exists for each. An example substantive procedure is to examine the gross profit percentage achieved this year; a fall might be caused by goods being dispatched but not invoiced.

Step 4   Only when you are confident that you are about to answer the question that has been set, should you start writing.

The examiner's answer

(a)   (i)   The following procedures should be in operation when accepting customers and setting their credit limits:

-    the customer should complete a standard form, which requests a credit limit, supplies the most recent set of financial statements of the business, provides details of the bank and gives at least one customer reference

-    this information should be checked by the credit controller. If a large credit limit is being given, it should also be authorised by the Financial Director

-    references should be requested from the bank and a customer

-    a credit reference should be obtained from a reputable credit rating company (eg, Dun and Bradstreet in the UK)

Based on this information, the credit controller should recommend an initial credit limit for the customer (which will be approved by the Financial Director if it is above a specified limit). A high credit limit may be set for a reputable and well-known company (such as Marks & Spencer in the UK), but for smaller businesses, a low credit limit will probably be set, which will be increased quite quickly if the customer pays the amount outstanding on time. The credit limit would depend on sales to the customer. Obviously, it would be unrealistic to give a credit limit of £3,000 when each of the customer's orders is £6,000. If the customer's financial stability is questionable, or if it is a new business, no limit may be given, and the customer will be required to pay in advance or when the goods are received.

The credit controller should retain these documents so they can be inspected by the Financial Director (and myself, as auditor). To provide a check on the Credit Controller's work, the system may require the Chief Accountant to authorise the credit limit for all new customers.

Once the credit limit has been set, a customer account will be set up on the computer with the customer's name, address and credit limit. The computer system should allow only the credit controller to set up this information on the sales system (by requiring the credit controller's password).

Did you answer the question?

Note that there should always be a system for determining credit limits; they should not just automatically be granted to the value of the first order received from a new customer.

(ii)   A form should be completed which requests an increase in a customer's credit limit. This may come from the customer, the sales or accounting departments or the credit controller. The credit controller will scrutinise this request by looking at sales to the customer and the payment record. If sales are increasing and the customer is paying within the company's credit terms, an increase in the credit limit will probably be authorised (even if the current credit limit is being exceeded). However, if the customer is slow at paying his debt the increase in the credit limit will probably be rejected. An alternative will be to give a smaller than requested increase in the customer's credit limit.

A reduction in the credit limit is likely to arise when sales to the customer are falling, or the customer is slow at paying off the balance on the account. The Credit Controller should keep a written record of the reasons for reducing the customer's credit limit.

Where the customer has ceased trading with the company, the credit controller may delete the customer from the computer's list of credit customers. The computer system should not allow deletion of a customer when there is a balance on the sales ledger. If there is a balance, the credit controller can stop further sales by setting a customer's credit limit to zero.

The credit controller should authorise an increase or decrease in the customer's credit limit, and if the limit is above a specified level, it should be authorised by the Chief Accountant or Financial Director.

The credit limit on the computer will be changed by the Credit Controller, using her password to gain access to the system. Where authorisation by the Chief Accountant or Financial Director is required, the computer will require their authorisation before the credit limit is changed.

(iii)   It is the credit controller's responsibility to ensure bad debts are kept to a minimum (without significantly prejudicing sales). Customers should be telephoned just prior to payment being due for a large invoice. This should ensure the payment is received on time.

If goods are ordered which would put the customer over the credit limit, the credit controller should ask for a cheque from the customer (and receive it) before the goods are sent. The procedure of not sending the goods can be used when the customer has an old outstanding invoice on the sales ledger.

If the customer is over the limit or there are old outstanding invoices on the sales ledger, the customer should be contacted by telephone and a letter written, pointing out the problem and asking to receive payment.

If payment is still not received, there should be a system which progressively increases the action taken against the customer. This will include:

-    threats of action being taken if payment is not received in a specified period (eg, seven days)

-    going to the customer's premises to collect the cheque

-    using a solicitor or debt collector to write to the customer

-    using a debt collector to attempt to receive payment

-    taking legal action against the customer (ie, requesting the debt to be paid)

-    applying to the court for the customer's business to be wound up

The procedures used by the company will be based on their success in using the techniques and the costs and time involved in the debt collection procedure. The credit controller will probably deal with small debts, but the Chief Accountant or Financial Director may become involved with large debts. Monthly reporting of the aged debtors to the Financial Director (using a printout from the computer) should ensure the Financial Director is aware of all debtors where there is a risk of a bad debt.

(iv)   The system should automatically put customers on 'stop' when they are exceeding their credit limit or there is a significant value of old unpaid invoices. The credit controller will put customers on 'stop' when she believes they are a serious credit risk, usually when they are either having liquidity (going concern) problems or they are refusing to pay an outstanding invoice. Information about going concern problems will come from a number of sources including credit agencies and other businesses.

Customers will be taken off 'stop' when the risk of invoices being unpaid is reduced (ie, usually when outstanding invoices have been paid). Putting customers on 'stop' does not prevent sales to that customer, but it does require the credit controller to authorise dispatch of goods (or refuse authorisation). The credit controller may over-ride the computer's decision to put a customer on 'stop' in a number of situations. This may be either when a large sale increases the debtor balance above the credit limit, or there are old invoices which are unpaid, but are subject to negotiation. In this situation, the credit controller will consider whether goods should be dispatched to the customer, and if she considers it is a low risk, she will authorise the dispatch using a secret code.

In each of the situations above, the credit controller should gain access to the system through her unique password, and the authorisation will be by means of a secret code. The computer system should record:

-    when customers are put on and taken off 'stop'

-    when the credit controller authorises dispatch of goods (when the customer is on 'stop' or the standard credit criteria are being exceeded)

The computer should have the facility for printing out details of dispatch notes and invoices relating to dispatches which have been authorised by the credit controller.

(b)   The first question to ask is 'can goods be dispatched with no dispatch note'. I will check the company's instructions to the dispatch department to verify the dispatch department staff are authorised only to dispatch goods when there is a dispatch note. Also, I will ask the dispatch department staff whether they dispatch goods with no dispatch note. If they say this can happen, I will investigate the situation and try to quantify the value of goods dispatched with no dispatch note. It is probably not possible to identify when goods are dispatched with no dispatch note from tests of controls (ie, the only way of detecting it is to be present in the dispatch department when it happens). However, this weakness can be detected as it will result in a difference between the physical stock and the computer stock records. This audit test is described in part (iii) below.

A weakness of the sales system is that a dispatch note can be produced without a sales invoice being raised. The question says the sales department produce the dispatch note, which is printed in the dispatch department. However, the sales invoice is not produced until the dispatch department record on the computer that the goods have been dispatched. If the dispatch department fail to record the dispatch of goods on the computer, no sales invoice will be produced.

The dispatch of goods without a sales invoice being raised can be detected in one of the following ways:

(i)   the computer system may record dispatch notes where there is no sales invoice (eg, by including them in a pipeline file). If this is recorded, printing these items will highlight this type of error. Using test data on the sales system could confirm that the computer accurately records when there is a dispatch note but no sales invoice. I will have to ask whether it is possible to delete the records of dispatch notes with no sales invoice. If this can happen, it could reduce the effectiveness of this test. However, if there is a printout of the pipeline file (of dispatch notes with no sales invoice) before it is deleted, I would inspect this printout and record details of goods dispatched with no invoice.

(ii)   as a test of controls, I would select a sample of dispatch notes and check there is a sales invoice. These could be a number in sequence during certain periods of the year, say 50 dispatch notes at each of four times during the year. Alternatively, I may select apparently larger value dispatch notes so that my tests cover a larger percentage by value of good dispatched. However, it can be difficult to identify large value dispatches of goods from the dispatch note.

(iii)   as a substantive procedure, I would investigate differences between the physical and computer stock quantities. These differences could arise from goods being dispatched and a sales invoice not being raised, as the computer stock records are only updated when the invoice is issued.

As a further check, I would ask the company's management if they check that a sales invoice has been raised for each dispatch note. If there is evidence they perform this check, I will reduce my tests in (ii) above.

A further substantive procedure is to compare the gross profit margin with previous years. If this year's gross profit margin is less than previous years, it could indicate that goods are being dispatched without a sales invoice being raised. However, there are many other explanations for a fall in the gross profit margin, including the situation where the company had not raised its selling price as much as the increase in its costs.

Did you answer the question?

Note that the examiner has covered both tests of control and substantive procedures in his answer to part (b), as required.

---

59   (Answer 3 of examination)

Examiner's comments and marking guide

Question 3: concerned fixed assets.

The answers to part (a) on checking the valuation of land and buildings were good. Some of the answers could have gone into more depth. For instance, it would be better to say you would check to the register of members whether the valuer owned shares in the company, rather than just stating 'checking the valuer does not own shares in the company'. Also, it would be unwise to rely on the management's statement that the valuer does not own shares in the company. Candidates were given credit for suggesting a valuation should be obtained from another valuer, despite the fact that this would be unusual to occur in practice (particularly in view of the cost to the auditor).

The answers to part (b) on verifying the existence and completeness of plant and machinery were disappointing. Candidates should have suggested physically checking the existence of fixed assets and, in particular, checking the serial number. Very few candidates suggested selecting fixed assets and checking they were in the fixed asset register. The word 'completeness' caused candidates problems, although this is an important aspect of audit work.

Most answers to part (c) were very poor. Part (i) was concerned with checking that additions to fixed assets are not of a revenue nature (eg, repairs), and part (ii) was concerned with the opposite, checking that additions to fixed assets are not treated as an expense in the year. Many candidates suggested checking all expense invoices, which would be excessively time-consuming. They should have suggested expense accounts where capital expenditure may have been charged, such as repairs and renewals. The boundary between capital and revenue can be imprecise, but hardly any candidates considered this problem.

Frequently, the answers to parts (b) and (c) were an example of candidates including everything in their answer that they knew about auditing fixed assets. This approach gains very few marks, and candidates' time would be better spent answering the question on the exam paper.

		Marks
(a)	Audit of valuation of land and buildings Generally 1 mark a point up to a maximum of:	9
(b)	Audit of existence of plant and machinery Generally 1 mark a point up to a maximum of:	5
(c)	Checking the correct treatment of capital items Generally 1 mark a point up to a maximum of:	6
Total		20

Step by step answer plan

Step 1   Read the question again and make sure that you focus on precisely what is required.

Step 2   Part (a) offers easy marks for the well prepared candidate. Focus on both the words 'accurate' and 'independent' eg, accuracy can be compared with indices of property prices in the area, and independence can be checked by ensuring that the valuer is not a shareholder in the company. With 9 marks available, you will need to describe at least, say, 10 audit procedures to be confident of earning a good mark.

Step 3   Existence and completeness are two of the standard financial statement assertions listed in SAS 400. Physical inspection can confirm existence, while testing from observed plant to the register will confirm completeness.

Step 4   The direction of testing is important in part (c). In part (i) the sample must be taken from recorded additions, while in part (ii) the sample must be taken from fixed asset expenses for the year (eg, repairs, motor expenses, etc).

Step 5   Only when you are confident that you are about to answer the question that has been set, should you start writing.

The examiner's answer

(a)   Firstly, I will obtain the letter from the valuer stating the value of the property (ie, land and buildings). This should be the original letter sent by the valuer to the company (and not a photocopy). I will check there has been no amendment to the valuation and that the letter is signed by the valuer. I will check the existence of the valuing firm by checking its name to the telephone directory.

Then I will consider the independence of the valuer:

(i)   the question says the valuer is not an employee of the company. To confirm this, I will check if the name of the valuer is on the company's payroll. I will carry out further investigations if I find an employee's name is the same as the valuer's (this seems unlikely)

(ii)   if the valuer has the same surname as a director or senior employee of Newthorpe Manufacturing, I will determine whether the valuer is related to that employee. If they are related, it could prejudice the independence of the valuer. If the valuation has been by a firm of valuers, I will check that none of the surnames of the partners are the same as directors or senior employees of the company.

(iii)   I will ask the directors if they are connected to the valuer, either by a blood relationship or by being directors or partners in a common business. I may ask the same questions to the valuer.

(iv)   I will include a note in the letter of representation saying the directors have no business or blood relationship with the valuer (or partners in the firm of valuers)

(v)   ideally, the valuer should not own shares in Newthorpe, and I can check to the register of members (shareholders) that the valuer is not a shareholder. If the valuer does own shares in Newthorpe Manufacturing, this should not be a problem provided the number and value of the shares is small, but it could be a problem if the valuer owns a substantial number or value of shares of Newthorpe Manufacturing.

(vi)   I will consider whether the fee for the valuation is a substantial proportion of the fees of the valuer. This may be apparent from my local knowledge of the firm of valuers. I may contact the valuer if I believe the valuation fee is a substantial proportion of the valuer's income.

To check the qualifications and experience of the valuer, I will:

(i)   check the qualifications of the valuer by inspecting his/her qualifications on the headed paper with the valuation (it will either be given in the list of partners, or when he/she signs the letter). If there are no qualifications given on the letter, I will contact the valuer. If I am concerned that qualifications may not be valid, I will contact the valuer's professional body. If being a valuer requires the member to have a practising certificate (like members of the ACCA), I will check to the professional body that the valuer has a current practising certificate.

(ii)   consider whether the valuer is experienced in valuing properties like those owned by Newthorpe Manufacturing. I will probably have to ask the valuer for these details. If the valuer normally values houses and has little experience of valuing industrial properties, then his/her valuation will be less reliable than if he/she commonly values industrial properties. Newthorpe Manufacturing's property is likely to be quite large, and it may be specialised, so I will check the valuer has experience in valuing this type of property.

(iii)   the valuer should have experience in valuing properties in the same geographical area as Newthorpe Manufacturing's property. If the valuer is a local firm, then it is more likely to produce an accurate valuation than from a valuer in a different area where there are large differences in property prices (eg, a London valuer valuing properties in Chesterfield).

I will ask the company for a copy of the letter appointing the valuer. This should show the terms of reference set for the valuer, and I will consider whether there have been any limitations placed on the valuer's work. The letter by the valuer which includes the valuation is likely to include any limitations placed on the valuer's work, assumptions concerning the valuation and the basis of valuation used.

On the valuation, I will consider the basis of the valuation and the current value:

(i)   the property should have been valued on an existing use basis (or similar basis). A basis like development value would probably not be appropriate as it is likely to be anticipating future profits. If development use is used, I will have to discuss the matter with the directors and seek further evidence and consider whether it is appropriate. A replacement cost valuation would not be appropriate, as the cost of replacing the building will probably be more than its current (second hand and used) value.

(ii)   as I am concerned the property appears to be over-valued, I will ask the valuer the basis he/she has used to value the property (eg, land and buildings on a £ per square metre basis). I will look at any documents the valuer has used in the valuation to check their authenticity and reliability.

(iii)   I will check the prices being asked for similar properties at other industrial estate agents and see if they are consistent with the value placed on Newthorpe Manufacturing's property. The rental value of a similar property could be used to estimate the current value, as with rentals at (say) 5% of capital cost, a rent of £100,000 a year would indicate a capital cost of £2 million.

(iv)   if local or national statistics are available which provide indices of property prices, I will use these indices to determine whether the increase in the value of the freehold land and building is reasonable.

Based on this work, I will decide whether the value of £5 million is reasonable. As valuation of properties can be subject to considerable error, quite a large difference between my estimated figure and that estimated by the valuer may be acceptable. However, if I feel there is a material over-valuation of the property, I will first ask the directors to reduce the value (or obtain another valuation which gives a lower value), and if they refuse I will have to qualify my audit report. If the difference is material, but relatively small, I may include an additional reference in my audit report on the valuation of the property, which refers to the notes in the financial statements.

Did you answer the question?

Note the large number of audit procedures suggested by the examiner to earn the 9 marks available, dealing with both the accuracy of the valuation and the valuer's independence.

(b)   Firstly, I will check the opening balances (cost and depreciation provision), closing balances, additions, disposals and depreciation charge on the fixed asset register agree with the accounting records and the draft financial statements.

Before deciding the number of items to check, I will ask the company how frequently it checks the existence of plant in the fixed asset register. I will look at documents recording details of the company's checks. I will select a larger sample of fixed assets if they are checked infrequently, or if only a small proportion of fixed assets are checked by the company or a large number of discrepancies are found in the company's tests.

To check the existence of plant and machinery, I will select items from the fixed asset register. The items selected will probably be weighted towards larger value fixed assets. Ideally, some statistical basis should be used for selecting the fixed assets such as monetary unit sampling or stratified sampling, probably based on the net book value of the fixed asset. When I have selected the items, I will ask the production manager the location of each fixed asset (this may be given in the fixed asset register). Then I will physically check the existence of the fixed asset. The fixed asset should be consistent with the description in the fixed asset register, and it is important that I check the serial number on the fixed asset is the same as that given in the fixed asset register. I may need help to find the serial number, as frequently they are inaccessible or are difficult to find. The fixed asset register should give the age of the fixed asset, and I will check this appears reasonable. By checking the fixed asset, I will be able to assess its condition and how much it is being used. The check from the fixed asset register to the fixed asset confirms the existence of fixed assets in the fixed asset register.

In addition, it is necessary to select a sample of plant and machinery from the factory (including their serial number and a description) and check they appear in the fixed asset register. It is probably not possible to use a statistical basis for selecting these items, but a pseudo monetary unit sampling basis could be used by biasing the sample towards newer and higher value items. It is important the serial number is recorded, as this is unique. This test checks that fixed assets which exist appear in the fixed asset register (ie, completeness of plant and machinery in the fixed asset register). If my tests highlight discrepancies in the fixed asset register, I will either perform more checks or ask the company's staff to perform more checks (and test check their work). If serious problems are highlighted, I will include the matter in my letter to the directors, and it could result in either the financial statements being amended (to correct errors) or an audit qualification (if the error or uncertainty is material).

(c)   In considering whether additions to fixed assets and certain expenses should be capitalised, I will consider whether the company's treatment is consistent with the Statement of Principles and Companies Act definitions of a fixed asset, namely that it is expected to yield future economic benefit and is intended to be retained for use in the business. In addition, I will consider whether the company's treatment of additions to fixed assets and charging items as an expense is consistent with previous years.

In checking additions to fixed assets in the year, I will vouch the purchase invoice to the nominal ledger and fixed asset register. The value of the invoice should agree to the amount posted to the nominal ledger and fixed asset register. The description of the fixed asset per the purchase invoice should agree to that in the fixed asset register, and the serial number of the asset should be correctly recorded in the fixed asset register.

(i)   when vouching additions to fixed assets, I will consider whether it is validly an addition to fixed assets or should have been an expense in the year. This can be quite difficult to decide. However, if it is a repair of the fixed asset, it should not be included in additions to fixed assets (as this would overstate fixed assets and profit for the year). If I believe this is happening, I will include details of the items which should be included in repairs in my list of unadjusted errors. I will discuss these with the directors. If they are material, I will ask the directors to amend the financial statements, and if they refuse, I may have to qualify the audit report.

(ii)   I will confirm with the directors and last year's audit file that items of under £500 are not capitalised. With the limit of £500, there may be a large number of items under this value, and not capitalising them may materially understate the value of fixed assets in the financial statements. If this is happening, I will consider whether the financial statements need amending.

To locate items which were included as an expense but should have been capitalised, I will look at certain accounts in the nominal ledger. These will include:

-     repairs and renewals
-     sundry expenses
-     motor and travelling expenses

Firstly, I will compare the charges in each of these accounts to previous years, both in terms of total value and as a percentage of the company's turnover. If the expense charge in each of these accounts is similar to previous years and audits in previous years have shown that the company has an appropriate split for capital/expense items, then I will reduce the number of items I check. However, if the expenses this year are significantly greater than previous years, I will increase the number of items I check.

From these accounts, I will select a sample of items over the minimum capitalisation value (ie, over £500) and check to the purchase invoice whether they are capital and should be included in fixed assets. I will obtain a list of items which I consider should be included in fixed assets and discuss them with the company's management. Following this discussion, I will prepare a final list of items which should be capitalised and include their details in my list of unadjusted errors. If I find a large number of errors, I will either increase the sample of items I check or ask the company's staff to check more items (and I will check their work). As I have only checked a sample of items, I will probably have to extrapolate my sample to estimate the potential error in the population. Most auditors would accept writing off certain fixed assets in the year of purchase, as this tends to understate profit for the year. Auditors are more concerned that profit is not overstated, so some understatement of profit in this way would be acceptable.

Finally, based on this work, I will decide whether the value of additions to fixed assets in the year is reasonable. If I feel there is a material understatement or overstatement of additions to fixed assets (which has a material effect on the profit for the year), I will ask the directors to amend the financial statements, and if they refuse, I will consider qualifying my audit report.

Did you answer the question?

Note that the direction of testing has been stressed in the answer to part (c).

---

60 (Answer 4 of examination)

Examiner's comments and marking guide

Question 4: was concerned with closure costs of a factory and the consequences of dismissal of a director. Many of the answers to this question were quite good.

In part (a) (i) some candidates were unclear about net realisable value. A few candidates wrongly thought that the net book value of the fixed assets would be the same (or is the same) as the net realisable value. Frequently, the answers were weak on consideration of the selling price of products which were unsold at the time of the audit. Many candidates failed to consider costs of sale. A disappointing number of candidates considered the original cost of the fixed assets and stock, which is not relevant in determining net realisable value.

In part (a) (ii) many candidates provided a good answer. For the normal redundancy payments, the auditor should check the length of service to the personnel records and the wage to payroll. Few candidates suggested starting from the payroll as the basis of auditing the redundancy cost.

The answers to part (b) (i) on disclosure of a contingent loss were variable, with some candidates giving the correct answer and others providing very little or incorrect information. The answers to the first half of (b) (ii) were generally good, with many candidates suggesting the auditor should obtain legal advice. The answers to the second half of this part were less good, as very few candidates considered a range of alternative situations.

Marks

(a)   (i)   Audit of NRV of plant and stock
              Generally 1 mark a point up to a maximum of: 7

      (ii)   Audit of redundancy cost
              Generally 1 mark a point up to a maximum of: 4

(b)   (i)   Treatment of contingent losses in financial statements
              Generally 1 mark a point up to a maximum of: 3

      (ii)   Audit of contingency relating to dismissal of director
              Generally 1 mark a point up to a maximum of: 6

Total   20

Step by step answer plan

Step 1   Read the question again and make sure that you focus on precisely what is required.

Step 2   SSAP 9 gives the definition of NRV for part (a). Book values are clearly irrelevant. The work on the redundancy cost will centre around the schedule prepared by the client calculating their estimate.

Step 3   Part (b) (i) is standard bookwork on FRS 12. Obtaining independent legal advice is a good point to start from in part (b) (ii).

Step 4   Only when you are confident that you are about to answer the question that has been set, should you start writing.

The examiner's answer

(a)   Firstly, I will ask the company to identify the assets and employees who are being made redundant as a result of closure of the factory. It will be easier to identify these items if the whole factory is being closed, the plant and machinery is identified in the fixed asset register and the employees are either on a separate payroll or are separately identified.

         (i)   For the plant and machinery, I will obtain a schedule of the fixed assets and the estimated or actual disposal proceeds. In most cases there is likely to be a loss on disposal, unless the fixed asset is fully written off.

                  To check completeness of the population being examined, I will check that the cost and depreciation on the fixed asset register agrees to or can be reconciled to the figure in the company's accounting records and the draft financial statements.

                  The company will probably have separate schedules of plant which is sold and plant which is unsold. I will test check completeness of plant and machinery on the schedules by selecting items of plant from the fixed asset register and checking they are on either the plant sold schedule or the plant unsold schedule. For plant which has been sold, I will check that the sale proceeds are the same as (or similar to) the figure on the company's schedule. The sale proceeds should be recorded on a sales invoice and in the cash book. There may be costs of disposal (eg, unfixing or dismantling the plant) which will have to be deducted from the sale proceeds if Newthorpe has agreed to pay these costs. If the item has not been sold, I will obtain details of the plant and its estimated sale proceeds. If the sale proceeds are small (eg, scrap value) I will probably perform little audit work. However, if they are substantial, I will have to consider whether they are realistic, by asking the company's staff why they are so large and whether potential buyers have expressed interest in purchasing them (I will try to get evidence of this interest by buyers). From this work, I will consider whether the sale proceeds are reasonable.

                  I will increase the sample of items I check if I find that the company's estimates are unreliable. Based on this work, I will decide whether the company's estimate of the sale proceeds of the plant and machinery is realistic. If I feel there is a significant difference, I will discuss the matter with the directors. If they refuse to change the figure in the financial statements, I will include the difference in my schedule of unadjusted errors (and I will probably qualify my audit report if the total of the errors is material).

(ii)   I will obtain a schedule from the company of the actual and estimated proceeds of sale of the stock. As stated in the question, the stocktake was carried out at the year end, so stock quantities do not have to be checked.

Details of year end stock from the stocksheets can be used as a basis for identifying the stock which is sold after the closure.

I will select a sample of items of stock, probably using monetary unit sampling. For stock which has been sold by the time of my investigations, I will check the sale proceeds to the cash book and other evidence of the sale. For some of these items of stock, it may not be possible to identify the selling price as a number of products may have been sold in a single transaction. If this has happened, I will check the sale proceeds have been correctly allocated against the stock sold.

For stock which is unsold at the time of my audit, I will consider whether the company's estimates are realistic. I will probably accept the company's estimates if the sale proceeds are small. For items where the estimated sale proceeds are large, I will ask the company's staff details of the stock and why such a high price is being used. From this information, I will try to obtain an estimate of the sale proceeds by either obtaining information from potential customers of their offers for the stock, or using judgement based on my knowledge of the products, and my experience in other audits. For instance, if the item is a valuable material (eg, lead), I could obtain the estimated value from a scrap merchant. For items which are unsold, net realisable value will be the sale proceeds less costs of sale, so the costs of sale will have to be deducted from the estimated proceeds. I will consider whether these costs of sale are realistic. They will include costs of advertising the stock and possibly the costs of transporting the stock to the customer.

Unsold work in progress is likely to have a low value. I will check cases where the items have been given a high value and the stock is unsold at the time of my audit. I will consider whether these estimated sale proceeds are reasonable.

If the value of unsold stock is significant, I could check the ratio of net realisable value of stock sold to its cost, and check that a similar ratio applies to the unsold stock. For instance, if stock has been sold at 20% of cost, then it is unlikely that the remaining stock will be sold for 25% of cost, but a figure of 15% of cost for the unsold stock would probably be realistic.

If there is a significant difference between my estimates and the company's figures, I will discuss the matter with the directors. If they refuse to adjust the financial statements, I will include the difference in my schedule of unadjusted errors.

Did you answer the question?

Note that some of the plant and stock has been sold, but some remains unsold. The proceeds on disposal of the unsold items will obviously be less certain than those that have already been sold.

(iii)   I will obtain a schedule of the redundancy costs from the company. I will ask the company the basis for the redundancy payment (which should be the same as described in the question). I will check that employees on the payroll just before the factory closed appear on the list of employees being made redundant. For employees on the payroll who are not on the list, I will check they have been transferred to another factory (eg, they should appear on a current payroll for that factory). I will ask the company about any employees on the list of those being made redundant who do not appear on the factory's payroll at the year end.

I will select a sample of employees who have been made redundant and check the calculation of the redundancy pay:

-        for most employees this will be the weekly pay times the number of years service. I will find the date they started working for Newthorpe Engineering from the personnel records and calculate the number of years service. I will determine the definition of 'weekly pay'. It may be the basic pay (excluding overtime) or the employee's average pay over the past year.

Depending on what basis is used to determine 'weekly pay', I will obtain the figure either from the payroll, other information in the wages department or from the personnel department. Then I will check the redundancy pay is calculated correctly.

- for employees under a service contract. I will check the redundancy pay is the amount stated in their contract.

As employees under a service contract are paid more than the basic redundancy, I will ask the company for copies of the employees' service contracts and select a sample of these employees. I will check the calculation of the redundancy is correct.

I will test check the payments to the cash book to ensure they are the same as on the company's schedule and per my calculations. I will check the addition of the employees' redundancy pay and check this equals the provision in the financial statements.

Finally, I will ask if there are any disputes with employees over the amount they are to be paid (or have been paid), and I will obtain evidence of these disputes (ie, letters from the employees). I will ask the company their opinion of the final outcome, and I will check that the company's estimate of the additional amount it will have to pay for these claims is reasonable. If these claims are likely to be substantial, and there is no provision for them in the financial statements, I will ask the directors to amend the financial statements. If they refuse to make the change, I will include the difference in my schedule of unadjusted errors.

(b)   (i)   This case is concerned with a contingent loss. FRS 12 (Provisions, contingent liabilities and contingent assets) specifies the following disclosure requirements for contingent losses:

Unless the possibility of any transfer in settlement is remote, an entity should disclose for each class of contingent liability at the balance sheet date a brief description of the nature of the contingent liability and, where practicable:

- an estimate of its financial effect.

- an indication of the uncertainties relating to the amount or timing of any outflow, and

- possibility of any reimbursement.

(ii)   In auditing this item, I will have to determine:

- whether the possibility of the company having to pay the claim is 'remote', 'possible' or 'probable'.

- the sum the company may have to pay if it is successful or unsuccessful in defending its action in dismissing the Managing Director.

To determine the possibility of the Managing Director being successful in his claim, I will:

- obtain a copy of his service contract. I will consider whether he could make a successful claim in relation to this service contract. So, I will have to check the compensation for dismissal according to the service contract. If the contract has two years' to run at the date of his dismissal, this would probably be the maximum sum he could claim under this contract. I will look to see if there are any circumstances which would prevent him making this claim, such as being dismissed for gross misconduct.

- obtain details of the allegations of gross misconduct, and evidence to support those allegations. I will obtain a transcript of the disciplinary hearing held on 17th March. I will ask if there is any evidence from the Managing Director of whether he agreed or disputed the findings of the disciplinary hearing. Based on this work, I will discuss the situation with the company's directors and decide whether the company's evidence would provide a successful defence to the Managing Director's claim.

-     ask about any developments since 17th March which could quantify the company's potential liability relating to this claim. I will ask for details of any correspondence between the company and the Managing Director (or between their solicitors). If the company has agreed to make a payment, a provision should be included in the financial statements.

-     it seems probable that the company will incur legal costs in defending the claim by the Managing Director, and these should be accrued in the financial statements. I will ask the company for an estimate of these costs, or I may ask the company's solicitor (with the client's permission) for an estimate.

-     I will ask the opinion of the company's solicitor the likely outcome of the case, and I will obtain details of the outcome of similar cases. If the amount of the claim is very material, I may obtain independent legal advice.

-     I will consider whether insurance will cover the claim against the company and the legal costs. I will check that insurance cover is available by looking at the insurance policy and the circumstances it covers. Also, I will contact the insurance company (with the client's permission) to check the insurance company will pay the sum due. The insurance company may pay the legal costs, but it may not pay the damages awarded against the company. Any insurance cover will reduce the provision required in the financial statements for this item.

Based on these investigations, I will consider whether the company's treatment of the item in the financial statements is reasonable. The company will probably want to avoid mentioning dismissal of the director in the financial statements (because of the associated bad publicity). Although very few details of the dismissal are given in the question, it seems the probability of the company having to concede the Managing Director's claim is 'possible' or even 'probable', so it should either be included as a note to the financial statements or accrued in the financial statements. Also, the company will probably have to pay its own legal costs, and these should be accrued in the financial statements. Thus, I will probably have to insist the contingency is mentioned in the financial statements (ie, the crystallisation of the contingency is 'possible'). If no mention is made in the financial statements, I will probably have to qualify my audit report for non disclosure of the item.

Did you answer the question?

Note that the examiner has reached a preliminary conclusion in part (b) (ii) on the appropriate accounting treatment, based on the facts of the case given in the question.

---

61   (Answer 5 of examination)

Examiner's comments and marking guide

Question 5: concerned using PCs in audit work.

Many of the answers were quite good. Surprisingly, some candidates failed to suggest that spreadsheets could be used to calculate ratios. Also, some candidates appeared to have little or no experience and understanding of spreadsheets. On the use of computer assisted audit techniques, many of the suggestions were those which would be carried out on a mainframe or mini computer, rather than using a PC. However, candidates were given some credit for mentioning these points. Very few candidates mentioned downloading data from the client's computer into the PC for testing. Some candidates were not aware of the form of a memorandum, and thus failed to gain the appropriate marks.

Marks

Use of PC's in auditors work
Generally 1 mark a point up to a maximum of: 20

Note: in awarding marks, the points made by candidates should be relevant to the question.

If the candidate makes a short point, it may be worth only ½ mark, but longer than normal points may be awarded more than 1 mark.

In awarding the total mark, you should consider whether the candidate has given an answer to each of the categories listed in the question. An answer which concentrates on one of the categories may be worth less than one which covers all the requested topics. It is not necessary for the candidate's answer to each part to be the same length, as more points can be made in some topic areas than others. Each of the topic areas are not water-tight, so it is acceptable for candidates to make a point in one area when it is covered in another topic area in the model answer. Nevertheless, candidates should be given credit only once if they make the same point in two parts of the question.

Up to 2 marks may be given for layout and presentation.

Step by step answer plan

Step 1   Read the question again and make sure that you focus on precisely what is required.

Step 2   Write your answer in the form of a memorandum, using the headings given in the question with perhaps a 'summary' or 'conclusion' paragraph at the end of your memorandum.

Step 3   Give examples in your memo of where in the audit each PC application could be used eg, spreadsheets for analytical review via ratio analysis, statistical packages for selecting samples in tests of control, etc.

Step 4   Only when you are confident that you are about to answer the question that has been set, should you start writing.

The examiner's answer

Memorandum of A Audit Firm

To: Senior partner

From: A Auditor

Date: 9 June 1997

Re: Use of PC's in Audit Work

This memorandum suggests applications of PC's to audit work. It has been divided into the following sections:

(a)   use of spreadsheets
(b)   use of statistical packages
(c)   using computer assisted audit techniques and testing controls over access to the computer
(d)   use of word processors and other packages to record audit work

(a)   **Use of Spreadsheets**

The principal application of spreadsheets is to carry out analytical review of the financial statements. The financial statements will be input into the spreadsheet which will calculate ratios and changes from previous years. Any unusual changes (eg, an increase in the age of debtors) can be investigated by carrying out more detailed audit work on such areas as the doubtful debt provision and sales cut-off.

More sophisticated spreadsheets can be used to compare ratios with industry averages and similar clients. Significant differences from industry averages will be investigated. For instance, if the client is significantly more profitable this year when similar businesses have a poorer performance, then an investigation can be carried out to determine whether the current year's profits are materially overstated.

Spreadsheets can be used to calculate such measures as Z-scores which are used to assess the risk that the company may not be a going concern.

(b)   **Use of Statistical Packages**

Statistical packages can be used in the following ways:

(i)   to determine the number of items to select for a test. The statistical package will suggest the number of items which should be checked to achieve the auditor's required level of control risk (for tests of control) and detection risk (for substantive procedures). If errors are found in the test, the statistical package will suggest the number of additional items which should be tested. For instance, in order to achieve the required level of confidence in the accuracy of the population, the statistical package may suggest 40 items should be checked if no errors are found but 75 should be selected if one error is found and the auditor still wants to achieve the required confidence level.

(ii)   to select samples for audit. Random sampling using random numbers generated by the computer can be used to select items for checking in tests of control, such as selecting dispatch notes by using the dispatch note number. Other methods can be used, such as using monetary unit sampling for selecting debtors for circularisation.

(iii)   to analyse the results of the audit test. Normally, this will give a measure of the confidence in the accuracy of the population. For instance, it might say the auditor is 95% confident that the error rate in the population is less than 7%.

In addition, the statistical package may suggest a range of statistical techniques to use, and assist the auditor in deciding which is most suitable. For instance, for a given level of statistical confidence, monetary unit sampling usually allows a reduced number of items to be sampled compared with using pure random sampling, but selecting a sample based on monetary value could take more time.

(c)   **Using Computer Assisted Audit Techniques and Testing Controls over Access to the Computer**

Where the client's accounting data is processed by PC's, it may be possible to transfer the programs and data onto the auditor's computer. This will allow the auditor to:

(i)   interrogate and analyse the data on the files.

(ii)   check whether the accounting system processes valid data correctly and either rejects invalid data or gives a warning (this is equivalent to using test data on a larger computer system). In this way, the 'robustness' of the computer system can be checked.

By downloading the files from the main computer, the auditor can use computer audit programs to check the accuracy of this information. Thus, it could be used on the sales ledger to check that the addition of the individual outstanding items (mainly sales invoices less credit notes) equals the total balance. It can check the ageing of debtors is accurate. For larger computer systems, the PC could be used to assist in other computer assisted audit techniques. For instance, the PC could be used as a terminal to the main computer.

Then it could:

(i)   interrogate the accounting files on the computer (in a similar way to a computer audit program).

(ii)   input data into the accounting system to check the reliability of the accounting computer programs (like using test data).

The PC could be used to attempt to gain access to the system by using a variety of passwords, thus checking the security of access to the computer system. The passwords could be selected randomly, or common first names or names of domestic animals could be used. The PC would have a standard list of common passwords, which could be input into the computer more quickly, thus saving audit time. Also, the PC can be used, for example, with a sales department password using a terminal in the sales department to check that it is not possible to update purchase accounting records or enter the payroll system.

(d)   **Use of Word processor and other Packages in Recording Audit Work**

The range of tasks a PC could be used for is very extensive. The following list gives examples of using word processors for audit work:

(i)   in recording audit work. This may mean replacing handwritten schedules with those prepared on the computer. The computer may have pre-prepared forms (or templates) and the auditor can insert the audit work on the forms. These pre-prepared forms could include checklists and internal control evaluation questionnaires. The security of this data may be a problem:

-     it is easier to delete a computer file than destroy paper based audit work, so there is a greater risk of the computer files being accidentally destroyed.

-     hand written audit files seem more 'certain' than computer based ones. For instance a sheet of audit work will normally have the preparer's signature and the date prepared at the bottom, and subsequent amendments to this work are more apparent. With computer based data, it is less clear when data is amended. Usually, there is no indication of the amendment and only a change in the date of the file will highlight the change. However, the date of the file can be amended to the date the information was originally prepared by changing the system date on the computer.

-     computer files can become corrupted and all the data lost.

-     security of computer files may be a problem, as an unauthorised person may copy the file onto a floppy disc, and there is no indication that the copy has been made. Files containing a lot of information can be copied very quickly, whereas it is much more time consuming to copy hand written audit files.

(ii)   preparing documents for the audit, such as the audit planning memorandum, the report to the manager and partner on the audit work done including review of the financial statements.

(iii)   in cases, where the accountant also prepares the financial statements from the company's accounting records, a spreadsheet package can be used to help prepare the draft financial statements and the statutory financial statements can be prepared by combining word-processing and spreadsheet data.

(iv)   the computer can be used for recording the time spent on each of the parts of the audit and the total time. The actual time spent can be compared with budget. It is probable that a central computer in the audit firm will record the time spent by audit staff against each client, so that the practice can compare the charge to the client with the costs incurred.

(v)   in assisting in carrying out a debtors' circularisation. The computer can select the debtors from the sales ledger file using statistical criteria (such as monetary unit sampling), write the letters to the debtors and record and analyse the results. This technique would use a combination of statistical, CAAT and word-processing programs.

(vi)   in preparing flowcharts of accounting systems. The member of the audit team inputs the information and the computer produces the flowchart.

(vii)   the computer may contain the firm's audit manual and provide guidance on common problems found in the audit. The guidance can be updated for changes in legislation and items added when new problems arise.

Summary

This memorandum shows there are many ways in which PC's can be used in audit work. If you would like to discuss these matters with me, or you require any further information, please do not hesitate to contact me.

Note: an answer to this question cannot include all relevant points and topics. Candidates will be given credit when they suggest relevant points.

62   (Answer 6 of examination)

Question 6: was concerned with tendering for the audit of a mobile phone company. There was a lot of opportunity for gaining marks, and many of the answers were quite good.

The answers to part (a) on the risks associated with the audit were less good than expected. Some candidates explained the elements of audit risk and, if this was all they considered, they gained very few marks. A good answer would have considered most of the points (a) to (k) in the question. Few candidates considered the limited coverage of Phones Anywhere's current and projected reception areas.

The answers to part (b) were better with candidates mentioning a range of relevant points. In part (c) most candidates rightly suggested the audit firm should not tender for the audit because of the risks. Some candidates mentioned some points in this part (such as potential going concern problems) which they should also have mentioned in part (a) of their answer. The boundaries between the parts of the question were not always clear cut, so candidates were given credit for points made in one part which were considered in another part of the model answer.

		Marks
(a)	Risks of audit and capability of audit firm	
	Generally 1 mark a point up to a maximum of:	8
(b)	Consideration of ethical matters	
	Generally 1 mark a point up to a maximum of:	8
(c)	Conclusion - should you carry out the audit, and reasons	
	Generally 1 mark a point up to a maximum of:	4
Total		20

Note: candidates should be given credit for including points in one part, which are included in another in the model answer. In part (c), giving a conclusion without any supporting points would be worth only 1 mark. However, additional credit should be given if the supporting points are included in parts (a) or (b) of the answer.

Step by step answer plan

Step 1   Read the question again and make sure that you focus on precisely what is required.

Step 2   The best approach to part (a) is to go through points (a) to (k) in the question and discuss their implications on the components of audit risk ie, inherent risk, detection risk and control risk. The conclusion will necessarily be that this audit has high inherent risk.

Step 3   Refer specifically to the ACCA Rules of Professional Conduct in part (b), for example the 15% limit of the fees from one client. The question states that you are from a four partner firm ie, a fairly small business which might be stretched by the rapid growth of this client.

Step 4   As with all such questions, the actual conclusion you come to in part (c) is not important. What is being tested is your process of coming to that decision. In exams you can afford to be very prudent in your decision-making and reject risky clients such as these.

Step 5   Only when you are confident that you are about to answer the question that has been set, should you start writing.

The examiner's answer

(a)   There appear to be considerable risks associated with undertaking the audit. In particular, Phones Anywhere appears to have a very high inherent risk. Looking at the matters in (a) to (k) in the question:

(i)   the low coverage of the country will be a disincentive to new subscribers. Initially, subscribers will only be those who operate in the town with a population of 1,000,000. The service will not be available when the subscribers are outside that town. I will have to consider whether the company has the financial resources to develop to towns with a population of 250,000 in the next year and its planned developments to the year 2000. The company's plans for extending the network do not appear to be realistic, as many mobile phones are used on motorways and trunk roads. Motorways will not be covered until the year 2000, and coverage of other roads is not mentioned. These plans are likely to be a serious disincentive to new subscribers joining the system, when competitors cover most of the country.

(ii)   the central computer is pivotal to the organisation, as it relays the calls and calculates the bills for subscribers. Will this computer and its software be reliable? The consequences of a break-down of the computer will be very serious. Ideally, there should be more than one computer running the system, and the system should be able to continue if one of the computers fails.

(iii)   what is the capacity of the main computer? With the planned expansion, it is probable that it will run out of capacity in the near future. Is it possible to expand the capacity of the computer? Has the cost of upgrading the computer been included in future forecasts? Will the current software be able to process a large increase in subscribers, or will it have to be re-written (at substantial cost)?

(iv)   is it reasonable to amortise the cost of the relay stations and main computer over six years? Six years may be realistic for the 'buildings' part of capital expenditure, but it may be too long for electronic components including the main computer and transmitters.

(v)   is the discount paid to retailers for the purchase of the phones recoverable? The question says it is capitalised and amortised over four years. Do subscribers remain connected to a single operator for as long as four years (if many change in less than four years, this amortisation period is too long), and are subscribers likely to change their phones within four years (to update to a more advanced model)?

(vi)   paying the executive directors a bonus based on the number of subscribers of the system could encourage them to obtain as many subscribers as possible (by offering discounted prices) rather than charging a realistic price which will ensure the long term future of the company. However, the executive directors should be concerned with the long term future of the company, as this will ensure they continue to be paid (rather than have to find a new job when the company fails).

(vii)   in view of the planned high borrowings, and future trading losses, there is a very serious risk the company may not be a going concern. This increases the risk of my firm being sued for negligence. Also, Phones Anywhere will put severe pressure on me to give a completely unqualified audit report. This pressure will increase because my audit firm is small and Phones Anywhere is a relatively large and rapidly growing company.

(viii) as an alternative to the company not being a going concern, there is the risk that other investors may purchase more shares in the company (to provide additional equity finance) or purchase the company outright from the existing directors (or the administrator/liquidator). If this occurs, recent financial statements will be subject to close scrutiny. The standard of audit work will have to be high, and the problems mentioned above (eg, complex computer systems and depreciation rates which may be inaccurate) could lead to undetected material errors in the financial statements. Thus, there is a high risk that legal action for negligence could be taken against my audit firm following a take-over or purchase of shares.

(ix)   flotation of the company on the London Stock Exchange is a further risk. Immediately prior to the flotation, the audit work carried out by my firm will be subject to close scrutiny. So, I will have to be very careful in my work which would increase the cost of the audit and reduce its profitability. Also, when the company becomes quoted on the London Stock Exchange, it is probable I will be replaced as auditor, as my firm will be 'too small'. Almost all of the companies quoted on the London Stock Exchange are audited by one of the 'big 6' firms.

(x)   this is a high technology industry. The technology or customer requirements may change, which could make parts of the equipment obsolete. Alternatively, it could be expensive to modify the equipment or software to meet the demands of subscribers. Is the company currently providing a similar range of facilities to other mobile phone companies. If its service is not as comprehensive as other mobile phone companies, it may not be successful in breaking into the market.

(xi)   this appears to be a very competitive industry. Are the competitors profitable, or are they making losses to keep prices low to prevent other companies entering the market? Establishing Phones Anywhere as a major company in the market will probably require large expenditure on advertising and offering new subscribers a service at a lower price than competitors. Both of these factors will tend to make Phones Anywhere unprofitable (as note (j) in the question suggests).

(xii)   I will have to consider the reputation of the three major shareholders and the executive directors. If they have been directors of companies which have failed, or been involved in financial or other wrongdoings, this will increase the inherent risk. The reputation of the financial director and the quality of the accounting records are other factors which will have to be considered.

(b)   The professional and ethical matters I will have to consider will include:

(i)   the size of the audit fee. The Association of Chartered Certified Accountants' (ACCA) rules of professional conduct say the fees for audit and other recurring work paid by one client should not normally exceed 15% of the gross practice income (and 10% for listed and other public interest companies). If the planned audit fee is over 15% of the current practice income I should not accept the audit. However, the rate of expansion of Phones Anywhere will probably be much greater than the increase in income of my practice, so the 15% rule may become a problem in the next few years. When Phones Anywhere becomes a listed company in the year 2000, the audit fee from Phones Anywhere must be less than 10% of the fees of the practice. It seems probable that this limit of 10% will be exceeded. In practice, it is undesirable for the audit fee to approach 15% of the practice income, as reliance on such a large audit fee could be seen to affect my firm's independence.

(ii)   my audit firm may be able to audit Phones Anywhere at its current size. However, when the system covers all towns with a population of over 250,000, on occasions audit work will probably have to cover all areas of the country, and it is most unlikely that my audit firm will have sufficient staff to perform this work.

(iii)   whether my firm is technically competent to perform the audit, and whether the size of the firm being audited is too large for the experience of my practice. Mobile telephone companies are very complex and have specialised accounting procedures, both in terms of the accounting system and the ways matters are treated in the financial statements (eg, the advance payment of £200 given towards the purchase of phones purchased by new subscribers). My firm will probably not have experience in auditing the computerised accounting system which controls calls and generates bills for subscribers. This requires specialised computer auditing techniques. Also, my firm will be unfamiliar with many of the accounting treatments for fixed assets and they will probably not be able to decide whether the lives given to fixed assets are reasonable. This lack of experience will probably mean that the audit will be too high a risk for my audit firm (ie, my firm's inexperience will mean that a satisfactory audit cannot be carried out, so there will be a high risk of material misstatements in the financial statements, which increases the risk of litigation being brought against me).

(iv)   I will have to consider whether I have adequate professional indemnity insurance (PII) cover. This is unlikely in view of the size of Phones Anywhere, so there will be an increased cost of obtaining more PII cover. The insurance company may refuse to increase my firm's PII cover, because they perceive this is a high risk audit which is exacerbated by the small size of my firm.

Other matters I will have to consider will include ensuring:

(i)   partners of my audit firm have no family or personal relationships with the directors of Phones Anywhere. These relationships also apply to any staff involved in the audit. Ideally, no member of my firm should have relationships with the directors of Phones Anywhere.

(ii)   no-one in the audit firm should own shares or any investments in Phones Anywhere.

(iii)   no-one in the audit firm should be a beneficiary or trustee of a trust which holds shares in Phones Anywhere. The ACCA's rules of professional conduct do allow employees of the audit firm to be a beneficiary of shares in an audit client, but that employee must not be employed on the audit of that client. For trustees, the trust should hold less than 10% of the shares of the company, and the value of the shares should be less than 10% of the total assets of the trust.

(iv)   employees and partners of the audit firm must not vote on the appointment, removal or remuneration of a firm which is an audit client.

(v)   the audit firm should not make a loan to or accept a loan from an audit client (exceptions to this rule apply where the audit client is a bank or other financial institution which does not appear to apply in this case).

The audit fee has been considered earlier in this section. However, the audit fee should be sufficient for my firm to perform the audit to a satisfactory standard. Thus, it would not be acceptable to offer a very low fee (often called 'lowballing') in order to obtain the audit, as this would impose pressure on the time allowed to carry out the audit. This could lead to inadequate audit work being carried out which would increase the risk that material misstatements in the financial statements may not be detected.

Other matters covered by the ACCA's rules of Professional Conduct include:

(i)   when my audit firm is asked to accept the audit appointment, I must ask the client's permission to communicate with the existing auditor. If this permission is refused, my audit firm should decline to accept appointment as auditor.

(ii)   my audit firm should write to the existing auditor requesting all the information which ought to be made available to decide whether or not to accept the audit appointment.

(iii)   my audit firm should consider the reply from the existing auditor. If adverse comments are made by the existing auditor, I will have to consider whether to accept the audit appointment.

(iv)   if the existing auditor does not reply to my firm's letter, a further letter should be sent giving notice (eg, seven days) that if no reply is received in that time, it is understood that there are no professional or other reasons preventing my firm from accepting the audit appointment.

(v)   before finally accepting the audit, my firm should prepare a letter of engagement and ask the directors of Phones Anywhere to sign it.

Did you answer the question?

Note the large number of points that can be made in part (b). The answer above is much longer than would be expected from a candidate in the exam. However your approach should be to describe briefly a large number of points, at least 8 points given the 8 marks on offer.

(c)   From the discussion above, my firm should not offer itself nor accept the appointment as auditor of Phones Anywhere. The main reasons for this decision are:

(i)   Phones Anywhere appears to be too large a company for my firm to audit, and it is likely to grow faster than my audit firm. The audit fee will probably exceed the ACCA's limit of 15% of the practice income, and if this is not exceeded now, it is likely to be exceeded in the next few years.

(ii)   Phones Anywhere is a specialised company with complex computer systems. It is probable my firm will not have the skills to perform this work.

(iii)   the accounting conventions for Phones Anywhere will probably be unfamiliar to my firm, particularly the treatment of the £200 given to new subscribers to purchase the phones and the lives of the fixed assets. I will probably not have the skills to consider whether these treatments are satisfactory, and this could lead to me not detecting material misstatements in the financial statements.

(iv)   Phones Anywhere appears to be undercapitalised. Currently, gearing is 20% but this will increase substantially with expansion of the network and losses in early years of trading. Thus, there is a serious risk that Phones Anywhere will fail or be taken over, which could result in my firm being sued for negligence.

(v)   the large size of Phones Anywhere and the small size of my audit firm could compromise the independence of my firm. Third parties (including shareholders) will perceive my firm is not independent (on the relative size criteria), and Phones Anywhere could bring severe pressure on my firm which would be hard to resist (ie, they will ask for an unqualified audit report to be given when I should either give a qualified report or an explanatory paragraph which mentions going concern problems)

(vi)   the potential listing of the company on the London Stock Exchange increases the audit risk, as there will be greater scrutiny of the financial statements prior to listing, which could highlight problems in the financial statements.

(vii)   finally, because of the large size of Phones Anywhere and the large audit fee, Phones Anywhere may attempt to 'squeeze' the audit fee. I may have to accept this reduced audit fee (as I would be reluctant to lose such a large audit fee) and this could result in a reduction in the time to perform the audit and thus increase the risk of me not detecting material misstatements in the financial statements.

Note: candidates will be given credit for valid points which are not included in this answer.

DECEMBER 1997 QUESTIONS

Section A – ALL THREE questions are compulsory and MUST be attempted

63   (Question 1 of examination)

Your firm is auditing the financial statements of Newton Manufacturing Limited for the year ended 31 October 1997. You have been asked to consider:

(a)   which overheads may be included in the value of stock, and

(b)   the evidence you would obtain to determine whether the company is operating at a normal level of activity, and the effect on stock value if it is operating at less than a normal level of activity.

The company manufactures a single product, the Beta. The company carries out a stocktake at the end of each month, and records the number of units of Beta transferred to the finished goods store.

The company has the following departments:

–   goods received department and raw materials store
–   production department
–   finished goods store
–   dispatch department
–   accounts department
–   purchasing department
–   sales department
–   administration.

The accounts department's duties comprise:

–   recording and paying for purchases
–   recording and receiving cash from sales
–   paying wages of staff in the departments above
–   maintaining the accounting records and producing monthly and annual accounts.

In relation to part (a) of the question:

(i)   the managing director of Newton Manufacturing wants to include the maximum value of overheads in stock, provided it complies with SSAP 9 (Stocks and Long Term Contracts), and

(ii)   you should consider whether all, none or a fraction of each of the overheads in (a)(i) to (iv) below should be included in stock. If you believe only a fraction should be included, you should suggest a basis which could be used to calculate that fraction.

In relation to part (b) of the question, direct labour costs are the wages of employees in the production department.

You are required to:

(a)   Consider and explain the extent to which each of the following overheads may be included in stock value:
   (i)   selling and dispatch department costs (including staff wages)
   (ii)   rent of the company's premises
   (iii)   wages of the accounts department staff
   (iv)   purchasing department costs (including staff wages).

(10 marks)

(b)   (i)   Describe the evidence you would obtain to determine whether the company is operating at a normal level of activity, and

(5 marks)

   (ii)   Consider how the year end stock value should be adjusted, in relation to direct labour and overheads, if the company is operating at a lower than normal level of activity.   **(5 marks)**

(Total: 20 marks)

Note: **Ignore long term contracts.**

64 (Question 2 of examination)

You are the auditor of Furniture Retailers plc, which buys furniture from manufacturers and sells the furniture to the general public. There is a large computer system, and you have been asked to audit certain aspects of the computerised purchases and purchase ledger system.

The company comprises a central head office and warehouse, and many shops throughout the country which sell the furniture to the general public. Furniture is received from manufacturers either at the individual shops or at the central warehouse. Details of the goods received are entered into the computer either by the shop or the central warehouse. Data entered from terminals at the shops is transmitted to the main computer through the national telephone system.

With the computerised purchases system:

(a) the user department (i.e. shop or central warehouse) issues a purchase requisition and sends it to the buying department at head office

(b) the buying department issues a purchase order which it sends to the supplier, and it records the order on the computer system

(c) when the goods are received by Furniture Retailers, they are checked and a goods received note (GRN) is raised by the goods received department in the shop or central warehouse. Details of the goods received are entered into the computer system and allocated against the purchase order

(d) the accounts department at head office receive the purchase invoice. This is sent to the user department who authorise it and return it to the accounts department. The accounts department input the purchase invoice details into the computer which posts the invoice to the purchase ledger

(e) the computer system only allows payment of the invoice if the computer system has recorded:

    –   the purchase order (in (b) above), and

    –   receipt of the goods (in (c) above)

(f) when the purchase invoice is due for payment, the computer prints the cheques and remittance advices to the suppliers.

As cheques are automatically produced at the due date after the purchase invoice has been posted to the purchase ledger, the partner in charge of the audit has asked you to identify the controls over authorising purchase invoices and changing suppliers' details on the computer's standing data file. He has explained that 'application controls' comprise controls exercised by the company's staff and by the computer.

You are required to:

(a) describe the application controls you would expect to see in operation from raising the purchase requisition to the computer accepting the purchase invoice **(6 marks)**

(b) consider the controls which should be exercised over access to the main computer from terminals in the head office and at the shops **(6 marks)**

(c) describe the application controls which should be exercised over changing supplier details on the standing data file on the computer. You should consider:

    (i) why it is important that there should be strong controls over changing supplier details, and how a fraud could be perpetrated if there are weak controls **(4 marks)**

    (ii) the controls which should be exercised over changing supplier details and ensuring supplier details are correct. Your answer should include consideration of controls over access to the computer to perform these tasks. **(4 marks)**

(Total: 20 marks)

Note: In part (c), changing supplier details comprises:

    (i) adding new suppliers

    (ii) changing the names and addresses of suppliers

    (iii) deleting suppliers.

65   (Question 3 of examination)

Your firm is the auditor of Newpiece Textiles Limited and you are auditing the financial statements for the year ended 31 October 1997. The company has a turnover of £2.5 million and a profit before tax of £150,000.

(a)   The company has supplied you with the following bank reconciliation at the year end. You have entered the 'date cleared' on the bank reconciliation, which is the date the cheques and deposits appeared on November's bank statement.

				£	£
Balance per bank statement at 31 October 1997					(9,865)
Add: deposits not credited					

CB date	type	date cleared	
31 Oct	SL	3 Nov	11,364
24 Oct	CS	3 Nov	653
27 Oct	CS	4 Nov	235
28 Oct	CS	5 Nov	315
29 Oct	CS	6 Nov	426
30 Oct	CS	7 Nov	714
31 Oct	CS	10 Nov	362

14,069

Less: uncleared cheques

CB date	Cheque no.	type	date cleared	
30 Oct	2163	CP	3 Nov	1,216
31 Oct	2164	PL	18 Nov	10,312
31 Oct	2165	PL	19 Nov	11,264
31 Oct	2166	PL	18 Nov	9,732
31 Oct	2167	PL	20 Nov	15,311
31 Oct	2168	PL	21 Nov	8,671
31 Oct	2169	PL	19 Nov	12,869
31 Oct	2170	PL	21 Nov	9,342
31 Oct	2171	CP	3 Nov	964

(79,681)

Balance per cash book at 31 October 1997   (75,477)

Notes:

(i)   'CB date' is the date the transaction was entered in the cash book

(ii) type of transaction

–   SL – sales ledger receipt

–   CS – receipt from cash sales

–   PL – purchase ledger payment

–   CP – cheque payment (for other expenses)

(iii) all cheques for purchase ledger payments are written out at the end of the month.

You are required to describe:

    (i)   the matters which cause you concern from your scrutiny of the bank reconciliation

    (ii)   the investigations you will carry out on the items in the bank reconciliation which cause you concern, and

    (iii)   the adjustments you will probably require to be made to the financial statements if your investigations confirm the problems you have highlighted in (i) above.

(10 marks)

(b)   The manager in charge of the audit has asked you to consider the petty cash system and recommend what audit work may be necessary. You have found that petty cash is recorded in a hand written analysed petty cash book and it is not kept on an imprest system. From the petty cash book you have recorded the petty cash expenditure for each month:

1996	£
November	855
December	6,243
1997	
January	972
February	796
March	893
April	751
May	986
June	695
July	749
August	8,634
September	948
October	849
Total	23,371

You are required to:

(i)   advise the audit manager as to the desirability of performing further substantive procedures on petty cash. You should consider materiality and audit risk in relation to the petty cash system   **(4 marks)**

(ii)   assuming the audit manager decides that further audit work is necessary, describe the detailed substantive tests of transactions and balances you should carry out on the petty cash system.

(6 marks)

(Total: 20 marks)

Section B – TWO questions only to be attempted

66   (Question 4 of examination)

You are responsible for quality control in your firm of Certified Accountants. The firm has three offices and fifteen partners. The partner in charge of your audit firm believes quality control is important, and she has asked you to provide guidance on quality control under the following headings:

(a)   the importance of quality in audit work

(b)   training of staff

(c)   monitoring the performance of staff and providing additional training

(d)   reviews of audit work:

   (i)   by staff and the audit engagement partner before the audit report is signed

   (ii)   a 'cold' review of audit work some time after the audit report is signed.

The partner has explained that a 'cold' review is carried out periodically on a sample of audits after the audit report is signed, to check the quality of the firm's audit work.

You are required to write a memorandum to the senior partner of your audit firm on quality control, which covers the four topics listed in (a) to (d) above.

(20 marks)

---

67   (Question 5 of examination)

SAS 150 *Subsequent events* was issued in March 1995.

You are auditing the financial statements of Newbridge Trading plc, for the year ended 31 October 1997.

The senior partner of your audit firm has asked you to consider the auditor's responsibilities for identifying subsequent events. Also, he has asked you to describe the audit procedures which examine subsequent events. He has suggested that an example of one point in answer to part (b) below would be:

'checking sales ledger cash received after the year end to determine the realisability of debtors at the year end and highlight doubtful debts.'

The detailed audit work was completed on Friday 5 December 1997. It is proposed that:

(a)   the audit report is signed on Friday 19 December

(b)   the financial statements are sent to shareholders on Monday 5 January 1998, and

(c)   the company's annual general meeting will be held on Wednesday 28 January 1998.

You are required to:

(a)   consider the auditor's responsibilities for detecting material subsequent events in the periods:

   (i)   31 October to 5 December 1997

   (ii)   5 December to 19 December 1997

   (iii)   19 December 1997 to 5 January 1998

   (iv)   5 January 1998 to 28 January 1998

   (v)   after 28 January 1998   **(7 marks)**

(b)   list and briefly explain audit procedures which involve examination of subsequent events   **(10 marks)**

(c)   describe the audit work you will carry out in period (a)(ii) above.   **(3 marks)**

(Total: 20 marks)

Note: an alternative term for 'subsequent events' is 'post balance sheet events'.

---

68   (Question 6 of examination)

Mautz and Sharaf (1961) proposed eight Postulates of Auditing.

The following guidance is given in discussing the two postulates in this question.

Postulate (a) states:

   'Financial statements and financial data are verifiable'

   It is explained that financial statements comprise financial data, and you should consider:

   (i)   whether financial data is verifiable, and the consequences for financial statements if financial data is not verifiable

   (ii)   how auditors verify financial data

(iii)   the accuracy to which financial data can be verified

(iv)   the circumstances when financial data cannot be verified

(v)   the effect on the audit report when financial data cannot be verified or when the verification procedure shows errors in the financial statements.

Postulate (b) states:

'The existence of a satisfactory system of internal control eliminates the probability of irregularities'

This is about the effect of internal controls on audit work. The key words in this postulate are 'satisfactory' and 'eliminates the probability of'. The word 'irregularities' includes fraud and error. You should consider:

(i)   what is meant by internal control and its characteristics

(ii)   the extent to which internal controls reduce the risk of irregularities

(iii)   the circumstances when auditors test internal controls, and the procedures used for testing internal controls

(iv)   whether internal controls can be sufficiently strong to avoid carrying out substantive procedures

(v)   whether the postulate is correct, or whether alternative words should be used in place of 'satisfactory' and/or 'eliminates the probability'.

You are required to consider and critically discuss the following Postulates of Auditing:

(a)   Financial statements and financial data are verifiable   **(9 marks)**

(b)   The existence of a satisfactory system of internal control eliminates the probability of irregularities.

(11 marks)

(Total: 20 marks)

ANSWERS TO DECEMBER 1997 EXAMINATION

The model answers to the questions are longer and frequently more detailed than would be expected from a candidate in the examinations. However, the model answer may not include all valid points mentioned by candidates – credit will be given to candidates mentioning these points.

The model answers may be used as a guide to the form and standard of answer candidates should try to achieve. However, the answers may not be as detailed as one would find in text books on the subject.

63   (Answer 1 of examination)

Examiner's comments and marking guide

Question 1 was concerned with determining the extent to which certain overheads should be included in stock value, assessing whether the company was operating at a normal level of activity, and how overheads should be allocated to stock if the company is operating at a lower than normal level of activity.

In part (a), on determining the extent to which overheads should be included in stock, most of the answers were quite poor. Many candidates believed that either all or none of the specified overheads should be included in the value of stock, whereas this only applied to part (a)(i). The requirement of the question did not specify whether overheads should be included when determining cost or net realisable value, so in part (a)(i) candidates were given credit for saying that selling and distribution costs would be deducted from the selling price to determine net realisable value. Many of the answers were either confusing or contradictory (i.e. in one place a candidate would say the overheads should be included whereas in another he/she would say they should not be included). Also, many candidates restricted rental costs to raw materials and finished goods stores, whereas the rent of the production area should also be included. This part of the question was one where many candidates included long introductions about valuing stock at the lower of cost and net realisable value. This wasted valuable time and gained few, if any marks. If candidates feel an introduction is required, they should keep it very brief.

The answers to part (b)(i) on determining whether the level of activity was normal were better. However, many candidates said, for instance, 'I will compare actual production with budget and last year'. This would have been improved significantly if they had added 'and if actual production is similar to budget and last year, then the company is probably operating at a normal level of activity'.

Most of the answers to part (b)(ii) were very weak. Some candidates even suggested adding the inefficiencies to the stock value, rather than ensuring they are eliminated. Very few candidates appreciated the existence of and difference between variable and fixed overheads, and idle time in direct labour cost.

Marks

(a) Overheads included in stock

    (i)   selling and dispatch department costs

    (ii) rent of premises

    (iii) wages of accounts staff

    (iv) purchasing department costs

    Generally <u>1 mark</u> a point up to a <u>maximum</u> of   10

(b) (i) Is the company operating at a normal level of activity

        Generally <u>1 mark</u> a point up to a <u>maximum</u> of   5

    (ii) Effect on stock value of company not operating at a normal

       level of activity in relation to direct labour and overheads

       Generally <u>1 mark</u> a point up to a <u>maximum</u> of   5

                                                        <u>20</u>

Note: In part (a), it is suggested that up to <u>2 marks</u> should be allocated to part (i) and normally a maximum of <u>3 marks</u> allocated to each of the other parts. The total marks allocated to part (a) should not exceed <u>10 marks</u>. In order to gain <u>2 marks</u> for part (i), the candidate must both say the overheads should not be included and explain why they should not be included.

Step by step answer plan

Step 1   Read the question again and make sure that you focus on precisely what is required. The question concerns the valuation of stock in accordance with SSAP9.

Step 2   For each of (a)(i) to (iv), state whether the overhead may be included, and justify your opinion by bringing SSAP9 into your answer.

Step 3   Part (b)(i) offers 5 marks, so make sure that you list at least 5 separate pieces of evidence that you would seek. 6 or 7 pieces of evidence, properly explained, should earn you all the available marks.

Step 4   Part (b)(ii) requires you to consider fixed and variable labour and overheads separately. Some fixed overheads may need to be written off to profit and loss account if the overhead absorption rate was calculated on the basis of the normal level of activity, and in fact the company is operating at lower than the normal level.

Step 5   Only when you are confident that you are about to answer the question that has been set, should you start writing.

The examiner's answer

(a)   Considering each of the items in the question:

   (i)   selling and dispatch department costs are not 'production overheads' so they should not be included in the value of stock (but see below). Technically, these costs are considered to arise when the goods are sold, and not when they are in stock (prior to sale).

   The Appendix of SSAP 9 (para 3) says that where firm sales have been entered into for provision of goods, overheads relating to selling before manufacture may be included in arriving at cost. However, this is an unusual situation and does not appear to apply to Newton Manufacturing.

   (ii)   some of the rent of the company's premises can be included in the value of stock, but only that relating to production. The rent will probably be allocated on a floor area basis. 'Production' could include only the production department, but it could also include:

   –   the goods received department and raw materials store

   –   the finished goods store

   –   the purchasing department.

   Also, it could include a proportion of the accounts department, which provides services to the production department and the departments above.

   It should not include the sales department, and it would not normally include any of the administration department.

   (iii)   a proportion of the wages of the accounts department staff could be included in 'production overheads'. These would relate to the departments in (ii) above, namely servicing the production, goods received, finished goods and purchasing department. This would normally be a percentage of the total accounts department wages cost. For the categories in the question:

   –   recording and paying for purchases for production would be considered as 'production overheads'. However, it would probably not be appropriate to include overheads relating to purchases for non-production departments

   –   recording and receiving cash from sales should not be included in 'production overheads', as this process occurs when the goods are no longer in stock

   –   for paying wages, the cost would be allocated in proportion to the time spent preparing, processing and paying wages of 'production' staff. Production staff could include the 'production' staff mentioned in part (ii) above

- a proportion of the time spent maintaining the accounting records and producing the accounts could be included.

(iv)   normally, most of the purchasing department costs would be included in production overheads. Costs which may be excluded are those relating to purchases for the administration and sales departments. Various bases could be used for determining the proportion of purchasing department overheads which should be included in stock. These could include:

- the proportion of the value of purchases for production to total purchases for the company

- the number of purchase orders raised for production compared with the total number of purchase orders issued

- an allocation based on staff time processing orders for production.

The term 'production overheads' in SSAP 9 (Stocks and Long Term Contracts) is not precise and a range of interpretations can be used. A very prudent basis would be to include only overheads relating to the production department. The suggestions in parts (i) to (iv) above would apply to Newton Manufacturing, where the Managing Director wants to maximise the overheads which are included in stock, but remain within SSAP 9. As auditor, I would consider whether the bases used by the company were reasonable. Also, I would check the same bases were used last year. If there has been a change of basis since last year, I will have to consider whether the effect is material. If it is material, I will probably have to either ask the company to disclose the change or qualify my audit report.

(b)   (i)   The work I will carry out to determine whether the company is operating at a normal level of activity will include:

- I will ask the company's management if the company is operating at a normal level of activity. Indications that the company is operating at a lower than normal level of activity will include idle time, production staff not working the full number of hours or employees being 'laid off' (i.e. not working). As the evidence from the company's management may be unreliable, I may ask other employees, such as the production manager and production workers and the accounting department staff

- I will compare production in October with budget. If it is similar to budget, then the company is probably operating at a normal level of activity

- I will compare October's production with other months. If it is similar to other months, then the level of activity is probably normal

- I will compare October's production with the previous year. If it is similar to the previous year, then production activity is probably normal

- I will compare October's production with the capacity of the company's plant. If it is similar to the plant's capacity, then the level of activity is probably normal

- I will see if any overtime is being worked. If overtime is being worked, then the company is probably operating at above its normal level of activity (unless working overtime is usual). However, it is unlikely that working overtime will increase the cost per unit, as although variable overheads per unit may increase (because of the higher rate of overtime pay), fixed overheads per unit should fall

- I will compare the variable labour cost per unit with previous months. If it is similar to previous months, then the company is probably operating at a normal level of activity.

In the statements above, production activity in October has been considered. If overheads included in stock cover a longer period, or are based on a longer period's costs (i.e. based on annual costs), then the level of activity for the period the costs cover will be considered in determining whether it is normal.

Based on this work, I will decide whether the company is operating at a normal level of activity.

Did you answer the question?
The requirement is to <u>describe</u> the evidence that you would obtain, so a list of short bullet points would not be sufficient. You must say why you would look at each point that you identify.

(ii)   SSAP 9 (Stocks and Long Term Contracts) requires stock to be valued at a normal level of activity basis. If the company is operating at a lower than normal level of activity, if no adjustment is made to stock value, then stock will have a higher value per unit than if the company is operating at a normal level of activity. This is because the fixed overhead cost per unit will increase and any idle time will be included in the value of stock. These additional costs should not be included in the asset of stock, but written off to the profit and loss account (as the company is operating at a lower level of efficiency).

On direct labour cost, provided this cost is entirely variable, all the labour cost can be included in the stock value, even when the company is operating at a lower than normal level of activity. However, there may be a fixed element of direct labour cost or idle time. If these exist, then their effect should not be included in the value of stock. For instance, if the fixed labour cost in producing the stock is £5,000 and the company is operating at 90% of the normal level of activity, then only 90% of the £5,000 labour cost should be included in the value of stock. Also, if 15% of the direct labour cost is idle time, then only 85% of the direct labour cost should be included in the stock value.

Similar considerations apply to production overheads. For variable production overheads, if they are entirely variable, then they can all be included in the value of stock, even if the company is operating at a lower than normal level of activity. However, for fixed overheads, if the company is operating at 90% of the normal level of activity, then only 90% of the fixed overheads should be included in the value of the stock. Other overheads, which are non-production overheads should not be included in the value of stock (irrespective of the level of activity and whether they are fixed or variable overheads). Consideration of overheads which are production overheads and those which are not production overheads is given in part (a) of this answer.

64   (Answer 2 of examination)

Examiner's comments and marking guide

Question 2 was concerned with controls in a purchases system, controls over access to the computer, and controls over changing supplier details. Most of the answers to part (a) on controls from the purchase requisition to the purchase invoice were very good, with candidates making a lot of relevant points and gaining high marks. Some candidates restricted their answer to considering 'application controls' solely in relation to 'input, processing and output' from the computer system and thus gained few marks. The question did explain that 'application controls' comprise controls exercised by the computer and the company's staff.

The answers to part (b) on controls over access to the computer were good. However, such controls as locking the room containing the terminals, and locking the terminals are rather 'old fashioned' as in many companies each employee has a terminal on his/her desk. The major type of control over access to the computer is the use of passwords.

In part (c)(i) most candidates were good at explaining how a fraud could be perpetrated if controls over changing supplier details were correct. The answers to part (c)(ii) on controls over changing supplier details were quite good, with the best candidates considering each of the three operations listed after the end of the questions.

Marks

(a) Controls from purchase requisition to purchase invoice
Generally <u>1 mark</u> a point up to a <u>maximum</u> of   6

(b) Controls over access to the main computer
Generally <u>1 mark</u> a point up to a <u>maximum</u> of   6

(c) Controls over changing supplier details
(i)   why it is important controls should be strong to prevent fraud
Generally <u>1 mark</u> a point up to a <u>maximum</u> of   4

(ii) controls over changing supplier details
Generally <u>1 mark</u> a point up to a <u>maximum</u> of   4
                                                                                                    ___
                                                                                                    20

Step by step answer plan

Step 1 Read the question again and make sure that you focus on precisely what is required.

Step 2 Note the wide meaning of the term 'application controls' which this question has defined. Part (a) requires a description of far more than just the controls in the computer system.

Step 3 Part (b) is standard bookwork. With 6 marks available, you should be prepared to write down at least 10 separate controls to be sure of earning all the marks.

Step 4 Answer part (c) by considering each of the three aspects of 'changing supplier details' in each of (c)(i) and (ii).

Step 5 Only when you are confident that you are about to answer the question that has been set, should you start writing.

The examiner's answer

(a) The controls I would expect to see in operation from raising the purchase requisition to the computer accepting the purchase invoice would include:

(i)   there should be a division of duties between the user department ordering the goods, the goods received department, the buying department and the purchases accounting department

(ii) before issuing a purchase order, the buying department should check that the user department are authorised to purchase the goods they have requested.

(iii) with this system, goods should only be purchased from an authorised supplier (i.e. one which is on the purchases system standing data file). If it is a new supplier, this should be authorised by the appropriate procedure before the purchase order is issued

(iv) there needs to be a periodic independent check of the buying department to ensure they are purchasing furniture from the most appropriate supplier, in terms of quality, price and delivery date. With purchases systems there is the risk that bribes may be given by suppliers to the staff in the purchasing department. This independent check should prevent this happening (i.e. it should deter it from happening and may detect it if it is happening)

(v)   the purchase order should be input into the computer by the buying department (see part (b) below). The purchase order will be sent to the supplier and a copy sent to the user department and one retained in the buying department

(vi) when the goods are received, the goods received department should check they are in accordance with the purchase order, and, after checking they are satisfactory, they should enter the details into the computer (see part (b) below). A copy of the goods received note should be kept in the goods received department and one sent to the user department

(vii) when the accounts department receive the purchase invoice, they should record it in a register and send it to the user department

(viii) the user department should check the goods have been received and that the price agrees with that on the purchase order. They may provide an analysis of the item for posting to the nominal ledger. They should authorise the purchase invoice and return it to the purchases accounting department

(ix) the purchases accounting department should check the purchase invoice has been authorised by the user department, and they have performed the checks described above. The purchases accounting department should check the nominal ledger analysis of the invoice is correct and, from a terminal in their department, input the purchase invoice details into the computer which will post it to the purchase ledger. The computer should not accept purchase invoices where there is no supplier on the standing data file. Also, the computer should display the name of the supplier on the terminal when the employee enters the account number, so that the employee can check the supplier's name is correct

(x)   the computer should check that goods have been received for the invoice and that there is a purchase order. The purchase invoice should be matched to the goods received note and the quantities of goods received should be deducted from the purchase order before the computer allows it to be posted to the purchase ledger. For expenses where there is either no purchase order or no goods received (e.g. electricity invoices), a special code should be entered into the computer before it accepts the invoice and posts it to the purchase ledger. Alternatively, the system may allow certain types of invoice to be posted to the purchase ledger in this way without a goods received note or purchase order. These should be only for certain accounts, and there should be very strict controls over which accounts are allowed this facility (e.g. by requiring a senior person to authorise this function, and periodically checking that only certain authorised accounts are allowed this function)

(xi)   there should be a periodic check of:

-     invoices where no goods have been received

-     goods received where no invoice has been posted to the purchase ledger

-     purchase orders where not all the goods have been received

-     invoices which have been sent to a user department but which have not been returned to the accounting department, and

-     continuity of the numerical sequence of purchase orders and goods received notes.

(b)   The controls which should exist over access to the computer system should include:

(i)   passwords should be used to gain access to the main computer and the purchases accounting system. A number of passwords may be used. The first will allow the employee access to the main computer and the second will allow them access to the particular part of the purchases system. The purchases system should restrict access to particular parts of the system. For instance, only staff in the buying department will be allowed to input purchase orders, only staff responsible for receiving goods will be able to input details of goods received, and only the purchases accounting department staff will be allowed to enter purchase invoices. Passwords should be changed periodically. Staff should not keep a note of their password near their terminal or in another visible or easily accessible place (which could be used by another employee)

(ii)   as a further control, the location of the terminal from which the data is input should be used as a control over access to the computer. For instance, only terminals in the buying department should be able to input purchase orders, and terminals in the goods received departments will only be allowed to input details of goods received, and only the terminals in the purchases accounts department should be able to input purchase invoices

(iii)   all input of data should be restricted to the normal working hours of the company. However, input of data at other times may be allowed with the authorisation of a senior employee (e.g. the chief accountant) using his/her password and a secret code

(iv)   the computer should log off the terminal when it has not been used for a specified time (this period should be no more than 15 minutes). The software of the accounting systems should accept automatic log-off of terminals without corrupting the data (e.g. by not accepting the latest transaction or latest batch of transactions)

(v)   for input of data from the shops, a number of techniques can be used. Probably the most effective is to use a call-back system. With this procedure the terminal contacts the main computer and identifies itself. Then, the telephone line is disconnected. Following this, the main computer looks up the terminal's telephone number and rings it and contact between the terminal and main computer is established. If the terminal is unauthorised, the computer will not ring the terminal's telephone number, so contact with the main computer will not be achieved

(vi)   with some telephone systems, the telephone number of the sender is transmitted at the start of the call. The computer can check this number is authorised, and, if it is, it will connect with the main computer. This avoids the call back system (described above)

(vii)   the telephone number of the main computer should be ex-directory to prevent unauthorised individuals gaining access

(viii)   the computer should keep a log of users of each system. This will include the name of the employee (from the password), the terminal used, the time it was used and the system which was used. This should be reviewed periodically by a responsible official

(ix)   there should be a system for reporting when unauthorised passwords are being used. Ideally, the system should log off the terminal when an incorrect password has been used three times. Where there are repeated attempts at access in this way, the computer should permanently log off the terminal (or telephone line) until it is investigated by a senior employee in the computer department.

Did you answer the question?

The instruction in the question is to 'consider' the controls, which is rather unclear. From the examiner's answer, it appears that the instruction is intended to be the same as to 'describe' the controls.

(c)   (i)   The reasons why it is important there should be strong controls over changing supplier details on the standing data file are that otherwise there is a high risk of error or fraud.

Errors could take place if the supplier details are not kept up to date, or the details are not correct (i.e. the name or address of the supplier is incorrect). This would result in the cheque being sent to the wrong address, or the name of the supplier would be wrong on the cheque, so the supplier could not pay it into the bank.

If controls are weak, fraud could occur in a number of ways. Unauthorised addition of new suppliers (or changes to supplier details) could result in an employee getting the system to pay him/her a cheque. This would be perpetrated by the employee changing the supplier name and address to his/her own name and address. Alternatively, the employee could arrange a bank account in another name and arrange for the cheques to be sent to the name and address of the bank account. By posting credit items to the account (e.g. purchase invoices) the system will automatically pay the fraudster.

Thus, there should be strict controls over changing supplier names and addresses to ensure this is not happening. This will include periodically checking names and addresses of suppliers on the standing data file are correct (see part (ii) below).

It is important that dormant accounts (i.e. those from whom the company will not purchase any more goods) are deleted. Otherwise, this provides temptation to an employee, who could perpetrate a fraud by changing the name and address to his/her own address. Deleting the accounts prevents this happening. The system should not allow an account to be deleted when there is a balance, but in this situation, it should have the facility to prevent any more transactions from being entered on to that account and it should not allow any changes to the name and address of that account. At a reasonable time after the balance has been paid (or cleared), the account should be deleted (e.g. by the computer system asking for the account to be deleted).

(ii)   There should be strong controls to prevent unauthorised amendment of supplier details. This would normally be by means of a password. For instance, if the purchases accounting department change suppliers' details, each employee should have a unique password, and the computer system would only allow amendment of a supplier's details if this data had been input using an authorised password. As a further control, the computer may restrict these changes to a terminal in the purchases accounting department and changes would only be allowed to take place during the normal working hours of the company. As a further control, the staff in the purchases accounting department may input the changes, but the standing data files may not be changed until the chief accountant authorises the change using his/her password and a secret code. As a further control, each batch of changes should be given a sequential number, which is recorded in a book (with the date of the change and the name of the employee making the change). Any break in the sequence should be investigated as it could indicate an unauthorised change in the standing data file. The computer should print out all the changes to supplier details when they take place (i.e. new suppliers, changes to existing supplier details and deletion of suppliers).

It is important that names and addresses of suppliers who are no longer used are deleted from the standing data file. This will reduce the risk of an invoice being posted to the wrong account, and thus payment being made to the wrong supplier. However, it also prevents amendment of the supplier details to the name of a fraudulent supplier (who could be an employee), and it stops this type of fraud from taking place (see part (i) above). The computer should not delete a supplier where there is a balance on the purchase ledger. In this situation, the computer could keep the account open until the invoice is paid, and it could prevent any purchase invoices being entered on that account.

Periodically, a person independent of the purchases accounting department (e.g. the internal auditor) should check the names and addresses of a sample of suppliers to the manual records to ensure they are correct. Also, the computer should print out suppliers where there has been no transaction for a specified period (e.g. six months). Staff should consider whether this supplier will ever be used, and if this is unlikely, the supplier should be deleted from the standing data file.

65   (Answer 3 of examination)

Examiner's comments and marking guide

Question 3 was concerned with a bank reconciliation (part (a)) and audit of petty cash (part (b)). Many of the answers were quite poor, particularly to part (a).

In part (a) some candidates noticed the late banking of cash sales while others noticed the late clearing of cheques paying suppliers, but only a minority recognised both of them. The answers on investigating these two items were weak, with candidates relying too much on asking the company's management and checking controls. Very few candidates explained how they would check for a teeming and lading fraud (does the cash from the unbanked sales exist — if not, there is a fraud) and the late clearing of cheques to suppliers (check suppliers' statements, and the paid cheques, if they are available). Many candidates were concerned with:

(a)   the size of the bank overdraft, and

(b)   the small value of unbanked sales ledger receipts to the large value of purchase ledger payments

However, these matters were of very limited relevance, as the size of the bank overdraft depends on the value of other balance sheet items (which were not given in the question) and outstanding purchase ledger payments were for a month, whereas sales ledger receipts were for only a day.

Very few candidates got close to answering part (iii) of the question on the adjustments required to the financial statements.

The answers to part (b) were slightly better. In part (i), many candidates correctly determined that petty cash payments were material based on profit before tax (which is a better measurement of materiality than turnover). Also they mentioned the inherent riskiness of petty cash and an imprest system not being used. The answers to part (ii) on specifying the substantive tests on the petty cash system were weaker than expected. Some candidates gave answers which demonstrated little understanding of petty cash systems, with incorrect suggestions that petty cash would include receipts from cash sales. Also, a number of candidates incorrectly suggested checking transactions to the sales and purchase ledgers and the petty cash balance to the bank statement. Some of the tests suggested by candidates were checks of controls, whereas the question required substantive tests of transactions and balances.

		Marks
(a)	Checking the bank reconciliation Generally <u>1 mark</u> a point up to a <u>maximum</u> of	10
(b) (i)	Considering audit of petty cash for the year Generally <u>1 mark</u> a point up to a <u>maximum</u> of	4
(ii)	Audit work on petty cash Generally <u>1 mark</u> a point up to a <u>maximum</u> of	<u>6</u> <u>20</u>

Step by step answer plan

Step 1   Read the question again and make sure that you focus on precisely what is required. This looks an attractive question on the audit of the bank reconciliation and petty cash, which will be easier if you are confident on these topics from your accounting studies.

Step 2 In part (a), note the significant period of time between entering receipts in the cash book, and those receipts clearing on the bank statement. This is indicative of teeming and lading. Note also the period of time between entering cheque payments in the cash book, and those payments clearing on the bank statement. This suggests that cheques are written but then not sent out promptly.

Step 3 In part (b), any audit work on petty cash must be carried out with a view to the materiality of the amounts involved. These seem to be large payments in December and August which must be looked at in detail, but for other months the petty cash payments are not very material.

Step 4 Only when you are confident that you are about to answer the question that has been set, should you start writing.

The examiner's answer

(a) (i) The matters which cause me concern in the bank reconciliation are:

- the late banking of cash sales. The delay appears to be about a week. There could be a teeming and lading fraud
- the delay in clearing cheque payments to suppliers. The delay appears to be about two weeks. It seems probable that the cheques were sent out after the year end, rather than before the year end (as recorded in the cash book).

The delay in banking the sales ledger cash seems reasonable, as is the delay in clearing sundry cheque payments.

(ii) I will carry out the following investigations on the delay in paying cash sales into the bank:

- I will check the date stamped by the bank on the paying in slip. If this is the same date as on the bank statement (or the day before) then this is the actual date the cash was paid into the bank
- I will check the amount banked agrees with the cash sales invoices (or the till roll) for the date shown in the cash book (i.e. cash sales for 24 October were £653)
- if these checks show there is a delay in banking cash sales, I will perform similar checks at the date of the audit visit. Namely, I will check whether there is still a delay of a week in banking cash sales. Also, I will check each day's unbanked cash sales from the sales invoices (or till roll) to the cash book
- then, I will ask if there is cash for the sales which are unbanked. If there is no cash, then a fraud is probably taking place (i.e. a teeming and lading fraud). Only if all the cash is present is no fraud taking place. However, even if the cash exists, it should have been banked, so the problem would be included in my management letter
- if there is a fraud, it will be reported to senior management, who should carry out an investigation and take action. As auditor, I will write to the company's management informing them of the fraud.

For the uncleared cheques at the year end, it is probable that they were sent to suppliers after the year end. I will ask the company's staff about procedures for sending these cheques to suppliers. The evidence I receive may be unreliable. If the cashier confirms he/she sent the cheques after the year end, this confirms my suspicions. Also, if the cashier gave the cheques to the financial director, accountant or managing director at the year end, this indicates they were sent to suppliers after the year end. I will ask the person to whom the cashier gave the cheques when they were sent to suppliers. If they say they were sent after the year end, then the payment in the accounts should be after the year end. If they say they were sent before the year end, I would be suspicious of what they said. I would obtain suppliers statements (i.e. copies of outstanding items on the suppliers' sales ledgers) and check the date the cash was recorded on the statement. If this is similar to the date recorded on the bank statement, it provides further evidence that the cheques were sent to suppliers after the year end.

Finally, I would check the sales ledger cash received on 31 October (per the cash book) was actually received on that day. Evidence for the date of receipt could include the date stamped by the company on the remittance from the customer, the pre-list of sales ledger cash received in the day, and any details of post received in the day. However, it seems probable the sales ledger cash of £11,364 was received on 31 October, and it would be very difficult to argue it was received after the year end.

(iii)   It appears that two adjustments are required to the bank balance at the year end as a result of checking the bank reconciliation:

–   if the cash sales receipts from 24 to 31 October are a teeming and lading fraud, then these receipts should be excluded from the cash book (as the asset does not exist). Thus, cash receipts should be reduced by £2,705 at the year end. The value of the fraud at the year end would be charged as an expense in the profit and loss account. In the event of the fraud being repaid to the company by the perpetrator, it would not be charged as an expense in the profit and loss account

–   it appears that the purchase ledger payments recorded on 31 October in the cash book were really payments after the year end, as the date of the payment is the date the cheque was sent to the supplier (and not the date on the cheque). Thus, cheque numbers 2164 to 2170 should not be included in the cash book before the year end, which would result in £77,501 of purchase ledger payments being excluded from the cash book with a consequent effect on the bank balance at the year end. The value of these payments should be added to the purchase ledger balance at the year end (thus increasing creditors due within a year by £77,501)

–   so the cash book balance in the financial statements should be £681 (overdrawn), £77,501 should be added to creditors for the cheques sent after the year end, and £2,705 should be charged to the profit and loss account for the teeming and lading fraud on cash sales

(b)   (i)   By listing the monthly petty cash expenditure, some analytical procedures have been carried out.

The company's profit before tax is about £150,000. Thus, a material error of 5% of profit before tax would be £7,500 and 10% of profit before tax is £15,000. The total petty cash expenditure is £23,371, which is material in terms of profit before tax, so petty cash should be audited. However, August and December's petty cash payments total £14,877, and the remaining 10 months expenditure is only £8,494 (which is hardly material).

In terms of audit risk (and ignoring materiality), petty cash is a high risk area of the audit, as there is a high risk of fraud. However, if petty cash expenditure is small (as in 10 months of the year) it is most unlikely that any fraud or error would be material. Thus, from an auditor's point of view, little or no audit work need be carried out in these months. If petty cash expenditure in the 10 months (excluding August and December) is similar to previous years, this provides further evidence of the reliability of expenditure in the current year.

However, the high petty cash expenditure in August and December should be investigated, as it is unusually large compared with the other months.

As petty cash is not on an imprest system, this increases audit risk, so the auditor should check both a sample of transfers from the cash book to petty cash and the total transfer for the year.

It may be appropriate to test check additions in the petty cash book and posting of transactions from the petty cash book to the nominal ledger.

No mention is made in the question of the petty cash balance. I would have to consider whether the petty cash balance is reasonable. A year end balance of up to about £500 would be reasonable (i.e. about two weeks normal expenditure). However, if the balance is £2,000 or over, I would probably count it. Although a balance of £2,000 is immaterial in terms of profit before tax, I would probably be criticised by the client if the actual petty cash balance was £500 when the petty cash book was showing £2,000.

Did you answer the question?
The question requires you to consider both materiality and audit risk. But even if you decide that petty cash is not material, you must still do some audit work on it. An auditor would find it difficult to justify in court a decision to ignore petty cash completely.

(ii)   Firstly, for August and December I will find the reasons for the unusually large petty cash expenditure. There should be good evidence of the expenditure (e.g. invoices from suppliers). Hand written invoices from the company's staff will be less reliable audit evidence (and may be fraudulent). The petty cash expenditure should have been authorised by an independent member of staff (i.e. not the cashier or the person making the claim). If evidence of the petty cash expenditure is weak, I will report the matter to the company's management and probably include it in my management letter to the company at the end of the audit.

The amount of audit work I will carry out on other petty cash expenditure will depend on the results I have found from my investigations on August and December's payments, and the level of expenditure. Thus, except for August and December, I will carry out only limited audit work on the petty cash system (i.e. I will check only a small sample of items). My audit tests could include:

–   selecting payments from the petty cash book and checking there are supporting documents for the payments. This evidence could include invoices from suppliers (including meals etc.), and authorisation of the payment by a responsible official (e.g. department manager). The employee should have signed a receipt acknowledging receipt of the cash from the cashier

–   test checking additions in the petty cash book and posting to the nominal ledger. Checking additions of the total column is important (as it could be overstated to perpetrate a fraud), and the total of the analysed columns should be checked as being equal to the amount in the total column

–   test checking payments from the cash book to petty cash. As petty cash is not on an imprest system, this increases audit risk. With an imprest system the amount reimbursed equals the value of petty cash payments in the period. Also, each reimbursement is of a different value, so it is easier to check each payment from the cash book to petty cash. With a non imprest system, petty cash is likely to be reimbursed by the same amount each time, and it is difficult to be certain that each payment from the cash book is entered in petty cash. Thus, an additional (fraudulent) payment can be made from the cash book, which never appears in petty cash. The check of transfers should be from the cash book to petty cash, as this will highlight any payments from the cash book which were never recorded in petty cash (and thus constituted a fraud)

–   counting the petty cash at to-day's date. The amount of petty cash should equal the amount in the petty cash book. Allowance will be made for any petty cash payments which have not been recorded in the petty cash book. However, the petty cash book should be kept reasonably up to date (it should have been updated within the past week). If any IOUs are found when the cash is counted, these should be reported to the company's management, as they are a free loan and could become a fraud. Also, if the petty cash counted does not agree with the balance in the petty cash book, and the difference is significant, this should be reported to the company's management. Normally, petty cash should be counted as a surprise (i.e. no warning should be given), but it is difficult to make it a surprise when the auditor is on the premises and the staff are expecting it to be counted!

66   (Answer 4 of examination)

Examiner's comments and marking guide

Question 4 was concerned with quality control in audit work. Most candidates who structured their answers in the manner suggested in the question gained good marks, whereas most of those who did not failed to gain a pass. Some candidates failed to lay out their answer in the form of a memorandum, and thus lost easy marks.

In part (a) more candidates should have said quality work is required to minimise the risk of the auditor being sued for negligence. The answers to parts (b) and (c) were satisfactory. In part (d) some candidates were confused or unclear about the differences between the reviews in (i) and (ii). Most of these candidates incorrectly described review type (i) in their answer to part (ii).

	Marks
Layout of the memorandum – up to	2
For consideration of (a) to (d)	
Generally <u>1 mark</u> a point up to a <u>maximum</u> of	18
	——
	20

Note: you may give up to <u>5 marks</u> for each of the parts (a) to (d). However, the total mark awarded for the question should not exceed 20 marks.

Step 1   Read the question again and make sure that you focus on precisely what is required.

Step 2   Present your answer in the form of a memorandum, as required, using the four headings given in the question.

Step 3   Any knowledge of SAS 240 will help your answer, but even without any reference to this SAS you should be able to answer on the basis of common sense.

Step 4   Only when you are confident that you are about to answer the question that has been set, should you start writing.

The examiner's answer

MEMORANDUM

To: Senior Partner   8 December 1997

From: A Auditor

Re: Quality Control in the Audit Firm

Thank you for asking me to prepare a memorandum on quality control. The Auditing Practices Board have issued SAS 240 on Quality Control for Audit Work. The first statement in this Standard says:

'Quality control policies and procedures should be implemented both at the level of the audit firm and on individual audits.'

This memorandum considers quality control in the audit firm in the following sections:

(a)   the reasons why quality of audit work is important

(b)   training of staff

(c)   monitoring the performance of staff and providing additional training

(d)   reviews of audit work

         (i)   before the audit report is signed

         (ii)   'cold' reviews of audit work some time after the audit report is signed.

Did you answer the question?

Note how the answer is given as a memorandum, with the above introductory paragraph, then the detailed answers to (a) to (d), finished up with a conclusion.

(a)   **The importance of quality control**

Quality control is important in audit work for a number of reasons.

Principally, if high quality audits are carried out, this reduces the risk of audit failure, and the auditor being sued for negligence. Audit failure occurs when an unqualified audit report is given and subsequently material errors or fraud are found in the financial statements, or, less commonly, a qualified audit report is issued, but subsequently no material errors or fraud are found in the financial statements.

Audit failure can result in the audit firm being sued for negligence. Also, it is likely to result in a deterioration in the relationship with the client and possibly the loss of the audit. Adverse publicity from a negligence claim can result in losing other clients and not gaining new clients.

If the procedures over carrying out audits are good, the manager and partner can be more confident that the audit work has been carried out satisfactorily and that the audit staff report significant errors, uncertainties and fraud in the financial statements and records.

A high quality of audit work will minimise the occasions when review of audit work reveals weaknesses in the audit approach (or audit work). These weaknesses will require additional time spent by audit staff (usually of a senior level) which will increase the cost of the audit.

High quality audit work should increase the efficiency of the audit, and thus reduce costs. However, it should be appreciated that to a certain extent, auditing is a balance between audit risk and the cost of carrying out an audit. So there has to be a balance between the time spent on the audit and the risk that material errors and fraud are not detected. Nevertheless, if a 'high quality audit' means spending more time on significant audit areas (particularly those of a high risk) and spending little time on low risk areas, this increased efficiency should reduce overall audit risk (for a fixed time in carrying out an audit).

High quality audit work will ensure there are good records of audit work so that these can be produced in a court of law, if required.

Finally, high quality work will give confidence to the client of the standard of service provided. Client satisfaction is important, as the audit should have provided an accurate assessment of the quality of the company's financial systems, it should ensure the audit is retained, and it could attract new audits (because of recommendations by the audit client).

(b)   **Training of staff**

Training of staff is important, as it will ensure they have the highest level of competence in the work they carry out.

If the staff are unqualified, they should undertake the exams of a professional accounting body. Depending on the qualifications and ability of the staff, this could include a technician qualification or the full ACCA qualification. Staff may be given time off to study and take the professional examinations. Their performance should be monitored. This could be through reports from their tutors, or by the audit firm carrying out tuition sessions and assessed tests. Action should be taken where the employee's performance is unsatisfactory.

In addition, the firm should train staff in the company's auditing procedures. There should be progressive courses for staff studying for the professional accounting exams. This will start by explaining the firm's basic audit procedures, then cover more advanced procedures and finally include managing staff and the audit.

For new employees who are professionally qualified, there should be a more rapid progression of courses.

Also, there should be courses to familiarise staff with new legislation, including Companies Acts, accounting and auditing standards.

Finally, all qualified staff should attend sufficient courses for them to be eligible to obtain, and to maintain their practising certificate.

(c)   **Monitoring the performance of staff and providing additional training**

The performance of each employee should be assessed. This should be carried out more frequently than annually. Ideally, it should be at the end of each audit assignment (provided the assignment is not too short). The senior in charge of the audit should assess each member of his/her audit team and the manager should assess the senior in charge of the audit.

A number of factors should be included in the rating. These could include:

(i)   technical ability

(ii)   organising ability

(iii)   initiative

(iv)   quality of working papers

(v)   relations with the client.

The member of staff should be rated on each factor, using a rating system like 'A' to 'E' with 'A' being excellent, 'C' being satisfactory and 'E' being unsatisfactory.

There should be a 'feedback' procedure whereby an employee getting an 'unsatisfactory' rating should be seen by the manager or partner. The reasons for this low rating should be explained and suggestions made as to how the problems could be overcome. There may be a system for additional training when an employee's performance is unsatisfactory. For instance, if an employee has checked each sales ledger balance to the list of balances, when only a sample is required, it could be explained why only a sample should be checked, and which items would be checked.

In addition, there should be a feedback system which reports problems in audits, which are found during reviews of audit work. These problems may be reported to individual members of staff. Also, the system may report them to all staff when the problem is either frequent, or important (either in a training session or a staff newsletter).

For staff who have problems passing the professional accounting exams, there may be advice on examination technique (e.g. allocating the correct time to answer each question) and the member of staff may be allocated work in the area where his/her exam performance is poor (e.g. audit work if their exam performance in the auditing exams is poor).

(d) **Reviews of audit work**

The review type (i) in the question occurs before the audit report is signed by the audit engagement partner. The second type (ii) review is carried out on a sample of audits by staff not involved in that audit some time after the audit report is signed. These reviews are normally carried out annually (or more frequently if a significant number of problems are highlighted).

With the first type of review, the senior in charge of the audit should review the work of his/her staff. This will be reviewed by the manager of the audit. Finally, it will be reviewed by the audit engagement partner. The amount of review at each stage will depend on the competence of the staff at each stage. It is probable that the manager will check all the detailed audit working papers, and discuss the findings with the senior in charge. Where there are problems, they should be overcome either by discussion or additional audit work. Any outstanding problems should be listed in the audit working papers.

If the audit engagement partner believes the manager is competent, he/she may not check the detailed audit working papers. However, in this situation, the manager and senior in charge should prepare a memorandum which covers each stage of the audit. This memorandum should explain the figures in the financial statements and the audit work which has been carried out (including the conclusions of the audit work). Problems encountered in the audit should be noted. The audit engagement partner can review this memorandum and discuss the audit with the manager and senior in charge. Where problems are highlighted, the partner will probably refer to the detailed audit working papers. Staff should be informed when the review highlights weaknesses in the audit approach or in the audit work.

Based on this work, the audit engagement partner will decide whether an unqualified audit report can be given. When there are problems in the audit which might lead to a qualification, another audit partner should be consulted. Before issuing a qualified audit report, the audit engagement partner should discuss the matter with the client. Then, the client will be given the opportunity to amend the financial statements and avoid an audit qualification.

The second type of review, after the audit report is signed, should be carried out on a random sample of audits. These will include a selection of small, medium-sized and large audits. The reviews should be carried out by staff not involved with the audit. In an audit firm like the one in the question, where there are a number of offices, the review team should be drawn from managers and partners from other offices. The review will involve looking at the audit working papers and interviewing the manager and partner in charge of the audit. A written report should be prepared for each audit studied, which assesses the quality of the audit and reports any significant weaknesses. There should be a final report which notes the quality of the audits of the office and reports common and significant weaknesses. These weaknesses should be reported to staff, so they can be avoided in future audits.

Conclusion

This memorandum covers only the topics you requested in relation to quality control. Quality should permeate the audit firm. Thus, it should cover all aspects of the firm's work, and not just those considered in this memorandum.

I trust that I have provided the information you require. If you would like to discuss any points, please do not hesitate to contact me. I hope that some of the points I have raised will be incorporated into our firm's quality control procedures (where they do not already exist).

---

67   (Answer 5 of examination)

(**Examiner's comments and marking guide**)

Question 5 was concerned with the auditor's responsibilities for detecting post balance sheet events, and audit procedures which involve checking post balance sheet events.

The answers to part (a) on the auditor's responsibilities for detecting post balance sheet events were relatively poor. Some candidates talked about the accounting treatment of post balance sheet events, rather than the auditor's responsibilities, and thus gained very few marks. Up to the time the audit report is signed, most candidates gave the correct answer. However, few candidates correctly described the auditor's responsibilities once the audit report had been signed. Essentially, the auditor's responsibilities only arise if the company informs him/her of a material post balance sheet event. This part of the question was another example of many candidates producing an introduction describing the accounting treatment of adjusting and non-adjusting post balance sheet events, which usually gained no marks (as it is not relevant to what the question requires).

In part (b) on audit procedures involving checking post balance sheet events, most candidates raised very few points, whereas there are many which could be included, as is shown by the model answer. A number of candidates mentioned contingencies and little, if anything else. Most of the answers to part (c), on the audit procedures between completing the detailed audit work and signing the audit report, were very weak.

Marks

(a) Auditor's responsibilities in five periods

Generally <u>1 mark</u> a point up to a <u>maximum</u> of   7

(b) Examples of audit work involving examination of subsequent events

Generally <u>1 mark</u> a point up to a <u>maximum</u> of   10

(c) Audit work to carry out in period (a)(ii)

Generally <u>1 mark</u> a point up to a <u>maximum</u> of   3
                                                                                                                   ———
                                                                                                                    20
                                                                                                                   ———

Step by step answer plan

Step 1   Read the question again and make sure that you focus on precisely what is required. This question deals with the auditor's responsibilities concerning subsequent events ie, events occurring between the balance sheet date and the laying of financial statements before the members. (This is <u>not</u> the same as the SSAP17 definition of post balance sheet events.)

Step 2   SAS 150 splits up the subsequent period into three periods:

Period	Auditor's responsibility
Period end, to date of audit report	Full audit procedures required
Date of audit report, to issue of financial statements	Only necessary if auditors become aware of events; no specific procedures required
After issue of financial statements, but before they are laid before members	No specific procedures required, but may need to withdraw the audit report if become aware of events

Step 3   Part (b) offers 10 marks, so make sure you list and explain at least 10 separate audit procedures.

Step 4   Only when you are confident that you are about to answer the question that has been set, should you start writing.

The examiner's answer

(a)   The auditor's responsibilities in the periods listed in the question are given in SAS 150 (Subsequent Events).

   (i)   In the period 31 October to 5 December 1997, the auditor should carry out sufficient appropriate audit work so that he/she has a reasonable expectation of detecting and quantifying material subsequent events (SAS 150 para 5). Examples of the types of audit procedures carried out are included in part (b) of this answer.

   (ii)   In the period 5 December 1997 to 19 December 1997 the auditor's responsibilities are the same as in period (a)(i) above.

(iii)   The period from 19 December 1997 to 5 January 1998 is covered in paras 10 to 13 of SAS 150. The Standard says that the auditor should reasonably expect the directors to inform him/her of any material subsequent events detected in this period which may affect the financial statements. During this period auditors do not have any obligation to perform procedures or make enquiries regarding the financial statements (SAS 150 para 10).

When the auditor becomes aware of material subsequent events in this period, he/she should carry out appropriate audit procedures to determine whether the subsequent event has a material effect on the financial statements.

If the directors amend the financial statements, the auditor should produce a new report on the amended financial statements.

If the directors do not amend the financial statements, and the subsequent event is material, the auditor should consider how the shareholders can be informed of the subsequent event. This may include the auditors making a statement at the annual general meeting at which the financial statements are approved by the shareholders. SAS 150 para 19 suggests the auditor may consider taking legal advice, and it points out that auditors do not have a statutory right to communicate directly in writing to shareholders.

(iv)   In the period from 5 January to 28 January 1998, the auditors have no duty to seek out whether any material subsequent events have occurred in this period (SAS 150 para 14). However, if the auditor becomes aware of a material subsequent event in this period, he should consider whether he should withdraw his audit report. He will probably have to take legal advice on the matter. Also, he should discuss the problem with the company. It may be necessary for either the directors or the auditors to make a statement at the annual general meeting (AGM).

If the directors revise the financial statements, the auditor will have to audit these revisions and come to a conclusion on whether the revised financial statements show a true and fair view (SAS 150 para 17). The audit report on the revised financial statements should refer to the note in the financial statements which describes the changes, and it should refer to the earlier audit report. The audit report on the revised financial statements should not be dated before the date the directors approve those financial statements (normally, the dates are the same) (SAS 150 para 18).

If the directors do not revise the financial statements, and do not make a statement at the AGM, the auditor should take legal advice on the course of action he should take. Normally, he should make a statement to shareholders at the AGM. In the UK, auditors do not have the right to write to shareholders, but this right does exist if they resign as auditor (SAS 150 para 19).

(v)   SAS 150 does not provide guidance on the auditor's responsibilities after the financial statements have been approved by members at the annual general meeting. However, it does appear that the auditor has no responsibility for detecting subsequent events in this period. If, during this period, the directors find material mis-statements in the audited financial statements, and inform the auditor of the fact, the procedures will be similar to those described in part (a)(iv) above

(b)   The audit techniques which involve checking subsequent events include:

(i)   checking cash received from debtors after the year end to check recoverability of year end sales ledger balances. Any year end balances which are unpaid at the time of the audit will be potential bad debts, and further investigation should be carried out

(ii)   a debtors' circularisation carried out after the year end could be a post balance sheet check of debtors at the year end

(iii)   checking sales after the year end to check recoverability of stock at the year end. If, for stock held at the year end, the selling price after the year end is more than cost, then the stock can be valued at cost. However, if the selling price is less than cost, this stock should be valued at net realisable value

(iv)   checking sales cut-off. Starting from the dispatch note, for sales before the year end, the sales invoice should be posted to the sales ledger before the year end. For sales after the year end, the auditor should check the sales invoice is not posted to the sales ledger before the year end (technically, only this latter check is a check of a subsequent event)

(v)   checking purchases cut-off. Starting from the goods received note, for goods received before the year end, the purchase invoice should either be posted to the purchase ledger before the year end or included in purchase accruals at the year end. For goods received after the year end, the purchase invoice should be neither posted to the purchase ledger before the year end nor included in purchase accruals at the year end

(vi)   checking suppliers' statements to the balances on the purchase ledger. If the balances agree, this is good evidence that the purchase ledger balance is correct. If there is a difference, it should be reconciled and the auditor should consider whether the differences are reasonable. Suppliers' statements are an effective way of checking purchases cut-off, and of detecting late issue of cheques after the year end

(vii)   checking any sales or disposals of fixed assets after the year end. This will check whether these assets have been sold for more or less than their balance sheet value. If they are sold for less than their balance sheet value, normally they should be written down to their realisable value at the year end

(viii) checking returns of goods from customers and other sales credits given after the year end. This helps determine whether the provision for these items in the financial statements is reasonable. Similar checks can be made for purchases items, such as goods returned before the year end when the credit is received after the year end, and other credits received from suppliers after the year end

(ix)   checking about legal claims against the company which exist at the year end. This will involve asking the company secretary and the directors if there are any claims, and (with the client's permission) asking the company's solicitor. Inspecting board minutes (see item (x) below) could highlight any claims against the company. The bank letter may include details of a claim against the company or Companies House may have some information (but this is uncommon).

(x)   checking board minutes and management reports after the year end which relate to events at or before the year end

(xi)   checking management accounts after the year end for any items which should have been included at the year end (e.g. bad debts, stock write-downs etc.)

(xii)   checking cash book and petty cash transactions after the year end to see if there are any unrecorded accruals and prepayments at the year end, and to confirm those items in the financial statements. For instance, receipts after the year end may indicate sundry debtors at the year end and payments after the year end may highlight sundry creditors and accruals which existed at the year end (e.g. the payment of tax and national insurance in November would be good evidence of the liability at the year end)

(xiii) checking purchase invoices received after the year end. Some of these may relate to pre-year end transactions (i.e. those which are dated before the year end). Purchase invoices for gas and electricity received after the year end are an effective way of determining the accrual at the year end

(xiv)   checking the bank reconciliation to check if payments were actually before the year end and there is no teeming and lading fraud (see answer to question 3(a)). If there is a long delay in clearing a significant value of cheques issued before the year end, this indicates the actual payment (i.e. when the cheques were sent to the creditors) was made after the year end. A delay in lodging cash received into the bank indicates a teeming and lading fraud. The fact that the cash book balance can be reconciled to the balance on the bank statement is good evidence that the cash book balance in the financial statements is correct

---

Did you answer the question?

Although the examiner's answer to part (b) is perhaps longer than you would have time for in the exam, it illustrates the depth of answer that you must provide to earn a high mark.

(c)   As no detailed audit work would have been carried out during this period, there is a risk that material subsequent events may have occurred in this period. Thus, the auditor will have to ask the directors and senior management if any material subsequent events have occurred in this period, or whether further evidence is available for uncertainties existing at 5 December 1997. Also, the auditor should examine such documents as Board and Management minutes, management accounts and seek out further evidence relating to uncertainties at 5 December 1997 (e.g. whether a doubtful debt at 5 December has been settled).

68   (Answer 6 of examination)

Examiner's comments and marking guide

Question 6 was concerned with discussing two Postulates of Auditing by Mautz and Sharaf. Part (a) was concerned with determining whether financial statements are verifiable. Most candidates came to an appropriate final conclusion. However, candidates were weaker at describing how financial data is verified, tending to concentrate on internal controls rather than substantive procedures. Also, they were relatively poor at describing when financial data may not be verifiable to within the auditor's materiality limits. They mentioned loss of records because of fire or other catastrophe, rather than the more common situations of uncertainties about doubtful debts, stock valuation, depreciation rates and legal claims against the client company.

Part (b) was concerned with discussing whether a satisfactory system of internal control can eliminate the probability of irregularities. Many of the answers were quite good, with both an appropriate discussion and producing a good conclusion.

		Marks
(a)	Financial statements and data are verifiable	
	Generally <u>1 mark</u> a point up to a <u>maximum</u> of	9
(b)	Satisfactory system of internal control eliminates the	
	probability of irregularities	
	Generally <u>1 mark</u> a point up to a <u>maximum</u> of	11
		20

Step by step answer plan

Step 1   Read the question again and make sure that you focus on precisely what is required. This question concerns 2 of the possible postulates of auditing.

Step 2   Follow the answer plan suggested in the question. For postulate (a) there are 5 points to be addressed, and 5 further points for postulate (b).

Step 3   Only when you are confident that you are about to answer the question that has been set, should you start writing.

The examiner's answer

Considering each of these statements:

(a)   **Financial statements and financial data are verifiable.**

At first glance, this statement seems obvious. If financial statements and financial data are not verifiable, then we cannot say whether they are correct. Thus, they could have any value (i.e. we would not be able to say whether another value is correct or incorrect). A material change in the value of an item will change our view on the financial statements. Thus, if we say we cannot verify the value of an item in the financial statements, the financial statements in this respect become meaningless.

Auditors are concerned with verifying the value of items in the financial statements. They do this in a number of ways, including:

(i)   verifying the accuracy of the underlying accounting records (mainly by carrying out tests of controls)

(ii)   checking the item against the accounting records and supporting documents (e.g. checking purchase invoices for the cost per unit of stock)

(iii)   asking the company's staff and management

(iv)   asking third parties, including experts

(v)   physically examining the item.

A few items in the financial statements can be said to be 'exactly correct', and these can include cash in hand and cash at the bank (or bank overdraft). Other items in the financial statements are probably not 'exactly correct', but the potential error in their value is small and so is not significant (i.e. material). For instance, there are likely to be small errors in the value of debtors because the bad debt provision is an estimate and is most unlikely to be 'exactly correct'. Similar considerations apply to other assets and liabilities in the balance sheet. Thus, by the term 'verifiable' in the postulate, we really mean 'verifiable to within the materiality limits'.

There can be situations when financial data may not be verifiable to within the materiality limits, and it depends on an outcome of an event after the financial statements are authorised by the directors and approved by the shareholders. These items are uncertainties which exist at the date of the audit report. These include:

(i)   unsettled legal claims against the company

(ii)   amounts owing by debtors which are not settled at the time of the audit

(iii)   year end stock which is unsold at the end of the audit

(iv)   whether any fixed assets at the year end are worth less than their balance sheet value. Their value may not become known for many years, until they are sold

(v)   uncertainty about the company being a going concern.

Normally, items (ii), (iii) and (iv) should be verifiable within the materiality limits, but there could be situations when the potential error is material. The items in the list may be partly verifiable (e.g. there may be legal precedent and legal advice on a claim against the company), but there may not be sufficient evidence to conclude the item is stated to within the auditor's materiality limit for that company. If the amount of the uncertainty is material, the auditor should qualify his report.

There can be situations when financial data is verifiable, but it would result in a qualified audit report. This is where the auditor's verification procedures have confirmed the value of an item (or items) which is materially different from that shown in the financial statements. In this situation, if the directors refuse to amend the financial statements, the auditor should qualify his audit report.

In conclusion, by slightly amending the postulate, in most situations we can say that:

'Financial statements and financial data are verifiable to within the auditor's materiality limits'

Where the financial data is not verifiable to within the auditor's materiality limits, he should give a qualified audit report (or, in certain situations when there is a fundamental uncertainty, an unqualified report with an explanatory paragraph).

Where the auditor's verification procedures show a material difference between their estimate of the value of the item and that shown in the financial statements, he should qualify his audit report (if the directors refuse to amend the financial statements).

(b)   **The existence of a satisfactory system of internal control eliminates the probability of irregularities**

Essentially, this statement is concerned with internal control. Internal control can be divided into division of duties and internal check.

Division of duties is concerned with ensuring that no person is responsible for more than one of the following:

(i)   authorising or initiating a transaction

(ii)   recording the transaction

(iii)   custody of the asset.

If there is an inadequate division of duties, then there is a weakness in the system of internal control, which will allow fraud or error to occur. Weaknesses in the division of duties are quite common, as, for example, the till operator in a shop who receives cash from a sale also records the transaction. Because of the weakness in the division of duties, the till operator can commit a fraud by not recording the transaction (or under-recording it) and misappropriate the unrecorded takings at the end of the day.

However, a weakness in the division of duties can be overcome by a system of internal check. With this procedure, an independent person checks the employee's work. Frequently, this is on a test basis. For the till operator, a video camera could be used to observe the till operator. If a bar code system of recording stock is used, then shortages in stock could indicate unrecorded sales. The problems with a system of internal check include:

(i)   the person performing the checks may not perform the check properly or at all, and

(ii)   the checks may be on valid items, but not on those which are fraudulent. Checking totals of transactions tends to be more effective at detecting fraud and error than test checking individual items.

Auditors test internal controls when they believe they will be effective in reducing the risk of fraud and error. Auditors will not check internal controls where they are very weak or do not exist.

The procedures auditors use for checking internal controls comprise:

(i)   recording the accounting system (probably using a flowchart)

(ii)   evaluating the controls (probably using an internal control evaluation questionnaire)

(iii)   if the evaluation of controls show they are at least moderately strong, then the auditor will test the internal controls, usually by testing a sample of transactions.

Returning to the statement on internal control, the important words appear to be:

(i)   satisfactory

(ii)   eliminates, and

(iii)   probability.

As stated in the question, the word 'irregularities' is assumed to include both fraud and error.

It would probably be correct to say that 'with an unsatisfactory system of internal control, irregularities probably exist'.

The statement by Mautz and Sharaf appears to go too far in saying 'a satisfactory system of internal control eliminates the probability of irregularities'. Either the word 'satisfactory' is not strong enough, or 'probability' is too strong. Also, the word 'eliminates' is very strong.

Most auditors would agree with the statement 'a satisfactory system of internal control reduces the risk of irregularities'. Even this statement is not quite correct, as even with internal controls, errors take place. However, internal controls should detect these errors and correct them before they appear in the financial statements. Also, internal controls should deter fraud (as they increase the risk of the fraudster being detected). As a further point, the auditor (and the company) are probably not concerned when irregularities are immaterial, as the cost of eliminating all irregularities would be greater than the loss from those irregularities. So, the word 'material' should be included in the postulate. Thus, the postulate would be better if it said 'a satisfactory system of internal control reduces the risk of material irregularities appearing in the financial statements'.

If the words 'eliminates the probability' are retained in the statement, it appears that the word 'satisfactory' is too weak. If the probability of irregularities is to be eliminated the internal control system must be much better than 'satisfactory'. It should be either 'good', 'very good' or 'effective'. Nevertheless, re-phrasing the statement to 'an effective system of internal control eliminates the probability of irregularities' still seems to be too 'strong' - it is questionable whether an effective system of internal control would eliminate all irregularities. In fact, SAS 300 (Accounting and Internal Control Systems) says in statement 8 that 'regardless of the assessed levels of inherent and control risks, auditors should perform some substantive procedures for financial statement assertions of material account balances and transaction classes.' Thus, the Auditing Standard is saying that irrespective of the effectiveness of the internal control systems, the auditor should not rely entirely on internal controls and perform no substantive procedures. Also, SAS 300 para 25 lists six inherent limitations of internal control. These limitations include the cost of the internal control should not exceed the potential loss, internal controls tend to be directed to routine transactions rather than non-routine ones, and the problem of collusion. It concludes by saying 'these factors indicate why auditors cannot obtain all their evidence from tests of the system of internal control'.

Another statement which is unclear is 'eliminates the probability'. It seems the word 'probable' means 'occurs on over 50% of occasions'. However, what does 'eliminates the probability' mean. It does not mean that irregularities never occur. It seems to mean that 'irregularities are possible', when 'possible' means less than 50% of the time.

It is not clear whether this statement is concerned with individual transactions or the whole population which is used to prepare the financial statements. It does not appear to be concerned with individual transactions, as it is most unlikely that over 50% of transactions would have errors. Thus, it appears the statement is concerned with the financial statements as a whole. So, it seems to be saying that if there is a satisfactory system of internal control there is a less than 50% chance of material irregularities in the financial statements.

It is difficult to decide whether this statement is true. If internal controls are 'satisfactory', is it probable there are no material irregularities in the financial statements? In view of the number of accounting systems (e.g. sales, purchases, cash, fixed assets, stock) it seems that with a 'satisfactory system of internal control' there could be a more than 50% chance of material errors in the draft financial statements. The justification for making this statement is that if materiality is likened to taking balls out of a bucket, and there are five buckets for the five accounting systems. Then, if the probability of a material error in each system is about 13%, the probability of a material error in the financial statements is just over 50%. Achieving a confidence level of 13% in each system, entirely by testing internal controls is probably unrealistic. Thus, the statement by Mautz and Sharaf that 'a satisfactory system of internal control eliminates the probability of irregularities' is probably not correct. However, internal controls will reduce the possibility of irregularities.

It would probably never be possible to agree with the Mautz and Sharaf statement. However, it should be possible to say:

'The existence of a satisfactory system of internal control reduces the probability of irregularities'

or

'The existence of an effective system of internal control significantly reduces the probability of irregularities'.

Did you answer the question?
Do not be put off by the length of the examiner's answer; it is significantly longer than could be expected under the exam's time constraints. Concentrate on giving at least 2 points in response to each of the five areas required for each postulate.

JUNE 1998 QUESTIONS

Section A – ALL THREE questions are compulsory and MUST be attempted

69 (Question 1 of examination)

Your firm is auditing the financial statements of Hawkhead Textiles Ltd for the year ended 28 February 1998. The company purchases textile products from manufacturers and sells them to retailers.

You have been assigned to the audit of stock and you have been asked to identify and check the valuation of stock which may be worth less than cost. A full stocktake was carried out at the year end, and you have verified that stock quantities are accurate and there are no sales or purchases cut-off errors.

The computerised stock system:

(i)   records the quantity of goods received and the purchase price

(ii)   deducts the quantity of goods sold from the stock quantities

(iii) calculates the quantity of goods in stock

Control risk over the accuracy and reliability of information held on the computerised stock system has been assessed as low. Sales invoices are available, which include the quantity and the selling price of the goods sold.

In relation to part (a) of the question, the senior in charge of the audit has asked you to determine the value of the stock of Sweatshirts X at the year end. You have obtained the following sales and purchases information from the company's records:

Sweatshirt X

Date	Quantity purchased	Purchase price per unit (£)	Quantity sold	Selling price per unit (£)
31 Jan	80	10.30	90	13.50
14 Feb	70	10.40	80	13.00
28 Feb	65	10.50	70	12.00
14 Mar	60	10.50	60	10.80
28 Mar	40	10.30	50	10.40
11 Apr	30	10.10	35	10.00
25 Apr	20	10.10	10	8.00

Stock at 28 February 1998 = 150 units

The dates above are the sales and purchases in the two weeks ending on that date. All purchases and sales in the two weeks have been made at the same price.

You have ascertained the following costs as a percentage of sales revenue:

(a)   selling and marketing costs – 2% of sales

(b)   distribution costs – 3% of sales

(c)   administrative overheads – 10% of sales

Stock is valued in accordance with SSAP 9 (Stocks and Long Term Contracts) on a first in first out basis.

The company has two types of product, standard lines and fashion lines. The standard lines are competitively priced and it is the company's policy to keep the full range in stock so that it can claim to provide any standard product within 24 hours. As they are not fashion goods, the accountant claims that some items may remain in stock for more than a year, but they are eventually sold at the full price. Occasionally, these items may deteriorate due to damp and other environmental factors, when they will either be sold at a substantial discount or scrapped.

The fashion lines are sold at higher prices and profit margins. Fashion goods are purchased at the beginning of a season and they become obsolete if not sold within four months. Stock unsold at the end of four months is disposed of either to customers or to other wholesalers at substantial discounts, often at less than cost.

You are required, for stock held at 28 February 1998, to:

(a)   Calculate the value of the stock of 150 Sweatshirts X:

   (i)   at cost

   (ii)   at net realisable value

   (iii)   at the balance sheet value in accordance with SSAP 9 (Stocks and Long Term Contracts)

   (6 marks)

(b)   (i)   Describe the audit procedures you will carry out:

   – at the stocktake, and

   – at the final audit in June 1998

   to identify stock which may be worth less than cost

   (7 marks)

   (ii)   for the stock you have identified in part (b)(i) above, describe the audit work you will carry out to check the company's valuation of the stock:

   – at cost

   – at net realisable value

   and to ensure the stock has been correctly valued in accordance with SSAP 9 (Stocks and Long Term Contracts)

   (7 marks)

   (Total: 20 marks)

Note: Ignore long-term contract stock

70   (Question 2 of examination)

Your firm is the external auditor of Westwood Trading plc. The company has a turnover of £98 million. It sells all its products on credit, and the sales records and sales ledger are maintained on the company's computer. Year end debtors are £21 million and there are about 5,000 accounts with outstanding balances on the sales ledger.

You have been assigned to the audit of the company's sales and sales ledger system, and the engagement partner has suggested it may be appropriate to use the computer assisted audit techniques of 'test data' and 'computer audit programs'.

In the computerised sales and sales ledger system, there are the following procedures over dispatching goods to customers, producing sales invoices and posting them to the sales ledger:

(i)   the sales department input the customer's account number, the part numbers and quantities of goods to be dispatched and the dispatch date. Normally, the dispatch date is the date the details are entered into the computer, or the following day

(ii)   provided the goods are in stock and the customer's credit limit is not exceeded, the computer prints the dispatch note in the dispatch department, who dispatch the goods to the customer. The quantity of goods dispatched is deducted from the stock quantities on the computer

(iii)   the computer calculates and prints the sales invoice and posts it to the sales ledger. The accounts department send the sales invoice to the customer.

The sales ledger files and the print-outs from the computer comprise:

(i)   outstanding transactions for each account (sales invoices, credit notes, adjustments, unallocated cash and discounts). These can be printed for individual accounts or all accounts

(ii)   listing of sales invoices, credit notes, cash received, discounts and adjustments, which can be printed out for any specified month

(iii)   the total balance on each account and the debt aged into current month, 1 month, 2 months and 3 months old or over, which can be printed for all accounts or a range of accounts

(iv)   the total balance on the sales ledger

You are required to:

(a) (i) Briefly explain what you understand by the term 'Test Data', and

(ii) Describe the procedures you would carry out using Test Data to check the operation of the company's computerised sales and sales ledger system. Your answer should give examples of the valid and invalid Test Data you would use **(6 marks)**

(b) Explain how Computer Audit Programs may be used in performing substantive procedures on recorded debtors on the sales ledger at the year end, including selecting debtors for circularisation

(7 marks)

(c) Describe the circumstances when the use of Computer Assisted Audit Techniques in performing audit procedures would be:

(i) unnecessary or inappropriate

(ii) necessary or desirable **(7 marks)**

(Total: 20 marks)

Note: (a) an alternative term for 'test data' is 'test packs'

(b) an alternative term for 'computer audit programs' is 'audit software'

---

71 (Question 3 of examination)

Your firm is the external auditor of Eastwood Engineering plc which has a turnover of £100 million. The head office site includes the manufacturing unit, the accounting functions and main administration. There are a number of sales offices in different parts of the country. Eastwood Engineering does not have an internal audit department.

At the interim audit you have been assigned to the audit of the wages system. This will involve obtaining an understanding of the wages system, testing the controls and performing substantive procedures in order to verify wages transactions.

The wages records are maintained on a computer and all the wages information is processed at the head office. Some of the employees in the manufacturing unit are paid in cash and all other employees have their wages paid directly into their bank account.

Manufacturing employees are paid their wages a week in arrears. All other employees are paid at the end of each week or month.

There is a personnel department which is independent of the wages department. The personnel department maintain records of the employees, including their starting date, grade, current wage rate and leaving date (if appropriate).

Previous years' audits have revealed frauds by wages department staff which have been facilitated by weaknesses in controls in the wages system. These frauds have included:

(i) paying employees after appointment but before they commenced work

(ii) paying employees after they have left, and

(iii) paying fictitious employees

A check of current controls in the wages system has revealed that the company has failed to instigate controls to prevent these types of fraud recurring. So, the audit programme requires extensive substantive procedures to be carried out to ensure that recorded wages transactions have not been mis-stated by similar frauds taking place in the current year.

The existence of employees at the head office site can be verified by physical inspection. From a cost effectiveness point of view, only a small sample of sales offices will be visited. The audit manager has asked you to consider the audit procedures you would carry out to obtain sufficient appropriate evidence of the existence of employees at sales offices not visited by the audit staff.

The audit manager has explained that 'unclaimed wages' (in part (c) below) arise when manufacturing employees are not present to collect their wages (when they are paid out in part (b)). The unclaimed wage packets are given to the cashier who records their details in the unclaimed wages book and is responsible for their custody. Any employee who has not received his/her wage packet at the pay-out can obtain it from the cashier. You have ascertained that there is no system of checking the operation of the unclaimed wages system by a person independent of the cashier and the wages department.

You are required to describe:

(a) how you would verify that employees are not paid before they commenced employment or after they have left (a 'starters and leavers' test)   **(5 marks)**

(b) the audit procedures you would carry out in connection with attending a pay-out of wages in cash to manufacturing employees

(5 marks)

(c) the substantive checks of transactions you would carry out on the unclaimed wages system

(5 marks)

(d) the evidence you would obtain to verify the existence of employees whose wages are paid directly into their bank account, including those at sales offices   **(5 marks)**

(Total: 20 marks)

Section B – TWO questions only to be attempted

72   (Question 4 of examination)

SAS 500 has been issued on 'Considering the work of Internal Audit'.

Your firm is the external auditor of Sighthill Supermarkets plc. The company has a head office, central warehouse and a large number of supermarkets which sell food to the general public. The company's Financial Director has suggested the audit fee could be reduced if your firm was prepared to place greater reliance on the work of the internal audit department.

The Financial Director has explained that the duties of the internal audit department include:

(i) testing and reporting on the effectiveness of internal controls by maintaining up to date descriptions of the company's accounting systems and evaluating the effectiveness of controls in those systems. Recommendations are made of improvements in controls, and proposed changes in controls are assessed

(ii) checking the operation and reliability of the computer systems. The department uses the computer assisted audit techniques of test data and computer audit programs (audit software). Particular attention is paid to controls over access to the computer and checking payment of suppliers and wages, and receipt of cash at supermarkets

(iii) visiting the central warehouse to check operation of the systems and the effectiveness of controls. Stocktaking procedures are checked at the periodic stocktakes

(iv) visits to supermarkets. All supermarkets are visited at least once a year with more frequent visits to larger supermarkets and those where serious weaknesses have been detected. At the supermarkets, the internal auditors check the effectiveness of controls and carry out cash counts and test counts of the stock. Visits are made to supermarkets to attend the periodic stocktakes and check procedures

The Financial Director says the internal audit department would be willing to amend the timing of its work, so as to fit in with the external auditor's work. The results of the internal auditor's work can be reported directly to the external auditor.

In part (a) of the question, in considering the effectiveness of the internal audit department, you should consider factors which indicate the independence and competence of the internal audit staff, reporting arrangements and the extent to which their recommendations are implemented.

In part (b) of the question, you should consider the extent to which you can rely on the internal auditors' work and either reduce or eliminate certain aspects of the audit work carried out by your firm. The reduction in audit work will result in a reduction in the cost of carrying out the audit and thus allow a reduction in the audit fee.

You are required to:

(a) Describe the matters you should consider at the planning stage to assess the effectiveness of the internal audit department

(6 marks)

(b) Consider the Financial Director's proposals, namely the extent to which you can rely on the work of the internal auditors and thus reduce your audit work in:

(i) recording accounting systems and evaluating the effectiveness of the recorded controls

(ii) performing tests of controls

(iii) carrying out substantive procedures to verify assets and liabilities in the balance sheet

(iv) auditing the computer systems, including using computer assisted audit techniques

(v) visiting supermarkets

(14 marks)

(Total: 20 marks)

73   (Question 5 of examination)

The Senior Partner has asked you to explain the contents and importance of audit working papers to unqualified audit staff who have recently joined your audit firm.

It has been explained that audit working papers are divided into:

(a)   the permanent audit file, and

(b)   the current audit file

Your audit firm has a standardised method of organising and referencing working papers within each audit file.

You are required to:

(a) (i) List and briefly describe the contents of the Permanent Audit File and the Current Audit File

(ii) Suggest a system for referencing the different sections of the audit working papers and explain why it is important the audit firm should use a standardised referencing system.

(iii) Describe three types of checklist (excluding audit programmes) and three types of specimen letter which are commonly included in audit working papers **(10 marks)**

(b) Describe the reasons why auditors use working papers to record their work and consider whether it is necessary for auditors to record all their audit work **(4 marks)**

(c) Your firm is the auditor of Bestwood Trading Limited. The audited financial statements for the year ended 31 October 1997 show the company's turnover was £2.5 million and the profit before tax was £160,000. The part of the working papers which record audit work on the bank reconciliation at 31 October 1997 noted cash receipts of £7,000 recorded in the cash book before the year end which were not credited to the bank statement until a week or more after the year end. No further work was carried out as the amount was not considered material, and this conclusion was noted in the audit working papers. In May 1998 the company investigated delays in banking cash receipts and discovered a teeming and lading fraud of £18,000. The fraud was carried out by the cashier who was responsible for banking all receipts and preparing the bank reconciliation.

You are required to consider whether the auditor is negligent in each of the following situations:

(i) the auditor reported the late banking of cash receipts in the management letter and explained the risk of a teeming and lading fraud

(ii) the auditor did not mention the late banking of cash receipts in the management letter

(6 marks)

(Total: 20 marks)

74   (Question 6 of examination)

Your firm was appointed external auditor of Newton Electronics Limited in June 1997, and you are carrying out the audit of the financial statements for the year ended 30 April 1998. Newton Electronics is a small company with a turnover of about £1 million, which sells televisions, video recorders, audio equipment, video and audio tapes and accessories to the general public.

From recording and evaluating controls in the company's accounting systems, your investigations have shown that there are too few staff to provide a proper division of duties in the accounting systems, and checks to overcome the weaknesses in the division of duties are inadequate. So, you have concluded that control risk is moderate to high for most accounting systems. Thus, you have decided to adopt a predominantly substantive approach to the audit.

Your audit work on balance sheet items has shown there are no material errors. However, you are concerned that sales may be understated, and audit work has failed to obtain reliable evidence of some expenditure, the vouchers for which have been generated by the company's staff and provide very limited information on the expense incurred. Sales are made to the general public, who pay in cash, or by cheque or credit card (charge card).

There is no stock control system, and sales receipts are recorded using a till. The sales assistant records the value of each item sold, but no description. However, for high value items (e.g. televisions and video recorders) a hand-written invoice is made out which describes the product. A copy of this sales invoice is retained by the company. The sales invoice can be used by the customer when asking for a refund or repair of the product.

You have been asked to describe the substantive audit procedures which can be used to determine whether all sales income has been included in the financial statements. The audit manager has suggested your work on verifying completeness of sales income should include:

(i)   consideration of the relative risks of misappropriation by staff of sales income received in cash, cheques and by credit card

(ii)   observation of sales procedures

(iii)   checking the analysis of sales

(iv)   checking the gross profit margin on sales

A Management Representation Letter has been prepared in which the directors have been asked to confirm that all sales income has been included in the financial statements and that when there is weak evidence of expenditure, the expenditure has been for the benefit of the company and not for the personal benefit of any employee or director (i.e. completeness of sales income and validity of expenditure).

You are required to:

(a)   Describe the substantive audit procedures you would perform to obtain sufficient appropriate evidence that all sales income due to the company has been included in the financial statements. Your answer should include both tests of details and analytical procedures   **(10 marks)**

(b)   Consider the reliability of audit evidence provided by directors in the Management Representation Letter. You should consider whether you should rely wholly on the representations of the directors or whether you should obtain other evidence   **(5 marks)**

(c)   Describe the action you would take and the conclusions you would reach if the directors refused to sign the Management Representation Letter.

Your answer should specifically consider the statements in the letter concerning completeness of sales income and validity of expenditure.   **(5 marks)**

(Total: 20 marks)

ANSWERS TO JUNE 1998 EXAMINATION

The model answers to the questions are longer and frequently more detailed than would be expected from a candidate in the examinations. However, the model answer may not include all valid points mentioned by candidates – credit will be given to candidates mentioning these points.

The model answers may be used as a guide to the form and standard of answer candidates should try to achieve. However, the answers may not be as detailed as one would find in text books on the subject.

69 (Answer 1 of examination)

Examiner's comments and marking guide

Question 1: This question was concerned with calculating the cost and net realisable value of 150 sweatshirts (part (a)), with identifying stock which may be worth less than cost (part (b)(i)) and checking the valuation of such stock (part (b)(ii)). Generally, candidates who produced a correct answer to part (a) performed much better in part (b) of the question.

In part (a) a majority of candidates calculated the cost of the stock correctly. However, only a minority calculated net realisable value correctly. Net realisable value is determined from the selling price after the year end, from which selling, distribution and marketing costs must be deducted. Some candidates also deducted administration overheads, while others calculated net realisable value as the selling price after the year end and did not deduct the costs of sale. Almost all candidates stated the balance sheet value correctly as the lower of cost and net realisable value.

Part (b)(i) was concerned with identifying stock which may be worth less than cost at the stocktake and at the final audit. Some of the answers were quite good. However, many candidates listed the procedures the auditor should carry out when attending the stocktake, rather than answering the specific point about identifying stock which may be worth less than cost. Making points which are not answering the question gain no marks. More of the answers should have considered the special problems of fashion goods.

Most of the answers to part (b)(ii) were less good than part (b)(i). A number of answers considered labour costs and production overheads, which are irrelevant in this question when the company is a wholesaler. Many candidates were quite weak at checking net realisable value of the stock.

		Marks
(a)	Valuation of Sweatshirts X	
	(i) at cost (£1,565)	2
	(ii) at net realisable value (£1,480·10)	3
	(iii) at lower of cost and net realisable value (£1,480·10)	1
	Total marks for part (a)	6
(b)	(i) Identifying stock which may be worth less than cost	
	Generally <u>1 mark</u> a point up to a <u>maximum</u> of:	7
	(ii) Checking stock in (b)(i) is valued correctly	
	Generally <u>1 mark</u> a point up to a <u>maximum</u> of:	7
		20

Note: In part (a)(iii) the 1 mark should be awarded if the candidate makes the correct decision over determining the value of stock, even when his/her calculated figures are incorrect

Step by step answer plan

Step 1 Read the question again and make sure that you focus on precisely what is required. This question concerns the stock valuation of sweatshirts. Think about the specific factors that apply; fashion items may quickly go out of fashion so that their NRV falls below cost.

Step 2 In part (a), present your calculations clearly, in accordance with the principles of SSAP9.

Step 3 In part (b), slow-moving goods can be identified at a stock-take because they are often dusty or in a 'quiet corner' of the warehouse. Note that, since the company in question sells finished goods, there is no point discussing 'costs to completion' in any NRV calculation.

Step 4 Only when you are confident that you are about to answer the question that has been set, should you start writing.

The examiner's answer

(a) The value of Sweatshirts X at 28 February 1998 is:

(i) At cost

Purchase date	Units	Cost/unit	Total cost
28 Feb	65	10·50	682·50
14 Feb	70	10·40	728·00
31 Jan	15	10·30	154·50
Total	150		1,565·00

(ii) At Net Realisable value

Date of sale	Units	NRV/unit	Total NRV
14 Mar	60	10·26	615·60
28 Mar	50	9·88	494·00
11 Apr	35	9·50	332·50
25 Apr	5	7·60	38·00
Total	150		1,480·10

Note: NRV/unit is 95% of selling price, as selling, marketing and distribution expenses should be deducted from the selling price to obtain the net realisable value per unit

An alternative presentation would be:

Date of sale	Units	Selling price/unit	Total
14 Mar	60	10·80	648·00
28 Mar	50	10·40	520·00
11 Apr	35	10·00	350·00
25 Apr	5	8·00	40·00
Total	150		1,558·00

less: selling and marketing costs (2%)	(31.16)
distribution costs (3%)	(46.74)
Net realisable value	1,480.10

(iii) At lower of cost and net realisable value (in accordance with SSAP 9):
Net realisable value of 150 sweatshirts X = £1,480·10

(b) (i) To identify stock which may be worth less than cost at the stocktake I will:

- go round the warehouse and record stock which appears damaged, dusty or dirty, slow moving or which is in an area which is not often used

- note any fashion stock which appears to be for another season and any current season fashion stock where there are large quantities in stock
- ensure the company's staff record details of such stock on the stock sheets
- ask the warehouse staff if there is any stock which is slow moving or damaged or which may be sold at less than cost

At the final audit in June 1998, I will obtain a schedule from the company of stock which is worth less than cost. As an independent source of information on stock which may be worth less than cost, I will:

- note stock which has been recorded as slow moving, seconds or damaged at the stocktake from both the stock sheets and the notes made by the audit staff at the count
- consider the age at which stock may become worth less than cost. For fashion goods I will consider the 'season' when the stock is expected to be sold. As the final audit in June 1998 is over three months after the year end (28th February), most of the fashion stock held at the year end should have been sold by the time of my audit investigations in June 1998. Any stock held at 28th February which is still unsold in June 1998 will probably be worth less than cost. I will check to the computer records whether this stock has been sold. The stock is likely to be worth less than cost at the year end if either some stock remains in June 1998 or the stock was sold at a discount after the end of the season (i.e to another wholesaler or a retailer). I will record details of such stock. I will record details of any stock held at the year end where the 'season' finished before the year end as this is likely to be worth less than cost.

  For the non-fashion stock, I will consider how long the stock has to remain for it to become worth less than cost. The accountant says items may remain in stock for over a year yet be sold for more than cost. For a sample of items, I will check what happened to slow moving stock at 28th February 1997 which exceed the age when my tests suggest the stock may become worth less than cost.

- inspect management reports, sales reports and other written documents in the company which record stock which may be worth less than cost. For instance, sales and management reports may highlight sales of obsolete and old stock and special offers which may sell the stock for less than cost.
- ask the company's staff for details of any stock which may be worth less than cost. This will include the warehouse staff, sales staff and management.
- as the audit is being carried out over three months after the year end, I will look at stock levels at the year end and sales in the three months after the year end. For fashion lines, I will determine from the company's staff when they were expected to be sold (e.g. printed sweatshirts for an event in March). If the 'season' for selling the fashion product is passed by June, then it is probable that any stock held at the end of May will have to be sold for less than cost. My investigations will cover only stock which was held at 28th February 1998.
- I will ask the company the names of wholesalers and retailers to whom the company disposes surplus stock. I will record sales to these customers for further investigation (in part (b)(ii)).

From these investigations, I will have a list of stock which may be worth less than cost. I will note stock which is:

- on both my list and the company's
- only recorded on the company's list
- only recorded on my list

Did you answer the question?
Note how the examiner's answer deals with the specific circumstances of the question (selling clothes to retailers), rather than items of stock in general.

(ii) I will perform the following work to determine whether the stock identified in part (b)(i) above has been correctly valued at the lower of cost and net realisable value.

From the question, it is apparent that cost can be determined from the computer records. I will test check the accuracy of 'cost' on the computer records to purchase invoices. 'Cost' will be determined in a similar manner to that shown in part (a)(i) of this question. If the computer records are accurate (as the question indicates), I will use them for checking the cost of stock at the year end. If the computer records are inaccurate, it may affect the value of most of the stock, so I will perform more checks to quantify the inaccuracy on the valuation of the year end stock.

In the situation of Hawkhead Textiles, which is a wholesaler, there are no costs to completion so net realisable value is the actual or estimated selling price less selling, distribution and marketing expenses. I will ask the company how it determines selling, distribution and marketing expenses. I will check to the nominal ledger that selling, distribution and marketing expenses as a percentage of sales are the same as those stated by the company. If extra selling costs are required to sell the product or there are additional distribution costs, I will ensure these are included when determining net realisable value. As the selling price is similar to net realisable value, it is probably acceptable to compare the selling price with cost and only value stock at net realisable value when the selling price is less than cost.

To determine the actual selling price, I will look at sales invoices after the year end. Provided the selling price is more than cost, the stock can be valued at cost. Otherwise it will have to be valued at net realisable value.

Most of the fashion goods which were in stock at the year end should have been sold by the time of my audit visit in June 1998. For stock which has been sold since the year end, I will check the selling price to sales invoices. If the sales are to other wholesalers, it will probably be at less than cost. I will note any fashion stock which is unsold in June 1998. This stock will probably have to be sold at less than cost, and I will consider whether the company's estimate is reasonable. The company's estimate should be similar to sales of the stock just before the audit visit (provided it is being sold as obsolete at that time). If there are no recent sales, I will ask the sales department the price they expect to sell the stock. I will look at records of negotiations with customers over the selling price of the stock and offers made by those customers and consider whether the company's estimate of the selling price is reasonable. From this information, it should be possible to determine an estimated selling price. For stock where it is difficult to determine the estimated selling price, it may be possible to use some evidence from past sales of similar stock. For instance, if most stock is disposed of at about 30% of cost, then this slow moving stock is likely to be sold at a similar percentage of the original cost.

For the non-fashion stock, if not all the year end stock has been sold by the time of my audit checks, I will consider whether the remaining stock will be sold at a similar price. If this is the case, the remaining stock can be allocated the same value as stock which has been sold between the year end and my final audit visit.

If there have been no sales since the year end, I will look at the selling price before the year end. I will ask the company's staff if the year end stock is likely to be sold at this price. Provided I consider the company's representations are reasonable, I will value the stock in accordance with the selling price before the year end.

If there have been no sales for some time, the stock may be worth much less than cost. For this stock I will estimate its selling price and check the company's estimate is similar to my figure.

For the damaged and seconds stock, I will check the selling price of this stock after the year end and ensure it is correctly valued in the financial statements.

I will ask the company the names of customers to whom they dispose of stock which is difficult to sell (including damaged and seconds stock) and I will obtain copies of sales invoices since the year end. From these, I will check that this stock has been valued correctly (normally, this stock would be valued at net realisable value).

From the actual or estimated selling prices determined above, I will calculate net realisable value by deducting selling, distribution and marketing expenses from the selling price.

Finally, I will check that the stock is correctly valued at the lower of cost and net realisable value.

Based on this work, I will note any significant differences between my own valuation and the company's, and I will discuss them with the company's staff. If the difference in the valuation is material, I will ask the company to amend the financial statements, and if they refuse I will probably have to qualify my audit report.

70   (Answer 2 of examination)

Examiner's comments and marking guide

Question 2: This question was concerned with the use of computer assisted audit techniques. The answers to part (a) on test data were better than part (b) on computer audit programs. The answers to part (c) were very weak.

In part (a) most candidates' answers were quite good, with them mentioning the use of valid and invalid test data, and suggesting what this data might comprise.

The answers to part (b) were less good, although somewhat better than in past exams. Some candidates could not identify the difference between test data and computer audit programs. Others failed to produce a comprehensive list of how computer audit programs could be used on the sales ledger file. Some candidates suggested computer audit programs would be used to check transactions during the year (e.g., sales invoices, credit notes and cash posted to the sales ledger during the year). However, these points are less relevant than checking the sales ledger file, as the sales system files may contain only transactions in the current month, as earlier months' transactions would be deleted at the end of each month.

The answers to part (c) were quite weak. Candidates should read the model answer. Many candidates suggested computer assisted audit techniques (CAAT's) would not be used if it was a manual accounting system (which is obvious, but hardly answers the question), or where there were few transactions during the year. Very few candidates considered the effect on audit risk and audit time of using or not using CAAT's.

		Marks
(a) (i)	Brief description of use of test data	
(ii)	Examples of the use of test data in auditing sales system	
	Generally <u>1 mark</u> a point up to a <u>maximum</u> of:	6
(b)	Use of computer audit programs in verifying debtors	
	Generally <u>1 mark</u> a point up to a <u>maximum</u> of:	7
(c)	When is the use of computer assisted audit techniques	
(i)	unnecessary or inappropriate	
(ii)	necessary or desirable	
	Generally <u>1 mark</u> a point up to a <u>maximum</u> of:	7
		20

Note: In part (a)(i) you should award <u>up to 2 marks</u> for the definition of 'test data'

Step by step answer plan

Step 1   Read the question again and make sure that you focus on precisely what is required. This is a standard-looking question on computer assisted audit techniques (CAATs).

Step 2   Parts (a) and (b) require an explanation of test data and computer audit programs.

Step 3   Part (c) requires some thought to earn the 7 marks available. It is not enough to say that CAATs are inappropriate for a manual system!

Step 4   Only when you are confident that you are about to answer the question that has been set, should you start writing.

The examiner's answer

(a) (i)   'Test data' is data devised by the auditor to check the operation of the company's accounting systems (in this case, their sales ledger system). Test data comprises both valid data and invalid data. Valid data is used to check that the company's software processes the data accurately. Invalid data is used to check the company's software gives either a warning or rejects the data.

(ii)   Normally, test data is used on test files set up by the auditor. The company's live files are not normally used, as there is a risk the invalid data may corrupt the files.

Initially, the contents of the test files will be printed out.

Then, valid data is entered into the computer. This will include inputting, for a sample of accounts, sales details, credit notes, cash received, discounts and adjustments. Print-outs from input of this information will be retained, and the contents of the computer's data files will be printed out. I will check the results of processing are what I expect and record any cases when errors occur (which is unlikely).

The invalid data which could be input into the computerised sales system would include:

- an invalid customer account number. The computer should reject an account number which is not on the company's standing data file. When a valid account number is input, the customer's name and address should be displayed on the computer screen. This should ensure the operator enters the correct account number, as he/she should check the account name on the screen is correct

- a part number which is not on the computer's standing data file. The computer should not accept the invalid number. When the part number is input, the computer should display the description of the product so the operator can check it is correct

- a negative, zero or very large quantity of goods sold. The computer should reject these items. If the quantity is unusually large, it should give a warning and ask the operator to confirm the quantity is correct

- asking for dispatch of goods when there are none in stock, or the quantity of goods in stock is less than the quantity to be dispatched

- an invalid date. This could include a date with alphabetic characters, an unacceptable date such as 31/02/98, and a date some time in the future or in the past (e.g. 31/12/97 or 31/03/99). With the 'year 2000' problem, the auditor could see the effect of inputting a date in the year 2000 (or later). Normally, the computer should reject an invalid date, but it may be acceptable to give a warning. From the description of the system in the question, the computer should give a warning if the date is in the past (i.e. before to-day's date) or if it is more than a certain time in the future (e.g. more than a week after the current date)

- an invoice which would put the customer over the credit limit. A warning should be given if the customer is slightly over the credit limit, and the operator should be asked to confirm processing of the data (this may require confirmation by a senior person). If the sale would take the customer substantially over the credit limit, the computer system should either reject the data or ask for authorisation by a senior person (e.g. the credit controller or the financial director)

Following input of this data, I will print out the computer's data files and check the results are as I would expect. Also, I will record the action the computer takes when invalid data is input and note any exceptions I encounter. I will record any problems.

Based on this work, I will decide whether the company's sales system processes valid data accurately and takes appropriate action when invalid data is input. I will report any weaknesses I have found to the company's management, and I will consider whether any of these errors will lead to material errors in recording sales and sales ledger transactions.

(b) In verifying the accuracy of the reports produced by the company's software of the data on the sales ledger files, the computer audit program can:

(i) add up the individual transactions on each account and check the total equals the total balance on that account. As stated in the question, there are two files, one containing the transactions on each account (invoices, credit notes, unallocated cash, discounts and adjustments) and the other the total balance on each account. The auditor should perform this check, as a programming error or corruption of the data file may result in the total of the transactions not equalling the balance on the account. The computer audit program should print out any occasions when it finds the net balance of the individual transactions does not equal the balance on the account

(ii) adding up the balances on each account and calculating the total balance on the sales ledger. The total balance will be compared with that produced by the company's accounting software

(iii) the ageing of the debts can be checked with the company's computer print-out. The computer audit program will determine the ageing from the outstanding invoices, credit notes, unallocated cash and discounts and any adjustments. Occasionally ageing of debts by accounting software can be incorrect, particularly with unallocated cash, which most software allocates against the oldest invoices. The total ageing of debts per the auditor's computer audit program should be compared with that produced by the company's accounting software. I will investigate accounts where there is a difference. It is important that ageing of debts is accurate, as the auditor uses this to highlight doubtful balances for further investigation

(iv) the audit software can be used to determine the number of accounts with a balance on the sales ledger. This will be compared with that produced by the company's accounting software. Any difference between these two figures should be investigated, as it could indicate hidden accounts which are not printed by the company's software. Also, the computer audit program should determine the total number of accounts on the sales ledger (including those with no outstanding transactions). If there are a large number of accounts with a zero balance, the auditor should investigate the situation and he/she will probably suggest that many of these accounts should be deleted from the sales ledger standing data file

(v) the computer audit program can be used to print out accounts which are significantly over the credit limit, or those with a significant value of old outstanding items, for the auditor to investigate

In selecting debtors for circularisation, commonly both a random basis of selection and judgement would be used to select the debtors. The number of debtors selected in each of these categories would be based on the criteria in SAS 430 (Audit Sampling). The most appropriate method of randomly selecting debtors is to use monetary unit sampling where the sampling unit is £1. If 60 debtors are to be circularised using monetary unit sampling, one debtor would be selected for each £350,000 (or each £350,000 value of the band). SAS 430 Audit Sampling (para 22) uses the term 'systematic sampling' to describe a form of monetary unit sampling. It says systematic sampling involves selecting items using a constant interval between selections (£350,000 in this case), the first interval having a random start (the random start would be a random number between £0 and £350,000). A computer audit program can be used to select debtors from the sales ledger file using this method.

In addition, the auditor should select a sample of doubtful and other debts. The computer audit program would highlight doubtful debts as those over the credit limit, those with old unpaid items and those put on 'stop' by the credit controller. The auditor can select a sample of these items from those suggested by the computer. The number of debtors selected will depend on the perceived level of material doubtful or disputed debts on the sales ledger. 'Other debts' to be circularised will include a sample of zero and negative (i.e. credit) balances on the sales ledger, which would not be selected using monetary unit sampling.

(c) 'Auditing around the computer' comprises looking at documents recording input into and outputs from the company's software which processes accounting data. This procedure does not look at processing by the computer, only the results of that processing and it does not use any computer assisted audit techniques.

Using computer assisted audit techniques (CAAT's) looks more closely at processing of the accounting data by the computer.

The main matter to consider in deciding whether to use CAAT's is the effect on audit risk of not using CAAT's and whether alternative procedures (e.g. auditing around the computer) are able to reduce audit risk to an acceptable level.

It may not be necessary to use CAAT's in the following circumstances:

(i) if the company is small and uses standard software (which is used by many other companies), it is probably not necessary to use CAAT's. There should be evidence that the company is unable to amend the software. Most small companies would not have the staff with the skills to amend the software, and most standard software is designed so it cannot be amended by the user (e.g. by the program being compiled, rather than comprising statements in a high level programming language). With standard software, 'bugs' in the programs should have been detected by other users and corrected by the software supplier. Thus, the software should be reliable and process data accurately

(ii) where there have been no changes in the software since CAAT's were carried out, and those CAAT's have shown that the software is reliable, then it would be unnecessary to use CAAT's in the current year. The software should be checked as being unchanged by checking that the dates and sizes of the program files are unchanged from last year

In all other circumstances, it is probably necessary or desirable to use CAAT's. These circumstances include:

(i) when the company has recently installed a new computer system. As noted above, if the company is small and it uses standard accounting software, it is probably not necessary to use CAAT's. Where the company is the only user of the software (or one of a small number of users) it is desirable for the auditor to use CAAT's. The auditor will have to consider the effect on audit risk of not using CAAT's. For example, audit risk would be high for complex systems and those developed by the company's staff. In high risk situations, the auditor should use CAAT's

(ii) where the auditor plans to rely on the software to check for invalid data by giving either a warning or rejecting the data, he/she should check the effectiveness of the software by using test data

(iii) if the software has been changed in the past year, it is desirable for the auditor to use CAAT's. Most payroll systems are amended each year to incorporate annual tax changes by government, so it will probably be necessary to use CAAT's more frequently on payroll systems than on other systems.

(iv) if the standard software allows the company to change the programs or add procedures, it may be necessary to use CAAT's to check the correct operation of these procedures. It would not be necessary to use CAAT's if it can be demonstrated that the company has not made amendments to the programs or used these procedures (e.g. by the size of the program files being unchanged from last year)

(v) it is probably necessary to use CAAT's when there is a significant loss of audit trail in the computer system, as the loss of audit trail increases audit risk. The auditor may have to use CAAT's every year when a significant balance sheet or profit and loss account item is determined using calculations by the computer for which there is no audit trail. This could occur with calculation of interest on bank accounts, and the calculation of net debtors from gross debtors in a company which has hire purchase transactions (i.e. net debtors will be the gross debtor less unearned (or future) interest)

(vi) where the data is confidential, it is desirable to check the effectiveness of controls over access to the system. These controls will include the use of passwords and limiting access to certain terminals or during certain times of the day (e.g. normal working hours). For most systems there should be some controls over input of data and amending data files, and it would be desirable for the auditor to check the effectiveness of these controls by using both valid and invalid passwords and authorised and unauthorised terminals to gain access to the system

(vii) the auditor should check controls over amending accounting software. There should be a procedure for authorising and recording amendments to accounting software. Accounting software should only be amended when necessary and it should be used only when it has been tested and shown to overcome the reported problem (or to incorporate changes in tax rates for payroll systems). Any significant amendment to the software will probably require the auditor to repeat the CAAT's he/she carried out on the system

(viii) where the company's accounting software has known weaknesses (e.g. in ageing of debtors on the sales ledger) it may be necessary to use CAAT's every year.

Did you answer the question?
Part (c) is worth 7 marks, so make sure that you describe at least 3 (preferably more) circumstances for each of parts (i) and (ii).

---

71   (Answer 3 of examination)

Examiner's comments and marking guide

Question 3: This question was concerned with audit matters relating to a wages system. Many candidates tended to write all they knew about auditing wage systems, rather than answering the question on the exam paper.

Part (a) was concerned with performing a starters and leavers test. Many candidates failed to mention checking to the payroll, which is a very important document in a wages system. Many candidates mentioned checking that 'starters' were paid for the first week they worked, and 'leavers' were paid for the last week they worked. However, it is much more important to check that 'starters' were not paid the week before they started work and 'leavers' were not paid the week after they left (with appropriate adjustments for manufacturing employees who are paid a week in arrears).

Many of the answers to part (b) on attending the wages pay-out concentrated on procedures before the wages were paid, rather than on the topic of the wages pay-out. Very few candidates mentioned the important point of checking the unclaimed wages at the end of the wages pay-out to the unclaimed wages book (this point could be made in an answer to either part (b) or (c) of the question).

Most of the answers to part (c) on checking the unclaimed wages system were weak, in that they did not answer the question directly. Many candidates mentioned banking the unclaimed wages, but few candidates considered checking the unclaimed wages in part (b) were recorded in the unclaimed wages book. The answers on checks over employees collecting their unclaimed wages were quite good, but very few candidates suggested counting the unclaimed wages and checking them to the unclaimed wages book.

Most of the answers to part (d) on other checks of the existence of employees concentrated on checking the payment to the employee's bank account. Candidates should aim to produce a variety of checks, as per the suggested answers in the question and suggested answers booklets.

Marks

(a) Performing a starters and leavers test
   Generally <u>1 mark</u> a point up to a <u>maximum</u> of: 5

(b) Checks over payment of wages in cash
   Generally <u>1 mark</u> a point up to a <u>maximum</u> of: 5

Marks

(c) Checking procedures over unclaimed wages
Generally <u>1 mark</u> a point up to a <u>maximum</u> of: 5

(d) Checking existence of employees not paid in cash
Generally <u>1 mark</u> a point up to a <u>maximum</u> of: 5

         20

Step by step answer plan

Step 1   Read the question again and make sure that you focus on precisely what is required. This question concerns tests of control in a wages system that might be carried out at an interim audit.

Step 2   Each part of the question is worth 5 marks, so make sure that you offer the marker at least 5 points in your answer to each part.

Step 3   In part (b), the audit procedures on attending the pay-out would include work carried out on documents obtained before the pay-out, such as a full copy of the payroll.

Step 4   Only when you are confident that you are about to answer the question that has been set, should you start writing.

The examiner's answer

(a) To carry out a starters and leavers test, I will select two payrolls, the first at the start of the company's financial year and the second a recent payroll. I will note:

(i) employees not on the first payroll who are on the second payroll. These are 'starters'

(ii) employees on the first payroll who are not on the second. These are 'leavers'

For both starters and leavers, I will go to the personnel department and find the date each employee started or left.

For starters I will check to the relevant payrolls that they were not paid before they started employment. For most employees, the first payment should be at the end of the week or month they started work and not for the previous week or month For manufacturing employees, the first payment should be made the week *after* they started work and they should not be paid at the end of the week they started work.

For leavers I will check to the relevant payrolls that they were not paid after they ceased employment. For most employees, they should be paid at the end of the week or month they finished work but not for the subsequent week or month. For manufacturing employees, the last payment should be the week after they left employment and they should not be paid in the following week's payroll.

An alternative way of performing this test is to start from the personnel records of staff who have started or left during the period. I will check that starters have not been paid before they started employment and leavers have not been paid after they left employment in the same way as that described in the two paragraphs above.

> **Did you answer the question?**
> Where there are two possibilities (here, basing the test on the payroll or the personnel records), explain both approaches to earn all the marks available.

If I find any problems, I will discuss them with the company's management. If I detect a fraud, this will require further investigation and I should report it to the company's management and include it in my management letter. This will suggest there should be greater controls over preventing frauds over starters and leavers, such as the personnel department periodically checking the wages department are treating these types of employee correctly.

(b) I will carry out the following audit procedures when I attend the pay-out of wages to employees:

(i) before the wages are paid, I will take a copy of the payroll and check there is a pay packet for each employee. If the pay packet is transparent, it may be possible to test check the money in the pay packet agrees with the net pay on the payroll

(ii) when the employee is given his/her wage, he/she should sign for it. The signature should be test checked to the employee's signature kept by the personnel department. I will mark on my list when each employee collects his/her wage

(iii) I will check that no employee receives more than one pay packet or one for another employee. I will note if this is happening

(iv) at the end of the wages payout, I will check that there is a wage packet for each employee who has not collected his/her wage. These will be the unmarked items on my payroll list. These are 'unclaimed wages'

(v) I will check that these unclaimed wages are recorded in the unclaimed wages book. The information recorded in the unclaimed wages book should include the payroll date (and payment date, if different), the employee's name and number, and the net wage. I will note cases where unclaimed wages are not recorded in the unclaimed wages book. This is not unusual, as frequently wages collected in the day of payment are not recorded in the unclaimed wages book, and the unclaimed wages book records only those wages which are unclaimed at the end of the day. This creates a weakness in the wages payment system (although it is minimised by the employees signing for their wages)

As indicated above, one of the purposes of attending the wages payout is to check the existence of employees.

(c) In checking the procedures over unclaimed wages:

(i) I will have checked procedures for recording unclaimed wages in the unclaimed wages book in part (b)(v) above. To qualitatively check that the same procedures are carried out in the weeks when I did not attend the pay-out, I will check the number of unclaimed wage packets is about the same each week. If they are significantly less in other weeks, this indicates that some unclaimed wages are not recorded in the unclaimed wages book. If I am concerned that proper procedures have not been followed in other weeks, I will ask the company's staff if the procedures are different in other weeks and I may attend another pay-out of wages. I will report the matter to the company's management and include it in my management letter

(ii) I will check there is a wage packet for each unclaimed wage recorded in the unclaimed wages book

(iii) where employees have collected their wages, I will check that they have either signed for the wage or there is a letter from the employee authorising another person to collect the wage packet (e.g. when the employee is ill). I will check the employee's signature to the personnel records

(iv) the company should pay into the bank wage packets which have been unclaimed for more than a month. The date the wages were banked should be recorded against details of each wage packet in the unclaimed wages book. For a sample of bankings of unclaimed wages, I will check that the amount banked (per the cash book) agrees with the total net wages of the employees as recorded in the unclaimed wages book

(v) if there is a long delay before the wage packets are banked (e.g. over three months), I will report it to the company's management and I may include it in my management letter

I will report any weaknesses I find to the company's management. The unclaimed wage packets should be kept in a secure place, such as a safe. Ideally, unclaimed wages should not be dealt with by employees in the wages department, and there should be an independent check (probably by the accounts or personnel department) to ensure that proper procedures are carried out and there is no fraud.

(d) To verify the existence of employees, I will first select a sample of employees from the most recent payroll. The procedures I will use for checking the existence of the employees will include:

(i) for employees at head office and at sales branches my audit firm visits, I could go and see them, and ask for a signature which would be checked to the personnel records

(ii) employees could be checked to the personnel records, as being currently employed by the company. The question says the personnel department is independent from the wages department.

(iii) department managers could be asked to sign a list of employees who work for them and return it direct to me

(iv) if the employees are paid by cheque, the cheques could be inspected before they are given to the employee or sent to their bank. In the UK, most employees are paid by BACS where the bank is sent a list of employees to be paid. The name of the employee on the list should be the same as on the payroll

(v) other evidence of employees will include expense claims signed by the employee and records of tax and national insurance. For instance, there could be notifications from the Inland Revenue of changes in tax code, and there will have been an annual return to the Inland Revenue (at the end of the tax year) which lists each employee

Based on the results of these tests, I will decide whether all the employees on the payroll actually work for the company. It should be noted that the checks above are the variety of methods which can be used to verify employees on the payroll, and in practice not all of them would be used.

Did you answer the question?

Note the 5 points made by the examiner in his answer to each part of the question. Did your answer follow this same format?

---

72 (Answer 4 of examination)

Examiner's comments and marking guide

Question 4: This question was about internal auditors and the reliance external auditors could place on their work.

The answers to part (a) on assessing the effectiveness of the internal auditors at the planning stage were variable. The good answers considered the points included in the suggested answer and in the standard 'Considering the work of Internal Audit.'

Most of the answers to part (b) were very poor. Many candidates described the work of either the internal auditors or the external auditors. Some candidates incorrectly thought the question was about 'internal controls' rather than 'internal audit'. The key to answering this part of the question was that where the internal auditors have performed work in an area of interest to the external auditor, the external auditor should carry out a small number of similar tests. Where the results of the external auditor's tests are similar to the internal auditors' then the external auditor can place some reliance on the internal auditors' work. Thus, the external auditor can reduce the number of items he/she checks in order to achieve the required level of audit risk. Very few candidates approached the answer to this part in this way.

Marks

(a) Matters to consider in deciding amount of reliance on internal auditor's work

    Generally <u>1 mark</u> a point up to a <u>maximum</u> of: 6

(b) Extent of reliance on internal auditors:

    (i)   recording accounting systems and evaluating controls

    (ii) testing of controls

    (iii) verifying assets and liabilities

    (iv) auditing computer systems, including using CAAT's

    (v) visits to branches

    Generally <u>1 mark</u> a point up to a <u>maximum</u> of: 14

                        20

Step by step answer plan

Step 1   Read the question again and make sure that you focus on precisely what is required. This question concerns internal audit; any knowledge you may have of SAS 500 would be valuable.

Step 2   Part (a) only concerns the planning stage of the audit. Don't drift into operational matters.

Step 3   In part (b), treat internal audit like any other internal control that the external auditor might want to rely on. External audit would test some of the internal audit work, and if it appears sound, external audit can then reduce their amount of detailed testing in that area.

Step 4   Only when you are confident that you are about to answer the question that has been set, should you start writing.

The examiner's answer

(a)   SAS 500 (Considering the work of internal auditors) para 14 lists four important criteria in assessing the work of internal audit, which are listed in parts (i) to (iv) below

   (i)   Organisational status. The internal audit department's status in the organisation and the effect this has on its ability to be objective. Sighthill Supermarkets is a public company, and it may have an audit committee. If it does, ideally the internal audit department should report to them (or be able to report to them). In practice, it is probable that much of the work of the internal audit department will be controlled by the Financial Director. However, there should be some input from the Board (and audit committee, if it exists) to ensure that all important aspects of the company's operations are covered by the internal auditors. As stated earlier, the internal audit department should have the right to report to the audit committee, and the audit committee should review copies of reports by the internal auditors. Also, the internal auditors should be free to communicate with the external auditors. The independence of the internal audit department is important, and I will consider whether it has adequate independence both in terms of the work it carries out and the reports it makes

   (ii)   Scope of function. I will check what action is taken by the company as a result of the internal auditors' work. Action should be taken by the company when the internal auditors detect significant weaknesses in the accounting systems or errors in processing transactions. The internal auditors should re-test the systems to check that the problems have been corrected. The internal auditors' working papers showing weaknesses and errors and subsequent correction will provide me with evidence of whether action is taken following adverse reports by the internal auditors.

   (iii)   Technical competence. I will check the qualifications and experience of the internal auditors. If the internal auditors have appropriate qualifications (e.g. a member of the ACCA) their work is likely to be more reliable than if they are unqualified. Experience in auditing is important. They could have qualified with a firm of professional accountants and have performed audits of private and public companies, or they may have experience of internal audit in other companies. They should attend courses to keep up to date and learn about new developments. Unqualified staff should be studying for the exams of a professional body. I will check these matters by discussing them with the head of the internal audit department and obtaining appropriate evidence

   (iv)   Due professional care. The work of the internal auditors should be properly planned, supervised, reviewed and documented. I will scrutinise the working papers of the internal auditors. I will check the work they have carried out is appropriate and that the conclusions they reach are consistent with the results of the tests they have carried out. I will assess the work programme of the internal audit department and check it provides adequate coverage of the company's operations and that it is carried out at an appropriate frequency. For instance, checks should be carried out when new accounting systems are installed, and tests should be re-performed at a later date when serious errors or weaknesses in controls are found. There should be appropriate audit manuals for the internal audit staff.

(b)   The existence of an internal audit department will improve controls in the company. Firstly, this is because of the 'policing' effect, in that the existence of an internal audit department will make employees aware there is an increased risk the internal auditors will detect fraud or errors in their work. Thus employees will be more careful to minimise and correct any errors and they will be deterred from perpetrating a fraud. In addition, the internal auditors should improve the effectiveness and extent of controls as a result of the tests they carry out and the recommendations they make. Thus, the existence of an internal audit department reduces control risk. So, with an internal audit department, the external auditor should be able to carry out fewer tests of controls and/or substantive procedures in order to achieve the planned level of audit risk.

The extent to which I can rely on the internal auditors' work in relation to the matters listed in the question and thus reduce my audit work are:

   (i)   For recording accounting systems, it is likely that I will rely almost entirely on the internal auditors' work. Ideally, they should have the same system and use the same symbols for recording accounting systems as my audit firm. I will check the accounting systems have been recorded correctly by performing walk through tests using a sample of transactions. If the systems have been recorded accurately, I can use the flowcharts in my audit working papers.

   For evaluation of controls, the internal auditors' internal control evaluation questionnaire (ICE) (or internal control questionnaire – ICQ) should be the same or similar to my firm's. If they are the same or similar to my firm's, I will check to the flowchart that the questions have been answered correctly. If there are significant differences with my firm's questionnaires, I will check that the internal auditors' ICE or ICQ asks appropriate questions. I may fill in my firm's ICE or ICQ rather than use the internal auditors' as this will make it easier for the partner to review, and it would minimise the risk of missing weaknesses in the internal auditors' ICE or ICQ. As my firm is likely to be the external auditor for a number of years, it is desirable that the internal auditors should use my firm's ICE's or ICQ's rather than their own.

(ii) For tests of controls in accounting systems, I will review the internal auditors' work and check they are testing appropriate controls. In this area, the external auditor should not rely entirely on the internal auditors' work. I will perform additional tests, either on the same items as were checked by the internal auditor, or on a different sample of items. If I find the results of my tests are similar to the internal auditors' (particularly in terms of frequency and types of error found) then I will be able to place reliance on the internal auditors' work and I will reduce the number of items I check. If my checks detect either different types of error or at a higher frequency than the internal auditors', I will have to perform further work by increasing the number of items I test and I will probably ask the internal auditors to perform more checks

(iii) Internal auditors verify assets and liabilities by:

- checking the existence of fixed assets

- attending stocktakes

- checking debtors including carrying out debtors' circularisations (in a supermarket, there are likely to be very few debtors, so a debtors' circularisation may not be carried out)

- checking bank reconciliations

- counting cash in tills and petty cash

- checking purchase ledger balances to suppliers' statements

As stated in part (ii) above, I should not rely entirely on the internal auditors' work. I will check the internal auditors' work by either re-performing their tests, or performing tests on a different sample of items. Provided my test results are similar to the internal auditors', I can reduce the number of items I check (compared with what I would check if there was no internal auditor). Where the internal auditors find weaknesses or errors, I will check the internal auditors have re-checked the systems at a later date to ensure the weakness has been corrected. I may perform more checks in areas where the internal auditors have found weaknesses or an unacceptable error rate

(iv) The question says the internal auditors use computer assisted audit techniques. I will look at the programme and results of their work. The programme should ensure that new computerised accounting systems and significant changes to existing systems are tested by the internal auditors. I will check that any weaknesses or errors found as a result of these tests are acted upon and re-tested by the internal auditors.

I will inspect the CAAT work carried out by the internal auditors and consider whether it is appropriate and checks all the significant aspects of the computerised accounting systems. If certain aspects have not been covered, I will either ask the internal auditors to carry out the work or I will perform the tests myself.

Audit of the computer systems should not be limited to using CAAT's. The reliability of the computer system is vitally important, as any serious failure could create major operational and financial problems. Thus, the internal auditors should have carried out procedures to check the reliability of the system. For instance, there should be no 'bugs' in the software which either result in the system 'crashing' or data files being corrupted. As most large computer systems contain some 'bugs', the system should be 'tolerant' so that it can continue to operate when such problems occur. The internal auditors should have carried out tests of controls over access to the computer. The system should be able to detect errors in transmission of data (particularly over telephone lines to head office) and ensure the data is re-transmitted. I will check the internal auditors' work and consider whether it is sufficient for the purposes of my audit. If I believe it is inadequate, I will either ask the internal auditors to carry out the work or I will carry it out myself.

(v) The internal auditor is likely to carry out a substantial number of visits to supermarkets. The question says visits to supermarkets are carried out more frequently to large supermarkets and to those where problems have been found. I will inspect their work and check the frequency of their visits to supermarkets to confirm this is happening. I will check that all supermarkets are visited at least once a year. It would not be possible for my staff to visit all the supermarkets at every audit, so I will visit the large supermarkets on every audit and smaller ones on a rotational basis. I will compare the results of my tests with those of the internal auditors. If the results of the tests are similar, I will be able to place more reliance on the internal auditors' work than if there are significant differences.

The audit procedures carried out at supermarkets will include checking balance sheet items, such as stock quantities and cut-off details. Also, they should include checking controls such as receipt of goods, procedures at the cash check-outs, custody and banking of cash and the existence of employees. Checking procedures over employees is important, as the supermarkets are likely to have a large number of full-time and part-time employees, who work different hours. There should be evidence of their existence and the hours they have worked. It is apparent there is a high risk of a fraud being committed by creating fictitious employees, or, where the employees are paid in cash, of inflating the employees' hours and the fraudster misappropriating the wage for the overstated hours.

The internal audit department will be very helpful at the year end, as, with their assistance, it will be possible to visit a greater proportion of the supermarkets at the year end to attend the stocktake and obtain details of purchases cut-off (sales cut-off should not be a problem with a supermarket). Provided the work of the internal auditors is reliable, the external auditors may be able to reduce the number of supermarkets they visit at the year end and at the interim and final stages of the audit.

73   (Answer 5 of examination)

Examiner's comments and marking guide

Question 5: This question was about audit working papers. Part (a)(i) asked candidates to list the contents of the permanent and current audit file. Most of the answers were quite good, although some candidates were confused about whether items should appear in the permanent or current audit file. More candidates should have pointed out that the main contents of the current audit file are the tests carried out by the external auditor in the current year's audit. The answers to part (ii) on referencing of the audit file and the importance of it, were satisfactory, although less good than part (i). Most of the answers to part (iii) on checklists and specimen letters were quite good.

The answers to part (b) on why auditors use working papers were quite good. However, more candidates should have mentioned that audit working papers are used as evidence of work done. This will be used by the partner in deciding whether an unqualified audit report can be given, and audit working papers will be very valuable when legal action is being taken against the auditor for negligence.

Some of the answers to part (c) on whether the auditor was negligent in two situations were very brief. However, many of the answers rightly considered the materiality of the fraud, and usually they came to an appropriate conclusion on whether the auditor was negligent. It is probably better to say 'the auditor is probably negligent' or 'is probably not negligent', rather than be dogmatic in saying 'the auditor is negligent' or 'is not negligent'.

		Marks
(a)	Contents of audit working papers, examples of checklists and audit letters	
	Generally <u>1 mark</u> a point up to a <u>maximum</u> of:	10
(b)	Reasons why auditors have working papers. Is it necessary for all audit work to be recorded?	
	Generally <u>1 mark</u> a point up to a <u>maximum</u> of:	4
(c)	Is the auditor negligent in two situations?	
	Generally <u>1 mark</u> a point up to a <u>maximum</u> of:	6
		20

Step by step answer plan

Step 1 Read the question again and make sure that you focus on precisely what is required. This question on working papers is easier if you have had direct experience of audit.

Step 2 Part (a) is worth 10 marks and comprises the bulk of the question. If you have had direct experience of working on an audit assignment, feel free to describe the system for referencing working papers that you have seen.

Step 3 Part (b) centres on the fact that working papers are a source of audit evidence from which the reporting partner forms his opinion.

Step 4 Don't be too dogmatic in part (c), but discuss the possibilities in each situation.

Step 5 Only when you are confident that you are about to answer the question that has been set, should you start writing.

The examiner's answer

(a) Audit working papers are normally divided into:

(i) the permanent audit file, and

(ii) the current audit file

The permanent audit file contains information which is relevant to many years' audits. Its contents can include:

(i) the letter of engagement

(ii) the memorandum and articles of the company

(iii) a history of the company, a description of its business and details of directors and senior staff

(iv) copies of previous years' financial statements with ratio analysis and comment on the figures

(v) details of the company's accounting systems, flowcharts of those systems and completed Internal Control Evaluation Questionnaires (ICE's) or Internal Control Questionnaires (ICQ's)

(vi) copies of significant documents, including minutes of significant Board Meetings

The current audit file contains documents which are relevant to the current year's audit. This information includes:

(i) evidence of planning of the audit, including the audit planning memorandum

(ii) copies of board minutes, significant management reports, management accounts, the trial balance and draft financial statements. There should be a reconciliation of any difference in profit between the draft financial statements and the management accounts

(iii) consideration of audit risk for each area of the audit. This could include notes on high risk areas of the audit and decisions on sample sizes

(iv) copies of flowcharts and completed ICQ's or ICE's if they are not included in the permanent audit file. It may be preferable to include flowcharts and ICE's or ICQ's in the current audit file as there may be changes to the systems and including them in the permanent file may mean there is no record of the system two or three years ago (which may be needed if litigation is threatened against the auditor). The results of evaluation of controls will be used to estimate the sample sizes in part (iii) above

(v) records of the audit work done, problems encountered and conclusions reached (see below). The audit schedules should be initialled and dated by the member of staff preparing them and by the manager or partner who reviews them

(vi) a section for the manager's and partner's attention which lists significant problems encountered in the audit. This will include a summary of unadjusted errors. This section will direct the partner to these important areas, and to decide whether the financial statements need amending or a qualified audit report should be given

Did you answer the question?

Part (a) does not require a long list of bullet points. Note how the answer describes the purpose of each file before describing typical contents.

Recording audit work in working papers is usually divided into sections which have a reference letter or number. For instance, the letter 'D' could be used for Sales and Debtors work. Thus, for any audit carried out by the firm, any member of staff wanting to look at audit work on Sales or Debtors can go to the section with the letter 'D'. Within each section, there will be a sub-division whereby verification of debtors will be in pages D1 to D99 and audit work on the sales system will be on pages D100 to D199 (i.e. tests on balance sheet items will be on pages 1-99 and tests on accounting systems will be on pages 100–199 – these numbers will be preceded by a letter which signifies the area of the audit, with 'D' being for sales and debtors). The front page of the 'D' section of the audit file will show the value of debtors in the balance sheet, and references on the make-up of debtors will be to the pages where details of verification of these items is included in the working papers. For instance, the total value of debtors will be broken down into:

(i) verifying the gross value of debtors (e.g. given on page D2 of the audit file)

(ii) checking the bad and doubtful debt provision (e.g. given on page D5)

(iii) audit of sundry debtors and prepayments (given on page D10)

By using this standardised procedure for referencing audit files, all members of the firm's audit staff, including managers and partners, can review each section of the audit in a systematic manner. This should enable them to come to an appropriate conclusion on the audit work done and the form of audit report which should be attached to the financial statements. If no standardised procedure is used, the partner would find it time-consuming to find a particular matter in the audit file. By standardising audit files, the audit work should be carried out in a more systematic manner which should ensure a high quality audit is carried out.

Particularly important sections in audit files include:

(i) conclusions reached in each area of the audit and notes of any significant problems detected

(ii) matters for consideration by the partner and the summary of unadjusted errors (which should include significant uncertainties)

There are many types of checklist used by auditors. They include:

(i) Internal control evaluation questionnaires (ICE) and internal control questionnaires (ICQ) for evaluating controls in accounting systems

(ii) stocktaking checklists which are used to record work done and to ensure all aspects are covered

(iii) Companies Act and Accounting Standards checklists to ensure the financial statements comply with these statutory and professional standards

(iv) audit completion checklists to help the auditor ensure all material audit work has been performed and matters considered

Checklists are important, as they are a means of ensuring that all aspects of the audit work are carried out. A standard ICE on the sales system would be better than one prepared for each audit, as the standard ICE will be 'tried and tested' so there will be a lower risk of a matter being omitted than if the checklist was prepared by the auditor at each audit.

Specimen letters include:

(i) the engagement letter which the auditor should send to the client (and get agreed by the client) before the audit is accepted. The contents of this letter should be reviewed and a new one issued and agreed when there are significant changes in the auditor's responsibilities

(ii) management letters which are letters sent by the auditor to the company recording weaknesses found in the audit

(iii) management representation letter which is a letter drafted by the auditor, but on the company's letter heading and signed by the directors. It is used to enable the directors to confirm to the auditor certain matters where the auditor cannot obtain adequate evidence from other sources

(iv) bank letter, where the bank states the balances on the company's bank accounts and other matters

(v) debtors' circularisation letters and replies from debtors. The debtors' circularisation letter asks customers of the company to confirm (or otherwise) the balance on the sales ledger

(b) The reasons why auditors have working papers include:

(i) as a record of work performed on the audit, and to ensure a consistent, logical and reasoned approach to audit work by following an audit plan and recording work performed as the audit progresses.

(ii) to assist the manager in reviewing the audit work, and the partner in coming to an audit opinion. The audit working papers will provide evidence to the partner of work done. From the working papers it may become apparent that insufficient work has been carried out in certain areas and more work is required

(iii) to provide evidence of work done if there is a threat of or action taken against the auditor for negligence. The audit working papers should provide evidence that appropriate audit procedures have been carried out and conclusions reached. In the case of a material doubtful debt, it should show the evidence the auditor has obtained and the matters he/she has considered in deciding whether the company's estimate of the bad debt provision is reasonable

Generally, all audit work should be recorded in the audit working papers. Work performed on some immaterial items may not be included. However, as is noted in part (c) of this answer, it is desirable that all audit work is recorded, as an item which may appear to be immaterial may subsequently become material. For instance, an item which is checked in a test of controls may not in itself be material, but an error detected in a test will probably be material in terms of the conclusion reached on the population (using statistics). To a certain extent, audit working papers are a summary of work done, so a check performed in a test of control may be signified by an audit tick against the item, and the tick will be explained at the bottom of the schedule. If some audit work is thought to be unimportant (and thus there is the possibility of it not being recorded) the auditor should consider whether it is necessary to carry out that work.

It is important to record audit work, as, if legal action is taken against the auditor, it may be necessary for the auditor to demonstrate the items he/she has checked and the conclusions he/she has reached.

(c) If the late banking of receipts of £7,000 was a teeming and lading fraud at 31 October 1997, this is 4.4% of profit before tax, so it is unlikely to be material. When the fraud was found in May 1998, it amounted to 11.25% of profit before tax which is probably material. If the auditor did not report the late banking to the company which he/she found at 31 October 1997, then he/she could be held (partially) responsible for the loss between 31 October 1997 and when it was found in May 1998. The loss during this period is £11,000, or 6.9% of profit before tax, which may be material.

(i) In this situation, it appears the auditor is not negligent. The only matters which might be unsatisfactory in the auditor's work are:

   – it appears he/she has not determined whether a teeming and lading fraud was being carried out at 31 October 1997, and

   – the company should have been informed at the time the discrepancy was found, rather than leaving it to the management letter

   However, both of these criticisms of the auditor appear to be relatively minor.

   It may not be possible at to-day's date to determine whether there was a teeming and lading fraud at 31 October 1997, as the £7,000 of late banking could have been held by the cashier (although this seems unlikely). In conclusion, the auditor is probably not liable for negligence in this situation. The company has been warned of the risk of a teeming and lading fraud but appears to have taken no action until May 1998

(ii) In this situation, the auditor may have some liability for negligence. The late banking of deposits should have been reported to the company both verbally and in the auditor's management letter. Also, the auditor should have checked whether there was a teeming and lading fraud at 31 October 1997 (or at the date he/she checked the bank reconciliation). Thus, the auditor has some liability for negligence for not reporting the matter to the company's management and not carrying out further procedures.

   The auditor could argue the possible fraud at 31 October 1997 was immaterial as it is 4.4% of profit before tax, but by taking no action on the matter it has increased to 11.25% of profit before tax, which is material. The auditor should not be held wholly responsible for the extra loss of £11,000 (between 31 October 1997 and May 1998) as it is probable that the company's control procedures were inadequate. As the cashier was 'recording cash received and preparing the bank reconciliation' as well as 'having custody of the cash received' there was an inadequate division of duties, so another person in the company should either have prepared the bank reconciliation or checked it. It is apparent that either this check was not being performed or it was not performed competently. As the auditor was aware of the late banking of £7,000 of cash receipts and he/she should have been aware of the weakness in control over the cashier, the auditor should have reported these problems to the company, even though the fraud was immaterial at the time of the audit.

   Thus, in this situation, the auditor has some liability for the fraud continuing but this is mitigated by the fact that there was a clear weakness in the division of duties with the cashier, and the company should have established an effective system of internal check over the cashier's work. This was either not being performed or not being performed competently. Thus, the company must accept some liability for the fraud developing. If the case came to court, reference will probably be made to the audit working papers as one factor in determining the extent of the auditor's liability for negligence.

Did you answer the question?

The examiner discusses the issues involved in each situation in part (c), before coming to a tentative conclusion.

---

74 (Answer 6 of examination)

Examiner's comments and marking guide

Question 6: This question was concerned with verifying completeness of income and the reliance an external auditor can place on the management representation letter from the directors.

Most of the answers to part (a) on verifying completeness of income were very weak, and hardly covered the topic. Very few candidates used points (i) to (iv) which were helpfully listed in the question paper. The question asked for 'substantive procedures' but many candidates' answers concentrated on tests of controls, which are hardly appropriate in view of the weaknesses in controls in the company's sales system. Very few candidates suggested checking the gross profit margin on actual sales, by comparing the selling price with the cost on the purchase invoice. Similarly, very few candidates suggested checking, for high value items, the quantity purchased and the quantity sold. A significant number of candidates suggested checking sales ledgers, which is inappropriate in the cash sales business of the company in the question.

The answers to part (b) on considering the reliability of evidence provided by the management representation letter were satisfactory and much better than part (a). More candidates should have considered whether the evidence provided by the management representation letter is consistent with other evidence obtained by the auditor. If it is consistent, the management representation letter will provide additional positive evidence for the auditor. However, if it is inconsistent, the external auditor should be reluctant to accept the evidence provided by the management representation letter.

Many of the answers to part (c) of the question rushed to the conclusion that the auditor should qualify his/her report. Such answers gained few marks. Firstly, the refusal of the directors to sign the management representation letter should have 'put the auditor on enquiry'. The model answer describes how the auditor should try to persuade the directors to sign the management representation letter. However, if the directors still refuse to sign the letter, the auditor should carry out more work in the problem areas. If the auditor cannot obtain sufficient appropriate audit evidence to confirm the completeness of income and validity of expenditure, then the audit report will probably have to be qualified. Many candidates were good at considering the types of qualification which could be used.

		Marks
(a)	Audit techniques to verify completeness of income including verifying the gross profit margin	
	Generally <u>1 mark</u> a point up to a <u>maximum</u> of:	10
(b)	Reliability of Management Representation Letters as audit evidence	
	Generally <u>1 mark</u> a point up to a <u>maximum</u> of:	5
(c)	Action to take and conclusions to reach if directors refuse to sign the Management Representation Letter	
	Generally <u>1 mark</u> a point up to a <u>maximum</u> of:	5
		20

Step by step answer plan

Step 1 Read the question again and make sure that you focus on precisely what is required. This question concerns the gathering of audit evidence in a small company with poor controls.

Step 2 Part (a) is worth 10 marks, so forms the bulk of the question. Avoid tests of control, since we already know that the controls cannot be relied on.

Step 3 In part (b), the representation letter forms part of the audit evidence available.

Step 4 In part (c), there is a range of possible actions that you should discuss.

Step 5 Only when you are confident that you are about to answer the question that has been set, should you start writing.

The examiner's answer

(a) In checking whether all sales income due to the company has been included in the financial statements, I will consider the sources of income. The question says they are received in cash or by cheque or credit card. The risk of cheque and credit card receipts being misappropriated is low. The customer would make the cheque out to Newton Electronics and, in the UK, it is almost impossible to negotiate a cheque to another party. Similarly, for most receipts from credit cards a machine connected to the bank's computer is used, which will only accept 'payments' by customers which are directed to the company's bank account. For manual credit card receipts, the machine has a stamp which prints the company's name on the credit card voucher, and the bank would not make a payment into another bank account.

Thus, the greatest risk is that cash takings are misappropriated by staff or the directors.

To check that all sales are recorded on the till, I will:

(i) note the system for recording and banking cash from the till

(ii) observe the procedures over recording sales on the till. Each item purchased should be recorded on the till, payment should be received from the customer and the cash, cheque or credit card receipt should be placed in the till. Ideally, the till should record the type of payment, so this can be matched with the takings at the end of the day. There should be no evidence that sales are being made and not recorded on the till

(iii) at the end of the day, the takings should be counted and banked. As explained above, if the takings are divided into cash, cheques and credit card receipts, the amount of each of these should be the same as that banked. Normally, the cash and cheques will be banked and the credit card receipts will appear automatically on the company's bank statement. There should be a reconciliation of credit card receipts per the bank statement to the amount recorded on the till. I will test check that the amount banked agrees with the total on the till roll. Small differences are permissible, but larger ones should be investigated. There should be evidence of the company investigating larger differences and taking appropriate action. Cash from the till should be banked promptly and intact. If there is evidence of a delay in banking takings, there could be a teeming and lading fraud. There is an increased risk of fraud if part of the takings are used to pay other expenses (including the employees' wages)

(iv) perform a surprise count of the cash in the tills. The amount counted will be checked as agreeing with the sub-total produced by the till (after allowing for cash floats). This type of test can detect unrecorded cash sales which are misappropriated by the shop assistant at the end of the day (i.e. the amount to be misappropriated will be the difference between the cash in the till and that shown on the till roll)

Observation by the auditor of the company's procedures is a relatively weak way of detecting whether cash sales are being misappropriated, as the staff are likely to be honest while the auditor is watching. However, the use of a video camera and recorder which observes the till can both deter and detect misappropriation of sales cash. I will be more confident of completeness of sales income if such a video camera is being used.

Other techniques which can be used to verify completeness of sales income include:

(i) comparing the mix of cheque, credit card and cash income. If on occasions cash income is unusually small, this may indicate when it is being misappropriated

(ii) looking at total sales each day. There is likely to be a pattern of sales, probably with more sales taking place on Saturday (and Sunday if they are open). I will investigate when sales appear to be unusually low. Sales should be high before Christmas and during sales (i.e. when products are sold at a discount).

(iii) checking the gross profit margin, as described below

Checking whether the gross profit margin is reasonable is an effective way of determining whether all sales have been included in the financial statements. It is probable that purchases of products for sale as recorded in the financial statements will be correct, as the company will record them in the accounting records (as the payments will probably be on credit and the payment will be made from the company's bank account) and it is unlikely that the company will understate this figure (as otherwise the Managing Director or member of staff would have to pay for the items purchased himself/herself). If we have an accurate estimate of the gross profit margin and purchases are accurate, then, allowing for changes in stock, the sales can be estimated. These estimated sales can be compared with sales in the financial statements and the auditor can consider whether the difference is reasonable and thus whether sales in the financial statements are correct.

The gross profit margin can be estimated by:

(i) comparing this year's gross profit margin in the financial statements with last year. This is a weak way of checking the gross profit margin, as the proportion of sales misappropriated each year may be similar, thus giving a similar reduction in overall gross profit margin

(ii) determining the gross profit margin on actual sales and comparing this with the gross profit margin in the financial statements. As auditor, I will obtain the purchase price from purchase invoices and the selling price from the price of the product in the store. Allowance will be made, where appropriate, for the effect of VAT (value added tax) on sales and purchases. A weighted gross profit margin would be calculated using the mix of sales of types of product and their gross profit margins. The mix of sales would be found by checking purchasing records (if the categories of products are separately analysed when processing purchase invoices) or asking the company's staff (when I will consider whether their representations are reliable).

Using this method, it is probable that the gross profit margin I calculate will be higher than the figure in the financial statements. I will consider whether the difference is reasonable. The gross profit margin would be depressed by selling products at a lower than normal price (e.g. in a sale) or where products are returned by customers and later sold at a lower price or scrapped. Wastage of stock (or shrinkage), due to it becoming damaged or stolen by customers will further reduce the gross profit margin

As a further check on completeness of income from sales of high value items, I will select a sample of products (e.g. Sony 60cm television). For each item, I will note the quantity of opening stock and closing stock. From purchase invoices I will find the quantity purchased in the year, and the number sold will be found from sales invoices. From this information it should be possible to determine the number and value of televisions which 'disappeared' in the year. These would be the televisions for which there is no record of the sale. The sales invoices should be checked to the till rolls (and bank records if they are purchased by cheque or credit card) to verify that cash was received and banked for these sales.

Based on this work, I will decide whether the gross profit margin in the financial statements is reasonable and sales income is not materially mis-stated.

(b)   Normally, the Management Representation Letter is drafted by auditors, but it is written on the client's headed notepaper and signed by the directors. Alternatively, the letter may be written by the directors, but contain matters requested by the auditors. As audit evidence, it is written evidence (which is better than verbal evidence) but it is evidence from within the company. This evidence is from the directors, who are 'within the company' and thus it is not as independent a source of evidence as most other evidence obtained by the auditor (e.g. third party evidence and evidence obtained directly by the auditor). In some respects evidence from directors may be less reliable than evidence from the company's employees, as there may be more pressures and motivation for the directors to mislead the auditor (e.g. because they were misappropriating some of the takings). In another respect, statements from the directors may be more reliable than those from employees, as they may have a better understanding of the situation and, in their position as directors, they may better realise the importance of the statements they make to the auditor. The directors should be aware that the Companies Act 1985 s.389A(2) (as amended by the Companies Act 1989 s.120) states that a company director commits an offence if he knowingly or recklessly makes a misleading, false or deceptive statement to the auditor. This should make directors careful of what they say to auditors, particularly when it is in writing.

In some relatively immaterial areas, the auditor may accept the directors' statements without seeking further evidence. However, in most situations the auditor should attempt to find alternative evidence to support (or refute) the directors' representations. Thus, in determining whether all sales income has been recorded in the financial statements, the auditor should obtain other evidence and he would probably be negligent if he relied entirely on the directors' representations. In addition, the auditor must consider whether the directors' representations are consistent with the other information he has obtained. If this evidence is consistent, then the directors' representations will reinforce the evidence obtained by the auditor. However, if the other evidence obtained by the auditor is not consistent with the directors' representations, the auditor should be extremely careful before accepting what the directors say. He should seek further evidence to either refute or confirm the directors' statements. If there is a material difference between the other evidence and the directors' representations, the auditor will probably have to qualify the audit report, or give an unqualified report with an explanatory paragraph which explains the inherent uncertainty.

(c)   Where the directors refuse to sign the Management Representation Letter, I will ask them why they are refusing to do so. I will explain that:

(i)   it is a normal procedure for auditors to draft the Management Representation Letter and ask the directors to sign it

(ii)   my audit opinion will be based mainly on audit work which does not involve representations from directors. However, directors' representations are helpful in providing further evidence that the financial statements are free from material error

(iii)   the Companies Acts require the directors to sign the financial statements. This provides evidence that the directors believe the financial statements are free from material error. Thus, this is little different from the directors signing the Management Representation Letter

If they are still unwilling to sign the Management Representation Letter, I will ask them which paragraphs they are unhappy about. We will discuss the wording of these paragraphs and see if they will sign a letter with alternative wording. However, I will have to ensure the alternative wording provides what I require (i.e. it would probably be unacceptable to remove the paragraph where the directors confirm completeness of income).

If the directors continue to refuse to sign the Management Representation Letter, it makes me suspicious they are hiding something. Thus, I will have to carry out additional audit procedures in the areas where the matters have been excluded from the Management Representation Letter. There is a significant risk that the directors refusing to sign the Management Representation Letter will lead me to having either to qualify my audit report or include an explanatory paragraph in an unqualified audit report which explains an inherent uncertainty (e.g. I am unable to confirm the completeness of sales income).

DECEMBER 1998 QUESTIONS

Section A – ALL THREE questions are compulsory and MUST be attempted

75   (Question 1 of examination)

Your firm is responsible for auditing the financial statements of Hucknall Manufacturing Limited for the year ended 30 November 1998. The company operates from a single site. Its turnover is £5 million and the profit before tax is £110,000. There are no stock records so the stock counts at the year end will be used to value the stock in the financial statements. As Monday 30 November is a normal working day, it has been decided that the stocktake should take place on Sunday 29 November when there is no movement of stock.

The company has produced the following schedule to determine the value of stock at 30 November 1998 from that counted on 29 November 1998:

	£	£
Value of stock at 29.11.98		583,247
Add: Cost of goods received on 30.11.98	10,969	
production labour on 30.11.98	3,260	
overheads relating to labour at 120%	3,912	18,141
Less: cost of goods sold on 30.11.98		(36,740)
Value of stock at 30.11.98		564,648

The company keeps basic accounting records on a microcomputer using a standard software package. The accounting procedures for sales, purchases and wages comprise:

(a) dispatch notes are raised by the dispatch department when the goods are sent to customers. Sales invoices are produced from the dispatch notes. Sales invoices are input into the computer which posts them to the sales ledger and the nominal ledger

(b) when goods are received, a goods received note (GRN) is prepared. Purchase invoices are matched with the GRNs and purchase orders and authorised by the managing director. After the purchase invoices have been authorised, they are input into the computer which posts them to the purchase ledger and the nominal ledger

(c) for the wages system, the hours worked for each employee are input into the computer, which calculates the gross wage and deductions (e.g. for tax, national insurance etc.) and the net pay. All employees are paid weekly.

In part (b) of the question, you are required only to verify the *total value* of stock of £564,648 at 30 November 1998. You are not required to describe the procedures necessary to verify the accuracy of the individual values of raw materials, work in progress and finished goods, as required by SSAP 9 (Stocks and Long-term Contracts).

You are required to describe:

(a)   the audit procedures you should perform to verify the accuracy of the stock count:

   (i) before the stocktake, and

   (ii) on the day of the stocktake.

   (iii) Your answers to parts (i) and (ii) above should include details of the matters you should record in your working papers for follow-up at the final audit   **(11 marks)**

(b)   the substantive procedures you should perform to check the company's schedule, as shown above, which adjusts the value of stock at 29 November to that at the company's year end of 30 November 1998
                                                                                                      (6 marks)

(c)   the substantive procedures you should perform to check purchases cut-off at the year end.   **(3 marks)**
                                                                                          (Total: 20 marks)

---

76   (Question 2 of examination)

Your firm is the external auditor of Southwood Trading Limited, and you are auditing the financial statements for the year ended 30 November 1998. Southwood Trading has a turnover of £11 million and trade debtors at 30 November 1998 were £2·1 million.

The engagement partner has asked you to consider the relative reliability and independence of evidence from third parties and certain matters relating to a debtors' circularisation.

In relation to part (b)(ii) of the question the partner has explained that judgement would be used to select debtors which appear to be doubtful and those which would not be selected using the monetary unit sampling technique described in part (b)(i).

You are required to:

(a)   consider the relative reliability and independence of the following types of evidence from third parties:

   (i)   replies to a debtors' circularisation to confirm trade debtors

   (ii)   suppliers' statements to confirm purchase ledger balances   **(6 marks)**

(b)   in relation to selecting debtors for circularisation:

   (i)   explain how you would use monetary unit sampling to select the debtors to circularise

   (ii)   consider the criteria you would use to select individual debtors for circularisation using judgement

   (iii)   discuss the advantages and disadvantages of using monetary unit sampling (in (i) above) as compared with judgement (in (ii) above) to select the debtors to circularise. Your answer should consider the reasons why it is undesirable only to use judgement to select the debtors for circularisation   **(8 marks)**

(c)   describe the audit work you would carry out in following up the responses to a debtors' circularisation where:

   (i)   the debtor disagrees the balance and provides a different balance

   (ii)   no reply to the circularisation has been received from the debtor and all attempts at obtaining a reply have failed.   **(6 marks)**

                                (Total: 20 marks)

---

77   (Question 3 of examination)

Your firm is the external auditor of Bestwood Engineering Ltd which manufactures components for motor vehicles and sells them to motor vehicle manufacturers and wholesalers. It has a turnover of £10 million and a profit before tax of £400,000.

The company has a new financial director who has asked your advice on controls in the company's purchases system.

Bestwood Engineering has separate accounts, purchasing and goods received departments. Most purchases are required by the production department, but other departments are able to raise requisitions for goods and services. The purchasing department is responsible for obtaining goods and services for the company at the lowest price which is consistent with the required delivery date and quality, and for ensuring their prompt delivery.

The accounts department is responsible for obtaining authorisation of purchase invoices before they are input into the computer which posts them to the purchase ledger and the nominal ledger. The accounting records are kept on a microcomputer and the standard accounting software was obtained from an independent supplier. The accounting software maintains the purchase ledger, sales ledger, nominal ledger and payroll.

The company does not maintain stock records, as it believes the costs of maintaining these records outweigh the benefits.

The financial director has explained that services include gas, electricity, telephone, repairs and short-term hire of equipment and vehicles.

You are required to:

(a) describe the procedures which should be in operation in the purchasing department to control the purchase and receipt of goods   **(8 marks)**

(b) describe the controls the accounts department should exercise over obtaining authorisation of purchase invoices before posting them to the purchase ledger   **(6 marks)**

(c) explain how controls over the purchase of services, from raising the purchase requisition to posting the invoice to the purchase ledger, might differ from the procedures for the purchase of goods, as described in your answers to parts (a) and (b) above.   **(6 marks)**
                                                                                                      (Total: 20 marks)

Section B – TWO questions ONLY to be attempted

78   (Question 4 of examination)

Your firm is the external auditor of Eastfield Distributors plc, which has a turnover of £25 million and a profit before tax of £1.7 million. The company operates from a head office at Eastfield and has sales and stock holding centres in different parts of the country. The directors have decided the company has reached a size when it needs an internal audit department. As is becoming increasingly common, the directors have asked your firm to provide this service to the company as well as being the statutory auditor of the company's annual financial statements.

In answering the question, you should consider:

(i) the effects of the Association of Chartered Certified Accountants' Rules of Professional Conduct in relation to providing an internal audit service to Eastfield Distributors

(ii) the extent to which your audit firm can rely on the internal audit work when carrying out the statutory audit of Eastfield Distributors

(iii) the arrangements over control of the work and reporting of the internal audit staff:

–   the extent to which the internal audit staff should be responsible to Eastfield Distributors, and who should control their work

–   the extent to which the internal audit staff should be responsible to a manager or partner of the external audit firm, and whether the same manager and partner should be responsible for both the internal audit staff of Eastfield Distributors and the external audit.

You are required, in relation to your audit firm becoming internal auditors of Eastfield Distributors, to:

(a) describe the matters you should consider and the action you will take to ensure your firm remains independent as external auditor of the annual financial statements   **(8 marks)**

(b) describe the advantages and disadvantages to Eastfield Distributors of your firm providing an internal audit service   **(7 marks)**

(c) describe the advantages and disadvantages to your audit firm of providing an internal audit service to Eastfield Distributors   **(5 marks)**
                                                                                                      (Total: 20 marks)

79   (Question 5 of examination)

Your firm has been the auditor of Bridgford Products plc for a number of years. The engagement partner has asked you to describe the matters you would consider when planning the audit for the year ended 31 January 1999.

During a recent visit to the company you obtained the following information:

(i)   the management accounts for the 10 months to 30 November 1998 show a turnover of £130 million and profit before tax of £4 million. Assume sales and profits accrue evenly throughout the year. In the year ended 31 January 1998 Bridgford Products had a turnover of £110 million and a profit before tax of £8 million

(ii)   the company installed a new computerised stock control system which has operated from 1 June 1998. As the stock control system records stock movements and current stock quantities, the company is proposing:

  – to use the stock quantities on the computer to value the stock at the year end, and

  – not to carry out a stocktake at the year end

(iii)   you are aware there have been reliability problems with the company's products, which have resulted in legal claims being brought against the company by customers, and customers refusing to pay for the products

(iv)   the sales increase in the 10 months to 30 November 1998 over the previous year has been achieved by attracting new customers and by offering extended credit. The new credit arrangements allow customers three months credit before their debt becomes overdue, rather than the one month credit period allowed previously. As a result of this change, debtors age has increased from 1·6 to 4·1 months

(v)   the financial director and purchasing manager were dismissed on 15 August. A replacement purchasing manager has been appointed but it is not expected that a new financial director will be appointed before the year end of 31 January 1999. The chief accountant will be responsible for preparing the financial statements for audit.

You are required to:

(a)   describe the reasons why it is important that auditors should plan their audit work   **(5 marks)**

(b)   describe the matters you will consider in planning the audit and the further action you will take concerning the matters listed in (i) to (v) above.   **(15 marks)**
(Total: 20 marks)

80   (Question 6 of examination)

Your firm is the external auditor of Langar Computers Ltd and you are auditing the financial statements for the year ended 31 October 1998. The engagement partner is concerned that Langar Computers may not be a going concern. The company develops and sells computer equipment. In the past year it has been developing an 'archiving system', which uses a computer, a scanner with an automatic document feed to read the documents, and an optical CD (compact disk) writer to store the images. Software has been developed to enable the user to index the documents being stored and retrieve them.

The summarised draft financial statements for the year ended 31 October 1998 are shown opposite:

Profit and Loss Account
Year ended 31.10.1998

	£'000
Sales	8,524
Cost of sales	(6,774)
Gross profit	1,750
Other operating costs	(2,012)
Interest	(414)
Loss before tax and retained Loss	(676)
Retained profit b/fwd	516
Retained loss c/fwd	(160)

Balance Sheet
at 31.10.1998

	£'000
Fixed assets	
Tangible fixed assets	2,396
Capitalised development expenditure	3,172
	5,568
Current assets	
Stock	2,004
Debtors	1,847
	3,851
Creditors: amount falling due within one year	
Trade creditors and accruals	3,443
Bank overdraft	2,136
	5,579
Net current assets/(liabilities)	(1,728)
Total assets less current liabilities	3,840
Long-term bank loan	(2,000)
	1,840

	£'000
Capital and reserves	
Ordinary shares of £1 each	2,000
Reserves	(160)
	1,840

Ratios - year ended 31 October 1998	
Gross profit %	20·5%
Net profit %	− 7·9%
Interest cover	− 0·63
Stock age (months)	3·55
Debtors age (months)	2·60
Creditors age (months)	6·10
Current ratio	0·69
Acid test ratio	0·33
Gearing (including bank overdraft)	2·25

Debtors age is based on sales, and creditors and stock age are based on cost of sales. Gearing is the ratio of loan capital (including bank overdraft) to equity.

You have discussed the company's financial position with the financial director who says the company's future existence depends on the successful development and sales of the archiving system. Development of the archiving system commenced in January 1998, and £2·5 million has been spent on its development, which has been included as an intangible asset of development expenditure. The remaining development expenditure relates to older projects. The company estimates it will require an additional £300,000 in the year to 31 October 1999 to complete development of the archiving system. Development expenditure is amortised at an annual rate of 10% on cost, starting from the date of commencement of sales of the product. A number of potential customers have been using the development system and sales are expected to commence in January 1999. Because of the rapid change in technology in the computer industry, sales of the company's other products are declining. The current bank overdraft limit is £1·9 million. It is due for renewal on 15 January 1999.

You have ascertained that for the year ended 31 October 1997 sales were £10·2 million and the profit before taxation was £110,000. At 31 October 1997 the long-term loan was £2 million and the bank overdraft was £573,000.

Assume the financial statements for the year ended 31 October 1998 are correct, except for the capitalised development expenditure. The company has debited all development expenditure on the archiving system to capitalised development expenditure in the balance sheet, but this asset may be worth less than that shown in the draft balance sheet.

The engagement partner has pointed out that the principal criteria of SSAP 13 (Accounting for Research and Development) must be satisfied for Langar Computers to continue as a going concern. The principal criteria of SSAP 13 are:

(i)   the development project must be technically feasible

(ii) the project must be commercially successful, in that future revenues must be sufficient to recover future costs and amortisation of the capitalised development expenditure.

You are required, for Langar Computers Limited:

(a)   to describe the factors which indicate the company may not be a going concern   **(9 marks)**

(b)   in relation to your audit of the capitalised development expenditure of the archiving system, to describe the work you will carry out to determine whether:

(i)   development of the archiving system will be technically successful   **(5 marks)**

(ii) future revenues from sales of the system will be sufficient to recover costs and amortisation of the capitalised development expenditure.   **(6 marks)**

(Total: 20 marks)

Note: In answering the question, you should use the financial information provided, including the ratios.

End of Question Paper

DECEMBER 1998 ANSWERS

The model answers to the questions are longer and frequently more detailed than would be expected from a candidate in the examinations. However, the model answer may not include all valid points mentioned by candidates - credit will be given to candidates mentioning these points.

The model answers may be used as a guide to the form and standard of answer candidates should try to achieve. However, the answers may not be as detailed as one would find in text books on the subject.

75   (Answer 1 of examination)

(a) (i) Prior to the stocktake, I will confirm with the company's management that the stocktake will take place on 29 November. I will ask for details of the stocktake and the stocktaking instructions.

I will look through the stocktaking instructions and consider whether they are suitable for instructing staff on how the stocktaking should take place. I will inform the company of any weaknesses and, if required, ask them to make some amendments to the instructions. These instructions should be given to staff taking part in the count a few days before the stocktake. This will allow them time to read the instructions. The instructions should ensure that the stock is easy to count, so:

- the stock counting areas should be tidy
- identical items should be kept in one place, and, if possible, arranged so that they are easy to count
- where the stock is difficult to identify, a note giving its description and part number should be included
- stock which may be worth less than cost should be identified.

In addition to the instructions, the company should provide me with details of the staff involved in performing the count. Ideally, staff counting the stock should not be those who are responsible for custody of the stock, but they should be competent to identify the stock (and its state of completion if it is in work in progress). However, storekeepers often count the stock for which they are responsible. To overcome such a weakness in internal control, there should be adequate checks of the stock counts by independent persons (e.g. the company's management). Management should supervise the count and ensure procedures are carried out correctly.

If a significant value of stock is held by a third party, I will probably have to attend a stocktake at the third party's premises. Otherwise, it is probably acceptable to obtain written confirmation from the third party of the quantities held at the year end.

If the company holds stock on behalf of third parties, I will ask for it to be segregated from the stock the company owns. This stock should be counted at the year end, but its value should not be included in the value of the year-end stock in the financial statements.

(ii) At the start of the count, all staff taking part should be brought together and given verbal instructions of how the count should be undertaken, who is counting the stock and who is supervising the count. Staff should be allocated appropriate parts of the factory to count the stock. This is best done either by having a list of areas which each team should count, or a map of the factory with the names of staff who should count stock in each area.

Stock sheets should be sequentially numbered and the stock sheet numbers which have been issued to each counting team should be recorded.

At the stocktake, I will check the following procedures are being carried out:

- ideally the staff counting the stock should not be those who are responsible for the stock, as this would be a weakness in the system of internal control (i.e. they would be responsible for the custody of the stock and for recording the stock quantities).
- staff should count the stock in pairs with one member counting the stock and the other recording it. Stock should be marked when counted (e.g. with a chalk cross). The details on the stock sheet should record the part number, the description and the quantity. This should be recorded in ball point pen and any amendments should be initialled by the counters and the manager of the count. If there are problems in obtaining the part number or description, this may be

recorded on the products prior to the count, or obtained from an employee who is responsible for the product. For work in progress, it is important to record its state of completion. If stock is likely to be worth less than cost, the stocktakers should record details of the state of the stock (e.g. if it is damaged or slow moving)

- the stock should be counted systematically (e.g. from left to right along shelves) and the stock counters should ensure that all stock in their area has been counted by the end of the stocktake
- the stock sheets should be initialled by the staff performing the count, and ruled off after the last item if the stock sheet is not full (to prevent any items being added)
- management should perform test counts to check the work of the stock counters. If any differences are found, the stock should be re-counted and the agreed quantity included on the stock sheets. Details of the management's counts should be recorded.

During the stocktake, I will observe the stocktake and check the procedures as described above have been carried out, and I will record any situations when correct procedures are not being carried out. In addition, I will perform test counts, both from the stock sheets to the physical stock and from the physical stock to the stock sheets. Counting stock from the stock sheets to the physical stock checks that stock on the stock sheets exists and is counted correctly. Checking from the physical stock to the stock sheets verifies that stock which exists is correctly recorded on the stock sheets. If any significant differences are found between my counts and those of the company's staff, I will ask the stock counters to re-count the stock and the agreed quantity will be recorded on the stock sheets and in my audit working papers. I will note in my working papers the stock sheet numbers of the items I counted and include a mark on the stock sheets so that they can be found when checking the valuation of the stock at the final audit. I will contact the company's management at the stocktake if I find a significant number of errors in counting the stock

At the end of the stocktake, the company should:

- ensure all the stock sheets have been returned, by putting them in sequential number order and noting any that are missing. Stock sheets which have been issued to stock counters but not used should be recorded. All stock sheets should be retained at the end of the count (even those which are unused). I will obtain a copy of the stock sheets, which should ensure they are not amended after the stocktake (I will be able to use these copies to detect if it is happening). At the final audit I will check that only the stock sheets used in the stock count are used to value the stock
- check that all stock has been counted. Items of stock can be selected and counters asked who counted the stock and show on the stock sheets where they are recorded. The stock should have a mark to indicate it has been counted.
- I will record cut-off details. These will be the last dispatch note number, the last goods received note number, the last return to suppliers and the last return by customers. If they are available, I will record internal movements of stock, such as issues from the raw materials store to production and transfers from production into the finished goods store.

The answer to part (iii) is incorporated in the answers to parts (i) and (ii) above.

(b) I will carry out the following work to check the company's schedule which calculates the value of stock at 30 November 1998 from that determined at the stocktake on 29 November 1998:

(i) firstly, I will consider the materiality of the adjustments. The total adjustment is £18,599, which is about 17% of profit before tax. Thus, the adjustment is material, so the schedule should be audited. The adjustment is not large, so small errors may be allowed. It may be necessary to audit the adjustment, even if it was less than 10% of profit before tax, as the potential error could be material

(ii) the value of stock at 29 November 1998 will be checked to the value I have audited and the total value of the stock at 29 November per the stock valuation sheets

(iii) to check the cost of goods received on 30 November, I will:

- list details of the goods received from goods received notes on 30 November
- follow through from the goods received notes to the purchase invoices and list the value of those purchase invoices (before VAT)
- check the total value of the purchase invoices is £10,969

Alternatively, if the company has produced a schedule of goods received on 30 November, I will:

- check all goods received on 30 November are included on the schedule, and
- obtain a sample of invoices for the goods received and test check their value to the value of the invoices on the schedule

(iv) the production labour cost will be found from the print-out from the computerised payroll. I will ask the company the employees who comprise production labour, and I will consider whether these are the employees whose labour cost should be included in the value of stock. If the employees work five days a week, the production labour cost will be checked as being 20% of the labour cost of production employees in the week ending 4 December 1998

(v)   the overheads included in stock should be production overheads. I will check that the overhead rate of 120% is the same as that used to value the year-end stock. I will have checked the overhead rate when auditing the value of stock at the year end. I will carry out further investigations if the overhead rate in the schedule is different from that used to value the year-end stock. The overhead rate will be determined from either the costing records (if they exist) or the financial accounting records

(vi) sales on 30 November will be found from sales invoices or the computerised sales day book which lists invoices raised on 30 November. The sales invoices will be test checked to the dispatch notes to ensure they relate to goods dispatched on 30 November. I will check the adjustment equals sales on 30 November less the gross profit margin in the financial statements. Cost of sales in the financial statements will be checked as comprising the cost of raw materials, production labour and production overheads. If the difference between my calculated figure and that on the schedule is material, I will ask the company how it has calculated the figure, and I will consider whether their figure is correct

(vii) the additions of the schedule will be checked (those in the question are correct)

This schedule assumes that in relation to the £18,141 added to the value of stock (i.e. the cost of goods received, production labour and overheads) there is no wastage or inefficiency on 30 November 1998. The value of this wastage will probably be immaterial. However, I will check whether it is material by asking the company's staff, including the financial director, managing director and production manager and looking at any management accounting records (if they are available).

(c)   To check purchases cut-off at 30 November, I will check the numerical sequence of goods received notes before and after the year end. Ideally, the goods received notes should indicate whether they have been checked to purchase invoices. I will record any goods received before the year end which have not been checked to purchase invoices as they are likely to be purchases cut-off errors.

I will select a sample of goods received notes (GRNs) from before and after the year end. This will cover a period of about two weeks before to two weeks after the year end, and I will try to select larger value goods received. The last goods received note number for goods received before the year end will be recorded in my audit working papers when I attended the stocktake.

For goods received before the year end, I will trace the goods received note to the purchase invoice, and check the purchase invoice is either posted to the purchase ledger before the year end or included in purchase accruals at the year end.

For goods received after the year end, I will trace the goods received note to the purchase invoice, and check the purchase invoice is neither posted to the purchase ledger before the year end nor included in purchase accruals at the year end.

I will note details of any purchases cut-off errors I find, and I will increase the sample of items I check if I find a significant number of errors.

Checking suppliers' statements to the purchase ledger is an effective way of checking purchases cut-off. As part of my audit of creditors due within a year, I will check purchase accruals at the year end, which should be for goods received before the year end where the purchase invoices have not been posted to the purchase ledger before the year end.

76   (Answer 2 of examination)

(a) (i)   The replies to a debtors' circularisation should be independent of the company, as the auditor should send the circularisation letter direct to the debtors and the reply from the debtor should be returned to the auditor's office (i.e. not the client's premises). In terms of reliability, the replies to a debtors' circularisation are probably less reliable than checking purchase ledger balances to suppliers' statements. First, many debtors never reply to a circularisation, so this limits the value of this type of evidence. Secondly, in replying to the circularisation, debtors are looking at their purchase ledger. In most companies purchase ledgers tend to be less reliable than sales ledgers. Sales ledgers are more accurate, as the transactions of dispatch of goods and raising the sales invoice are under the control of the company, and sales ledgers need to be accurate in order to receive cash from sales promptly (to minimise cash flow problems). Purchase ledgers tend to be less accurate as the goods may be received at a different time from the purchase invoice (which is received through the post). Frequently, there are delays in processing the purchase invoice before it is posted to the purchase ledger. These create timing, and thus cut-off, errors which reduce the accuracy of the purchase ledger.

It should be noted that sales ledgers tend to overstate the amount owing by customers because of bad debts and disputes. Purchase ledgers tend to understate the amount owing to suppliers because of invoices which are not posted to the purchase ledger and invoices in dispute (commonly, these are not posted to the purchase ledger until the dispute is settled).

A debtors' circularisation does provide important evidence confirming the existence of debtors and that they are customers of the company. Verifying the existence of debtors from evidence obtained entirely within the company is less reliable than obtaining this information from replies to a debtors' circularisation.

A limitation of a debtors' circularisation is that although the debtor is agreeing or disagreeing the balance, it does not confirm the debtor is able to repay the balance on the sales ledger. However, in most situations when the debtor is unable to repay the balance on the sales ledger he/she will not reply to the circularisation. Thus, a balance which the debtor agrees is probably recoverable.

(ii) Suppliers' statements tend to be good evidence confirming the balance on the client's purchase ledger. The supplier's statement will be a copy of their sales ledger. As explained above, sales ledgers tend to be more reliable than purchase ledgers, so if there is a difference, it is more likely that the balance on the client's purchase ledger will be wrong than that on the supplier's statement, so suppliers' statements are good audit evidence. The main problems with suppliers' statements are:

- the supplier's statement has been received by the client (and not directly by the auditor) so there is the risk that it may be fraudulently amended, created or destroyed by the client. The auditor should inspect the statements and consider whether they have been issued by the supplier. If statements are photocopies or faxed documents, there is a greater risk that they have been amended by the client company.
- there may be no suppliers' statements for some of the purchase ledger balances. There is the risk the client may have withheld a supplier's statement for a material balance, because there is a large difference between the company's purchase ledger balance and that on the supplier's sales ledger. The auditor should obtain positive confirmation of the purchase ledger balances for all major suppliers or those with large balances on the purchase ledger. Where there is no supplier's statement, confirmation can be obtained either by:
  - contacting the supplier and asking for the balance to be confirmed, or
  - asking the supplier to send a statement direct to the auditor's office, or
  - circularising the supplier.

The auditor should reconcile suppliers' statements with the purchase ledger balances and determine whether the difference is reasonable. Suppliers' statements are effective at highlighting purchases cut-off errors and late dispatch of cheques to suppliers.

(b) (i) The most appropriate method to use for selecting debtors to circularise is monetary unit sampling (SAS 430 para 10). With this method, the sampling unit is £1, rather than individual debtors, so the probability of a debtor being selected is proportional to its value. If 50 debtors are to be circularised using this method, then with total debtors of £2·1 million, one debtor will be selected for every £42,000 value on the sales ledger. Using interval sampling (SAS 430 para 22 calls this 'systematic selection'), a random number will be found between 0 and 42,000, say £15,923. The debtors list will be obtained and the starting and ending cumulative total found for each debtor. The debtor balances which straddle £15,923, £57,923 (i.e. £15,923 + £42,000) and so on will be those which are circularised. This is shown in the following example:

Customer	Balance (£)	Cumulative opening balance (£)	Cumulative closing balance (£)	Select?
AB & Co	5,217	0	5,217	No
AD & Co	14,569	5,217	19,786	Yes
AF & Co	16,380	19,786	36,166	No
BB & Co	23,514	36,166	59,680	Yes

Customer AD & Co is selected because its balance straddles £15,923 (its balance lies from £5,217 to £19,786). Customer BB & Co is selected because its balance straddles £57,923 (its balance lies from £36,166 to £59,680).

A computer audit program could be used to select debtors using this technique.

A technique of selecting debtors entirely randomly (i.e. each debtor has an equal chance of being selected) would not be appropriate, as the auditor is concerned with the recoverability of debtors and larger value debtors have a higher risk of being materially mis-stated than small value debtors.

(ii) The debtors I would select using judgement would be those which have a high risk of being doubtful and those which would not be selected using the monetary unit sampling method described in part (b)(i) above.

The doubtful balances would be those where:

- the age of the debt is high. Usually, a slow paying debtor is one which is having liquidity problems and there is a high risk of the debtor failing
- there are old unpaid invoices on the sales ledger. There is a high risk of there being a problem with these items. Frequently, the items are in dispute, so the full amount of the debt will not be recovered
- the debtor is over the credit limit. It is important that credit limits are kept up to date. If credit limits are not being kept up to date, there may be increased sales to a customer which puts it over the credit limit, yet the customer is paying the debt within the agreed credit period
- any debtors which the credit controller and further investigations suggest may be doubtful. These debtors will be identified by inspecting correspondence with the debtors and reports from credit reference companies
- if considered desirable, a sample may be taken of high value debtors on the sales ledger which are not selected in part (b)(i) above. Generally, the higher the value of the debt, the greater is the risk of a material misstatement in its balance.

The debtors selected above would be biased towards those which have the highest risk of misstatement in terms of monetary value. Thus, a debtor with an invoice of £10,000 which is six months old at 30 November 1998 would have a higher chance of being selected than one where the invoice is £100.

The monetary unit sampling technique described in part (b)(i) above would not select debtors with zero or credit balances (i.e. where the company owes money to the debtor). A sample of these debtors will be selected using judgement.

The number of debtors selected using judgement will depend on two factors. If a large sample of debtors is circularised using monetary unit sampling techniques, then the auditor will probably select fewer debtors to circularise using judgement. The auditor will select a larger sample of debtors where he/she assesses the recoverability of debts on the sales ledger is poor.

(iii) Using the monetary unit sampling technique to select debtors to circularise provides a random and unbiased sample. Thus, it should be good at providing evidence of the quality (in terms of recoverability) of debtor balances on the sales ledger. The monetary unit sampling method of selecting debtors to circularise is given in part (b)(i) of this answer. Using the monetary unit sampling method to select debtors allows statistical techniques to be used to provide a conclusion on the recoverability of debtors on the sales ledger. This fits in well with a risk based approach to auditing. The problem of using the monetary unit sampling technique to select debtors is that it takes longer to select the sample than using judgement.

The argument against using judgement for selecting debtors is that the sample selected is likely to be biased (and non-random). The sample can be biased in a number of ways. If the auditor selects a high proportion of doubtful balances, as suggested in part (b)(ii) above, this creates the weakness that it may give the auditor the impression that a large proportion of the balances on the sales ledger are doubtful, which is probably not the case for a majority of debtors. Alternatively, if the auditor wants to select debtors who agree the balance (i.e. those within the credit limit) he/she would come to the conclusion that the recoverability of the debts on the sales ledger is better than is actually the case. A further weakness of using judgement in selecting debtors is that statistical techniques cannot be used to estimate the recoverability of debtors on the sales ledger. Using judgement to select the debtors to circularise does allow the auditor to direct his/her attention to doubtful balances, which are of high risk to the auditor. Also, selecting debtors using this method should be less time consuming than using the monetary unit sampling method described in part (b)(i) above.

It is undesirable only to use judgement to select the debtors, as the auditor cannot argue that the sample is entirely unbiased (i.e. entirely random), and this could create problems if the auditor was being sued for negligence. In practice, it is probably best to select debtors using both monetary unit sampling and using judgement. The monetary unit sample will provide evidence of the quality of debtors on the sales ledger, and the judgement sample will provide further evidence on sales ledger balances which appear to be doubtful. The number of debtors selected using judgement will depend on the auditor's perceived assessment of the recoverability of debtors on the sales ledger.

(c)   When I receive the reply to the debtors' circularisation, I will check the postmark on the envelope is consistent with the customer's address. Then I will carry out the following audit work on the replies (and non-replies):

(i)   where the debtor disagrees the balance and provides another (agreed) balance, it is probable the difference will be due to 'goods in transit' and/or 'cash in transit'.

Goods in transit (more correctly 'invoices in transit') are invoices on the client's sales ledger which are not on the customer's purchase ledger. If these items are near the year end, it is probable the difference is due to delays in the customer processing the purchase invoices and posting them to the purchase ledger. I will confirm the goods were sent to the customer before the year end by checking the date of the dispatch note. Further confirmation of the date of dispatch can be obtained from invoices from the carrier taking the goods to the customer and the date the customer confirms receipt of the goods. If the invoices are more than two weeks before the year end, they are likely to be in dispute. I will ask the credit controller about them and decide whether there is a risk that the full amount of the invoice is not recoverable. I may contact the debtor to ask about the invoices. Based on these investigations, I will decide whether the amounts due from the 'invoices in transit' are recoverable, or whether a provision should be included against them.

Cash in transit is cheques on the customer's purchase ledger which are not on the client's sales ledger. I will check the cheque was credited to the client's sales ledger shortly after the year end. If there is a significant delay in the cheque appearing on the client's sales ledger, I will see if a similar situation is occurring with other customers. If it is, there is a risk of a teeming and lading fraud. So, I will check that cheques received today are banked promptly (i.e. either today or tomorrow). If there is a significant delay in banking cheques, I will check the unbanked cheques exist, and if they do not exist, a teeming and lading fraud is probably taking place.

There could be other differences between the sales ledger balance and the customer's purchase ledger balance. If these differences are small, I may ignore them (although I must be careful that the small difference is not as a result of two large differences which almost cancel each other). If the difference is significant, I will discuss them with the credit controller and probably contact the customer. A provision would have to be made against these items if I believe the amount is not recoverable.

(ii)   Where the debtor does not reply to the circularisation, the existence of the debtor has not been confirmed. To obtain evidence of the existence of the debtor, I can:

– telephone the debtor and ask about the debt. I must be careful that my call cannot be intercepted by the company. This can be minimised either by direct dialling the debtor through the company's telephone system, or using a mobile phone
– inspect copies of correspondence from the debtor, including orders, remittances, cheques from the customer and headed notepaper. These documents should be originals and the name and address of the customer on these documents should be the same as that on the client's sales ledger
– check the existence of the customer in telephone directories and trade directories. The weakness of this approach is that although it provides good evidence of the existence of the debtor, it is weak at providing evidence the debtor is a customer of the client company.

Once the existence of the debtor has been confirmed, the recoverability of the debt on the sales ledger will be determined. Firstly, I will check the ageing of the debt. If it is within the credit limit and is being paid within the company's credit terms, then the debt is probably recoverable. I will check cash received since the year end which clears some of the pre year-end sales invoices. Any invoices for which cash is received after the year end can be considered to be good. However, if at the time of my audit investigation there are old outstanding pre year-end items or the age of the debt is high, some of the balance may not be recoverable. So, I will discuss the uncleared items with the credit controller. I will consider the information I receive from the credit controller and other evidence I have obtained and decide whether all or only some of the debt may be irrecoverable. If I believe the debt is wholly or partly irrecoverable, and the company believes it is fully recoverable, I will include details in my summary of unadjusted errors.

---

77 (Answer 3 of examination)

(a) The controls the purchasing department should exercise over ordering and control over receipt of goods and services should include:

(i) for all goods ordered, there should be a purchase requisition from a user department. The purchasing department should not be permitted to raise purchase requisitions, as this would create a weakness in the division of duties. For goods required by the purchasing department, they should request another department (e.g. the accounts department) to raise a purchase requisition. Before raising the purchase requisition, the accounts department should ensure it is for goods the purchasing department require and are authorised to order

(ii) the purchasing department should check the purchase requisition is for goods the user department is authorised to buy or consume. If the value of the order is substantial, the purchasing department should ensure there is a need for such a large order, by checking current stock levels and future orders to determine whether so large a quantity or value is required

(iii) the purchase requisition should use a standard form and be signed by an authorised signatory

(iv) the purchasing department should order the goods from an authorised supplier. Where there is a choice of supplier, or a new supplier is required, the purchasing department should obtain the product from the supplier who provides the product or service at the best price, quality and delivery. For audit purposes, it is desirable for staff in the purchasing department to record details of the suppliers contacted, the price, delivery date and perceived quality, and the decision on which supplier was finally chosen

(v) the purchasing department should raise the purchase order, which should be signed by the purchasing manager. For large value purchases, a director may be required to sign the purchase order. The purchase order should be sent to the supplier, the goods received department, the user department and the accounts department

(vi) the purchasing department should ensure the goods are received on time. This may require them to contact the supplier a week before the expected delivery date to ensure they are received on time, and allow action to be taken if the delivery date is later than specified on the purchase order

(vii) when the goods are received, the purchasing department should receive a copy of the goods received note (GRN) from the goods received department. They should record the goods received against the order. From this information, they will be able to take action when there are short deliveries or the goods are received late. Frequently, purchasing departments file purchase orders in three types of file:

   – where none of the goods have been received
   – where some of the goods ordered have been received
   – where all the goods ordered have been received (i.e. 'dead' purchase orders)

(viii) the purchasing department may be part of the system which authorises purchase invoices. They should check the goods on the invoice are consistent with the purchase order and the price per unit is correct

(ix) the purchasing department should be informed about short deliveries (i.e. the quantity of goods received is less than on the purchase order or advice note) and when there are quality problems. From this information, they can contact the supplier so that corrective action is taken. Also, such details may be helpful in determining whether the supplier should be used for future orders

(x) the purchasing department should be informed of situations when goods or services are received but no purchase order has been raised. With this information, the purchasing department should contact the 'offending' department and ensure that in future a purchase order is raised for all the goods they order. The supplier should be contacted and informed that an authorised purchase order must be received by them (the supplier) before any goods or services are provided by the supplier.

(b) The procedures the accounts department should undertake before the purchase invoice is input into the computer and posted to the purchase ledger and nominal ledger should include:

(i)   the accounts department will receive the purchase invoice, which they should record in a register

(ii) the invoice expense will be included on the invoice (for posting to the nominal ledger). The expense analysis will be checked by an independent department (e.g. the purchasing or user department)

(iii) the accounts department will either match the purchase invoice to the goods received note and delivery note, or ask the goods received department to check and authorise the purchase invoice

(iv) the purchasing department will be asked to confirm the goods are as described on the purchase order and the price per unit is correct

(v)   the user department may be asked to authorise the purchase invoice

(vi) an appropriate responsible official will be asked to authorise the purchase invoice

(vii) provided these checks are satisfactory, the accounts department should input the invoice details into the computer which will post it to the purchase ledger and the nominal ledger.

Where there is a problem with the invoice (e.g. concerning the quantity, quality or price of the goods received) the accounts department should put the invoice in a 'hold' file. They should contact the supplier (sometimes with the help of the purchasing or user department) and try to resolve the problem. When either a credit note is received or the correct quantity and quality of goods have been received, the accounts department will get authorisation (e.g. from the purchasing department) that the situation is resolved and they should input the purchase invoice into the computer (and credit note if this is required).

Periodically, an independent person should check suppliers' statements against the balances on the purchase ledger. Differences between these two balances should be recorded. If the transaction which created the difference is close to the date of the check, it is probable that no action will be taken. However, older items should be investigated to ensure that action is being taken to resolve the problem.

(c) Frequently, procedures over receiving services are less strong and less effective than those over receiving goods.

For some types of service, such as receipt of electricity, gas, water and telephone charges there may be no system for raising purchase orders. However, there should be a system for reviewing these costs, by comparing them with the previous year (or period), with budget and with amounts charged by alternative suppliers. In this way, the company can ensure these services are received at the most economical cost. For some of these services it may be possible to suggest ways in which these costs can be reduced (e.g. by turning off lights and reducing the temperature settings in winter). Costs of gas, electricity and water can be monitored by checking the meter readings monthly and determining whether the consumption is reasonable. For telephone expenses, the system should provide information on the cost for each department, and each department manager should review his/her department's costs. A risk with telephone systems is that they can be abused by staff, who make personal telephone calls using the company's telephone system. The department managers should be made responsible for checking this abuse is kept to a minimum.

For receipt of all other services, before the service is obtained, a purchase requisition should be raised by the user department, and the purchasing department should raise a purchase order. In emergency situations, it may be acceptable to raise a purchase requisition and order after the service has been received (e.g. the repair of a vehicle which has broken down). There should be a system whereby action is taken when no purchase order has been raised for a service which has been received. In many situations when a service has been received, it is probably appropriate that the department receiving the service should issue a goods received note and send it to the purchases accounts and the purchasing departments. In this way, the same system can be used for processing receipt of services as for receipt of goods.

78   (Answer 4 of examination)

(a) The matters I will consider and the action I will take to ensure the provision of an internal audit service does not conflict with my duties and the independence requirements of my firm being external auditor to the company include:

(i)   it appears that Eastfield Distributors is not a listed company, so my fees from the external audit, the internal audit and other work I perform for Eastfield Distributors should not exceed 15% of the practice income (the limit is 10% for listed companies)

(ii)   if Eastfield Distributors is a listed company, my audit firm should not prepare the annual financial statements (except in emergency situations). This requirement will apply to my firm's work as internal auditors. Even if Eastfield Distributors is not a listed company, it is undesirable that my audit firm (as either internal or external auditors) should prepare the annual financial statements

(iii)   the Rules of Professional Conduct of the Association of Chartered Certified Accountants (ACCA) do not specifically cover the independence of the internal audit work from the external audit work when the external auditor carries out both these functions. However, the situation seems to be similar to when the auditor both prepares the annual financial statements and audits them. So, it appears to be desirable that there should be some independence between the internal and external audit functions within the audit firm. Thus, it is desirable that different audit staff should carry out internal audit work from those who undertake the statutory external audit. Internal audit staff should report to a different partner from the engagement partner for the external audit. If the internal audit and external audit staff report to the same engagement partner, the audit firm may be criticised for a lack of independence

(iv)   if the internal audit staff prepare the annual financial statements, my audit firm should make it clear that the directors must accept responsibility for these financial statements

(v)   the internal audit staff should be careful not to assume the role of management when carrying out their work, as this would contravene the ACCA's Rules of Professional Conduct. This may create problems, as the internal auditors may be asked to design the company's accounting systems in order to provide adequate controls. This problem may be reduced by requiring the company's directors to confirm any recommendations by the internal auditors. The company's chief financial officer (i.e. finance director or chief accountant) will be an important person to be involved in this type of decision, as he/she will have the skills to make a responsible decision

(vi)   there may be problems about who the internal audit staff are responsible to. On a day to day basis, they will probably report to the finance director, but they should have the right to report to the board of directors. For the internal auditors to be truly independent of the external auditors, they should not report to partners in the audit firm. However, this is impractical and unrealistic. It is impractical, as the internal auditors will be employees of the audit firm and their promotion will be determined by the audit firm. Thus, the audit firm will have to be able to assess the quality of each employee's work. It is unrealistic, as external auditors use the work of internal auditors in coming to their audit opinion. Thus, the external audit staff will have to review the work of the internal auditors, and the internal auditors may be asked to carry out certain work to assist the external audit staff. There will need to be some agreement with the client about the extent to which the company and the external audit firm control the internal auditors' work. This should be included in the engagement letter

(vii)   there will have to be a decision about which members of the audit staff should perform this internal audit service. The staff should have a range of skills and range from junior to qualified staff. I will have to consider whether the staff should always work for the audit client, or whether different staff should be employed at different times. More staff may be provided for the internal audit service when the external audit work-load is low, and fewer staff when the external audit department is busy. It is important that the internal audit staff are competent, as otherwise this could adversely affect Eastfield Distributors' opinion of the audit firm. This will create the risk that Eastfield Distributors will want to change the external auditor with the consequent risk to the external auditor's independence

(viii)   there will have to be an agreement about how much should be charged for the internal audit service, and the services which will be provided. The charge will probably be based on the number of hours worked by staff at Eastfield Distributors and their level of experience

(ix)   other considerations will be similar to those for my audit firm being external auditor of Eastfield Distributors. These will include:

- staff undertaking the internal audit work should not own shares in Eastfield Distributors or have close family or other personal relationships with the directors or senior employees of Eastfield Distributors
- there should be an agreement over payment of charges for the internal audit work. If Eastfield Distributors is slow at paying these charges, it could adversely affect the independence of my audit firm

    – the internal audit staff will have to be careful in accepting goods, services and hospitality from Eastfield Distributors. Any benefit from these items should be modest. For instance, staff purchasing goods from the client should receive them at no more favourable rates than employees of Eastfield Distributors, and they should be only for personal use

    – internal audit staff should not accept loans from Eastfield Distributors

(x)   an engagement letter should be agreed with Eastfield Distributors for the internal audit work, which includes most of the matters listed above. It may be appropriate to have a trial period after which Eastfield Distributors will decide whether the service should continue. Following this, both parties should agree a new engagement letter, which seeks to overcome any problems and includes important matters which were omitted from the original engagement letter.

(b)   The advantages to Eastfield Distributors of having the external audit firm perform the internal audit work will include:

(i)   the new internal auditors should be skilled in carrying out audit work, so the learning time for the staff should be short compared with setting up an internal audit department within the company

(ii)   the audit procedures and standard should be consistent with those of the external auditor. Thus, the external audit staff should be able to use more of the internal auditor's work in coming to their audit opinion. This should reduce the cost of the external audit

(iii)   the audit firm may be able to provide staff with a wider range of skills than Eastfield Distributors may be able to recruit as employees. For instance, the audit firm may be able to provide specialists in computer auditing, where it would not be economical to have a computer audit specialist as an employee.

The disadvantages of the external audit firm performing the internal audit work will include:

(i)   there may be problems with who is in charge of the internal audit staff. The internal audit staff will be employees of the external audit firm. The client company will probably have less control over the internal audit staff, and this may create problems over the work they do and the reports they make

(ii)   because of the ACCA's Rules of Professional Conduct, the internal auditors may be restricted in the work they do. For instance, they may be prevented from preparing the financial statements and making management decisions. Thus, they may not be able to decide the form and controls for a whole accounting system

(iii)   the internal audit staff will be skilled at performing work similar to the external auditors, but they may have limited skills and experience of other work carried out by internal auditors (e.g. advising on the purchase of a business)

(iv)   using the external audit firm to perform internal audit work is likely to be more expensive than the company employing its own internal audit staff, as the external audit firm will want to cover its costs and make a profit on the work

(v)   there may be problems with the internal audit staff changing from time to time. The external audit firm will probably want to provide the maximum staff to Eastfield Distributors when the audit firm are less busy and fewer staff when they are busy. Having different staff at different times will require the new staff to learn about Eastfield Distributors' business. This learning time is likely to be greater than if Eastfield Distributors employed its own staff

(vi)   the requirement of the external audit firm to have to perform external audits (when it is busy) may mean that Eastfield Distributors does not have sufficient internal audit staff during periods when it wants them (e.g. at the year end for stocktakes and to help in preparation of the annual financial statements).

(c)   The advantages to the external audit firm are frequently similar to the disadvantages to the audit client. However, some advantages can apply to both the audit firm and the client. The advantages can be summarised as:

(i)   by having the internal auditors as part of the audit firm's staff, their audit procedures should be the same and the confidence of the audit firm in their work will probably be greater than if the internal auditors were employees of the client company. Thus, the external auditor will probably be able to achieve a greater reduction in the external audit work compared with if the internal audit work is being carried out by employees of the client company

(ii) the service will provide additional income and profits to the audit firm. It may provide a wider experience to the audit staff, but there may be problems with obtaining the appropriate work experience for staff to become members of the ACCA

(iii) it may be possible to use the internal audit work to fill in periods when there is little external audit work. For instance, in the UK, there is little audit work from July to early September, so more staff could be employed in internal audit work during this period.

The disadvantages to the audit firm in providing an internal audit service include:

(i) the firm must be careful that the professional rules on independence are not contravened. It may be difficult to ensure that none of the staff employed on internal audit work are part of the external audit team. It may be very difficult to ensure the rules of professional independence are complied with at all times, as the internal auditors may be required to make executive decisions or be involved in the preparation of the annual financial statements

(ii) if a dispute arises with the client over the internal audit work, this is likely to affect the audit firm's relationship with the client. Because of this, there may be implications on the external audit. For instance, if the audit firm is dismissed as internal auditor of Eastfield Distributors, it may be dismissed as external auditor as well.

79   (Answer 5 of examination)

(a) SAS 200, Planning, says in statement 200.1 that 'Auditors should plan the audit work so as to perform the audit in an effective manner'. It goes on to say that 'planning entails developing a general strategy and a detailed approach for the expected nature, timing and extent of the audit'.

As this is a continuing audit, the general strategy will probably be similar to last year's audit. However, it will be modified by problems experienced in last year's audit and significant events which have taken place in the company since last year's audit. The timing of the audit work is important, as time will be wasted if it is planned to carry out audit work when the appropriate information is not available from the company. The timing of the audit work will influence the make-up of the audit staff during the audit (i.e. the balance between junior and experienced audit staff). It will be necessary to agree a timetable with the company of when information will be available and this will determine when the audit work is carried out. Also, the following dates will be important:

(i)   the stocktake
(ii) when the full financial statements are available for audit
(iii) when the financial statements are agreed and signed by the directors and the auditor
(iv) the date of the annual general meeting when the financial statements are approved by the shareholders

The extent of the audit work in each area will have to be considered. This will be based on a number of factors, including the materiality of the item and the audit risk, based on experience in previous years' audits.

A budget will be prepared which suggests the time which should be spent on each aspect of the audit and the completion dates of each part of the audit.

During the audit, progress will be compared with the audit plan. Any adverse (and favourable) variances against the plan will be investigated, and the plan amended if it is considered appropriate.

Planning an audit is important. One would not build a house without a plan, so one should not carry out an audit without a plan. The requirement to plan an audit ensures senior audit staff have considered the work which is required to complete the audit, and the timing of that work so that it fits in with the dates information is available from the company and the planned completion date when the financial statements are approved by the directors and the auditor. By having a plan, the auditor should take a more considered approach to the audit which will improve the quality of the audit, and thus both minimise the time spent on the audit and the overall audit risk. When the audit is carried out, the progress can be monitored against the plan, and action taken when the audit starts to take more time than expected, both in terms of staff time and in reaching deadlines.

(b) The matters I will consider in relation to the items listed in the question and their implications on planning the audit will include:

(i)   the company's turnover for 10 months is £130 million, which given an annualised turnover of £156 million, is a 41·8% increase over the previous year. The annualised profit before tax is £4·8 million, compared with £8 million last year, which is a fall of 40%. It appears the company is increasing sales at the expense of profits. If profits are falling, the actual profit for the 10 months to 30 November 1998 may be even less than the £4 million shown by the monthly accounts. The fall in profit indicates problems which may not be fully reflected in the monthly accounts

(ii) audit work will have to be carried out on the new computerised stock control system. Computer audit specialists within the audit firm will probably have to be used. It may be appropriate to carry out this work before the year end, so that any problems with the system can be highlighted and either overcome or allowed for at the year end. The company says it will not be carrying out a stocktake at the year end, so as auditor I will have to place considerable reliance on the accuracy of the stock quantities reported by the stock control system. I will have to determine from the company how frequently they count the stock, the proportion of the stock counted at each stocktake, and the checks they make to the stock quantities on the computerised system. If there are a large number of differences between the physical stock quantities and those on the computer, stocktakes should be carried out more frequently and on a larger proportion of the stock than if differences are infrequent. This information will have to be determined before the year end, as, if differences are frequent, it may be necessary to carry out a full stocktake at the year end. Otherwise, there is a high risk the audit report will have to be qualified

(iii) reliability problems with the company's products could create the following problems:

–   certain stock being unsaleable, and thus worth less than cost (or even being worth only scrap value)
–   legal claims against the company
–   customers not paying for the products

These last two points are mentioned in the question. Further details will have to be obtained about legal claims against the company and customers refusing to pay their outstanding debts. Information can be obtained for this by inspecting correspondence with customers and discussing the matter with the company's staff, including the company secretary, sales director and the credit controller.

The audit risk with these problems include:

–   the difficulty in estimating the costs (i.e. the costs of defending legal claims and damages which may have to be paid, and the cost of the bad debts)
–   the risk that there may be more claims and bad debts, which relate to the year under review, but may not become apparent until after the audit report is signed
–   the value of the faulty stock held at the year end. The selling price of stock sold between the year end and the audit will have to be checked to ensure it is valued at the lower of cost and net realisable value. There may be problems with determining the value of year-end stock which is still held at the time of the audit

(iv) the large increase in debtors' age will have resulted in a large increase in debtors, from £14·7 million at 31 January 1998 to an estimated £53·3 million at 31 January 1999. The increase of £38·6 million will probably have come from increased borrowings. Thus, the increase in the credit period and sales to new customers will result in the following audit risks:

–   new customers tend to have a higher risk than existing ones, thus increasing the risk of bad debts
–   increasing the credit period tends to attract customers who are a poor credit risk. This is for two reasons, firstly the longer credit limit will reduce the customer's cash flow problems, and secondly it attracts customers who already have cash flow problems, as these customers are unable to pay other suppliers within the shorter credit period (e.g. the one month credit period previously allowed by Bridgford Products)
–   a potential bad debt, or dispute about a faulty product, may not become apparent until after the credit period is being exceeded. Thus, it will probably take at least three months before the doubtful debt becomes apparent, rather than the one month with the previous credit period. So, doubtful debts from sales immediately prior to the year end may not become apparent until after the audit report has been signed

In addition, the actual age of debtors is 1·1 months in excess of the current credit limit (of three months) compared with 0·6 months over the credit limit in the previous year. This indicates there may be problems with collection of debts from customers and thus an increase in bad debts.

With the large increase in debtors, the company is probably experiencing liquidity problems. Are the company's borrowing facilities adequate, and is there a risk the company may not be a going concern?

(v) the reasons for the dismissal of the financial director and purchasing manager will have to be ascertained. Were they carrying out a fraud (separately or together?) or were they contravening financial procedures. If this was happening, what are the financial consequences? Is it possible for this type of fraud to recur? Could our audit firm be liable for not detecting these events? If the dismissed employees are claiming unfair dismissal and compensation from the company, the likely outcome from these claims would have to be investigated and an appropriate provision included in the financial statements. This could be a high risk area of the audit.

In addition, I will have to consider the consequences of the company being without a purchasing manager from 15 August until the new purchasing manager was appointed. There is the risk that controls during this period will have been weaker than normal, thus increasing the risk of a fraud. The new purchasing manager will take time to become effective in his post, which could increase the risk of fraud. Also, the wrong products may be purchased, or products may be purchased at an inflated price. This could mean that some products in stock at the year end may be worth less than cost.

The effect of there being no financial director between 15 August and the year end may mean that financial records and controls may not be as effective as in previous years. The chief accountant will probably be much busier than when there was a financial director, which could mean that, with less time to prepare the financial statements, the annual accounts are less accurate and less complete. If the financial director prepared the annual draft financial statements in previous years, does the chief accountant have the skills and experience to prepare this year's financial statements?

---

80 (Answer 6 of examination)

(a) For Langar Computers, the following factors indicate the company may not be a going concern:

(i) large research and development expenditure which may not be successful, for any of the following reasons:

- the product may not be technically feasible within time and financial constraints
- it may not be possible to sell sufficient quantities of the product at a price which recovers costs and the capitalised development expenditure
- sufficient finance may not be available to complete either of the two stages above

(ii) the company has made a loss of £676,000 in the current year. If these losses continue, the company will probably fail

(iii) the gross profit margin is low (at 20·5%). It is difficult to specify when gross profit is low, as it depends on the type of business. However, a gross profit margin of 20% would be low for most businesses, except those with a high turnover compared with working capital (e.g. supermarkets). The net profit margin is negative at −7·9% (see item (ii) above)

(iv) a high stock age. The company's stock age is 3·55 months which appears high for this type of business. A high stock age uses working capital and requires higher borrowings

(v) a high creditors age. At 6·1 months, the creditors age is very high and it appears that the company is using creditors to finance the business so as to minimise its other borrowings

(vi) a low current ratio. With this type of business, the current ratio should be within the range 1·6 to 2·0, but it is 0·69 which is very low (current liabilities exceed current assets)

(vii) a low-acid test ratio. One would expect the acid test ratio to be about 1·0 but it is very low at 0·33 which indicates severe liquidity problems

(viii) high gearing. The gearing ratio is 2·25 (including bank overdraft). Most lenders start to express concern when the gearing reaches 1·0 (i.e. borrowings are equal to shareholders' funds). With Langar Computers borrowings are 2·25 times shareholders' funds, which is very high

(ix)   a high bank overdraft which is above the limit specified by the bank. The financial director has said the bank overdraft limit is £1·9 million, but the bank overdraft in the financial statements is £2·136 million which is £236,000 over the limit. Also, the bank overdraft has increased by £1·563 million (i.e. from £573,000) over the past year which is another indication of going concern problems. The fact that the bank overdraft facility is due for renewal on 15 January 1999 creates further going concern problems, as there is a high risk it will not be renewed at the current level of £1·9 million (it is likely to be substantially less than £1·9 million)

(x)   sales are falling. In the year ended 31 October 1997 sales were £10·2 million while they were £8·524 million in the year ended 31 October 1998. This represents a 16·4% fall in sales over 1997. Also, the financial director has said that sales of other products are falling. Unless sales and profit margins increase, the company will continue to make losses which will result in it not being a going concern.

If the development expenditure of £3·172 million is worthless, then shareholders' funds will become £1·332 million negative, which will probably result in the immediate failure of the company.

From further discussions with the company, it is probable that other going concern problems will become apparent

(b)   The question says the capitalised development expenditure for the archiving system has been correctly recorded in the accounting records, but it may be worth less than £2·5 million (for the archiving system) at 31 October 1998 (out of a total capitalised development expenditure of £3·172 million at 31 October 1998).

(i)   To check whether the archiving system is technically feasible, I will ask the company's staff the specification of the system and to demonstrate it. I will try to operate the system myself to see if it works and is easy to use. The speed of operation of the system will be checked against the specification. I will check that documents which have been archived can be retrieved and printed. I will check the space used on the optical disk for the documents. From these investigations, I will decide whether the archiving system operates reliably and quickly. I will ask about the experiences of trial users of the system, and for any reports they have produced. With the client's permission, I may contact the trial users to obtain their independent opinion of the system. I will ask them if they will purchase the system when it is fully developed, or whether they would buy an alternative system or none at all. I will ask about amendments to the system to overcome problems experienced by the trial users. Have these amendments been implemented and do they overcome the problems? A statistic in the computer industry is that the error rate of programmers is about 2% per instruction, but their error rate in correcting mistakes is about 30%. So, there is a significant risk that modifications have not overcome problems experienced by users.

As further development work is required, I will ask for details of this work and consider whether the estimate of £300,000 is reasonable. As £2·5 million has already been spent, the amount of additional work required to overcome the current problems should be small. If it looks as though a considerable amount of work will be required to perfect the system, then the estimate of £300,000 looks too small. Any additional expenditure over £300,000 and further delay will aggravate the company's going concern problems. Also, this further development work should have been completed by the time the product goes on general sale in January 1999.

I will consider the company's experience with past software products. If they have experienced problems when they are first used, then this is likely to happen with the new archiving system. If they have been relatively error-free, then the prospects for the archiving system are good. However, it appears this new archiving system is much larger than previous systems (I will check whether this is the case), and increased complexity increases the risk of problems when the product is introduced.

(ii)   In auditing this part I will obtain from the company its estimated revenues and costs from selling the archiving system.

The sales revenue will be the product of the number of systems sold and the selling price. I will ask about customer interest in the product and whether any sales have been made by the time of my audit (the question says that no sales have taken place at the time of my audit visit). I will ask the company and obtain information from other sources (e.g. computer magazines) to determine whether there are any competitors. If there are, I will ask for details of the client's selling price and that of competitors. The client should be charging a similar price to competitors. If the selling price is significantly higher than competitors and the performance of the system is similar, then the selling price is unrealistically high. In addition, I will check whether past estimates of sales and selling price have been realistic. With computer products, the price tends to be high when a new product is introduced and reduces as more competitors enter the market. Thus, I would expect the company's estimates of the selling price to fall in future periods. Based on this work, I will decide whether the company's estimate of sales revenue is realistic.

I will check the company's estimates of costs. The direct costs will include hardware and software costs. The hardware cost will be checked against the company's costing records. Software costs are likely to be relatively small, as this is likely to comprise optical CDs for the software and instruction manuals. The other major direct cost is likely to be advertising. I will ask the client the sources of advertising it proposes to use and obtain details of the costs for each source. Advertising is likely to be in journals and in printed material which is sent to potential customers. In addition to these costs, the company must recover the capitalised development costs over the life of the archiving system. The Financial Director has said that the amortisation rate on development expenditure is 10% on the original cost, and amortisation is charged from the start of sales of the product. Thus, the company is estimating a life for the product of over 10 years, which seems very long. Also, the company is likely to have to spend more money updating and improving the product to keep up with competitors. The budgeted income statement should incorporate such expenditure, and I will consider whether it is reasonable.

From the question, it appears the archiving system will comprise a majority of the company's future sales. Thus, for the company to continue to be a going concern, it will have to break even or be profitable from these sales. So the sales revenue will have to recover not only direct costs and amortisation of the development expenditure but a significant proportion of other overheads.

Based on this work, I will decide whether the capitalised development expenditure will be recoverable against future sales. If I have reservations about future net revenues being sufficient to recover the development expenditure, I will probably have to qualify my audit report. This will increase the risk the company is not a going concern.

Certificate Examination – Paper 6(U)   **Marking Scheme**
Audit Framework (UK Stream)

For most questions the marking scheme suggests you award 1 mark a point. However, the mark you award for each part will depend on its relevance and the depth of the candidate's discussion. So, a brief point may be worth 1/2 mark or less while a point with a longer and deeper discussion could be worth 2 marks.

Also, marks are not allocated to specific points, as the candidate may mention a valid point which is not given in the model answer – obviously, the candidate should be given credit for the point.

Many questions require candidates to include a range of points in their answer, so an answer which concentrates on one (or a few) points should normally be given a lower mark than one which considers a range of points.

Finally, in awarding the mark to each part of the question, you should consider whether the standard of the candidate's answer is above or below a pass grade. If it is of pass standard it should be awarded a mark of 50% or more, and it should be awarded less than 50% if it does not achieve a pass standard. When you have completed marking a question you should consider whether the total mark is fair. If you decide that the total mark is not a proper reflection of the standard of the candidate's answer, you should review the candidate's answer and adjust marks, where appropriate, so that the total mark awarded is fair.

			Marks
1	(a)	Audit procedures over attending the stocktake Generally *1 mark* a point up to a *maximum* of:	11
	(b)	Checking schedule adjusting stock value to 30 Nov Generally *1 mark* a point up to a *maximum* of:	6
	(c)	Checking purchases cut-off Generally *1 mark* a point up to a *maximum* of:	3
			20

2	(a)	Consideration of reliability and independence of two types of third party evidence Generally *1 mark* a point up to a *maximum* of:	6
	(b)	Methods of selecting debtors to circularise – monetary unit sampling v judgement Generally *1 mark* a point up to a *maximum* of:	8
	(c)	Audit work on checking responses to a debtors' circularisation (i) debtor disagrees the balance (ii) debtor does not reply to circularisation Generally *1 mark* a point up to a *maximum* of:	6
			20

3	(a)	Controls in purchasing department Generally *1 mark* a point up to a *maximum* of:	8
	(b)	Controls by accounting department over purchase invoices Generally *1 mark* a point up to a *maximum* of:	6
	(c)	Controls over receipt of services Generally *1 mark* a point up to a *maximum* of:	6
			20

Note: *For brief points, without an explanation, you should award 1/2 mark a point. For longer points with an appropriate explanation you may give 1 mark a point.*

Marks

4   Provision of internal audit service to audit client:

   (a)   Matters to consider to ensure auditor's independence
       Generally *1 mark* a point up to a *maximum* of: 8

   (b)   Advantages and disadvantages to audit client
       Generally *1 mark* a point up to a *maximum* of: 7

   (c)   Advantages and disadvantages to audit firm
       Generally *1 mark* a point up to a *maximum* of: 5
                                                                                                    —
                                                                                                    20
                                                                                                    ≡

5   (a)   Why planning an audit is important
       Generally *1 mark* a point up to a *maximum* of: 5

   (b)   Matters to consider in relation to items (i) to (v) in question
       Generally *1 mark* a point up to a *maximum* of: 15
                                                                                                    —
                                                                                                    20
                                                                                                    ≡

6   (a)   Factors which indicate going concern problems in Langar Computers Ltd
       Generally *1 mark* a point up to a *maximum* of: 9

   (b)   Checking capitalised development expenditure:
      (i)   will project be technically successful
         Generally *1 mark* a point up to a *maximum* of: 5
      (ii)   will future net revenues recover capitalised development expenditure
         Generally *1 mark* a point up to a *maximum* of: 6
                                                                                                    —
                                                                                                    20
                                                                                                    ≡

ACCA
AT FOULKS LYNCH

HOTLINES
Telephone: 0181 844 0667
Enquiries: 0181 831 9990
Fax: 0181 831 9991

AT FOULKS LYNCH LTD
Number 4, The Griffin Centre
Staines Road, Feltham
Middlesex TW14 0HS

Examination Date:
☐ June 99
☐ December 99

	Publications			Distance Learning	Open Learning
	Textbooks	Revision Series	Lynchpins	Include helpline & marking	
Module A – Foundation Stage					
1 Accounting Framework	£17.95 [UK] [IAS]	£10.95 [UK] [IAS]	£5.95 ☐	£85 ☐	£89 ☐
2 Legal Framework	£17.95 ☐	£10.95 ☐	£5.95 ☐	£85 ☐	£89 ☐
Module B					
3 Management Information	£17.95 ☐	£10.95 ☐	£5.95 ☐	£85 ☐	£89 ☐
4 Organisational Framework	£17.95 ☐	£10.95 ☐	£5.95 ☐	£85 ☐	£89 ☐
Module C – Certificate Stage					
5 Information Analysis	£17.95 ☐	£10.95 ☐	£5.95 ☐	£85 ☐	£89 ☐
6 Audit Framework	£17.95 [UK] [IAS]	£10.95 [UK] [IAS]	£5.95 ☐	£85 ☐	£89 ☐
Module D					
7 Tax Framework FA98	£17.95 ☐	£10.95 ☐	£5.95 ☐	£85 ☐	£89 ☐
8 Managerial Finance	£17.95 ☐	£10.95 ☐	£5.95 ☐	£85 ☐	£89 ☐
Module E – Professional Stage					
9 ICDM	£18.95 ☐	£10.95 ☐	£5.95 ☐	£85 ☐	£89 ☐
10 Accounting & Audit Practice	£22.95 [UK] [IAS]	£10.95 [UK] [IAS]	£5.95 ☐	£85 ☐	£89 ☐
11 Tax Planning FA98	£18.95 ☐	£10.95 ☐	£5.95 ☐	£85 ☐	£89 ☐
Module F					
12 Management & Strategy	£18.95 ☐	£10.95 ☐	£5.95 ☐	£85 ☐	£89 ☐
13 Financial Rep Environment	£20.95 [IAS]	£10.95 [IAS]	£5.95 ☐	£85 ☐	£89 ☐
14 Financial Strategy	£19.95 ☐	£10.95 ☐	£5.95 ☐	£85 ☐	£89 ☐
P & P + Delivery UK Mainland	£2.00/book	£1.00/book	£1.00/book	£5.00/subject	£5.00/subject
NI, ROI & EU Countries	£5.00/book	£3.00/book	£3.00/book	£15.00/subject	£15.00/subject
Rest of world standard air service	£10.00/book	£8.00/book	£8.00/book	£25.00/subject	£25.00/subject
Rest of world courier service†	£22.00/book	£20.00/book	£14.00/book	£47.00/subject	£47.00/subject

SINGLE ITEM SUPPLEMENT: If you only order 1 item, INCREASE postage costs by £2.50 for UK, NI & EU Countries or by £10.00 for Rest of World Services

TOTAL					
Sub Total £					
Post & Packing £					
Total £					

Telephone number essential for this service   ***Payments in Sterling in London***   **Order Total £** [   ]

DELIVERY DETAILS

☐ Mr ☐ Miss ☐ Mrs ☐ Ms Other

Initials _____ Surname _____

Address _____

_____

_____

Postcode _____

Telephone _____   Deliver to home ☐

Company name _____

Address _____

_____

Postcode _____

Telephone _____ Fax _____

Monthly report to go to employer ☐   Deliver to work ☐

PAYMENT

1 I enclose Cheque/PO/Bankers Draft for £_____
Please make cheques payable to AT Foulks Lynch Ltd.

2 Charge Mastercard/Visa/Switch A/C No:

Valid from: [   ]   Expiry Date: [   ]

Issue No: (Switch only) [ ]

Signature _____   Date _____

DECLARATION

I agree to pay as indicated on this form and understand that AT Foulks Lynch Terms and Conditions apply (available on request). I understand that AT Foulks Lynch Ltd are not liable for non-delivery if the rest of world standard air service is used.

Signature _____   Date _____

Please Allow:	UK mainland	- 5-10 w/days
	NI, ROI & EU Countries	- 1-3 weeks
	Rest of world standard air service	- 6 weeks
	Rest of world courier service	- 10 w/days

Notes: All delivery times subject to stock availability. Signature required on receipt (except rest of world standard air service). Please give both addresses for Distance Learning students where possible.